CHARLES VALENTIN ALKAN

To S with much

love and affection

Charles Valentin Alkan
His Life and His Music

WILLIAM ALEXANDER EDDIE
The Open University and University of Edinburgh, UK

ASHGATE

© William Alexander Eddie 2007

All rights reserved. No part of this publication may be reproduced, stored in a retrieval system or transmitted in any form or by any means, electronic, mechanical, photocopying, recording or otherwise without the prior permission of the publisher.

William Alexander Eddie has asserted his moral right under the Copyright, Designs and Patents Act, 1988, to be identified as the author of this work.

Published by
Ashgate Publishing Limited
Gower House
Croft Road
Aldershot
Hampshire GU11 3HR
England

Ashgate Publishing Company
Suite 420
101 Cherry Street
Burlington, VT 05401–4405
USA

Ashgate website: http://www.ashgate.com

British Library Cataloguing in Publication Data
Eddie, William Alexander
 Charles Valentin Alkan : his life and his music
 1.Alkan, Charles–Valentin, 1813–1888 2.Alkan, Charles–Valentin, 1813–1888 – Criticism and interpretation 3.Composers – France – Biography 4.Pianists – France – Biography
 I.Title
 780.9'2

Library of Congress Cataloging-in-Publication Data
Eddie, William Alexander.
 Charles Valentin Alkan : his life and his music / William Alexander Eddie.
  p. cm.
 Includes bibliographical references (p.), list of composer's works (p.),and discography (p.).
 ISBN 1–84014–260–X (alk. paper)
 1. Alkan, Charles–Valentin, 1813–1888–Criticism and interpretation.
 2. Piano–Performance. I. Title.
 ML410.A442E33 2006
 786.2092–dc22

2005026463

ISBN 978-1-84014-260-0

Printed and bound in Great Britain by MPG Books Ltd, Bodmin, Cornwall.

Contents

Acknowledgements		*vii*
Preface		*ix*
Abbreviations		*xi*
1	Alkan – The Historical and Social Background	1
2	Apprentice Works	27
3	Development of a Personal Voice	39
4	*Études*	53
5	Sonata Types for Piano	77
6	Morceaux Caracteristiques	93
7	The *Esquisses*	121
8	Arrangements and Cadenzas	131
9	Organ and Pédalier Music	143
10	Piano and Strings	157
11	Miscellaneous Compositions	167
12	Reception	173
13	Performance Practice	199
14	Epilogue	215
Notes to Chapters		219
Bibliography		237
Archival Sources		245
List of Works		247
A Basic Alkan Discography		255
Index to Musical Works		257
Name and Subject Index		265

Acknowledgements

I am much indebted to an ever widening association of Alkan scholars including Hugh Macdonald, Richard Shaw, Ronald Smith, François Luguenot, David Conway, Raymond Lewenthal, Brigitte François-Sappey, Constance Himmelfarb and Britta Schilling. The encouragement of David Charleton at a very early stage in my interest in Alkan and also Jeremy Dale Roberts at London University and Ruth Nye my most inspirational teacher needs to be recorded here. Raymond Monelle made me aware of the importance of semiotics in music.

Thanks are also conveyed to the staff at the universities of London and Edinburgh and also the British Library and Bibliotheque Nationale as well as Dr Leonard Henderson. I also appreciate the patience and encouragement of Rachel Lynch of Ashgate and also the excellent work of Sheila Cochrane who typed the chapters and Jan Forrest, John Purchase and Fiona Watt who helped complete the other parts of the book.

William Alexander Eddie

Preface

Until the appearance of Ronald Smith's studies of Alkan there have been no detailed accessible accounts of either the life or music of this fascinating erratic, eccentric French romantic composer. Academic writing on Alkan has fared better however and includes important dissertations by Joseph Bloch, Richard Shaw, Dennis Hennig and Brigitte Schelling listed in the bibliography. All were consulted for the present study. Other distinguished writers such as Hugh Macdonald, Constance Himmelfarb, Brigitte François Sappey and François Luguenot have provided essential material for the present volume.

Outside purely academic circles interest in Alkan has been stimulated in the UK by the *Alkan Society Journal* founded by John White and in France by the *Société Alkan Bulletin* edited by François Luguenot. Both journals have brought biographical, style analysis, concert and CD reviews to the attention of a wider audience of professionals and amateurs.

My own interest in Alkan goes back to a research paper delivered at a conference at Glasgow University in 1969 entitled 'Fact and fiction about Alkan'. This was prompted by Raymond Lewenthal's invaluable Alkan collection, commentary and recordings. Lewenthal's enthusiasm proved invaluable in prompting this study on Alkan. Even today with many superb performances of the *Symphonie* op 39, *Quasi-Faust* op 33 and *Le Festin d'Esope* op 39, Lewenthal's stylish and dynamic performances are essential in any Alkan collector's discography.

The musical texts of Alkan throw up far fewer editorial problems than those of Chopin and Liszt. Most of the music exists as a single source with very few existing composer's autographs. Alkan's first editors Delaborde and Philipp made a judicious selection of his music. Their edition is unfortunately very incomplete but consultation of other publishers' catalogues and studies of depositions in the various libraries mentioned in the list of works appendix have resulted in a fairly complete picture of Alkan's oeuvre. Several modern editions are also worthy of note including Hugh Macdonald's edition of the *Cello Sonata* op 47, Georges Beck's *C.V. Alkan: Oeuvres choisies pour piano* and Ronald Smith's and John White's *Alkan in Miniature*. The latter is essential for pianists of average ability.

The approach in this text is generally style analytical, although the importance of more modern motivic and semiotical studies is acknowledged where relevant. But throughout this study the sound of the music is emphasized particularly from the middle period onwards of the massed effect of block chords often texturally altering which produce such 'orchestral' pianistic potency. To this end Alkan shares a similar sound world with Schubert rather than Chopin. Indeed Alkan shares the 'innig' intimate sonority of the German school of Schumann and Mendelssohn as well as the morphological form building of Beethoven. These composers haunted Alkan from mid-career onwards and provided the focus for the programmes of the 'Petits Concerts' performances in later life.

Alkan the performer cannot be neglected. As a virtuoso Alkan was probably only equalled by Liszt, and Alkan also excelled like Chopin as a poet of the piano. These romantic composers shared reclusive tendencies but Alkan demonstrated the most extreme sense of introversion in performance withdrawal. Nationalistic eruptions in mid-century provoked in him an almost catatonic state. Essentially a creature of the *ancien régime*, the stability and reassurance of baroque and classical musical structure were fundamental starting points of his own compositional outpourings.

Alongside this background for Alkan must be added the 'Jewish element'. This is not just a question of directed impositions of Jewish chant in his music: such tendencies are relatively rare. It is the more general Jewish qualities of intense melancholic brooding, the sharpest sense of wit and orgiastic joy which permeate his music. This partially explains the stylistic consistency of his music after the apprentice years period. So Judaic culture, the French baroque and German classicism were the main sources for his imagination. Extramusical art forms did not interest Alkan. The music of composers such as Liszt and Wagner whose world was stimulated by art and literacy held little interest for Alkan. It would be unfair to dismiss Alkan as a regressive romantic composer: it may be meaningful to regard Alkan as discussed in this study as a 'conservative radical'. This term allows us to merge influences with reactionary forces manifested in his finest music.

It is hoped that the following chapters ignite the reader's desire to explore the music of this non-establishment romantic composer.

Abbreviations

AMZ	Allegemeine Musikalische Zeitung
ASJ	Alkan Society Journal
GM	Gazette Musicale de Paris incorporating Revue Musicale (RM) to form RGM
LFM	La France Musicale
LSA	La Société Alkan bulletins
MMR	Monthly Musical Record
ML	Music and Letters
MM	Music and Musicians
MQ	Music Quarterly
MT	Musical Times
NBM	Neue Berliner Musikzeitung
NZFM	Neue Zeitschrift für Musik
RR	Records and Recordings
RGM	Revue et Gazette Musicale de Paris
SR	Stereo Review
SM	Studia Musicologica Academiae Scientiarum Hungaricae
SMA	Studies in Music, University of Western Australia

Chapter 1
Alkan – The Historical and Social Background

During the early years of the nineteenth century, post revolution French musical taste had moved away from baroque and classical music. Audiences now preferred a simpler more melodious mode of musical expression epitomized by the romance where a vocal type melody was gently accompanied by arpeggio-like figures.[1] This type of musical style was pursued by early nineteenth-century piano composers composing for the rise in bourgeois audience numbers. The romance, lyrically and intellectually undemanding was the basis of song-like piano music in the salon where Chopin, Liszt and Alkan made indelible musical impressions.

On the other hand conservatoire-trained professional musicians of the conservative type staunchly defended the superiority of eighteenth-century (and seventeenth-century) music against the newer romance-based styles of music. The re-opening in 1816 of the Paris conservatoire and the appointment of many distinguished academics and composers to the professorial staff reinforced the importance of Haydn's and Mozart's music especially as the model of classicism in music. Additionally, Austro-Germanic baroque music especially that by J.S. Bach was performed and techniques of harmony, counterpoint and fugue studied. These theoretical disciplines were re-established by Cherubini, the director of the Paris Conservatoire. Equally Choron's *Principes de composition* (1808–1810) was influential as was his teaching based upon the editing and performance of pre-eighteenth-century vocal music. These studies laid the foundations for a sympathetic reception and ingestion of early music for students such as Alkan at the beginning of the nineteenth century.

*

Returning to the question of counter-Conservatoire culture, the music and popular craze for Rossini was an important force too in shaping the compositional habits of Parisian musicians. To this Italian operatic influence and the French romance tradition for Alkan's musical heritage should be added the influence of Jewish culture and music and a short examination of this is now appropriate.[2]

During the *ancien régime* in France Jewish customs were barely tolerated. Post-revolution Jews however were granted full civil rights in 1791 by the Abbé Gregoire.[3] Previously in 1780, Alkan's grandparents settled in Paris and were still able to give the civic name Alkan to their son, the father of the composer and the subject of this book. Post 1791, Jews in France could employ French Christian names for their children.

Youthful virtuosity and early successes (1813–1845)

Details regarding Alkan's birth are well established since the birth certificate[4] clearly dates his precise time and place of birth as 30 November at 1500 hours, rue de Braque no. 1. Named Charles Valentin, Alkan was the second of six children. He had one older sister Céleste and four younger brothers Ernest, Maxime, Napoléon and Gustave. A family tree diagram (see Diagram 1.1) gives details of the Alkan ménage.

We need to clarify some confusion regarding Alkan's full name. The repeated error of expanding the Ch. into Charles Henri, persists in English musical dictionaries up to 1954. The addition of Henri is incorrect as can be seen from inspection of his birth certificate. From the beginning Charles Valentin Alkan experienced a high quality of musical training at his father's boarding school which acted as a pre-Conservatoire course where (mostly Jewish) young children received elementary musical instruction and learned the rudiments of French grammar.[5] Significantly at this school Jewish students did not have to compromise any religious practices. Alkan's musical contemporaries included the pianist Ravina[6] and pianist and composer Honoré.[7] Marmontel,[8] a distinguished teacher at the Conservatoire perceptively remarks[9] on Alkan's psychological nature at that early life stage: 'He was not yet a recluse: [he was] happy joyous [and] full of zest for life. He had, like all of us ... the foolish enthusiasm and cherished illusions of youth.'

Diagram 1.2 shows the musical talent of Alkan's siblings. None of their achievements surpass those of Charles Valentin however.[10] Easily the most precocious of the Alkan household, Charles Valentin was admitted to the Conservatoire on 6 October 1820 winning first prize in solfège in 1821. On 3 October 1821 he commenced studies in piano with Zimmerman[11] gaining an accessit prize in 1823, a second prize in 1823 and a first prize in 1824. Admitted on 1 October 1823 to Dourlen's[12] practical harmony and accompaniment class, he gained first prize in 1827. As well as these prizes for piano and practical musicianship skills he gained a first prize for organ in 1834 after studying with Benoist[13] from 15 May 1832. Clearly a student of remarkable talent, Alkan was duly rewarded with some academic teaching within the Conservatoire and on 10 April 1829 he was initially appointed repetiteur before becoming assistant professor of solfège, a post in which he remained until 1836 when he was replaced by Batiste.[14]

Interestingly, Alkan's first concert appearance was as a violinist not a pianist. At his début[15] recital in 1821 he played an air and variations by Rode.[16] The exact Rode piece is not known but it is likely to have been the *Ricordanza* no. 6 (1815) which was very popular with performers at that time. For example during the 1817–1818 season in the Italian opera house in Paris Mme Catalani[17] sang this set of variations and her performance took her audience by storm.[18] Thereafter there are no further reports of Alkan as violinist: all his musical energies were now directed towards becoming a piano virtuoso. To this end Alkan's piano professor Zimmerman organized his piano début recital at the salon of the piano manufacturer Henri Pape on 2 April 1826. The original concert announcement[19] claimed that Alkan was eleven years old when he was in fact thirteen. Alkan shared this concert with several other instrumentalists and singers who were already established artists including Mme Pasta,[20] Rubini,[21] Galli[22]

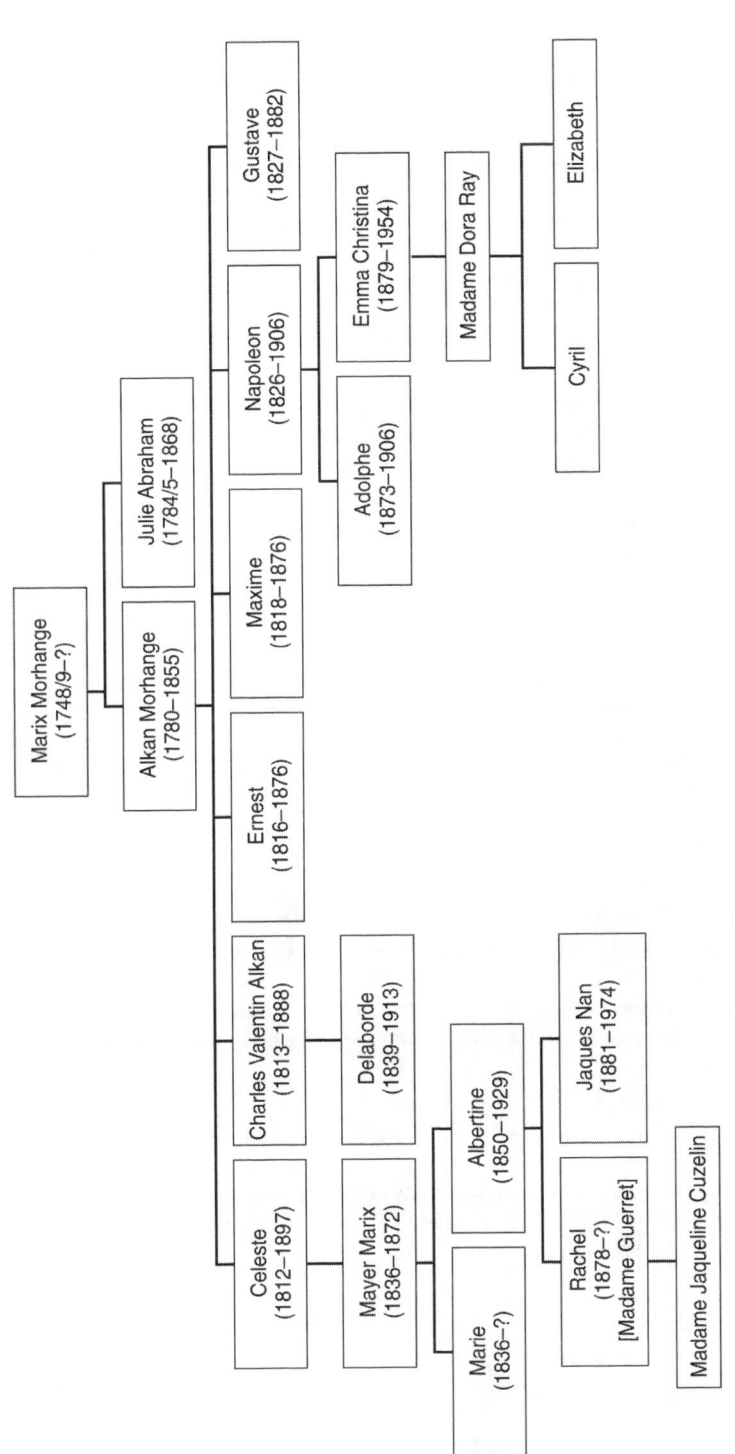

Diagram 1.1 Alkan's Family Tree

Celeste Alkan (born 25 February, 1812)

- admitted to the solfège class of Mlle Croisilles on the 3 July 1819; won second prize in 1822, first prize in 1823.
- admitted to the figured bass class of Mlle Foulon on 2 October.
- admitted to the vocalisation class of M. Henry on 17 May 1828; terminated studies in 1830.
- upper-second prize in the ensemble class of Kuhn, October 1830 to 1831.
- admitted to the vocal class of Pellegrini on 23 November 1829; struck off on 14 January 1832 without gaining any prize because of absences and illness.

Ernest Alkan (born 11 July 1816)

- admitted on 31 January 1828 to the solfège class of Bienaimé; *accessit* in 1829, prize in 1831, second prize in 1831, first prize in 1832.
- admitted on 18 June 1828 to the flute class of Guillou (later Tulou); second prize in 1831, first prize in 1832.
- admitted on 28 December 1837 to the counterpoint and fugue class of Millet; terminated course 9 November 1839.

Maxime Alkan (bom 28 May 1818)

- admitted on 21 April 1829 to the piano class of Laurent and on 10 November 1830 to the piano class of Zimmerman; second prize in 1832, first prize in 1834.
- admitted on 29 November 1832 to the harmony class of Dourlen; struck off on 13 June 1836 by the decision of the Committee.

Napoléon Alkan (born 2 October 1826)

- admitted on 21 October 1835 to the solfège class of C. V. Alkan; second prize in 1836, first prize in 1837.
- admitted on 26 October 1835 to the piano class of Laurent and on 8 October 1838 to the piano class of Zimmerman; second prize 1842, first prize in 1843.
- admitted on 4 October 1848 to the organ class of Benoist, resigned 29 October 1850.
- admitted 10 October 1848 to the counterpoint and fugue class of Adolphe Adam; first prize in 1849.

Gustav Alkan (born 24 March 1827)

- admitted on 17 January 1849 to the harmony and practical accompanying class of Bazin; moved to the composition, counterpoint and fugue class of Halévy on 19 October 1850, left this class on 30 October 1852.

Diagram 1.2   Achievements of Alkan's musical siblings

and Massart[23] as well as accompanying his sister Céleste. *Le Mentor*[24] remarked that Alkan had 'astonished [the audience] by the marvellous manner in which he played variation and his [original] composition'.

On a personal front, Zimmerman in 1827 took a paternal interest in the young Alkan introducing him to Parisian aristocratic figures which led to various musical successes in the salons. So to promote his gifts as a young virtuoso Alkan in the spring of 1827 made a triumphant tour of Belgium playing in all the main cities. Reports of his outstanding gifts were frequent[25] and he was favourably compared with Herz and Moscheles. In Belgium on one occasion he shared a concert with local violin virtuoso Massart who he had met at his Parisian piano début described above. This occurred at the end of March 1827 in Liège at a special concert for the Société Grétry. The Liège reviewer lauded both the talent of Alkan and Massart and this furthermore is the first report of Alkan's performance of his op 1 *Variations sur un thème de Steibelt*: 'in his charming piano variations [op 1] Alkan has proved through his effortless, light brilliant and rapid playing ... achieving such perfection at a tender age ... it became doubly interesting to see and hear [Massart] after young Alkan'.[26]

After Liège Alkan gave three concerts in Brussels. The success of these concerts was brought to the attention of many of London's music critics and the *Harmonicon* (a leading contemporary music journal) commented[27] that the concerts attracted all the best musical amateurs and even more prestigiously the Royal Highness gave his highest approval and satisfaction to Alkan's talents. On return to Paris Alkan – again at the instigation of Zimmerman – was introduced to the Princesse de la Moscova and de Bertha reports[28] that Alkan played at several musical evenings organized by the Princesse.

Alkan now attracted the full enthusiasm of the Parisian press and his pianistic and composition career appeared to go from success to success. Fétis, the important Parisian academic and critic reviewed Alkan's op 1 very favourably.[29] Like many musicians of the time (including Beethoven) Alkan's primary reputation was as a performer but it is interesting that despite Alkan's brilliant piano playing his concerts even at this stage of his career always included an input of chamber music. He also promoted the cause of high quality symphonic music and opera. On 1 November 1829 in the Salle Favart Alkan's contribution included therefore several excerpts from Weber's *Der Freischütz* (the overture, a vocal duet and sextet) as well as original chamber and piano compositions by Alkan and Franchomme.[30]

1830 was an important date for musical life in Paris. On 30 July revolution broke out causing the bourgeoisie to achieve political and social power. Effectively too this marked the end of *ancien régime* attitudes in music although Alkan in social custom, formality and musical taste clung on to the habits of the old regime. Nevertheless the musical atmosphere in Paris was romantically charged and there was now an insatiable demand for virtuoso piano players. This generation of pianists was of course headed by Franz Liszt, but Liszt respected Alkan enormously attributing to Alkan 'the finest technique of anyone ... but he [Alkan] preferred the reclusive life to that of the concert platform'.[31] Made retrospectively, of course, after Alkan's retiral from the concert platform in 1838 this is still an astonishing tribute to a rival and fellow artist. In later life conversely Alkan recalled the phenomenal impact which the young Liszt had made upon him but their relationship was a distant one. Both artists nevertheless abandoned the career of a travelling virtuoso and both turned to the life and more creative rewards of that of a composer. Even by the 1830s both Liszt and Alkan were growing weary of the atmosphere of 1830s Paris which has been brilliantly described by Rittermann.[32] Apparently although it was a mecca for pianists, many non-French musicians such as Clara Schumann viewed Paris disapprovingly. Yet despite the multiplicity of visiting pianists many established pianists such as Alkan, Zimmerman Hallé, Onslow, Chopin and Liszt made Paris their long stay venue. Paris attracted many pianistic 'asses and virtuosi' (Chopin's comments) but with over six hundred concerts in 1838 there was certainly a public demand for both types of pianists. Alkan was typical of the young virtuoso who would later mature into a fine composer. Alongside his contemporaries such as Chopin and Liszt, the initial fusion of pianist-composer would later separate into pianist and composer.

Temperamentally Alkan was more attuned to the introverted Chopin than the extroverted Liszt. The relationship and friendship between Alkan, Chopin and George Sand has been traced in some detail.[33] Alkan was present at Chopin's first concert in Paris in February 1832 and this was the start of their friendship. In Paris, due to a letter of recommendation to Ferdinand Paër, Master of Music at the court of Louis Philippe, Chopin had been introduced to many of established composers such as Cherubini, Meyerbeer and Auber and pianist-composers such as Hummel and Kalkbrenner. In turn the younger pianist-composers with whom Alkan was mostly closely linked were Hiller, Osborne, Mendelssohn, Liszt and Chopin. Just as Chopin on 26 February 1832 had introduced himself as pianist-composer to Parisian audiences through his F minor concerto op 21, Alkan on 29 April 1832 at a Conservatoire concert gained considerable success by performing his first *Concerto da Camera* op 10. By 1832 Alkan's talents were sufficiently developed to merit Fétis summarizing his achievements in these words ... 'This artist has become a commendable artist not just as pianist but as a composer for his instrument'.[34] Alkan was now deemed to be in the higher ranks of pianist and composer. He achieved further success during 1832 including an honourable mention in the Prix de Rome for the cantata *Hermann et Ketty* and the election to the *Société Académique des Enfants d'Apollon* with the (regressive) title of pianist-composer. Up until the summer of 1836 Alkan enjoyed the academic and professional benefits of this society whose members included distinguished musicians such as Clementi, Viotti, Rode, Baillot, Auber, Cherubini, Habaneck, Halévy and Kalkbrenner, a venerable mix of French and Italian composers and instrumentalists. This society[35] gave Alkan an opportunity to première his new compositions – the *Rondo Chromatique* op 12 was dedicated to the Society and performed at an Apollan Society concert[36] on 16 May 1833 along with the Septet of Ries. On 28 May 1835 the concerto for piano [possibly the second *Concerto da Camera* op 10] was performed and on 12 May 1836 the Trio of Mayseder[37] was played. At the monthly evening concerts Alkan participated in Beethoven's piano quintet in November 1832 and in December 1832 in his Concerto [no 1 in A minor op 10]. In June 1833 the Quintet op 53 by Spohr and in September 1833 a trio by Lamatre[38] and a sextet by Moscheles were performed.

In order for a French composer to achieve academic success it was necessary to win the Prix de Rome. After his minor Prix success in 1832, Alkan made a second attempt with the cantata *L'entrée en loge[s]* but this time without any success. Nevertheless, he continued to move within literary and artistic circles within Paris. He now lived in the square d'Orléans and residents there included many of the most important figures of Parisian artistic life including Dumas, Zimmerman, Kalkbrenner, the Viardots,[39] Ortigue[40] and of course George Sand and Chopin. This period of Alkan's life included making music with some of the most distinguished of contemporary composers including Pixis, Liszt and Franck. Alkan was also now a celebrated Parisian composer since Liszt had in 1837 reviewed his *Trois Morceaux dans le genre pathétique* op 15 in glowing terms observing that[41] 'these compositions could not be more distinguished'. As will be discussed in Chapter 3 these are remarkable pieces marking out the beginning of a more creative introverted, melancholic nature to Alkan's style.

Alkan continued to participate fully in Parisian concert life in 1838 and further engagements included a concert[42] at the salon of M. Pape on March 1838 where a second performance of the Mayseder second piano trio from a St Cecilia concert of 23 November 1835 was given. The other players were the violinist Ernst[43] and the cellist Batta.[44] Alkan played several of his own works including the third [sic] *Concerto da Camera* and two of his own études, *Le Vent* [op 15/2] and the C sharp [op 13/1], both of which had been published in 1837. Most importantly, Alkan had transcribed part of Beethoven's *Seventh Symphony* for two pianos (eight hands). The other players were Zimmerman, Gutmann[45] and Chopin and this was the first time Alkan had shared a concert programme with Chopin. This concert shows the catholic range of Alkan's musical sympathies.

From 1839 until 1844 Alkan voluntarily retired from the concert stage. There are several reasons for this decision. Firstly, he found the musical tastes of Parisian bourgeois audiences deplorable. These were the years of the Liszt/Thalberg duel[46] and the famous but musically jejune concert[47] where six virtuosi pianists Thalberg, Herz, Pixis, Czerny, Liszt and Chopin composed and performed a variation of a theme from Bellini's *I Puritani*. Liszt was commissioned to compose the introduction, the links between the variations and the finale. Alkan was easily the equal of any of these pianists but he was reluctant to participate in this type of musical fodder. Quite simply, his championing of chamber music was out of phase with Parisian mass audience taste. A second reason for Alkan's retreat from public concerts may have been the birth of his natural son Elie Miriam Delaborde on 9 February 1839. Very little is known about the father-son relationship save to say that Elie was a pupil of the father and became a brilliant pianist and a piano professor at the Paris Conservatoire from 1873. Much information regarding Delaborde seems to have been suppressed. De Bertha mentions[48] that Delaborde introduced him to Alkan in 1872 without any suggestion of filial connections. The eminent Alkan scholar-pianist Raymond Lewenthal had conversations with his teacher Olga Samaroff[49] who had studied with Delaborde at the Paris Conservatoire. The existence of a blood relationship is strengthened by the following facts. Firstly, Delaborde was an amazingly gifted pedal-pianist playing the same type of repertoire as Alkan. Secondly, both Delaborde and Alkan were parrot enthusiasts – Alkan compared a tombeau to a parrot in 1859 – the *Marcia funèbre sulla morte d'un papagello* and one hundred and twenty one parrots and cockatoos accompanied Delaborde on his London trip in 1870.[50]

During the 1840s Alkan moved to the St Lazare district.[51] Chopin still lived in the elegant square d'Orleans. The two composers now tended to communicate by intermediaries or by letters. For example Chopin wrote to Fontana: 'give him [Alkan] my greetings if you see him'.[52] 1843 saw Alkan assisting in a private performance of Franck's oratorio *Ruth* in the Salle Eraud. The audience consisted of many well known contemporary musicians including Adam, Halévy, Spontini, Meyerbeer, Moscheles and Liszt but not Chopin who by 1843 was very ill. Chopin was also absent from a performance of the Adagio and Finale of Beethoven's *Seventh Symphony* at Erard's on 1 March 1843. Despite Alkan's written invitation Chopin seems to have declined.

1844 was a most significant year for Alkan. His judaic beliefs were manifested by an invitation from the Paris Consistoire (the Jewish Governing body), to become a committee member in order to evaluate the skills of a proposed new cantor, Samuel Naumbourg. Also in this year Alkan started teaching Deleborde, now aged five. Additionally, Alkan's return to the concert platform in 1844 was trumpeted by *La France Musicale* on 25 February 1844. Curiously the announcement predated the concert by only two days, and the journal clearly had a very short memory since Alkan had an active concert career up until 1839. Alkan relied on his old teacher Zimmerman for promotional support and it was Zimmerman in turn who organized his next concert in March 1844. Alkan's choice of repertoire showed a further retreat from brilliant pièces d'occasion and an increasing bias towards baroque and classical works. The March 1844 recital included the *Air de ballet dans le Style ancien* [op 21], a nocturne [op 22] and the *Saltarelle* op 23. All these works were given public premières in 1844. Alkan continued to programme baroque transcriptions and his own works for his April 1844 concert, announced in *La France Musicale* on 14 April 1844. As well as the op 21, 22 and 23 works he included the *Alleluia* op 25 as well as the first two movements of his second concertino [the *Concerto da Camera* no. 2 in C sharp minor op 10], a gavotte by Bach [from the *French Suite in G major BWV 816*], an allegro by Scarlatti, the minuet from the *Symphony no. 40 in G minor* by Mozart and the rondo from Beethoven op 31 *Sonata* [op 31/1]. The only concession to virtuosity was the inclusion of Weber's *Movement perpétuel*. Apparently none of the non-Alkan works had ever been previously performed in Paris. Alkan's *Saltarelle* op 23 was predictably very popular and was his only work to have been frequently performed by other pianists including Josephine Martin whose performances were apparently 'interrupted at each reprise with frantic applause'.[53] In spring 1845 Alkan gave two more concerts which further consolidated his reputation as an enthusiast of pre-romantic music as well as a presenter of his own most recent compositions. His concerts in March and April 1845 consisted of the following programmes: 1 March 1845: *Adagio of the Hummel Concerto in B minor* accompanied by four horns, 'cello and bass, a Schubert minuet, a Mendelssohn fugue, the *Marches funèbres et triomphales* [op 26/1, op 26/2] and the *Romance du phare d'Eddystone* [for voice and piano, now lost]; 30 April 1845: *Étude in C sharp* with accompaniment by double quartet [probably the *Andante con moto* op 13/2], the *Marche Triomphale* op 27 and the *Saltarelle* op 23, the *Trois morceaux dans le genre pathétique* op 15, the Andante of the Mozart *Sonata in C* [K 521] for one piano/four hands and the Allegretto of Beethoven's *Seventh Symphony* for two pianos/eight hands with Zimmerman, Pixis and Napoléon Alkan. Chapter 12 will examine in more detail the divergence of critical opinion towards Alkan as pianist and composer but there was an overall general feeling that he was lacking in originality in presenting transcriptions and all his performances were bereft of romantic feeling.

The beginnings of personal and musical reclusivity (1846–1853)

Between April 1846 and the end of 1848 Alkan disappeared from the Parisian musical press as a performer and turned his attention fully to composition and in particular, to chamber music. The *Duo Concertant* op 21 published in 1841 and the *Piano Trio* op 30 published in 1842 were to be followed according to Kreutzer[54] by trios, quintets and sextets. Kreutzer also announced a symphony, the review of which is lengthy and detailed and will be considered in Chapter 10 – Piano and strings. Neither manuscripts of the symphony nor the trios, quintets and sextets exist. The manuscript of the symphony may possibly have been given to Napoléon Alkan's brother, and then to Napoléon's son Adolphe who died in 1904. Adolphe's wife Emma Christian (1879–1954) may have hidden the manuscript of the symphony and the aforementioned chamber works during the invasion of France in 1940.[55]

By 1847 Alkan was a sufficiently eminent composer for the *Revue et Gazette Musicale (RGM)* to invite him to contribute to an album tribute to Stephen Heller (1813–1888). The album's six pieces comprised an *Andante amoroso* by Liszt [no 9 of the *Harmonies poétiques et religieuses*], an impromptu by Prudent,[56] a polonaise by Wolff,[57] a nocturne by Chopin and Alkan's *Vaghezza* [published as op 32/1 in 1848]. In 1847 too Fétis wrote several articles in the *RGM* praising especially the two *Marches* op 26 and op 27 commending him for his originality.[58] Of Alkan's most recent compositions the 25 *Preludes* op 31 were critically discussed and this enthusiastic review will be evaluated in the Chapter 6.

Revolution again erupted in Paris in 1848. During the insurrection in June of this year many musicians had fled from the French capital. For musicians who decided to stay, the atmosphere was summed up by the public cry of 'vive la republique'. Chopin for example writing to Mlle de Rosières complained that:

> Poor Gutmann is in the National Guard – he might easily stop a bullet – and Grzymala, Delacroix, Pleyel and Alkan who own all those houses in the Rue Rochechouart neighbourhood. What horrors! May God grant that order has now been restored for a long time to come ... .[59]

In his Memoirs Berlioz evoked an even more pessimistic statement on the future of music: 'the art of music long since dying is now quite dead. They are about to bury it, or rather throw it on the dung heap. France and Germany have no further existence for me'.[60] Also, writing to J.M. Davison, the music critic of *The Times*, Berlioz bemoaned the general cultural decline of music in the French capital:

> I am very badly affected by the deplorable state in which I have found the music and musicians in Paris ... all the theatres closed, all the artists ruined, all the professors idle, all

the students in flight, poor pianists sweeping the streets, poor pianists playing sonatas in the public squares, historical painters sweeping the streets.[61]

To ameliorate these deplorable conditions a petition was signed by the Association Nationale des artistes et musiciens and presented by Victor Hugo to the home office minister which implored the authorities to improve the general conditions of musicians and to champion the cause of French musicians.

In 1848, Alkan decided to improve his economic position and artistic status by applying for head of the piano faculty at the Paris Conservatoire as successor to Zimmerman. His main rival was Antoine Marmontel who as will be seen was to employ underhand tactics to obtain the post. Possessing many academic distinctions from the Paris Conservatoire Alkan, at least on paper, was Zimmerman's most brilliant pupil. Letters from Alkan to Fétis however demonstrate that although Alkan had been once his favourite pupil Zimmerman had not supported Alkan's candidature for the head of faculty post.[62] Alkan was not silent in voicing a preference for the *ancien régime* rather than the current apparently more democratic climate. But Alkan thereafter took rather draconian measures to try to prevent his main rival Marmontel being appointed. He (Alkan) asked George Sand to write on his behalf to Charles Blanc, the director of Department of Fine Arts.[63] Sand's intervention however was to no avail. Blanc did not reply because he was mentally and emotionally concerned with the political future of his politician brother Louis. Alkan was also worried about the influential Auber (the Director of the Paris Conservatoire 1842–1871) and Auber's friendship with Marmontel.[64]

On 1 September Alkan wrote to the Ministry of the Interior informing them that Auber was about to appoint a man with little musical status. Further letters were sent by Alkan to Charles Blanc, the first on 3 September clearly stating that Marmontel's pupils had been mainly taught by other teachers including Henri Herz, Chopin and Alkan himself. In particular, a testimonial[65] from M Leroy was enclosed to state that his daughter helped by the tuition of Alkan had gained second prize for piano at the Conservatoire in 1848. In a second letter dated 3 September 1848 Alkan set out the reasons for his own appointment to the post:

> If you uphold the administrator of the Department of Fine Arts, I will be elected. If you discover public opinion instead of a small faction, I will be elected. If you gather the votes of all the leading musicians of Europe, I will be elected. If you judge the competition on three aspects – performance, composition and teaching – I will be elected. If you would postpone your decision until the new plan for adjustment takes place despite the influences exercised over a significant portion of teachers, I would still be elected by a large majority and would very likely inspire the unanimous vote of students.[66]

Further letters in an even more canvassing tone were unsuccessful. Marmontel was finally and emphatically elected, but he probably used several ingratiating tricks to help him secure the appointment by holding pre-competition lessons for students at the Salle Erard to enhance their chances of success. Furthermore, Marmontel parted company with other members of the music panel when, at the entrance examinations, he invited competitors to play their own compositions, which was a test not required by the Conservatoire. Bizet for example, gained an advantage through this advice from Marmontel.[67] The only connection between Bizet and Alkan however seems to have been through Crohare's solfège class accompanied by Alkan and attended by Bizet. It appears in fairness that within traditional limits Marmontel was an excellent teacher (particularly of solfège) but his pianistic and pedagogic skills were negligible compared with Alkan's.

Conservatism and mediocrity were rife in academic institutions in France in the nineteenth century. Berlioz gives a vivid account of this tendency in his *Memoirs*:[68] 'I have had the teachers at the Conservatoire against me stimulated by Cherubini and Fétis whose pride and principles were outraged by my heterodoxy in matters of harmony and rhythm.' (Both Berlioz and Alkan met French conservatism in the Prix de Rome: Berlioz winning it in 1830, Alkan attempting it twice, but never winning it.) Both composers solicited important references but Alkan needed more direct help since his merits were outlined in a letter from Charles Blanc dated 29 August 1848 where he said that 'M. Alkan does not owe his popularity to publicity, to the flattering of women, to an air varié on popular tunes ... [he] loves art for art's sake and he has opposed charlatanism for twenty three years ...'.[69] Furthermore, a second letter gives specific details of Auber's preferences: Auber had placed Marmontel at the top of his list whereas Alkan was placed only third.[70]

Ten years later, in 1858, Auber still promoted Marmontel, suggesting that Marmontel be awarded the Légion d'Honneur.[71] This further demonstrates that Auber was single-minded in overruling the Director of the Department of Fine Arts. Marmontel naturally was later to bear Alkan no grudges! In *Les Pianistes Célèbres*[72] for example he is full of sycophantic praise for Alkan. So Alkan's own professional relationship vis-à-vis Auber was weak.[73] Given the unstable political situation in Paris in 1848 with much social upheaval and its concomitant effect on musical life, Alkan had much about which to be depressed. His infrequent concert life from 1838 caused several musical critics to comment on his reclusive state but to support his credentials Alkan decided to return to Parisian musical life by giving a concert on 5 May 1849 at the Salle Erard. There were several distinguished artists in the audience including Delacroix and Meyerbeer. Henri Blanchard,[74] congratulated Alkan as a progressive artist and as someone who maintained the exact rules in writing music.

After summer 1849 Chopin was moved from the square d'Orleans to the periphery of Paris in order to escape the cholera outbreak. Once Chopin had ceased to live in the Alkan neighbourhood there is no indication that Alkan wrote or visited him. Following his death on 17 October 1849 Chopin left instructions to the affect that his unfinished manuscript of a piano method be bequeathed to Alkan and Reber.[75] The dedication to Alkan is however cryptic. Perhaps since several of Chopin's pupils studied with Alkan after Chopin's death his piano 'method' might in essence be a guide to maintain his style of teaching for posterity.

With the loss of Chopin Alkan sank into a deeper depressive state refusing to play the piano for his circle of friends despite encouragement from George Sand[76] and Ambroise Thomas. Nevertheless Alkan indicated in a letter to Thomas[77] that he would take pleasure in Thomas's company. Along with social interaction, Alkan furthered his interest in pre-classical music becoming one of the first French subscribers to the *Bachgesellschaft* founded in the centenary of Bach's death. In 1851 Alkan was appointed organist at the Paris Temple in Paris, but he resigned from the post several weeks later for reasons unknown. Perhaps increasing public reclusiveness was a factor. This decision to resign probably denied Alkan acclaim as first official organist at the main Paris synagogue. Alkan now turned to Fétis, the influential French academic.

By invoking the interests of Fétis on Alkan's own musical preoccupations Alkan considered he might further his own career. Several letters to Fétis in the *RGM* are evidence of this. The first letter of 1852[78] was written on paper headed 'Erard' since Alkan had been visiting the Erard offices in order to study the organ works of J.S. Bach on the pedal piano. Despite the fact that Alkan had taken a first prize in organ at the Paris Conservatoire in 1834 he seemed to prefer the pedal piano composing several works for this keyboard instrument.

The bulk of his second letter to Fétis[79] concerns Alkan's conversation with a certain Spanish friend [unspecified] who, on the subject of rhythm, was aware of the two and three beat bar, Alkan previously having admitted that he was not averse to the five beat bar. The Spaniard quoted an example from *La Dame Blanche*[80] and then proceeded to inform Alkan of the Zorzico, a dance prevalent in the Basque country which he had learned to play on a certain flute with only three holes but with a range of two octaves.[81] This flute was played with one hand, the other hand loudly beating a certain [unstated] rhythm on a tambourine. It appears that this five beat bar was often extended and became a 6/8 bar, or had one of its beats prolonged. Alkan, at this point, refers to Chopin who played in certain rhythms which alter when 'crossing a river'(!). On playing a Zorzico to a native, the dance was recognized at once. The example given, which was later quoted by Fétis,[82] subdivides the 5/4 bar (clearly) into 3/4 and 2/4. Alkan, however, mentioned in the same letter that in the second book of *Impromptus* (published by Brandus) he placed the accent differently in each of the three airs in five time. In the air in seven time Alkan realized that it was basically in 6/8 time with a slightly extended rest on the last beat. As an appendix to the letter Alkan adds that some people including his friend Hiller, seemed to enjoy the first of the airs in five time, but others found it to be disagreeable. Another letter,[83] compliments the article by Fétis on five time. Alkan notes that since the beginning of 1852 he had not received a single musical newspaper but that would not, apparently, have prevented him missing anything which Fétis had written.

The Fétis-Alkan correspondence contains many remarks about the inadequacies of Marmontel as pianist, teacher and arranger, thus Alkan's opinion of Marmontel remained poor. In a second letter Alkan recounts his struggle to prevent Marmontel from becoming head of piano at the Conservatoire. He told Fétis that Marmontel was: 'one of the poorest musical minds which had been reared on solfège and piano classics ... Embellishments, changes and additions were made (by Marmontel) to various competition pieces ...'.[84] Alkan longed for a revitalized French piano school at this time to counteract the empty virtuoso school in mid-fifties Paris: this would encourage some knowledge of the significant piano composers. Notably, Alkan along with Liszt and Hallé were all instrumental in promoting a more serious classical attitude to programme building. Alkan's most significant act towards this aim was the inception of the Petits Concerts given towards the end of his life. But Marmontel typically became chameleon-like apparently embracing the classics albeit through his own arrangements. Surreptitiously perhaps Marmontel acquiesced to some of

Historical and Social Background

Alkan's criticisms of the shallow pianistic practices in Paris. Marmontel had now, according to Alkan, conveniently 'become a scholar, a man of tradition who intended to produce and edition of all our classical masters not just purged of all the printing errors but with fingering, accents and annotations'; Alkan, therefore, considered that Marmontel had not changed his devious ways and showed no musical integrity whatsoever. Alkan complained that: 'He [Marmontel] will take an Adagio by Mozart which he does not understand, and only release it decked out with a feather, dressed up in riding boots and adorned with spurs. ...' He continues:

... Hummel, Mendelssohn and Beethoven (especially in his later works) can defend themselves to a certain extent because of the more numerous markings in their music and the greater exactness of their notation, but Mozart whose method of notation corresponds to the ideas expressed, whose restrained expression marks and genius in accentuation is so attuned to his divine genius ... such care will never be paid [by Marmontel] to Mozart's work.

Alkan felt that Scarlatti, Handel and Bach would also suffer under the 'scholarship' of Marmontel and he realized that these editions by Marmontel would be potentially disastrous in the hands of provincial piano teachers, who would be duped by the presence of Marmontel's name as editor on the title pages. Alkan pointed out that the editions of Mozart and Beethoven by Brandus and Richault were generally the most reliable, but he thought that it was unlikely that these publishers would protest at Marmontel's alterations to the basic texts because of Marmontel's academic prestige. Alkan then noted that Ambroise Thomas (the Director of the Conservatoire) added his name to approve the appointment of Marmontel. Alkan, additionally, remarked that a small group of teachers at the Conservatoire decided that Henri Herz would receive no votes at the public competition despite a pupil of Herz's informing the public, and despite the influence of Auber and two others (unspecified). In this letter Alkan asks Fétis to observe all these opinions and carefully make a note of them.

Finally, a third letter written a month later[85] includes Alkan's thanks to Fétis for his quoting of Alkan's letter of 24 October in the sixth article 'Dans le domaine du rhythme'.[86] Alkan continued his tirade against Marmontel stating that he (Alkan) could never understand that Auber's sympathies were with Marmontel, and that all Zimmerman's efforts were to prevent Alkan from taking over from him as head of piano. This was a further reason for Alkan to become even more reclusive. In his own characteristic depressed manner he mused: 'I am burning away without giving out any light.' He further commented that he was totally opposed to the 'Lanner-Czerny-Scarlatti' piano prospectus, a Marmontel headed edition of selected music from these composers reflecting Marmontel's idiosyncrasies as scholar-editor.

Nevertheless, despite Alkan's psychological state he gave two concerts during the next year (1853). At a matinée musicale with his friends, Hiller and Tellefsen[87] he played Bach's *Concerto for three pianos* accompanied by a string quintet. Inspired no doubt by the prospects of a complete Bach edition Alkan continued to study and perform Bach's music giving a performance of a duo sonata[88] in February 1853. The 1853 season's concerts were entitled 'Séances de musique classical et retrospective'. The emphasis on classical and (presumably) baroque music often involved works for organ played on the pedal piano for the instrument was fired by the Belgian organist

Lemmens[89] who commented on Alkan's excellent pedal piano playing[90] in 1853 and several years later judged the pedal piano to be important in chamber music as well as having great effects and novel sonorities.[91]

Academic vicissitudes and compositional maturity (1854–1873)

The two outstanding qualities of virtuosity allied to musical intelligence and a keen interest in the music of the past[92] which Alkan developed in the years 1844–1853 continued in the following years. Also, Alkan continued his criticism of contemporary musicians and music but composition became his principal activity from 1854–1873. Conversely, several members of the Alkan family achieved academic distinction or compositional success. Napoléon, Charles's brother was acclaimed as the 'worthy brother of the conscientious and celebrated pianist'.[93] Maxime, Charles's sister, capitalized on the Strauss mania sweeping through Paris in the 1850s and her collection of waltzes, polkas and mazurkas were published in 1854. The death[94] of Alkan Morhange on 3 January 1855 caused Alkan to become even more secluded and inward reflecting.

Among other musicians performing Alkan's music was Franck, a keen advocate of Alkan's music arranging and who performed[95] an Alkan nocturne [op 22] in a concert on 8 March 1855. This also included a choral piece by Alkan [the *Stances de Millevoye*?] and the *Air de Ballet* op 24 in a vocal arrangement sung by Mme Massart[96] and Viardot.[97]

1857 saw the publication of the gigantic op 39 *Études* and the large scale violoncello sonata op 47 as well as the op 38 *Chants*, the *Marches* op 40 and *Fantaisies* op 41. Great insights into the psychological state of Alkan are obtained by examining the Alkan-Hiller correspondence from 1857 onwards. All the correspondence shows great rapport between the two composers and Hiller seems to have been a willing receptor of Alkan's views on music and musicians alike. For example in a letter[98] to Hiller in 1857, Alkan indicated that he would be pleased to visit Cologne to support Hiller's crusade against Liszt. Additionally, Alkan lost no opportunity to make very thinly disguised tirades against his old rival Marmontel by writing: 'Why do I not have the means of pulling apart these dreadful little scoundrels who have recently taken to publishing classical works whilst at the same time vilely besmirching them?' But Alkan commented favourably on Hans von Bülow the noted pianist who had published a very positive review of Alkan's op 35 studies.[99] In the meantime Alkan informed Fétis of several works published or about to be published by Richault ie the 12 *Caprices* in four books, op 12, 13, 15, 16, *Les Mois* and the *Études* op 76.

Throughout his correspondence with Hiller Alkan's views on composers are made apparent. Sometimes composers such as Gounod were dismissed cursorily as 'mournful': more usually Alkan gives reasons for his critiques. For example he was enraged by Berlioz's nomination to the Institute[100] because of the excesses expressed in his Treatise of Instrumentation. Berlioz's writings astonished Alkan because alongside interesting and amusing views there were unbelievable inanities.[101] Other contemporary compositions, in particular Meyerbeer's *Dinorah* premiered in Paris in 1859 was described in an 1859 letter to Hiller as making one 'red in the face: ...

for example a symphony with voices in the guise of an overture which is one of the most atrocious things I know in music'.[102]

Without doubt the substance of the 1859 Alkan-Hiller correspondence concerns Alkan's melancholic state which was further deteriorating. His correspondence reflected his hatred of Wagner's music and his writings to Hiller in 1859 are probably the gloomiest of all in tone: 'huge numbers of otherwise level headed people seem strange and at the same time melancholy'.[103] Nevertheless, and despite an unpromising environment, Hiller intended to revive the Düsseldorf Music Festival. He sent Alkan an invitation to participate, but Alkan had severe doubts that any members of the festival committee would have heard of him: furthermore, he was reluctant to travel, but conveyed the warmest feelings to Hiller and in return invited him to Paris at the earliest possible opportunity.

Unfortunately Alkan's state of health and mind further deteriorated in 1860. During this year Wagner arrived in Paris and attempted to achieve the maximum possible musical impact by sending free tickets for his concerts to several important Parisian composers. For example, Berlioz wrote to Pauline Viardot on 25 January 1860: 'I think I shall be stronger this evening for Wagner's concert ... he has sent four tickets.'[104] Wagner had arranged three concerts, all with the same programme: the overtures *The Flying Dutchman* and *Tannhäuser*, the preludes to *Lohengrin* and *Tristan and Isolde* which was announced as a new work. Six other extracts from *Tannhauser* and *Lohengrin* were also played. Berlioz wrote:

> If a thing is worth doing, it is worth doing boldly: Wagner has just proved it as this programme, devoid of any of the bonbons which lure children of all ages to musical galas, was nonetheless listened to with constant attention and a very lively interest.

Berlioz found the *Tristan* prelude at odds with his idea of harmony, since the very fundamentals of tonality were being undermined. Alkan was a strongly tonal composer and his reaction against Wagner was therefore violent. In writing to Hiller he managed to dismiss Wagner as well as taking a few sideswipes against Berlioz after attending Wagner's concert on 25 January 1860 in Paris. Alkan wrote: 'I had imagined that I was going to meet music of an innovative kind but I was astonished to find only a pale imitation of Berlioz ... I do not like all the music of Berlioz while appreciating his marvellous understanding of certain instrumental effects ... but here he was imitated and caricatured.'[105] More vehemently Alkan continued, 'in his second piece [the *Flying Dutchman*] one hears a kind of horribly vulgar singing, the only concession this school can make to old prejudices. At that moment, Auber who was in the box next to d'Ortigue,[106] leaned over to the latter and said: "that will probably be tomorrow's polka"'. Alkan accurately noted Wagner's unpopularity in Paris but 'found it impossible to explain why such rubbish happened in Germany'. Apparently Alkan had met many people, artists and amateurs, who shared the same viewpoint, even if it were not openly expressed. Finally, with an appropriate verbal flourish, Alkan declared that Wagner was 'not a musician but a sickness'.

Having dismissed Wagnermania, Alkan's critical faculties targeted other virtuosi. For example in 1860 when Anton Rubinstein[107] visited Paris Alkan commented on his excellent piano playing:[108] to return the compliment Rubinstein dedicated his

Fifth Piano Concerto op 94 [composed in 1874] to Alkan. There is no evidence to suggest that Alkan played this work in public, yet the scale of its virtuosity is a testament to Alkan's ability. Meanwhile Alkan's compositional skills continued with several important highly incisive works including the *Sonatine* op 61 and the *Esquisses* op 63 but Alkan's state of mind was kept stable with his correspondence with Hiller being supported by Hiller's artistic existence, his influence and creativity. Yet the letter of 25 April 1860 indicates a further decline in Alkan's health and the disastrous effect this was having on his current compositions.[109] He complains also about his financial state but envies Hiller's having a wife and children but Alkan did not feel inclined to confess to Hiller the existence of his illegitimate son Elie Miriam Delaborde.

Letters of 1861 and 1862 briefly deal with Alkan's musical tastes and mental states. The 1861 correspondence with Hiller yields more evidence of Alkan's preference for baroque music preferring the [Matthew] *Passion* of Bach to anything that Wagner had produced. Alkan wryly notes that 'we have sent B[erlioz] to Germany and Germany has imposed on us conversely W[agner]'. The Alkan-Hiller 1862 letters[110] continues the melancholic trend relieved partially by the piano playing of Clara Schumann whose bold approach pleased Alkan. Her anti-academic approach as will be seen in an 1863 letter clearly delighted Alkan. But the 1862 correspondence marks a further descent into melancholia. Alkan now mused to Hiller that 'were it not for a little reading, I should be living rather like a cabbage or a mushroom', but nevertheless he reserved some energy for cryptograms and music and he kept financially solvent by teaching piano to wealthy princesses, including Princess Orloff, who enthused over Hiller's compositions. With the Princess at the second piano Alkan played a Mozart concerto[111] from score not in 'the horrible Hummel arrangement'. Alkan moreover wanted very badly to have Hiller's compositional presence in Paris, then he [Alkan] 'would no longer be left out blowing his solo horn'. Hiller in his turn was reluctant to visit Paris given the anti-Germanic atmosphere. Only Alkan was sufficiently moved to defend Schumann against French critical strictures even given that Schumann had earlier been highly critical of Alkan's op 15. Some French music with Germanic pretensions conversely caused Alkan real distress. For example, in a letter of 1863 to Hiller, he despaired about Gounod's success in Germany. Despite Gounod's ability to 'contrive effects from time to time', Alkan felt that Gounod 'had not written anything of real value'.[112] German pianists and composers of distinction were not assured of a sympathetic reception in France in 1863. For example Alkan worried about the reaction 'of our grand doctors of music' to Clara Schumann's playing and their opposition to the music of Robert Schumann in favour of works of 'Wagner, Liszt and company' (presumably including Berlioz). Alkan reserved his most severe strictures for critics stating that music criticism was a haven for failed and insensitive musicians. In a later letter he described French critics as 'pedants, ignoramuses, asses, beasts and outright rogues'.[113]

From 1864 Alkan's personal state continued to decline as did his compositional desire and he even felt unable to complete a letter to Hiller.[114] His house also was in the process of being expropriated since he was unable to pay the vast increase in rent. Being entirely unmaterialistic, Alkan was unwilling to give five or six thousand piano lessons just to keep a roof over his head. He now planned to look out for a small flat in the Latin Quarter, dividing his energies between study or taking courses and household chores. A later letter to Hiller in 1864 reinforced his lack of concentration and direction, and if Hiller visited Paris he would find Alkan in a retrospective mood surrounded by his portraits.[115] This inertia filtered into his compositional activity and for the period up until 1870 Alkan abandoned composition. Further introspection set in, as shown by his later writings to Hiller and he now turned to intensive biblical study.[116] Translation of the Apocrypha occupied him and he was now starting to translate the second Evangelist from the Syriac. Alkan commented that 'in order to understand the New Testament one has to be a Jew'.But Alkan never made any outward demonstration of his Jewish religious belief. He did not need the display of monastic discipline of Liszt and, indeed, he was rather shocked by his actions. Rather wistfully he remarked: 'I shall not accept the authority of the synagogue, but I shall become a monk in an entirely disinterested spirit; for if Paris is worth a mass, perhaps the authority of St Peter is worth a conscience.'[117] Other musical interests of Alkan included Bach and Beethoven compositions: for example letters of 1869 found him discussing points with Hiller on the *Hammerklavier* sonata of Beethoven and also the adagio of Bach's *Triple concerto*.[118]

To summarize the 1860's, Alkan grew dispirited, feeling ill at ease with the radical changes in Parisian life under the Second Empire. Social instability continued for several years and the French political situation in 1870 was inflammatory. On 4 September a republic was declared. An assembly of archconservatives had earlier in the year moved from Bordeaux to Versailles and were plotting to restore the inequalities of the *ancien régime*. Paris had been attacked by German troops and the city was ripe with revolutionary fervour. The National Guard had been armed for a siege and when the Versailles government attempted to withdraw, the guns from Montmartre offered strong resistance. By May 1871 the Paris commune emerged and went about the destruction of capitalistic principles. The terrorists made a shambles of Paris, burning the Tuileries and the Hôtel de Ville. Several French musicians now fled to Britain including Elie Miriam Delaborde who despite an extremely successful concert season in Paris during 1870–1871,[119] left the city accompanied by an enormous retinue of parrots in late 1871.[120] Alkan, however, firmly resisted leaving Paris and painted a totally doleful picture, writing to Hiller that:

> ... out of every hundred Frenchmen ninety nine have lost their heads ... I no longer feel French except out of custom caused by age. ... In this time of patriotic fervour one must be moved to compose even more; for myself, I cannot even try to at this time. I have gone through forty eight nights and fifty days of unbroken fighting and flying bullets and have only had holes in a shutter and a piano.[121]

1873–1882 (Petits Concerts and The Final Years)

Musical life in Paris was regenerated by the ending of the artistic restriction of the Second Empire in 1870. Therefore three years later Alkan returned to the concert platform after a recital silence of some fifteen years to play the 'Petits Concerts de musique classique'. These were intended to be a series of six concerts per year which, with the exception of 1876 lasted until 1880. For these concerts Alkan was offered a small concert room at 13 rue de Mail. The organization of the concerts was left to Alkan's brother Gustave (also a musician) but Charles Alkan decided the contents of each recital and also included on the programme the timing of each work played. There was much excitement in the Parisian musical journals regarding Alkan's return to Parisian concert life. Typically the *RGM* proudly announced in January 1873 that:

> Ch-Valentin Alkan, the eminent pianist and composer, who has self imposed retirement for too long, is returning to the forefront with the news, which will be received with a great deal of interest, of six little concerts of classical music for solo piano or four hands on one piano, for the pedal-piano or along with other instruments. These performances will take place on the Saturdays of the 15 February, the 1, 15 and 29 March, the 12 and 26 April. All concerts will take place at the Salle Erard at 9 pm prompt.[122]

This advance notice was intended to remind sensitive friends and musicians of Alkan's gifts, since this was his first concert appearance for many years. His 'Six Petits Concerts' however consisted of anything but 'little programmes'. All the programmes were very exacting for performer and audience alike including rather daunting baroque, classical and romantic works and Alkan's own compositions. At the first programme of the 1873 series the *Sonata in A flat major* (op 110) by Beethoven was performed and the virtuosic *Toccata in F* by J. S. Bach was played on the pedal piano. This programme also included three pieces by Rameau, the allegro of a concerto by Handel and some studies by Chopin and Hiller. Of his own works, Alkan played the first piece from the first volume of *Chants* and the *Deus Sabbaoth*. His uneasy personal relationship with Delaborde had been put aside and they collaborated with a performance of Alkan's march [*Trois marches* op 40]. To end the concert, Alkan played the *Introduction and Rondo* [op 70] by Schubert with Alard. The audience at the Salle Erard was a select one consisting of artists, and the warmest of receptions was given to the composer.

After such a long absence from the concert platform, the first concert's memory lapses in a Heller study and the Bach *Toccata in F* were possibly caused by stage fright. To alleviate this Alkan decided, then, to preview the next Petit Concert. On Monday and Thursday afternoons he rehearsed these recital programmes in the company of old friends. This procedure seems to have been successful since he negotiated the *Bach Toccata in F* at the second concert on 1 March flawlessly. Two additional excerpts from the two concertos of J.S. Bach for three pianos were also played as well as a fugue in C minor by J.S. Bach [possibly book 1 of the '48'], an allegro by Domenico Scarlatti, a *Nuit d'Été* (No. 7 of *Les Mois* recently published c 1872), the first piece from the first volume of *Chants* and the study in C sharp major op 13. The final pieces were the *Chorale* and the *Toccata in F* by J.S. Bach. Interestingly, Delaborde gave a recital in the very same month which also included the same Bach toccata. Delaborde's programme also contained a Beethoven sonata (in A major op 101), a suite [*Partita?*] in B flat by J.S. Bach, several pieces by Durand,[123] Mathias,[124] Gouvy[125] and Delaborde himself and on the pedal piano two canons by Schumann [op 56?], a prelude and prière by Alkan.

Delaborde seems to have been a rather more extroverted performer than Alkan since he, unlike Alkan, was accused[126] of over indulging in excesses of virtuosity in his performance of a transcription of the minuet from Bizet's *L'Arlésienne*. Delaborde in common with Alkan programmed chamber music and at this same concert Delaborde played the rondo of a Schubert violin sonata with Pablo Sarasate.[127] The third Petit Concert found Alkan below par because of an illness.[128] He was however in good health for the fourth concert on 29 March 1873 playing a Mozart fantasy for four hands (with Saint-Saëns) and the *Trio* [op 7] by Hiller along with Léonard[129] and Franchomme. Alkan displayed his liking for serious solo piano pieces by including two fantasies by C.P.E. Bach and Chopin, some pieces by Mendelssohn, Schumann (for pedal piano) and Schubert. Of his own music, the *Hymn* from the second volume of *Chants* and the F sharp *Impromptu* were played.

The fifth Petit Concert contained a wide-ranging programme. Given on 12 April 1873[130] Alkan played a prelude from his op 66 [on the pedal piano] as well as the *C major fugue and Pastorale* by J.S. Bach. On the piano he performed Hummel's *B minor Concerto* with orchestral accompaniment, a romance (F sharp major op 28) by Schumann, also the first piece of *Kreisleriana* by the same composer, a prelude by Mendelssohn, two movements from Mozart's *Sonata in A minor* (K310), and three pieces from his own (as yet unpublished) fourth volume of *Chants*: the *Barcarolle, Allegro con bravura* and *Le Chanson de la bonne vieille*. Finally, two pieces by Haydn and the *Variations for four hands* op 35 of Schubert were performed with Mme Massart. The audience as usual gave the virtuoso and composer a very warm reception. The end of the 1873 series was marked by a recital on 26 April and this event was only marred by the inclusion of a bizarre concerto for seven trumpets and timpani by Altenburg.[131] At this concert Alkan also played studies by Clementi, Berger,[132] Aloys Schmitt[133] and Moscheles, the largo from the *Sonata* op 35 of Chopin, a prestissimo by Czerny and finally the *Sonata* op 110 by Beethoven. On the pedal piano Alkan played the *Prelude and Fugue in F minor* by J.S. Bach (already played at the second concert) and the *Esquisses* [Blumenstück] in D flat by Schumann and a minuet and passacaglia by Handel. A quintet for piano, flute, clarinet, horn and bassoon by Spohr opened the concert.

The first 1874 concert[134] included the Beethoven op 109 sonata, three Chopin preludes, transcriptions from *Iphigénie en Tauride* (following their popularity in the 1873 season) as well as Alkan's own *Nocturne* op 22, *Barcarolle* op 65 and no. 8 of the *Prières* for pedaliér. Alkan also included two pieces from the *Mährchenerzählungen* of Schumann for piano, clarinet and viola with M. Grisez and M. Mas. At the second concert[135] on 5 March 1874 Alkan performed the adagio and saltarella from his *Violoncello Sonata* op 47. For pedal piano Alkan performed two Mendelssohn works and two Bach chorales. For piano solos Alkan played one of the Beethoven sonatas op 2, a polonaise and scherzo by Weber and various pieces by Schubert and Scarlatti. The third and fourth concerts[136] on 19 March and 3 April included the first *Étude* op 35, the first part of the *Second Concerto da camera*, the ancient Jewish Melodies [from *Preludes* op 31], some chants, prières and the two *Marches* op 26/27. Vocal items were provided by Mlle Marix, and other musicians included M. Alard, M. Jacquard and M.G. Pfeiffer. The last[137] of the Petits Concerts of 1874 consisted of a performance of Mozart's *Wind Quintet* and the slow movement of Chopin's *E minor concerto* as well as Alkan's *Violin Sonata* op 21. On the pédalier Alkan played a

Handel minuet and passacaglia, the Bach *Ich ruf dich* chorale and as in the 1873 series returned to the virtuoso Bach *F major Toccata* for the finale.

The first of the 1875 concerts of 19 February had been preceded[138] in the Parisian musical calendar by Alkan's presenting prizes at the Salle Taitbout and also performing movements from the Hummel *B minor concerto*, the Bach *F major Toccata* and a Kessler polonaise. The last two works were performed on the pedal piano. The Hummel and the Kessler repeated in the 1875 concerts. Inspection of the overall programme planning in the 1875 series (see Diagram 1.3) shows an astonishing range of composers and styles from the baroque to the romantic. The individual programmes were not specifically chronological and Alkan was sufficiently modest to place the performance of his own compositions during the interval. Also, he did not always now conclude his programmes with a virtuoso work and several programmes ended modestly with an original baroque work or transcription. The choice of romantic music is very selective and reflects Alkan's own predisposition for early romantics. The omission of Liszt and Brahms from the programmes is especially interesting: we may conclude that Alkan showed no temperamental desire to perform their piano works. Vocal music features only in the third programme but chamber music or chamber arrangements feature in all the programmes.

The first 1875 concert[139] took a chronological overview of all the most important keyboard composers from Couperin to Schumann taking in Scarlatti, Rameau, Handel, J.S. and W.F. Bach, Clementi, Mozart, Moscheles, Field, Weber, Czerny, Schubert, Mendelssohn, Chopin and a few others. Details of the programmes for the 1875 season are given in Diagram 1.3. As the series progressed we can observe that romantic music apart from the composer's own compositions feature less. For the last two programmes Alkan's final items are baroque works and the last concert of the 1875 series is a particularly well balanced programme with Bach chorales and other works including Haydn, Mozart (the F major sonata for four hands with Saint-Saëns), and Mendelssohn works as well as Alkan's magnificent violoncello sonata op 47. The austere F minor mazurka and the radiant third ballade of Chopin provide the romantic period works.

The 1876 series was cancelled[140] because of alterations to the Salle Erard. The *RGM* announced early in 1877 that Alkan was to resume his Petits Concerts with a similar programme structure as in previous concerts. These continued to be therefore in two parts with Alkan's own compositions being played at intermission time. Before the start of the 1877 season a recital was given to honour Alkan on 21 January. At this concert Alkan played several of his own works including his duo for piano and violin [op 21] and his second chamber concerto [op 10] accompanied by colleagues of long standing including Turban[141] and Verrimst.[142] The first concert proper[143] of the 1877 series took place on 21 February, although Alkan had previewed the programme on 14 February at the Salle Pleyel. The programme's contents were exactly the same as requested of Alkan two years previously. Beethoven's *Sonata in D* op 10/3, the adagio from Field's *A minor concerto*, the Chopin *Nocturne in C minor* op 48/1, his own *Chants* op 38/1 and 6 (played during the first intermission) and on the pedal piano a movement from a Bach [Trio] sonata and his own transcription of Gluck's *Ballet des Scythes* again.

Historical and Social Background

SIX PETITS CONCERTS DE MUSIQUE CLASSIQUE
CH: V^{IN} ALKAN

PROGRAMME I
Première Partie

I	LA FINE MADALON	COUPERIN
II	VIVACE de	D. SCARLATTI
III	LES SAUVAGES de	RAMEAU
IV	ADAGIO d'un CONCERTO Pour Clavecin de	HANDEL
V	1er MOU'VEMENT de la 6me SONATE de	J.S. BACH
VI	POLONAISES de	FRIEDMANN BACH

Premier Intermède:

I	N.1 du 4 Recueil de CHANTS pour Piano	CH: Vⁱⁿ ALKAN
II	N.2 du 4 Recueil de CHANTS pour Piano	CH: Vⁱⁿ ALKAN

Deuxieme Partie

I	N. 61, du GRADES, de	CLEMENTI
II	1er MORCEAU de SONATE de	MOZART
III	LARGO, de l'oeu: 10 de	BEETHOVEN
IV	ETUDE, en Mi mineur, de	MOSCHELES
V	ROMANCE en Mi bemot, de	FIELD
VI	SCHERZO, en Mi bemot, de	WEBER

Deuxieme Intermède

A	MARCHE des GRANDS-PRÊTRES, de l'ALCESTE: et:	
B	CHOER des SCYTHES, de l'IPHIGENIE EN TAURIDE: avec Clavier de Pèdales obligé	GLUCK

Troisieme Partie

I	PRESTISSIMO de l'oeu: 7, de	CZERNY
II	PENSEE MUSICALE, de	SCHUBERT
III	2 POLONAISE, de l'oeu: 25, de	KESSLER
IV	ETUDE, en Fa min: de	MENDELSSOHN
V	POLONAISE, de l'oeu: 26, de	CHOPIN
VI	FANTAISIE, de l'oeu: 111, de	SCHUMANN

PROGRAMME II
Première Partie

I	SONATE oeu: 78, de	SCHUBERT
II	FANTASIA: op: 77, de:	BEETHOVEN
III	POLONAISE, en Mi bemot, de	WEBER

Intermède

A	DEUX MORCEAUX RELIGIEUX pour Piano à Clavier de Pédales	
B	3 NUMÉROS des 48 MOTIFS, pour Piano seul	CH: Vⁱⁿ ALKAN
C	UNE TRANSCRIPTION du SAMSON, de	HANDEL

Deuxieme Partie

I	FANTAISIES, pour Clarinette et Piano; oeu:73, de	SCHUMANN
II	PRÈLUDE, ADAGIO, et PASTORALE, pour Piano à Clavier de Pédales, de	J.S. BACH
III	FANTAISIE, en La *min:* de	MENDELSSOHN

PROGRAMME III
Première Partie

I	SONATE: oeu: 110, de	BEETHOVEN
II	PRIÈRE PENDANT LA BATAILLE; Chant et Piano	WEBER
III	CHORAL, et FUGUE en Ré, pur Piano à Clavier de Pédales, de	J.S. BACH

Internède

	DUO, Pour Piano et Violoncelle:	CH: Vⁱⁿ ALKAN

Deuxieme Partie

I	DEUX PRELUDES, de Foeuvre 28, de	CHOPIN
II	RÉCITATIF, et AIR, pour Voix de Basse et Cimbalo obligato, de	J.S. BACH
III	MENUET, et 3 POLONAISE, de l'oeu:25; pour Piano à Pédales	HANDEL, & KESSLER

PROGRAMME IV
Première Partie

I	TRIO, pour Piano, Violon et Violoncelle, de	MOZART
II	CHOEUR de l'OBERON, transcrit pour Piano à Clavier de Pèdales	WEBER
III	DEUXIEME SONATE, de	CHOPIN

Intermède

A	IMPROMPTU	
B	MARCHE FUN9RRE	CH: Vⁱⁿ ALKAN
C	MENUET SYMPHONIQUE	
D	FANTAISIE, pour deux Pianos à Clavier de Pèdales	SAINT-SAËNS

Deuxieme Partie

I	SONATA, pour Piano et Violon, de	J.S. BACH
II	MAZURKA, et 1er BALLADE, de	CHOPIN
III	DEUX TRANSCRIPTIONS, pour Piano; de l'ARAMIDE, de	GLUCK
	Et de la SYMPHONIE en Mi bemot, de	MOZART

PROGRAMME V
Première Partie

I	A. CHORAL, et: B. CANON, pour Piano à Clavier de Pèdales, de	BACH & SCHUMANN
II	SONATE: op: 109, de	BEETHOVEN
III	A. CHORAL, et: B. VARIATIONS, pour Piano à Clavier de Pèdales, de	BACH & HANDEL

Intermède

A	PRÉLUDE VI, pour Piano à Pèdales	
B	La Chanson de la bonne Vieille Du 4 RECUEIL de CHANTS pour Piano	CH: Vⁱⁿ ALKAN
C	L'ETUDE en un dièse, avec accompagnement d'Orchestre	

Deuxieme Partie

I	CONCERTO, en Si min: avec accompagnement d'Orchestre; oeu: 89, de	HUMMEL
II	MENUETS, de	RAMEAU
III	A. CHORAL, et: B. ANDANTE, pour Piano à Pèdales, de	BACH, & HAYDN

PROGRAMME VI
Première Partie

I	SONATE, à 4 Mains, de	MOZART
II	DEUX TRANSCRIPTIONS pour Piano à Clavier de P&dales, de	WEBER, & J.S. BACH
III	PRÈLUDE, et FUGUE V; de	MENDELSSOHN

Internède

I	MARCHES, A 4 Mains; et	
II	SONATE, pour Piano et Violon	CH: Vⁱⁿ ALKAN

Deuxieme Partie

I	MAZURKA, et 3 BALLADE, de	CHOPIN
II	ROMANCE SANS PAROLES, de	MENDELSSOHN
III	CHORAL, et FUGUE, en Sol: pour Piano à Pèdales, de	J.S. BACH

Prix du Billet (numéroté): 6 francs
Abonnement. pour let Six Séances: 30 francs

Diagram 1.3

The second Petit Concert of the 1877 series included[144] the first movement of the Bach *Triple Keyboard Concerto* played by Alkan and Fissot with double quartet. For the rest of this programme Alkan duplicated his op 21 *Violin Sonata* and the Bach *F major Toccata* from the 1873 and 1874 series as well as performing at this 1877 concert a Bach fugue and a Mendelssohn capriccio and fugue.

For the third 1877 concert[145] Alkan narrowed the range of composers, concentrating on Chopin in the first half and Schubert in the second. As in all the Petits Concerts Alkan played his own compositions. The Schubert works included extracts from the *G major D894 Sonata* and some lieder – *Thécla* and a song from *Die Schöne Mullerin*. During the interval Alkan revisited some of his earliest compositions including *Une Nuit d'Été* from *Les Mois* op 74 and a march in D [op 40?] for four hands adapted by Alkan for pédalier. The Chopin works for this concert included the first part of the *F major Ballade* op 47 and the scherzo of the op 35 sonata.

Piano music by Beethoven and Weber was paired for the fourth 1877 Petit Concert.[146] Alkan selected the *Fantasie* op 77, the adagio from the *C minor Concerto* and the *A flat Sonata* op 110. The Weber items were more diverse and included Alkan's own *Filles de la mer* transcription from *Oberon*, the *E major Polonaise*, the adagio of the *C major sonata* op 24 and the rondo of the first concerto in Bülow's solo piano arrangement. For the first time in the Petits Concerts Alkan performed one of his largest pieces: the *Concerto* op 39, as well as a prelude from the op 66 *Preludes* and an extract from the *Prières* op 64.

A more mixed programme was devised for the fifth 1877 concert.[147] The first half was principally devoted to baroque music comprising two chorales and a fantasie and the pédalier D major fugue by Bach plus the *Dagon* chorus from Handel's *Samson*. Romantic piano music represented included the larghetto of a Hummel concerto [possibly the B minor concerto] and, as in the third Petit Concert, works by Chopin. This time Alkan played the largo of the op 35 *Sonata*, the *Fantasy* op 49 and the first ballade. From his own compositions he performed the *Barcarolette* op 63, the *Marche funèbre and Minuet* from the op 39 *Études*. Interestingly Alkan performed this programme twice on Thursday afternoon then as per usual for the Petits Concerts on Thursday evening.

The final concert[148] of 1877 consisted of several chamber works of Schumann, the A minor violin sonata and two pieces for clarinet, viola and piano. The *A major Mozart violin sonata* also featured as did many pédalier works, a Bach chorale and sicilienne, a Handel passacaglia and a Kessler polonaise. Compared with other 1877 concerts Alkan chose smaller examples of his own works playing on this occasion the opening piece of the third book of *Chants*, the *Super flumina* psalm and two marches for four hands with the pianist Fissot.

From 1877 to the termination of the Petits Concerts in 1880, journal reports become less frequent. The 1879 series in fact lack any critical reviews whatsoever. From 1878 onwards Alkan was inclined to repeat programmes or reduce the number of concerts per season. As an example of the former, the programme of the Salle Pleyel concert of 9 March 1878 was repeated as the first of the 1878 Petit Concert.[149] Following the least recital of the 1877 series the keyboard and organ (pédalier) music of Bach featured strongly and included were a chorale and sicilienne and the *G minor alla breve Fugue*. At these concerts Alkan probably played fewer of his own compositions: only the *Minuetto alla tedesca* [op 46] and the *Voix de l'instrument* [*Chants* op 70] were mentioned in the *RGM* report, although Alkan programmed works by Mendelssohn, Haydn, Field, Hummel and Chopin as well.

The *RGM* gave a rather fuller acount[150] of the second 1878 concert mentioning that Alkan performed his *Anciene Melodie de la Synagogue*, his *Petit Canon à l'octave* (*Chants* book 3) and *Le Chant de guerre* (*Chants* book 2). The rest of the programme comprised music by Schumann and Mendelssohn. Special mention was made in the *RGM* report of the Schubert *Variations* again with Fissot as Alkan's duo pianist.

Less detail is available for the third 1878 concert[151] on 13 April 1877. Piano music by Bach, Mozart, Haydn and Chopin featured in the first half with Beethoven as sole composer in the second. During the interval as always Alkan devoted himself to his own music including a march funèbre [op 39/6?] and the finale of the *Symphony* op 39. This 13 April concert was previewed one week earlier at the Salle Pleyel.

The fourth and last Petit Concert[152] of 1878 on 27 April consisted of Alkan's transcription of Marcello's *Psalm 18*. The other baroque items included the Handel passacaglia and movements from a Bach concerto as well as a Bach bourrée. Romantic music played at this concert included the Cramer *35th Study* (book 2), Alkan's own *Super flumina* paraphrase, his op 35/1 étude and his *Chanson de la bonne vielle*. Because of the illness of the violinist Mme Szarvady, Alkan changed the programme performing two Schubert marches with Fissot, Chopin's *Allegro de concert* op 46 and two of Schumann's op 56 pieces on the pédalier.

During the rest of 1878 Alkan's concert appearances seem to have been confined to a June chamber concert[153] when he performed several pieces including *Prière du matin* [op 31/10], *les Moissonneurs*, *la Journée* and *le Retour au village*. The *Violoncello Sonata* op 47 (with Jacquard) was also performed. The quality of Alkan's music is mostly commended in this concert and also at another one on 19 June where he played several pédalier works including the ninth of the *Onze Grande Preludes*.

No reports exist of any concerts given in 1879 and the final series in 1880 contained only three concerts each repeated in the Salle Erard. Alkan continued his indefatigable championing of the pédalier playing several pieces by Bach and the ninth of his *Grand Preludes*. The rest of the first programme[154] centred on several *Chants*, the Beethoven op 110 sonata and other works by Beethoven, Schumann and Chopin. There is from this programme contents and the rest of the 1880 series an air of retrospection to the programme planning. The second Petit Concert[155] thus contained music by Hummel (the *Adagio* from the *B minor concerto*), a favourite of Alkan's since his early concert days. Baroque keyboard works played at this petit Concert included a Bach-Vivaldi concerto, a Bach fugue and movements from a keyboard concerto. A Mendelssohn sonata and his presto scherzando in F sharp minor and a Kessler polonaise represented the Romantic era of piano music. During the interval Alkan performed his *Symphonie* op 39 for piano as in the 1877 series.

For his final 1880 recital of the series[156] Alkan played at the Salle Pleyel on 17 April and at the Salle Erard on 24 April. For both concerts he chose an austere programme consisting of fugues by Handel, Bach and Mendelssohn, a Bach chorale, a Handel passacaglia, canons by Schumann and his own *Air de Ballet* [op 24] and a prière (played on the pédalier). The only romantic works which appear to have been performed were a Chopin mazurka and the *F minor Ballade*.

This was Alkan's last Petit Concert and the end of his public concert career. He moved deeply into seclusion playing only to selected friends at the Salle Erard twice weekly.[157] Attempts were made by de Bertha on Alkan's behalf[158] to provide him with some official recognition. A diplomat, Prince Orloff, on the suggestion of de Bertha, called on Alkan several times to discuss the question of the Légion d'Honneur. When Alkan returned the call the prince was not at home. Thereafter Alkan lost interest and therefore never received the decoration. He did not have the humiliation of witnessing the honour being bestowed on his brother Napoléon who received the decoration in 1895 a few years after Charles's death. De Bertha again tried to come to Alkan's aid by approaching the administrators of the Conservatoire and suggesting that a post of Professor of Pédalier be created for Alkan. Alkan showed some interest but later on changed his mind: possibly at this stage in his life he was not prepared for a repetition of his previous troubles with the Conservatoire administration. Several important contemporary musicians, nevertheless, were welcomed by him at the Salle Erard rather than at his home. Frederick Niecks,[159] for example, was advised by a certain Mme Dubois[160] to appear at the Salle Erard on Monday or Thursday afternoons at 3 pm if he wanted to meet Alkan. On the stated occasion Alkan rose to greet Niecks and addressed him in the warmest possible manner. Niecks reported that Alkan's playing was on this occasion totally free from extravagance and his primary aim was fidelity to the music. Tributes to the sincerity of Alkan's playing also came from the founder of the *Schola Cantorum*, Vincent d'Indy who enthused about the clarity and expressiveness of Alkan's playing of Bach on the pédalier. When Alkan played Beethoven's op 110 *Sonata*, d'Indy compared his performance more than favourably with that of Liszt, writing that:[161] 'this [performance] was perhaps less technically skilled [than Liszt] but more personal and humanly moving'. With relentless energy Alkan may have continued his Monday and Thursday afternoon recitals[162] for his own pleasure right up until 30 March 1888, the day of his death, although no press reviews of these concerts exist.

If general music lovers know anything about Alkan they recount the bookcase/ death story. In the Alkan literature an unusual amount of interest too has been engendered regarding the exact circumstances of Alkan's death and this issue, moreover, has acquired something of the flavour of a Victorian melodrama. The most popular and dramatic version is the notion that Alkan was in the process of stretching up to the top of a bookcase for a volume of the *Talmud*, the books of Jewish law. There are many volumes of the *Talmud* and by tradition, no other book can be placed higher. It is therefore reasonable to assume that given Alkan's devout nature, these volumes would be kept at the top. It was believed by some apparently that this bookcase fell on Alkan and he was found, crushed to death, holding a volume of the *Talmud*. The source of this melodramatic tale can be traced to a verbal account by Isidore Philipp, recounted to Robert Collet, a piano professor at the Guildhall School of Music in London. Philipp,[163] according to the legend, dragged Alkan out from beneath the bookcase. Philipp was also one of the four mourners along with Blondel (the head of Erard's), the violinist, Maurin,[164] and de Bertha. Since Philipp's tale is verbal it may have become elaborated along the way and indeed Delaborde and Philipp may have been in collusion regarding this version. De Bertha's account however contains no such melodrama. He reported merely that 'Alkan was found stretched out, lifeless in his kitchen'.[165] It might be assumed that Alkan was about to prepare his evening meal since he was found in front of his cooker. A more modified version of the Philipp story was given by a relative of Alkan Mme Guerret[166] who reported 'yes, to my knowledge, it was his cupboard certainly which fell on him and caused his death'. The ambiguity here is 'to my knowledge' which may not have been first hand knowledge. Mme Guerret employed the French noun 'armoire' which is certainly not a bookcase but could possibly be translated as a 'kitchen cupboard'. To complicate the issue is Alkan's pupil José Vianna da Motta's account[167] of a natural death reinforced by the lack of any police record of an unusual mode of death.

The most recent research on the issues surrounding Alkan's death has been provided by Macdonald.[168] He reports that Jean Yves Bras, the French Alkan scholar, discovered a letter from Marie-Antoinette Colas dated 4 April 1888, several days after Alkan's death. Accordingly she reported that Alkan had failed to collect his lunch around 11.00 am on 29 March 1888. Alkan especially in later years was extremely predictable in upholding practical and domestic details so the omission of this domestic routine was unusual. At about 11.00 am the concièrge heard faint moans from Alkan's apartment. After forcing an entry, the concièrge observed Alkan prostate in the kitchen with the heavy umbrella stand on top of him. Possibly he may have fainted and had reached out for an object to support him. The concièrge had carried him through to his bedroom but Alkan died at about 8.00 pm.

Tributes to Alkan after his death were both sincere and intense. The obituary in the *RGM* 15 April 1888 is typical:

> Charles-Valentin Alkan (Alkan the elder) was an artist truly worthy of that name who in the purity of his inspiration and modesty of his lifestyle is reminiscent of the late lamented Stephen Heller who has just died aged seventy four. Alkan's musical talent was quite extraordinary. A highly distinguished student of Dourlen and Zimmerman at the Conservatoire he took first prize in solfège at seven, first prize in piano at ten and first prize in harmony at twelve. He abandoned concert life because public acclaim prevented him form composing and teaching. His concertos, sonatas, études – caprices, studies and preludes in all keys testify to a super fine talent, sober to the point of austerity. Alkan's music lacked the humour to make it popular. His thorough pedagogy produced numerous celebrated pupils including Ravina and Gavi.

This tribute sums up the rather special attributes of the outstanding French piano composer of the nineteenth century.

Chapter 2

Apprentice Works

'Now that instrumental writing has become the most important part of music, sonatas are very much in fashion, and all sorts of symphonies equally so; vocal music is scarcely more than an accessory.'[1] These thoughts of Jean-Jacques Rousseau, that most radical and protoromantic of all the *philosophes* reflect the state of late-eighteenth-century musical aesthetics in France. More conservative *philosophes* such as D'Alembert on the other hand regarded instrumental music as speaking neither to the spirit nor the soul. The expansion of instrumental music particularly for solo piano nevertheless is a phenomenon of French nineteenth-century music history simultaneously accompanied by an equal growth of piano music and piano teaching methods. Of special importance in France is the *Méthode de Piano du Conservatoire*,[2] which influenced all French piano composers, pianists and teachers of the nineteenth century. Yet French conservatories in the nineteenth century were musically conservative: at the start of the century the harpsichord was still preferred to the piano and this naturally delayed the emergence of a French school of piano virtuosi.

Radical French composers looked towards foreigners such as Dussek who settled in Paris in 1806. These composers were to provide the type of facile virtuosity, bravura effects and cantabile style which is to be found in the apprentice piano works of Alkan. Dussek made a huge impression on the Parisian critics such as Fétis. '[Dussek's] broad and grand style, his manner of making the instrument sing ... and the neatness and delicacy of his playing, all contributed to a triumph such as never has been seen.'[3] If Dussek represented the patrician approach, Steibelt, who settled in Paris in 1805, was the leader in stimulating bourgeois desire for a more popular approach to piano composition. The first works of Alkan may be viewed in a context of Steibelt's fashionable style. Conversely the classic piano works of Haydn, Mozart, Clementi, Beethoven, Cramer, Dussek and Hummel were now discarded by Steibelt: Alkan followed suit in his apprentice works. Not until 1837, the period during which Alkan developed a personal voice, is there any evidence of Alkan rediscovering the classics.[4]

It is to Steibelt directly that Alkan turned for his first composition,[5] his *Variations pour pianoforte composées sur un thème de Steibelt* op 1, published in 1828. This employs the rondo pastoral theme of Steibelt's *Third Concerto in E Major* (L'orage) of 1799. By incorporating the theme of a popular concerto by a well established composer, Alkan might confidently predict pianistic and compositional success. The type of audience enthusiasm in the early part of the nineteenth century is vividly portrayed by Alkan's friend and compatriot Chopin. A propos the latter's concert, it is reported 'as soon as I appeared on the stage the bravos began; after each variation [of his *Là ci darem là mano* op 2] the applause was so loud that I couldn't hear the orchestra's tutti'.[6]

Indeed on surveying the apprentice works of any early-nineteenth-century piano composer, variation and rondo feature strongly. Alkan's op 1 dedicated to his teacher and mentor Zimmerman shows off the virtuosic talent of a fifteen-year-old who possesses some glimmerings of compositional promise. The theme of the work itself is anchored to tonic/dominant tonality and is rather repetitive in phrase structure: it is capable therefore of ornamental and florid treatment beloved of contemporary Parisian virtuosi and their audiences.

Ex. 2.1   *Variations* op 1, theme, bars 1–4

Castil-Blaze[7] in 1825 succinctly described the stereotypical manner of variation writing: 'first there are simple quavers and triplets, then arpeggios, syncopations and octaves, not forgetting the adagio [variation] in the minor key and the tempo di polacca'. This gives the broad schemata for Alkan's early sets of variation and the six variations of op 1 which generally follow this decorative pattern. Variation one employs broken chords, arpeggios and scalic passages. Variation two features repeated notes (capitalizing on Erard's double escapement invention of 1821), passages in thirds and some brilliant Lisztian-type left hand octaves. Variation three has graceful and lyrical passage work with extensive scalic and chromatic coloratura. A higher point of musical interest is Alkan's deployment of the 'orchestral' link from the end of the theme as a modulation for the sustained fourth variation. The Adagio variation four itself is in *bel canto* mode with much filigree scalic figuration which focuses on the upper register of the 1820/1830 French piano. Variation five consists of thematic re-statement set against left hand arpeggio and scalic accompaniment. The final variation of Alkan's op 1 however is rather anti-climactic. Although it has a truly bravura character so much brilliant figuration has been utilized in previous variations that the impression here is rather repetitive. The coda adheres slavishly to the Orage theme and the end of the work (a fff scale over the whole range of the instrument) is a conventionally brilliant end.

The most unusual feature of op 1 is the frequent use of a *piacere* passages in small notehead notation in free rhythm giving some improvisational freedom to the performers. Alkan's op 1, in summary, is typical of the early-nineteenth-century set of variations designed for a bourgeois audience. Adding to Castil-Blaze, one might deduce that the formula of this type of variation writing invariably consisted of a grandiose introduction, then a simple statement of an operatic-type theme, several melodically and technically decorative variations then a brilliant finale often completed by a triumphant coda with cascading arpeggios or scales or thundering chordal passages.

These stylistic markers are also found in Alkan's next composition, his op 2 *Les Omnibus* set of variations. Like op 1 these variations are clearly the work of an aspiring pianist-virtuoso rather than a composer-prodigy given their emphasis again on *stile brilliante*. Published in 1829 op 2's title refers to the *Dames Blanches* which were Baudry's horse-drawn carriages[8] which ran from the Madeleine to the Bastille. As with the op 1 set, *Les Omnibus* relies on contemporary pianistic fireworks to make an impact. This is especially found in the introduction with a typical Rossinian 'orchestral crescendo' over an extended tonic pedal. Other stylistic features of the c1830 era used here are bravura arabesques and polacca-type rhythms. As for the theme itself, its direct harmonic simplicity in the introduction and a I–II–V chordal closure in the first half of the theme with long stretches of tonic harmony in the second half is appealing if rather naïve.

Ex. 2.2   *Les Omnibus* op 2, theme, bars 1–8

Nevertheless Alkan's careful calculation of the dynamics, the continuation of the introduction's Rossini-type crescendo and the (implied) glissandi in thirds are all brilliant examples of French early piano writing. Compared with op 1 the variations of op 2 provide a more cumulative impulse for the finale. As to the variations themselves, variation one expands the theme linearly in the upper range of the piano and makes much more use of figures in thirds (staccato and glissandi) and employs a faster harmonic rhythm, variation two re-decorates the theme with brilliant octave passage work and chordal textures, variation three follows the fashionable c1830 *alla polacca* style with much pointing of the polonaise rhythms, and this variation is even more prone to surface contour then any of the earlier ones. Perhaps the most interesting event in op 2 is the adroit harmonic preparation of the E flat major episode. Then a brief recitative passage provides temporary respite with a slowed down trumpet call, in imitation of the *Dames Blanches* perhaps before several bravura passages with glissandi in parallel and contrary movement round off the work. Overall, op 2 might be considered to be a worthy youthful virtuosic essay exploring contemporary piano sonorities: that is, broken octave figuration, *alla polacca* rhythms and multiple use of glissandi which are really the unifying narrative points of this set of variations and others in this early composition phase.

Alkan's next composition is his first example of a rondo-type structure: this is the rondoletto *Il était un p'tit homme* op 3, published in *c*1830. An obvious comparison and influence on op 3 is Chopin's *Rondo in C Minor* op 1 which was published five years earlier in 1825. Compared with the Chopin work, Alkan's rondoletto is more primitive and less imbued with a personal voice, although Chopin's op 1 has been dismissed as having 'its materials lacking [in] distinction and its structure [being] insecure'.[9] Similar if not greater, criticisms may be applied to Alkan's op 3. Contemporary reviews[10] of op 3, the *Rondo brillant* op 4 (published *c*1833) and the Rondo on Rossini's *Largo al factotoum* from *Il barbiere di Siviglia* op 5 (published *c*1833)[11] proclaimed that they were less subject to prolixity and shortage of new ideas compared with his earlier works. On closer inspection Alkan's op 3 does possess several strong features. Its introduction has an orchestral grandeur with many quasi-brass fanfares which implies that op 3 might have been originally planned for piano and orchestra. The rondo theme itself, although rather weak rhythmically, has attractive poise and well directed harmonic sequences not found in previous compositions. Within the basic rondo theme, there is an unexpected asymmetric phrase structure and, despite much meandering material, Schubertian major-minor key shifts and unpredictable augmented sixth harmonies add some colour to the harmonic palette. Moreover, there is a delightful use of accented passing notes in the first episode giving a piquant flavour to the melodic contour: this shows the influence of the French melodic style operatic of Auber[12] The direct application of passing notes becomes ingested into Alkan's later style. The final section of op 3 employs an embryonic locked chord figuration which Alkan was to develop in a much more excitingly dissonant format in the *Étude* op 39/12.

Finally, Alkan's desire to unify op 3 is shown by a reference back to the introduction reintroducing the theme in skeletal form in rhythmic augmentation. In short, although the influence of Rossini in tonic/dominant crescendo effects and direct imitations of Weber's pianistic glitter are derivative and granted that the work is perhaps overendowed with showy passage work, cadential trills, and a mock tutti,[13] Alkan's op 3 demonstrates a more personal style and much promise for compositional maturity, particularly towards the form of 'concerto without orchestra' in the *Études* op 39.

Alkan's *Rondo brillant* op 4 with *ad libitum* string quartet accompaniment was published *c*1833. Fétis had described this[14] as having 'energy and finish which belied the age of its composer'. The introductory theme of op 4 is elegantly sculptured in a more classical manner[15] and there is now a new confidence in melodic contour, controlled decoration within the basic theme and much more interesting piano texture particularly in the left hand as the opening paragraphs show.

Ex. 2.3   *Rondo brilliant* op 4, introduction and rondo theme, bars 1–29

This individuality is perhaps diminished by a deterioration into genre scalic bravura and arpeggiated chinoiserie, and although the rondo theme itself has an attractive rhythmic verve, as this section progresses, surface brilliance again takes over. Passage work in double thirds and martellato chordal figuration is stereotypical for 1833. So for the main part this work is representative of early nineteenth century pianistic *stile brillante* style,[16] but op 4 shows a more disciplined approach to thematic construction with episodes well differentiated from thematic material.

Less developed in thematic construction are Alkan's *Concerti da camera* but both maintain *stile brillante*. Like both Chopin concerti the Alkan examples are more original in detail rather than structure or rhetoric. For the latter Alkan along with Chopin depended on Mendelssohn, Hummel and Weber but most of all Mozart whose concerti (especially the brilliant types such as the *K537 Coronation*) judiciously balance bravura figuration, thematic power and potent long range harmony. Bravura composers of the early-nineteenth century mentioned formed a direct and contemporary model for Chopin and Alkan who were unable or unwilling to sustain Mozart's lofty musical parameters. In Alkan's concerti, like Chopin's, the Mozartian balance is now displaced in favour of more mechanically based rhythmic blocks, recessed accompaniments and pianistically brilliant but predictable scalic and arpeggiated contours.

Alkan's *Concerto da camera* op 10/1 in A minor was premièred in Paris on 29 April 1832 at the Société des Concerts du Conservatoire: the concerto was an unqualified triumph for the composer and it is strange that this work has vanished from most pianists' repertoires. Described as 'un grand concerto'[17] it is one of Alkan's most weighty and dignified works of this period using a full sized orchestra including four bassoons and bass trombone. The concerto also found favour in 1832 as a competition piece: part of the concerto was selected for the piano concours at the conservatoire according to the original title page. The opening orchestral tutti has a quiet but insistent energy in the style of the Weber/Hummel model. There is certainly a similarity between the opening of the Alkan *A minor Concerto* and the Chopin *E* minor.[18] Both have similar ascending patterns and this is common *rappel à l'ordre* in the early romantic piano concerto. The brilliance of the piano writing is as always present but there is equally very little tendency to develop themes. All the material is contained within a telescoped sonata principle where exposition themes do not reappear in full in either the development or the recapitulation. Alkan draws on the one movement concerto prototypes such as Weber's *Konzertstück* to link concerto movements together. Hence the Allegro opening movement's development merges into the central slow movement which is a cantabile adagio in E major of only forty bars' length. This movement is very simply constructed in aria style. The first half of the adagio owes much to Field and his nocturnes: the adagio's second half presents new material in A major with Weber-like *rollfiguren*. This then dissolves into the type of writing found in op 3 with added repeated notes and chromatic scalic passages. Despite these standard patterns there is nevertheless a better balance between technical effects and musical shape than most of Alkan's early works in this style. Unusually for a concerto of this period the longest movement is the finale. This is full of conventional contemporary gestures such as polacca rhythms (as per op 2) tonic/dominant chordal alternations in the Rossini

Apprentice Works

manner and *passim* an indulgent virtuosic verve. Hints of Alkan's originality and sensitivity do exist however in this movement – a well turned melodic episode with an asymmetric phrase shape delights the ear.

Ex. 2.4   *Concerto da camera* op 10/1, finale, bars 65–?

Superficially this movement may appear to resemble the finale of Chopin's *E Minor Concerto*, but already Alkan is exhibiting a more relentless driving energy with block chordal massed style to be developed further in works such as the *Concerto* op 39. There is also a convincing order of sections with related tonal regions giving rise to the feeling that Alkan can compose in larger forms.

The second *Concerto da camera* in C sharp minor was composed for Henry Field of Bath. Dedicated to the same individual, he performed it in Bath on 11 April 1834. Compared with the first concerto this concerto is shorter in length but not in musical weight or formal innovation. Contemporary reviews described it as a 'concertino ... especially delightful for the novelty of its style and technique'.[19] This concerto immediately gives a hint of the darker, more macabre, more compressed and massed style of the later more mature Alkan. The strongest influence in the opening is undoubtedly that of the operatic world of Weber.

Ex. 2.5   *Concerto da camera* op 10/2, first movement, bars 1–5

Also, Mendelssohn supplies the influence for the principal subject and filigree piano writing,[20] and the figuration itself just escapes from the formulaic by means of subtle metrical shifts. An attractive siciliano slow movement replaces the formal development. This short adagio movement is one of Alkan's freshest early inspirations – melodic fragility, piano texture and natural organic growth are now in perfect balance.

Ex. 2.6   Concerto da camera op 10/2, Adagio, bars 1–?

If the hand-crossings anticipate Liszt's well known *Au bord d'une source*, the use of the thumb melodies in this movement are Thalberg-derived. The adagio eloquently recedes to be followed by a dramatic piano entry marking out the final section which is a compressed recomposition of the opening section. The principal subject now in the tonic major is rejustified by invertible counterpoint. Alkan's desire to demonstrate compositional ingenuity is further evidenced by a rather unusual combining of the opening section's principal subject with the adagio's main melody. However, some splendidly athletic pianistics in the shape of locked hand textures, left hand octave work and broken octaves return the mood to a more mundane level. This ternary-designed concerto had a special place in Alkan's early compositions and was one of his favourite works for public performance. It is a flexible work: a solo piano version[21] was published in 1859 and it could also be played in a chamber version (string quartet plus double bass).[22]

The success of both the first and second *Concerto da camera* may have prompted Alkan to compose a third *Concerto da camera*, the first performance of which was announced for the concert[23] in Paris on 3 March 1838. Even given the imprecision of Parisian music journals no concerto was mentioned. But a review in *Le Pianiste* reveals the identity of the work from the description of the piece 'a simple gracious muted song for strings is accompanied by a series of chords which, passing from octave to octave, sustains the melody and produces an effect as original as it is ravishing'.[24] There is only one Alkan work which fits this description. This is the second of the *Trois andante romantiques* op 13 published in 1837 which was then republished[25] in 1838 with the title *Caprice ou Étude* in C sharp major. The simplicity and gentleness of this work is a remarkable demonstration of Alkan's rejection of the over-florid, over-extended practices of his early period of composition.

The *Rondeau chromatique* op 12 of 1833 is indicative of his further concise composition. Some aberrations such as undirected cadential passages and over-reliance on the direct imitation of orchestral instruments do not lessen the impression of op 12. The title indicates some desire to be slightly more adventurous.[26] Although the left hand tremolando quasi-orchestral effects is redolent of *Les Omnibus* op 2, there is now a stronger chromaticism at the start of op 12, although the model is still Rossinian. The rondo theme itself is much stronger melodically than previous works and is attractively coloured chromatically. Also, modulation (to the relative major) and a strategically placed Neapolitan sixth are well executed. The first episode with its massive orchestral texture looks forward very strongly to Alkan's massed chordal density found in the *Études* op 39 as does a frequent use of locked chord figuration. The structure of the work is enhanced by the climactical conversion of the rondo theme to the tonic major key to herald the coda section and a daring use of enharmonic modulation provides a drive to the final cadence amidst intensive pianistic bravura.

The next sets of variations were published in 1834 as op 16/4, op 16/5, op 16/6, the earlier op 16 sets being missing. All of these variations continue the *bel canto* Italianate influence but all are much more compactly written than earlier sets. Probably the most interesting of the op 16 sets is that on *La Tremenda Ultrice Spada* op 16/5 from Bellini's *I Capuleti i Montecchi*. Although this opera had its first performance in Venice in 1830, it is likely that Alkan's first contact with it was its first Parisian performance at the Théâtre Italien in the autumn of 1833. Bellini, awaiting a new commission for an opera, mingled with salon habitués[27] including Chopin, Paër[28] and Carafa[29] and may have been introduced to Alkan. Consequently Alkan might have been impressed by Bellini's ability to build broad melodic arches in his characteristically *bel canto* idiom from small metrical phrase units providing a much freer lyricism for Alkan compared with the rigid melodic units of earlier sets. Indeed, an examination of Bellini's theme of *La Tremenda* shows a fine control of melodic phrasing, major harmonic inflections predominating although minor harmony (via the submediant) is briefly employed, and in keeping with his Italian operatic contemporaries, a smoothing out of rhythms. Chiefly, however, is the magnificently structured melodic arch on which imaginative variations are constructed.

The background to op 16/5 is interesting. Alkan's setting of *La Tremenda* is dedicated to Miss Isabella Field[30] and the title page notes that Alkan was an honorary professor at the Royal School in Paris and was a member of the *Société Académique des Enfants d'Apollon*, having joined the Society in 1832. This *Tremenda* set is clearly designed to be 'brilliant but not difficult', a phrase much used by English musical publishers[31] of the early-nineteenth century to widen the appeal and increase demand by amateur pianists. Despite the obsessively scalic variation, one where the writing is much more compact then earlier compositions by Alkan, there is a wider ranging key scheme in this set of variations and stronger textural contrasts. Variation two is a lively chordal staccato minore, and variation three forms a submediant tonal relationship with the theme and internally moving chromatic notes, a rather quaint use of an Alberti bass figuration and a Mendelssohnian sense of drama are prominent. Variation four shows a control of structure and brilliance in a Mendelssohn-type 'hunting' manner.

Op 16/4 is that on *Ah, segnata e la mia morte [sorte]* (1834) from *Anna Bolena* by Donizetti. This opens with an effective dramatic arrangement of the ritornello, but the theme marked *con disperazione* (with despair) is very primitively organized with a very simple piano texture. Variation one returns to the pianistic brilliance highly reminiscent of Weber.

Ex.2.7a   Donizetti/Alkan *Ah segnata*, op 16/4, bars 1–9

Ex. 2.7b   Weber – *Sonata in C major* op 24, finale, bars 1–4

Variation two rhythmically augments the theme promisingly, but repeats the rather primitive accompaniment used in the theme itself and, later in the variation as per op 3, Italianate grace notes are added. (Later, Alkan, in his introduction to a first set of classical transcriptions published in 1847, chided Weber for a similarly indecorous treatment!) The final variation neatly transforms the theme into a graceful *mouvement de valse* followed by a prophetic hymn-like section before an exhilarating *alla polacca* final part rather akin to the finale of the op 2 variations.

The final set of the op 16 variations is the op 16/6 *Variations quasi fantaisie sur une barcarolle napolitaine*. Perhaps the most interesting features about this set is the sinuous bass chromatic movement in the introduction 'imitant le bruit des rames'[32] and the Neapolitan barcarolle melody[33] which may have provided a blueprint for Liszt's much more extended version in the middle section of the *Tarantella* from his *Venezia e Napoli*: particularly pertinent is the comparison with the earlier version (1840) contained in the *Tarantelles Napolitaines* and Alkan's chromatic decoration and rhythmic verve in the finale anticipate Liszt's setting quite strongly.

In conclusion, Alkan's apprentice works are the usual 1820's mixture of bravura, operatic *bel canto* and decoration. His own compositional progress within this apprentice phase was necessarily inconsistent and reliance on the contemporary pianistic models was fairly constant. Nevertheless there are individual touches of the unexpected in harmonic turns and in a colourful and direct approach to the piano texture which was later to become very much an Alkanian characteristic to suggest that he is to transcend the mundane vocabulary of the 1820's virtuoso pianist composer and become a vital force in the history of Romantic piano music.

Chapter 3

Development of a Personal Voice

Although Alkan remained faithful to the *stile brillante* models and the Rossinian operatic world, in developing a personal voice one finds a marked reduction in pianistic fioriture and passage work for its own sake. During this short period from 1835 to 1838 Alkan eschews contemporary bourgeois taste by discarding the ubiquitous rondo and variation genre. We now see a real musical identity developing with sparser classicism and symphonic grandeur predominating. Significant too is Alkan's return to his Gallic clavecin roots with an associated interest in reviving and energizing the miniature. Generally speaking after 1835 there is a reduction of musical prolixity and a greater sense of formal and motivic discipline.

This discipline arose from the wide influence and interest in Beethoven in 1830's France. Of special importance to this phenomenon is the empathy of Berlioz and others.[1] Berlioz in his many writings promoted Beethoven's music relentlessly against the sceptics.[2] Audiences, other critics and composers were made aware of Beethoven's innovations in harmonic procedures, dissonances and his sense of epic drama. Liszt also took up the cause of Beethoven by transcribing *Symphony No. 5* for two pianos in 1837 and Alkan arranged part of *Symphony No. 7* for two pianos which was performed[3] in the same year.

Towards a personal voice: ops 12, 13, 15 and 16

A Beethovian sense of the dramatic is present in all of Alkan's *Trois improvisations dans le style brillant* op 12 published in 1837. Despite the title, these pieces are neither improvisations nor in the *stile brillante* of apprentice days. As quasi études all three are carefully and rigorously planned and all are uncluttered by the excessive ornamentation of previous times. There is now an original sense of stylistic articulation by means of motif, modulation and mood. The first étude of op 12 projected at a heady prestissimo is effectively a study in arm octave and staccato chordal techniques. The opening page demonstrates a concision and precision. Fundamentally, there is a fine balance of dynamics, sounds and silences, and arpeggiated octaves feature with subsequent internal scalic movement as statement and response. From earlier works Alkan brings decorative melodic chromaticisms, sudden unprepared modulations, relentless rhythmic cells,[4] prepared silences and tonal ambiguity. Unprepared modulations, in this case in the mediant key, launch the opening paragraphs of op 12/1.

Ex. 3.1   *3 Etudes de bravour* op 12/1. bars 1–46

Alkan begins to unify by monothematic/monorhythmic procedures. The second theme is rhythmically and melodically allied to the opening theme, but the former is now decked out with added sixths and is harmonized by a succession of dominant seventh to tonic progressions. On the return of the opening theme the ornamentation is tightly controlled and the étude ends with a piano repeat of the dactylic rhythm before a fff percussive tonic chord using the extremities of the piano. This emphatic 'full-stop' was to become a thumbprint of later works.[5]

The second étude of op 12 is a lyrical allegretto and it is another excellent example of Alkan's now more uncluttered melodic line. Features which are now to be characteristic of Alkan's developed approach are found here including a melodic tendency to centre around one note, a liking for asymmetrical phrasing, an inbuilt rallentando and a Schubertian tendency to slip from major to minor tonal centres.

Another important style marker is that op 12/2 is the first example of Alkan's block structure, that is, his tendency to mark off contrasting sections with strongly marked double bars. In this étude this marker is also accompanied by a sudden but quite unpredictable melodically-led tonal shift.

Ex. 3.2   *3 Etudes de bravour* op 12/2, bars 36–42

Of all Alkan's early études this is the one which is most influenced by a Schubertian attitude to inversion of texture, namely, on repetition, the opening melody is now transferred to the left hand accompanied by right hand triplet filigree ornamentation.[6] But the most radical aspects in op 12/2 are the harsh dissonances before the triplet ornamentation and the passionate restatement of the opening theme now in a transformed 6/8 variant which alternates in the final page with an echo of the opening 3/4 section, and a delightfully rustic use of drone basses which are further explored in the Trio section of the *Scherzo* op 16/1.

The remarkable impact of op 12/3, an allegro marziale, is caused by its incessant Gallic revolutionary march rhythms and its dense uncompromisingly direct style. This is the most original of the op 12 *Études* and virtuosity and music content are now in equilibrium. Despite a deliberate lyrical parody and a banal quality of some of the figuration, nothing can diminish the triumph of the minor-major shift to the 'superbamente'[7] final section. This has a grandeur quite unparalleled in Alkan's piano output up to 1837. Undoubtedly, Alkan has rejected the shallowness of the French early-nineteenth-century school. As Bellamann comments, op 12 'emphasise the immediate steps Alkan was making at this time towards a much more free piano technique'.[8] One might add that Alkan's op 12/3 is his first example of a really original approach to composition.

The *Trois Andantes Romantiques* op 13 published in 1837 are more intimate pieces than the virtuoso op 12 set but these show a similar advance in compositional confidence. The opening with its rising melody and increased level of dynamics moves towards a French sixth harmonic tension. Perhaps the 'romantic' nature of this étude is typified by the principal melody at bar 9 which is almost a self-parody given its short-breathed, repetitive, over sequential and highly triadic nature. This neutral melody is then subjected to extensive 'vocal' decoration and transferred into the left hand with a Schubertian use of the Neapolitan sixth harmonic shift (F/G flat major): thereafter follows a further decorated version in G flat major. Also Schubert-like is the broken chord figuration[9] whereas the gently undulating right hand figuration owes more to Weber.[10] But the most original part of this étude is its final section, an adroit conversion of the principal melody into B flat minor which uses left hand chromaticisms highly reminiscent of a similar section in Liszt's *Mazeppa*. On closer inspection, too, Alkan's use of shifting chromatic block chords is even more prophetic of *Mazeppa* and it is virtually unthinkable that Liszt would not have known the Alkan work.[11]

Ex. 3.3   *3 Andantes Romantiques* op 13/1, bars 62–65

Many other texturally interesting passages are apparent in the second étude of op 13 which first existed[12] as a version with strings con sordini. The 1833 review described this étude in glowing terms.[13] The arrangement for solo piano is no less effective with the implied melody being sustained by pedal. For 1833, this is a novel textural effect. Moreover, Alkan's evanescent harmonies with applied suspensions, chromatic shifts and a delicate transference of the implied melody into stereotypical arpeggios are all remarkably innovative given the early date of composition. The middle section of op 13/2 is notable for a continuation and expansion of the arpeggios, this time over a richly sonorous bass melody in the submediant key, before the return to a densely chordal version of the opening section and a finely executed decay of the arpeggio figuration towards an altered plagal cadence which is the focal point of the whole étude. In summary, op 13/2 is certainly one of the finest of the early period works of Alkan and deserves a place in any pianist's repertoire. Perhaps this fusion of strong compositional direction and shimmering textures gave rise to Blanchard's designation of the op 13/2 *Étude* as 'both austere and pleasing'.[14]

Less interesting is the final étude of op 13 which is much more mundane musically, and merely functions as a thumb and second finger trill étude. Its opening melody is curiously similar to Beethoven's setting of the *Ode to Joy* in the *Symphony No. 9*. This étude has an over long dominant pedal but some internal harmonic shifts and applied sixth harmonies give the piece a degree of freshness and the pastoral atmosphere of op 13/3 is reflected in later pieces by Liszt such as the *Eglogue*.

Alkan's next set of études, the *Trois Morceaux dans le genre pathétique* op 15 published in 1837, represents a most interesting set of stylistic contrasts. Broadly speaking, the first, *Aime-moi*, is in romantic nocturne style; the second, *Le Vent*, is a terrifying étude in chromatics which looks forward to Liszt's more extended essay in *Chasse-Neige* of 1851 and the third is a desiccated desolate étude employing the *Dies Irae* motif. These études are not easily classified as either purely technical genre pieces or as concert études. Schumann writing in Music and Musicians found Alkan's op 15 difficult to comprehend: 'a glance at the contents of this collection gives us a fair idea of the taste of this disciple of young France; it has a considerable flavour of Sue and Sand. One is startled by such false, unnatural art'.[15] Schumann went on to compare Alkan unfavourably with Liszt and Berlioz: 'Liszt caricatures intellectually; in spite of his occasional lapses, Berlioz has a human heart; he is a voluptuary full of strength and daring; but here we find little more than weakness and unimaginative triviality.' Schumann's final comments are particularly harsh: 'we always make allowances for erring talent, providing only that talent exists, and a little music besides; but when the former is doubtful, and nothing of the latter is to be found but black on black, we turn away in discouragement'. If Schumann was unsympathetic Alkan found a greater sense of encouragement in the reviewing of Liszt. Op 15 was dedicated to Liszt and he received them with grace and understanding. 'The caprices of M. Alkan after reading and re-reading them many times ... are compositions which could not be more distinguished, and, even given friendly rivalry, are likely to invoke great interest with musicians.'[16] Interestingly, Alkan may have a desire to unify these works by a motive announced at the beginning of the first étude which returns near the end of the third étude: this cyclic relationship was also noticed by Liszt. These three études nevertheless operate perfectly satisfactorily separately: In fact, Alkan played the second étude *Le Vent* at a concert at the salon of M. Pape. Liszt also commented that: 'taken singly, each one of them [op 15], forms a complete work in which the main motive, expertly manipulated, developed with wisdom, always dominates the luxuriant subsidiary melody'. The op 15 études in short show an individual distinctiveness as well as a tendency towards unification preventing the occasional occurrence of prolixity. The first étude of op 15, *Aime-moi*, opens with an appropriate rappel à l'ordre with an insistent march rhythm and upward sliding chromatics: a combination of discipline and hopefulness, then the main theme follows pejoratively dubbed by Schumann as 'a watery French melody' but, very differently by Liszt as 'simple, tender [and] full of melancholy'. Such are the highly subjective differences of opinion of two great composer-critics!

Ex. 3.4 *3 Morceaux dans le genre pathétique* op 15/1, bars 1–8

Objectively, the melody cited has the typical Alkanian tendency to stabilize around one note. But the recall of the main theme as a fragmentary idée fixe near the end of *Morte* op 15/3 is an interesting derivative of its famous precursor in Berlioz's *Symphonie Fantastique*. It is conceivable that *Aime-moi* may have a hidden amorous meaning.[17] Also interesting in *Aime-moi* is its progressive energy from successive decoration of the main melody to sustained figuration in the middle E major section related to the opening through the similar use of rising appoggiaturas. The section also demonstrates Alkan's confident handling of line and texture, tonality and modulation. The rising appoggiatura as linking motive features also in the next section in the left hand with the Schubertian melodic climax in a German sixth modulation into B major which acts as the enharmonic C flat major for the next section. This section is notable for its fine sense of dramatic climax with some extraordinary passages of left hand agility and some transcendental broken chord figuration truly worthy of Liszt.[18] In cumulative bravura *Aime-moi* marks a turning point in Alkan's stylistic maturity and massed style. This factor further exemplified by a triumphant conversion of the main melody into the tonic major with a seven page extended use of this motive as a coda. Although Alkan might be easily blamed for excessive length which sometimes characterizes all his music, the sincerity, passion and the skyscraping pianistic tessitura of the final bar with its intriguing cadence, a plagal IV-I tinged with a flattened sixth is exhilarating. To sum up, this étude is truly effective in its varied intensity. Liszt enthused that many of the elements of this piece are: 'delightful things which, if played well, should result in an excellent effect'.[19]

The second of the op 15 set offers simpler and more direct rewards. Unashamedly virtuosic and imitative *Le Vent* was the most played of Alkan's études. Sorabji[20] comments on the familiarity of this étude and Lewenthal relates[21] a charming story about a female vaudeville artiste who apparently made a career out of performing *Le Vent* from coast to coast, three shows daily for many years! It is an incredibly atmospheric work prophetic of Liszt's *Chasse-Neige* with combinations of perpetual chromatics and tremolando figuration.

Ex. 3.5   *3 Morceaux dans le genre pathétique* op 15/2, bars 56–57

Schumann had little patience with *Le Vent* decrying it as: 'a chromatic howl over an idea from Beethoven's A major symphony'. On examining this statement carefully there is real evidence that Schumann was over hasty in judging this piece. Firstly, the variety of range, dynamics and textural aspects of the chromatics throughout is considerable and, secondly, although there is a passing similarity of the left hand of *Le Vent* to the allegretto movement of Beethoven's *Seventh Symphony*, the likeness is mainly rhythmic. Blanchard's review is more sympathetic, describing *Le Vent* as: 'a delicious conception of descriptive music ... all the whistling of the wind is infinitely varied in the most pleasant way by M Alkan'. This piece is a first class study for the agility of the right hand, and, as a composition, it combines unity of thought and harmonic richness. Blanchard had correctly noted the innovative nature of *Le Vent*, and, moreover, realized its formal simplicity and satisfying unity: the essential structure of the piece is basically ABA-1 with A returning varied as A-1. There is undoubtedly considerable harmonic beauty within the middle section, where the unresolved series of diminished seventh chords are surrounded by tremolando figuration and arpeggiated swirls. *Le Vent* strongly impressed Liszt. It is worth quoting in full his pictorial analogies:

> [*Le Vent*] is the most romantic of the three [études]. By uninterrupted flurries of chromatic semiquavers, the composer has wonderfully portrayed the eternal sound of those winds which monotonously wail for days on end, laying waste the heath and grasses of forests. One can picture the rain pouring down oak trees and one listens with peaceful contemplation to the melody which soars above those quiet murmurs, like the song of the poet or lover, who looks on at life's tragedies without sadness, because he feels within himself the sweet radiance of a memory or a hope.

The melody to which Liszt refers may be that instanced by Blanchard above: certainly the 'harmonic richness' and textural layout is very much akin to Liszt's own musical style. *Le Vent* certainly is one of the finest of the early period études in successfully combining quasi-impressionistic patterns, coherent structure and dazzling pyrotechnics. A later étude *Comme le vent* emulates, but does not surpass, *Le Vent*.

The final piece in the op 15 set is named *Morte* and is one of the most stylistically interesting and forward-looking of all Alkan's early period piano works. Its dark, funereally macabre style anticipates works such as the 1846 *Marche funèbre* and the 1847 *Prométhée enchaîné*. *Morte* is especially open-ended from a performance viewpoint since no expression marks or dynamics indications are provided.[22] It is difficult, therefore, to ascertain whether the opening *Dies Irae*[23] plainchant is to be presented powerfully as in Liszt's *Totentanz*, or in a more discreet manner. Perhaps the latter is more likely since texturally the solemn incantation of *Dies Irae* at a very low bass level at soft volume would be shattered by the dramatic outbursts fortissimo and crescendo with its quasi-Lisztian bravura.

There is a metrical freedom similar to early Liszt,[24] and it is possible that Alkan may have known this work through social contact in the salons or, more likely, through its publication as a supplement to the *Gazette Musicale*, a leading Parisian music journal of the period. Alkan evokes the atmosphere of recitative pathétique after the Lisztian bravura manner. The inversion of the *Dies Irae* motif[25] leads to a broad melody with the now familiar tendency to centre around one note. Also texturally, the tendency of Alkan towards bass biased dense chords looks forward to his middle period works – especially *Quasi-Faust*.

Alkan's fondness for notational eccentricity is well demonstrated by the next section described by Liszt as: 'tolling like the knell of the dying'. The repetition of these B flats acts as a rhythmic cell[26] for the surrounding bass triplets built on the inverted *Dies Irae* motive: this anticipates the polyrhythmic procedures of Charles Ives.[27] There follows a well constructed episode with a Lisztian feeling for pianistic rhetoric which, with much heavy chordal bravura, leads to a passionate finale although this is considerably less inventive in style because of obsessive rhythms and a same note-centred approach. Liszt noted that several of the transition passages are 'a bit careless'. Extending Liszt's critique it has to be said that some of the harmonies also are ill matched and the musical flow seems somewhat directionless. Perhaps Alkan's obsession with the motif caused lack of concern with other details. These uneven sections are however redeemed by a pithy summary at the end of *Morte* of the *Dies Irae* now decorated with grace notes, a recapitulation of the elements of the *Aime-moi* étude and the combination of the recitative pathétique from *Morte* against elements of *Le Vent*'s chromaticisms.

Compared with op 15, Alkan's next set of études, the *Trois Études de Bravoure* (also of 1837) offers a more conventional overview of Alkan's early virtuosic style. The extremes of Lisztian virtuosity in *Le Vent* are absent in the op 16 set. Also, these études are far more primitive and concise in structure. Some of the flavour of Schubert (particularly of the fast dances)[28] is detectable in op 16/1 but compared with Schubert, Alkan's introductory eight bars is much more fluctuating tonally. This tonal restlessness is admirably counter-balanced by a characteristically tight rhythmic cell and a powerfully dramatic use of silence worthy of the rhetoric of Beethoven. Powerful too is the sforzando use of diminished seventh chords which do not resolve directly. This marks a more adventurous use of harmonic colouring and a strong influence of Beethoven.[29] The main part of the étude marked 'con impassibilità'[30] has a naive but engaging brashness with rather square structures and predictable chordal textures. But the delicatemente section is quite delightfully delicate, and is tinged with augmented chords particularly I$^{5\#}$ and I$^{7\#}$ in G major which provides strong forward movement in the left hand. Unlike op 15/1 and op 15/2, op 16/1 has specific expression markings which aid the problems of interpretation. In this étude dynamics acts as formal divisions: the sordamente section marks the return of the introductory material in the relative minor. Alkan successfully advances his previous use of silence to mark out an abrupt introduction of the impassibilité theme in the flat submediant key, the relative remoteness from the key of C major being reinforced by the pianissimo dynamic.

An important feature of op 16/1 is Alkan's anticipation of the turbulent end of Chopin's *Ballade in F major* op 36.

Ex. 3.6a *3 Etudes de bravoures* op 16/1, bars 189–193

Ex. 3.6b Chopin – *Ballade in F major* op 38, bars 188–191

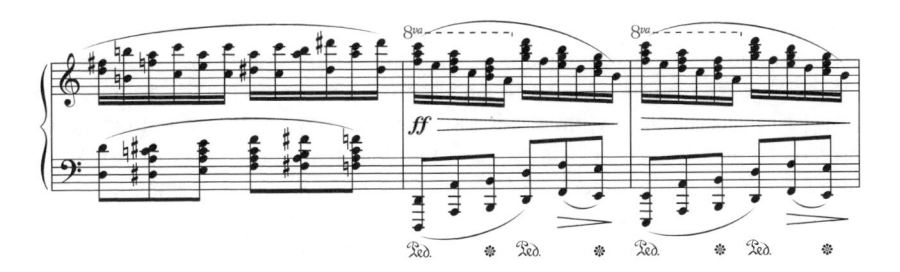

But undoubtedly the most innovative sections in op 16/1 are the approaches to the trio and the trio per se. After the Chopinesque passage described, there is no sense of modulation or direct cadence as such, but just the surprising effect of bell-like sonority with the alto and soprano line marked campane[31] and scampanio[32] respectively. Additionally, Alkan disrupts phrase symmetry so that the pedal A flat octave acts as an anchor for the floating harmonies above which in simple bass deficient ways imitate the sound of a music box. The alto line acts as a simple basis for varied repetition in gently moving chromatics, and on the next variant there is a shift to minor tonality and a shimmering use of syncopation which is highly distinctive. This is certainly one of the most memorable parts of the étude. Just before the stretto closing section, a cycle of fifths incorporating a variant of the alto line is produced. This stretto is chiefly notable for some experiments in pianistic timbre with greater chordal densities at the lower end of the piano. Despite the innovations in pianistic technique, Smith is correct in noting that this étude 'requires interpretative pleading of a high order'.[33]

The second étude of op 16 is marked quasi menuetto and demonstrates a rather severe pedantic style. Cast in Beethoven-like intense mould, it runs the full technical gamut of gruelling double thirds, octaves and chromatic fourths' the latter bearing a curious resemblance to a passage in the scherzo of Chopin's *Piano Sonata No. 2 in B flat minor* op 35. To counteract this intensity, the next section in op 16/2 is in easy going 'tune and accompaniment' style with a simple but effective motto rhythm and, in common with op 16/1, another example of cycles of fifths. The trio section of op 16/2 derives much of its rhythmic character from the rhythmic persistency of Schubert, in particular the trio section of his sonata in E flat major D568. Notable too near the end of the trio of op 16/2 is an implied melodic movement by harmonic release, a feature also to be found in Schumann's *Papillons* op 2. Alkan's early use of massed style is evident in the final page of op 16/2 with motives of the minuet following closely those of the trio.

The op 16/3 étude is certainly the most adventurous of the op 16 set. This étude is set in Alkan's reckless prestissimo vein, and the insertion of 2/4 bars appears to be disruptive but it is carefully calculated to provide a cadential release and repose. In op 16/3 the elliptical modulations with unresolved dominant sevenths and even more complex dominant sevenths on the flattened supertonic are stunningly original for the composition date of 1837. In textural lightness there are points of similarity with Mendelssohn's *Hunting Song* (op 19/3 of his *Lieder Ohne Wörte*) and this particular section of op 16/3 is memorable because of rhythmic variety and changes of harmonic rhythm within broken chord figuration.

An example of Alkan's anticipation of his more mature style in the *Scherzetto* (No 47 of the *Esquisses* op 63) is the left hand op 16/3 perpetuum mobile figuration set against part of the motto rhythm alluded to above. But by far the boldest innovation in op 16/3 is the astonishing switch to 2/8 time for the trio, a forerunner perhaps of a similar tendency in the scherzo of Bruckner's *Symphony No. 4* (Romantic). Alkan directs that two of the 2/8 bars are to equal the 3/4 (and 2/4) bars of the scherzo. Also entirely new in piano literature of 1830/1840 is the incredibly quick changes of pianistic texture almost presaging the Schoenberg idea of *Klangfarbenmelodie*, and moreover rhythmic conflicts continue with the bi-rhythmic juxtaposition of the scherzo's 3/4 rhythmic motto against the trio's 2/4 amidst a flurry of semiquaver bravura. Alkan's knowledge of Chopin's oeuvre may have resulted, moreover, in the latter being influenced directly by an episode in op 16/3 for his scherzo and lead in to the trio of the *Sonata No. 3 in B minor* op 58: especially striking are similar enharmonic changes from E flat to D sharp and thereby to B major. But Chopin's line is more typically melodious compared with Alkan's freer chromatic expressions.

The final section of op 16/3 uses a long dominant pedal and there is victory for the 3/4 rhythmic material over the previously intrusive 2/8 and 2/4 motives. With a return of broken chord figuration in the tonic and moderate variety of piano range, the pianistic bravura of op 16/3 is more tightly controlled than in earlier études, and op 16/3 builds on the ideas of *Morte* op 15/3 where blocks of contrasting character texturally and rhythmically are juxtaposed and superimposed. It is a tribute to Alkan's growing confidence as a composer that he has thrown off the ubiquitously decorative virtuosity of generic nineteenth- century style, and is content to forge an individual style and voice with contrasting blocks which nevertheless are well organized and possess a technical confidence the equal of but quite different to Liszt. These two stylistic features, and especially the positive use of differing material, points towards Alkan's mature compositions.

Op 8: the personal voice discovered in the miniature

Having developed a personal voice in the études, Alkan now turned to shorter, simpler, more concentrated pieces. Truly characteristic of Alkan the miniaturist is the set of *Six morceaux caractéristiques* published c1838 as op 8. Despite the low opus number 1838 is a plausible date because of stylistic congruity with other pieces up to 1838. The op 8 pieces both summarize Alkan's development as a composer of miniatures and point to the direction of his mature miniatures. The flavour of these pieces in their concentrated fragmented nature recalls late Beethoven, and the concision and wit of Haydn, although in melodic flexibility and romantic innocence they nearly approach Mendelssohn. Far removed from the facile style of Herz or Kalkebrenner and without the gemüth of Schumann the op 8 pieces are echt-Alkan. Schumann's views on these six pieces are instructive: He complained of a lack of gemüth although he admitted that compared with 'his last publication but one [which] we treated somewhat severely at the time and the recollection of it is still terrible to us, these six characteristic pieces are of a far gentler morality, and please us infinitely more'.[34] Schumann marked out Alkan in this review as 'one of the ultra romantic French school and copies Berlioz on the pianoforte'. Nevertheless Schumann had little understanding of the leaner textures, more abrupt melodic lines and more dissonant harmonies of Alkan. Schumann, in fact, interpreted Alkan's stylistic features as technical incompetence rather than a completely different style of composition.

The first piece of the six, *Une Nuit d'Hiver* is described by Schumann as 'characteristic; a cutting frost breathes in it'. This presumably refers to the desolate, singularly isolated melodic line accompanied only by the lightest of pizzicato effects in the bass of the piano with subtly rising chromatic line, and unlike some of the other sequential effects of Alkan's early works, the considered use of the chromatic augmented Italian sixth nearly leads back via the characteristically French minor dominant ninth to C minor. The rest of this piece includes tremolando variants of this isolated melodic line[35] and a less successful diatonic variant of the three-note cell substructure of the opening melody. But the growth and decay of complementary chromaticisms in melody and harmony and the resulting shapeliness of this piece is a[36] mark of Alkan's growing compositional stature.

The next piece, *La Pâque* (*The Passover*), creates a purely meditative atmosphere. Its plaintive tonic-centred melody over a drone bass is to be played 'bien chanté et bien soutenu', providing a sharp contrast to *Une Nuit d'Hiver*. *La Pâque*, in company with the earlier étude *Morte*, presents completely contrasting blocks of material.[37] For example, *La Pâque*'s pastoral atmosphere is violently interrupted by a declamatory recitative passage which is mollified by a return of the calm textures.

Ex. 3.7   *La Pâque* op 74/4, bars 45–58

The *Sérénade* in Schumann's terms 'would answer the purpose of its title agreeably, but marks of expression are wholly wanting; in regard to this, however, something is to be said for and against'. Evidently Alkan's rather reluctant romanticism is in polar opposition to Schumann's own views. The *Sérénade*'s musical material is rather four square but there are some attractive doublings, decorations and melodic chromaticisms. Simply constructed, as are most of *Les Mois*, the piece is in ternary structure. The middle section is characterized by several undistinguished sequential repetitions but, as often with Alkan, the mundane is counter-balanced by the extraordinary. The latter, in this case, is a recitative passage circling elements of whole tone scale tonality before the return of the opening section modified towards the end of the piece by persistent Neapolitan relationships.

Une Nuit d'Été, translated by Schumann as 'Spring Night' rather than 'Summer Night', falls prey to Schumann's censure who commented that he [Schumann] 'could have wished it [to be] more warm and odorous, though it is pretty enough'. Stylistically, the diatonically smooth parallel sixths are interrupted by chromatic melodic excursions with flattening of the seventh. Two other features stand out here: firstly, Alkan's fondness for melodic centricity and secondly his real feeling for smooth parallel textures giving a unity to the piece. Smith sees a resemblance with some conflicting inflections (F natural/F sharp) in Chopin's posthumous *Prelude in A flat major* written for Pierre Wolf in 1834. One feels that Alkan may also have known the Chopin *Prelude in F major* where the figuration and harmonic blocks are very similar.

The next piece, *Les Moissonneurs* (The Harvester), epitomizes Alkan's pastoral early style but again points the way forward to a direct and more uncompromising style. Typical of Alkan's earlier style is a Gallic lyric melody which often returns to a specific centre with minimal decoration although Alkan does allow himself an occasional Chopinesque melodic arabesque and harmonic quirkiness with sudden chromatic alterations. But in general there is here a tighter use of rhythm, a less meandering phrase structure and a starker approach to texture. Especially fine is the second half of the middle section with a repeat of the Alkan's rhythm which characterized a particularly important section of the op 16/3 *Étude* previously mentioned. Less appreciated in the development of a personal voice is the fact that Alkan is a composer with an excellent musical sense of humour. The final piece of the *Six morceaux caractéristiques* accordingly is a superb parody of all bombastic operatic stereotyped formulae of French opera of the 1830s. Schumann fully appreciated the piece, deeming it to be 'an excellent jest on operatic music ... that a better one could scarcely be imagined'. It is easy to understand that Schumann appreciated the march-like rhythms and clear textures. These are very much within his own aesthetic. A comparison between Schumann's symphonic studies and Alkan's similarly dotted chordal textures is particularly telling.

Ex. 3.8a   *L'Opéra* op 74/12, bars 20–27

Ex. 3.8b Schumann – *Symphonische Etuden* op 13, finale, bars 70–77

In summary, the elegant harmonic, melodic and rhythmic charm of these morceaux is most appealing and represents the quintessentially Gallic side of Alkan's musical personality which is more fully developed in his magnificent set of *Esquisses* of 1861. Certainly the period up to 1838 is one of the most significant of all in Alkan's compositional career. His personal voice is established by much compositional originality in both étude and miniature. Disdaining French contemporary decorative pianism, Alkan in embracing the classicism and directness of Beethoven along with developing his own personal voice laid the foundations for a series of transcendal piano compositions unique in the history of piano music. This is fully manifested in the series of études starting with the astonishingly precocious op 76 *Études* to be discussed in the next chapter.

Chapter 4
Études

Alkan's principal contributions to the piano étude literature are the three monumental op 76, op 35 and op 39 sets. Precedents to the major key op 35 and minor key op 39 collections do exist: Clementi (1790), Field (1816), Kalkbrenner (1826) and Moscheles (1826) wrote studies in major and minor keys. But Alkan in structure, scale and rhetoric far transcended these earlier examples. Op 35 and op 39 need to be set alongside the études of Chopin and Liszt. The genre in the hands of these three masters fulfilled the expansive definition of Marx as

> … a composition which may have the structure of a sonata allegro, or rondo, or at times the free style of a fantasy. Sometimes it develops consistently, a very capricious thought: sometimes it seems to tend towards lively playing style or towards a very particular figuration or manner of playing that must be specially practised'.[1]

Examples of this 'sonata allegro' type can be found in the huge first movement of Alkan's *Concerto* op 39, the 'fantasy' type in the first two *Études* op 76 and 'particular figuration' type in the *Festin d'Ésope* op 39/12 variations. This set of variations demonstrates many imitative touches popular with contemporary French audiences.

Other programmatic études such as battle études also had some degree of popularity. A rather tawdry piece, the *Étude de bataille* op 35, published in 1845, by Meyer[2] is typical of the genre with its imitation of rifles, cannon shots and galloping horses to name but three effects! Possibly Alkan was aware of this type of battle étude when writing the Étude op 35/7 *L'incendie au voisin*,[3] but crude mimesis plays a very small part in Alkan's études or other compositions.

Études op 76 (c. 1839)

Alkan's gigantic op 76 set of études[4] surpass any written by his contemporaries. His op 76 is equalled compositionally only by Liszt's *Études de Concert* of 1849. Transcending all his early virtuoso works in scale and content the op 76 *Études* are a prelude to the op 39 set. How characteristic of Alkan the innovator is his decision to open op 76 with an étude for the left hand alone.[5] Although the opening of op 76/1 is influenced by Thalberg's[6] 'thumb melody' stereotype, the approach of Alkan is much more purposeful and possibly influenced Liszt's first *Étude de Concert*. Of enormous significance to all piano literature in the 1830s was Paganini[7] and Alkan's own fascination by the Paganini-like devilish tremolando effects is well illustrated in some extended passages of op 76/1.

Ex. 4.1   3 *Grandes Etudes* op 76/1, bars 1–18

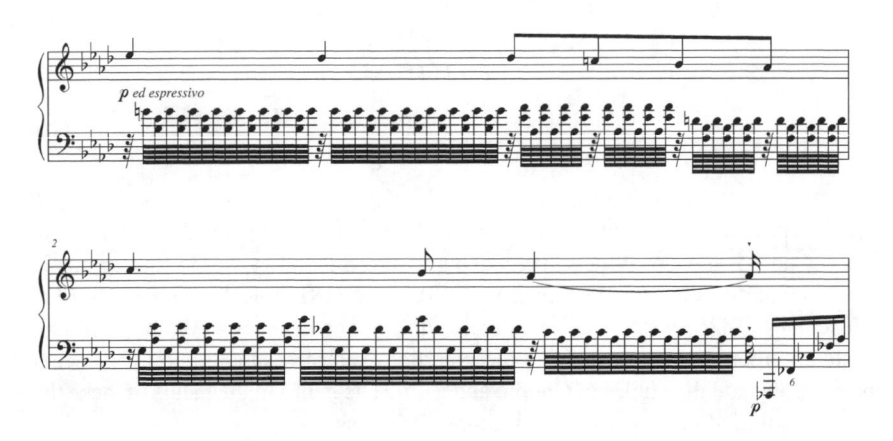

This section moves with considerable ease into an 'alla vivace' which effectively provides a speeded up variant of the opening of the étude. All this improvised opening rhetoric acts as a vast structural upbeat to the main body of the étude, a gravement Gallic march, but much more introverted in character than the earlier op 12/3 étude. Op 76/1 looks forward to the massed, macabre style of the *Marche funèbre* op 26, and is wonderfully orchestral in layout.[8] The opening gravement octaves now act as a passacaglia-like scaffolding for a powerfully dotted rhythmic variant which antedates Liszt's *Wilde Jagd* and the similarity of Liszt's étude to Alkan's figuration is very striking. Especially fine is Alkan's compression of the passacaglia to provide a rhythmic skeletal outline with very obvious harmonic changes. Alkan's insistent onward movement to a chordal triplet 'vivamente' restatement of the march time is impressive, as is the stretto's finally exuberant reprise of the march now firmly transformed to the major before a very truncated reference back[9] to the opening prologue which, like the op 15 études, serves to unify the musical materials. How different op 76/1 is compared with Dreyschock's[10] *Variation pour la main gauche seule* op 22. This étude is quite formless and superficially brilliant in thematic and variational construction.

If Alkan's left hand étude, op 76/1, is remarkable constructionally, op 76/2, an étude for the right hand alone, must be adjudged to be even more astonishing in its form, range, power and technical demands. Running to some twenty-one pages of concentrated energy, it combines all Alkan's prior expertise in étude and variation writing and it is subtitled 'Introduction, variations et finale'. The opening of op 76/2 is sustained, dignified and, in its arpeggiated grace, looks forward to the chorale from Franck's *Prelude, Chorale and Fugue* (1884) but totally unlike Franck is the skyrocket arpeggiated figure outflanking even the virtuoso exuberance of Liszt. Alkan now transfers a sequential melody to the fifth finger which eventually leads to some quite incredibly expressive chordal clusters with splendid romantic bravura and the density of the texture looks forward to Messiaen.[11]

Ex. 4.2   *3 Grandes Etudes* op 76/2, introduction, bars 47–48

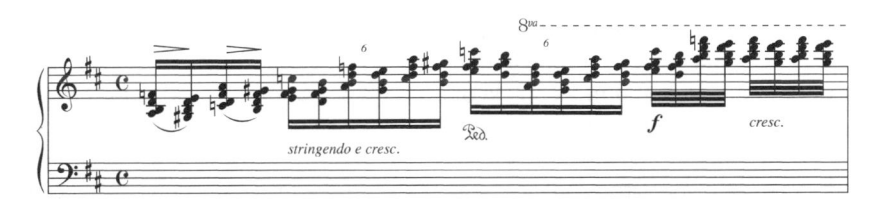

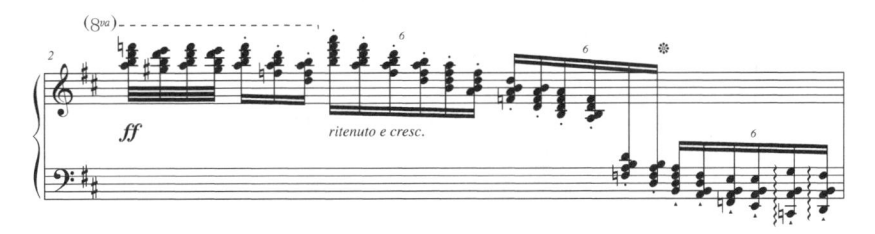

The scene is now set for a charmingly simple theme in two-part style which looks forward to the middle period études.[12] Stylistically consistent with the latter are the judicious balance of diatonic/chromatic melody notes, although there is a surprising harmonic switch to the mediant major which is only slightly signalled by its incomplete dominant seventh. Marked 'portando',[13] this is the highest point of harmonic tension in the theme. Variation one is concerned with a divided melody between treble and bass registers and its light, wrist staccato chords provide an admirable contrast to the smooth contours of the theme. The transient modulation in the theme to the mediant major is put into relief in variation one by a soft dynamic and a detached touch. Textural continuity of the introduction and variation one is assured by reference back to the chordal clusters mentioned above. Variation two is in serious quasi-imitative two-part style set in the darker flattened submediant key which has, of course, augmented sixth potentialities for the tonic key of the theme. The rest of this variation is concerned with delicate left hand filigree against a simple statement of the theme in the right hand. The most immediately obvious influence in variation three (based in the dominant key of variation two) is that of Paganini and, more exactly, there is some resemblance of this variation of Alkan's to the Paganini-Liszt *La Chasse*. The final variation of op 72/2 provides harmonic closure in returning to the tonic key of the theme, and is slightly altered melodically by chromatic passing notes. The influence of Paganini's virtuosity is everywhere apparent: arpeggios, tremolandos, scales in thirds are used freely, but perhaps the most original section in this variation is the sustained rapidly arpeggiated passage culminating in a climactic full piano range arpeggio looking forward to the exciting textures of Alkan's middle period works.[14] The finale of op 76/2 is heralded by the chordal clusters from the introduction, and then follows an imposing chordal transformation of the theme of the introduction, marked 'superbamente', which is appropriately cumulative and provides a harmonic summary of the previous variations. Most impressive of all, is the fusion of the themes of the introduction and that of the variations. This right-hand étude, op 76/2, is easily the finest of all the early period Alkan études, and must be included along with the mature op 39 set (published in 1857) as some of the most important examples of the nineteenth-century concert étude.

Op 76/3 is the uniting of both hands in similar and perpetual movement and, as a technical étude, it is unparalleled in the history of piano music. A precursor to this work might be found in the finale of Weber's *Sonata no. 1 in C major* (1812). Alkan was probably influenced structurally by Weber, as both these Alkan and the Weber examples are cast in rondo form. Alkan's theme has a circular contour and its spacing of the two hands at a two octave rather than one octave distance is unusual. The first episode uses virtuosic broken chords and octave figurations and elements of the opening pages but the second episode has a emergent theme in the relative major which is then transferred to the submediant. But the climax of this étude is the reappearance of the second episode in the tonic major which moves relentlessly onwards towards the final splendid glissando passage and, appropriately for the conclusion of these early style études leads to an emphatic plagal cadence. That perceptive Alkan critic, Sorabji, has described Alkan's op 76 set as a tour de force of considerable musical character and more particularly op 76/3 as 'one of the most memorable études in all piano literature'.[15] Perhaps Alkan's op 76 is the most neglected of all the sets of concert études. Given its marvellous combination of musical intensity and technical demands this neglect is indeed puzzling.

Études op 35 (1848)

Alkan's next contribution to the étude is the set of *Douze Études dans tous les tons majeurs* op 35: two books of six études each. Alkan organized the tonal structure of the set in ascending fourths starting from A major. The études are organized moreover such that the first book functions as a type of technical preface to the longer more involved second book. The first étude is a pastoral prelude in A major. Smith[16] notes as a possible influence the Lisztian nature painting in *Au lac de Wallenstadt* but the similarity is really confined to the gentle Aeolian harp-like arpeggios in the left hand, since the Liszt piece involves a broken chord figuration whereas the Alkan is concerned with legato hand turning and fifth finger sliding. Op 35/1 is characterized by a transparency of texture, an unforced harmonic naturalness and a symmetrical ternary structure. Op 35/1 is also a model of formal elegance with the second part of the ternary structure presenting a left hand version of the opening of the étude in the dominant key. Some piquant chromatic inflections follow with an obsessive ostinato chiming through the texture by means of a thumb melody between the hands. Contributing to the beauty of this passage is the oscillating harmony converging towards the dominant. The coda is simply but effectively organized with a bass octave gravely stabilizing the movement by its intenzionato instruction and its ascending bell-like preparation of the final plagal cadence.

Quite different in style is the second op 35 étude, an unusual echo étude with alternate staccato and legato touches. This piece cannot escape the accusation of being a purely genre étude with merely didactic third ascent motives. Bülow, however, comments that 'in the repetition of the three notes of the motive the third note is sustained hence complicating the repetition's rehearing'[17] and he feels that this is a unique device. Harmonically, there is a Mendelssohnian elegance in the well turned modulation to the mediant and in the strategic use of the Neapolitan. Structurally, as in the first étude, there is a real sense of clarity, but compared with op 35/1 there is a far wider modulation scheme with a joyous restatement of the basic motive transferred into the enharmonic mediant major (G flat major). When the recapitulation of the opening is achieved it is artfully altered to less stable second inversion triads, then is metrically altered to 2/4 which heralds the final presto section of this étude which in octave descending sequences outlines the motive of the third. One of the most interesting areas of op 35/2 is its final line with non-functional dominant harmonies delaying the tonic resolution.

The third étude of the op 35 set is a freely expressive andantino in G major marked 'doux, chantant et soutenu' with a glistening tremolando figure worthy of Rachmaninov and Alkan's op 35/3 demands great evenness of this technical device over the duration of the outer parts of this étude since the middle is concerned with rapid alternating chords. There is a well prepared launch of the Neapolitan statement of the opening melody, particularly effective at pianissimo dynamic 'con dolcezza' before similar tremolando effects in the left hand. The rapid alternating chord passage starting in the flat submediant key of E flat minor is particularly apt in expanding the tremolando concept to both hands and is more widely modulating. As the texture stabilizes, the B flat of the dominant of E flat major is employed to launch a G minor melodically varied treatment of the main theme and thereby to applied left hand appoggiaturas to ornament the restatement of the main theme. Texturally, the passages towards the end are finely calculated with the tonic key being encircled with ever decreasing and rhythmically augmented broken chord figurations.

Technically op 35/4 has in Bülow's opinion 'a very original way with alternate fingering on each pair of notes'. This fingering methodology applies to early nineteenth century pianos only, since at the very rapid tempo of minim = 108 this alternate fingering is impossible on modern pianos with heavier key resistance. Bülow even suggests a possibility of a cut for those of 'more modest staying power'.

This fourth étude of op 35 is a scintillating and delicate étude looking backward to the French clavecinists and forward to the twentieth-century neo-classicists. Indeed op 35/4 with its crisp accentuation, its mainly 'white note' harmony spiced with the occasional diminished seventh, looks forward to the opening of *Pour le piano* by Debussy. The extreme activity of op 35/4 is decreased by the emergence of a melody in the alto voice marked 'avec une grande expression' which gives way to a closely packed figuration and a restatement of the expression theme in the oblique key of the Neapolitan of the subdominant thus providing a harmonic elliptical relationship to the tonic key via VII^7 of V, but as often with Alkan, oblique relationships are effected by melodic chromaticisms. When the main theme returns it is lightly decorated with grace notes in a featherlight manner which may have influenced Liszt in his *Feux Follets* étude (from his *Transcendental Études*). The coda of op 35/4 shows a remarkable flurry of contrary movement broken chord figurations and a final harmonic twist using the melodic E to assert E minor, a voice leading up to G which harmonically is filled out with the dominant seventh of C major and thereby to a perfect cadence in the tonic key. The fifth étude of op 35 is subtitled 'Allegro barbaro' and is the most immediately dynamic and concise of all the op 35 set of études. Dille[18] provides convincing evidence that Bartok possessed a copy of the op 35 études of Alkan, so the influence of op 35/5 on Bartok's own 'Allegro barbaro', composed in 1911, is very likely. Sorabji's view of op 35/5 is of a piece with vehement, explosive vigour and crude, harsh strength'.[19]

Conversely, Bartok's work demonstrates similar ferocity, prolonged use of Lydian modes and grim octaves texture. Set in rondo variation structure the powerful directness of the opening is remarkably simple but effective. The first episode marked 'sostenuto ... con una certa espressione' is in the Phrygian mode but still maintains the original rhythmic impetus with the characteristic cell dotted crotchet/quaver/four quavers. This is contrasted with a sostenutissimo second episode with minimal movement but perfectly complemented by a sprightly staccato right hand: both factors give the sensation of temporary respite from the fury of the main theme. The modal stasis of this episode is also reinforced by repeated pedal notes before an extended and even more texturally brilliant version of the main theme. The final episode in Dorian mode has a surface brilliance in its parallel ascending and descending triplets and in its cellular five finger span which reaches back to the opening of 'Quasi Faust'. The final statement of the opening with stupendously brilliant passage work in counterpoint with the theme is unsurpassed in any of Alkan's études and provides an inevitability of direction towards the final cadence.

Ex. 4.3   *Etude* op 35/5, bars 116–125

Alkan's 'Allegro barbaro' in summary is a very well balanced étude in structure, technique and expression. Bülow enthused 'it is very much to our personal taste and no one will deny its great individuality'.

The sixth étude of op 35 is more of a genre piece. Smith[20] conjectures that Alkan's op 35/6 was known by Brahms when the latter was refurbishing the first movement of his first piano concerto but although there are technical similarities, the Brahms' example is more harmonically adventurous than op 35/6. In Alkan's op 35/6 there is rather too much reliance on dominant seventh harmony and perhaps the only interesting area of op 35/6 is the section marked 'avec expression' where melodic chromaticisms, dominant seventh harmonies and the sonorous sf pedal notes combine to give a musical equilibrium.

The second book of the op 35 études, nos. 7–12 is some twenty pages longer than nos. 1–6 and is generally of a higher inspirational level than the first set. Possibly the most remarkable as a programmatic étude is no. 7 itself, subtitled *L'incendie au village voisin*. Its eighteen pages encompass an adventurousness and emotional range prefacing the Lisztian symphonic poem of the next decade. The initial model is clearly derived from the third movement of Beethoven's *Pastoral Symphony*, Alkan substituting a fire in place of Beethoven's storm. Alkan's op 35/7 has sharply divided Alkan commentators. Beck dubs the piece as having 'a flat style and effects that are mere noise'.[21] Bülow is even more dismissive: 'after a somewhat prolonged fire alarm, to which a quantity of thunder and lightning seems gradually to be added, and in which ... an unnecessary abundance of water is splashed around in an attempt to put out the flames, we have a cantica, a kind of prayer of thanksgiving in which, likewise, we can find little which pleases us'. This has to be set against the view of Sorabji of op 35/7 as 'very remarkable, most original in form, and practically a fantasy'[22] and the praise of van Dieren who thought this étude to be 'an exquisite tone painting like one of the movements in Harold in Italy'.[23] A compromise view is possible and undoubtedly a sympathetic performance will bring this amazing piece of nineteenth-century tone painting to life. The étude's opening calm is admirably conveyed by means of a peaceful diatonic siciliano rhythm with no awkward chromaticisms to disturb the peace but soon eight drum beats on low E flats persist interrupting the tranquillity. The mood becomes increasingly dissonant with the entry first of diminished sevenths and harsher chordal clusters before the eruption of flames with appropriately tempestuous figurations of scalic and arpeggiated bravura. Later, the arrival of the soldiers marked 'soldatescamente' is resplendent in its military D major guise and trumpet fanfares. The fire again erupts with a harsh 'clamando' diminished seventh passage before finally being extinguished (musically!) by a finely judged use of tremolando figures. Despite Bülow's stricture of the final cantica, this author considers that the final section of op 35/7 in its devotional six part hymn style, while redolent of the thanksgiving section in Beethoven's *Pastoral Symphony*, is itself moving in its tender, diatonic chordal style rising finally to a powerfully launched plagal cadence.

That most perceptive commentator on Alkan, Lewenthal, has perfectly described the next étude, the A flat major op 35/8 as follows: 'by far the most poetic ... is no. 8 ... a perfect work, perfect as music, perfect as the étude it sets out to be. It is an exquisite garden scene, a love duet accompanied by softly plucking lutes ...

60 Charles Valentin Alkan – His Life and His Music

in a fabled land of griffins, fountains and unicorns'.[24] Despite the rather exotically perfumed language, Lewenthal's description gives an excellent overall view of this étude's opening.

Ex. 4.4   *Etude* op 35/8, bars 1–11

Texturally the success of the op 35/8 étude results from a fineness of balance between left and right hands and hands together. Also, the melodic content is of memorably high quality with a graceful elegance worthy of Fauré as the subtle chromaticisms before the melodic reprise shows. The intertwining delicate staccato accompaniment, moreover, perfectly complements the smooth melodic contour. Furthermore, Alkan's choice of modulatory sequences for the left hand contribution reflects the right hand contribution and the use of the asymmetric three bar phrase gives an unpredictability to the structure. Hence when the hands do unite a particular sense of calm and sonority is produced. An especially memorable point in the étude is the enharmonic transition to the Neapolitan key at slower tempo which acts as a breathing space to the forward momentum. The final bars show a melodic tribute to Chopin: Alkan's cadence is very similar to that of Chopin's *Nocturne in A flat major* op 32/2[25] which was published in 1837.

The ninth étude of op 35, entitled *Contrapunctus*, is a severe essay in octaves and double thirds and appealed strongly to Bülow who enthused that it is 'a most superb piano piece, full of strength, vitality and wit'. Sorabji also had positive feelings about op 35/9 describing it as: 'a vigorous and powerful contrapuntal study abounding in interesting detail, rhythmic and harmonic'. In structure this étude is a concise ternary format, virtually a scherzo and trio, or, more exactly, a ponderous octave contrapuntal minuet and canonic trio in thirds. The C sharp melody is scalic with considerable rhythmic impetus in baroque fugal style with a modulation to the dominant and later given much to two-part invention treatment. Carefully built into this section is the use of dramatic silence after and unresolved dominant seventh then some closely argued counterpoint ending the minuet with widely spaced texture at the cadence which is the most effective punctuation point noted by Sorabji. The trio is even more intriguing: nominally like the variation in thirds from Beethoven's 32 Variations in C minor as observed by Smith,[26] but in the Alkan oeuvre this is paralleled by the children's motto in the *Grande Sonate*. Alkan's reprises often are irregular: there is here a Haydnesque false recapitulation initially with a quintuple time bar then a merging of the scherzo minuet material via rapid dominant seventh changes. As in several Alkan works, there is the briefest recall of earlier material which equally often is rapidly swept away, in this case by two menacingly heavy chords.

Entitled *Chant d'amour – chant de mort* and subtitled 'et quando expectavi lumeni venit caligo', étude no. 10 is one of the most lyrically appealing of the op 35 set of études given its well balanced Bellini-like melody, its finely adjusted chordal accompaniment and its merging of left- and right-hand melodic chromaticisms at the end of the eight bar sentence. With the utmost grace, light ornamentation is added to the repetition of the opening section. The reply to the statement of coquettish love is a more passionate chordally involved passage marked 'fort et soutenu' with some unpredictable rates of change in harmonic rhythm. This is swept away by a duet section expressing the intertwining of two delicate ideas with a rare tenderness: perhaps texturally Alkan was aware of the Chopin Prelude in E flat major, although the Chopin example is of superior craftsmanship. But Chopinesque also is the variant of the duet section now rhythmically varied with subtle cross rhythms.

The most extraordinary part of op 35/10 is the final page which is heralded by a dissolution of the love theme by questioning pauses and silences before the death theme in funeral march style enters. Bülow concedes that 'the funeral march ... shows a quite remarkable treatment of the instrument plus an undoubted depth of feeling. But it is something of a problem to translate this totally in performance since the composer has not notified his intention by means of the necessary programme'. In texture and range this author agrees it is 'quite remarkable'. In brittle chordal style with low gruppetti it is curiously similar to the parallel passage in the Liszt *A major Concerto* started in 1839, revised between 1849 and 1861 and published in 1863. Hence it is possible that Liszt may have been indebted to Alkan given the publication date of 1847 of the op 35 études.

Alkan's penultimate étude of op 35 is an excellent study in sustained chords and moving inner parts. It is of the same simplicity as the first prelude of his op 31 and perhaps the liking for 'internal melody' anticipates the more famous example of Brahms in his *Intermezzo in E flat major* op 117. The technical requirements of Alkan's op 35/11 are inherent in the performance instruction 'la partie du milieu ressortant constamment' and 'doux et bien soutenu': the latter referring to the softly pulsed chordal accompaniment. This piece is a wonderful essay in the textural notion, as Bülow says, that 'the middle voice becomes ... an upper or lower voice in turn, so that only variety of shading can make it perceptible to the ear'.

Harmonically too this is one of Alkan's inspired creations with much confidence in handling large scale tonality through modulation in thirds in a Schubertian manner and a smoothness of flow from the opening section into the darker middle section with ostinato basses and flattened sixths. This gives a piquant tang to the melody and a completely natural transference of this melody to the bass. Masterly indeed is Alkan's building of the final climax in the reprise of the opening section with textural massed style density characteristic of his largest works in this middle period. As an expression of joyful pianism this étude is unrivalled in the Alkan output, and is only paralleled in the twentieth century by Messiaen, whose *Regard de l'Église d'amour* (1944) is a direct descendant of this Alkan work.

The twelfth and final étude of op 35 is a Kullak-type octave composition in simple ternary design. Alkan, however, provides a quintuple 10/16 time signature influenced perhaps by the *Impromptus* op 32/2 and his general interest in the five beat bar.[27] Furthermore, at the tempo indication of crotchet tied to semiquaver = 88, this final étude becomes a real test of endurance since the blend of mainline harmonies and symmetrical phrases is disrupted by the quintuple metre. The middle section shows a considerable degree of textural invention: the five group is divided between repeated octaves and chords and provides a textural and technical relief from the first section. The recapitulation furnishes a graceful added accompaniment to the right hand octaves.

It is typical of Alkan that in op 35 as in many other of his collections there is no set division of étude type, so technical and programmatic études are mixed together. Of all the middle period works the op 35 études at their finest show alongside the massed effects of the Grande Sonate the way forward to the final period of composition after 1847 in particular to the truly transcendental companion set, the *12 Études in all the minor keys* op 39.

Études op 39 (1857)

From the biography in Chapter 1 it is clear that Alkan suffered serious professional setbacks from 1848 which made him more introverted and led to him becoming deeply reclusive. During this period Alkan evolved the op 39 set, certainly the most neglected masterpiece of all nineteenth-century piano literature. Surveying the set as a whole, one finds an expansion of the symphonic and large block style of constructions of the op 35 *Études*, but the op 39 *Études* are much more gigantic, consisting of a full scale scherzo (étude 3), a symphony for piano (études 4 to 7), a concerto for piano (études 8 to 10), a large overture for piano (étude 11) and a huge set of variations (étude 12).

The first étude of op 39 is more in the style of a technical étude harking back to the op 15/2 étude, *Le Vent*. Op 39/1 is also a most remarkable finger study, named *Comme le Vent*, which is more refined melodically with the étude tempo advanced to quaver = 160: a prestissimamente speed with 160 2/16 bars to a minute, effectively sixteen notes per second. This étude must be counted as one of the fastest ever conceived. Apart from the pace of the demisemiquaver triplets, the off beat chords, added sevenths and quickening of the harmonic rate of change via a chromaticization of the supertonic chord just before the end of the eight bar sentence, all contribute to the lightest étude imaginable. Alkan's predilection for Neapolitan relationships occurs towards the end of the repeat of the opening section and can be compared harmonically to the contrary broken chord figuration with the parallel passage of the finale of Schubert's *Sonata in A minor* D784, from which Alkan may have drawn harmonic inspiration. There follows simple but effective parallel staccato massed blocks with alternating eight-bar periods of tonic and dominant harmony. Furthermore, the Schubertian influence is shown by the transference of these blocks up a third. Harmonically more radical is Alkan's non-functional harmonic application of unresolved dominant sevenths followed by added sixths. Up to this point *Comme le Vent* has been predominantly a whirlwind right hand étude but now the left hand engages in five finger C major scalic passages at a leggierissimo. This section is harmonically vitalized by the violent eruption of cadential chords which direct the tonality to the dominant, then the tonic, dominant and tonic respectively. The apex of virtuosity of *Comme le Vent* is its rapidly moving coda in parallel octaves, scalic but with modal inflections. The étude ends extremely quietly with well timed silences. *Comme le Vent* overall is the most obviously finger technique centred of all the op 39 set.

En rhythme molossique op 39/2 is described by Smith[28] as 'one of Alkan's most original conceptions'. Busoni[29] apparently had premiered it in Berlin to seemingly outright hostility: perhaps this étude's combination of quasi-Brahmsian D minor chordal masses and French melodic elegance was too much of an uncomfortable hybrid for the Berliners! The étude propels a motivic minuet by a ponderous rhythmic cell. Smith[28] notes the relationship between this étude and the statement of the minuet theme from Haydn's *String Quartet in D minor* op 76/2. This minuet was published *c*1870 in a transcription by Alkan, although classical dance form had a subliminal influence on him for several years prior to this date. From a form viewpoint, op 39/2 bears little relationship to a minuet although there is something potentially trio-like about its quaint first episode, albeit with a sentimentally upward rising melody, an almost Gothic use of diminished sevenths over the tonic pedal points, and, not least, with drooping suspensions. One can imagine that Busoni's Berlin audience would have balked at this Gallic reappraisal of Mendelssohn! Moreover, Alkan's harmonic quirkiness coupled up to the florescent melody might have provoked even more comprehension problems.

For the second episode Alkan truncates the molossique rhythm then returns to the opening version to give out a variant in brilliant double counterpoint. The momentum of op 39/2 is enhanced by a combination of two episodes in counterpoint. This étude also has a particularly fine coda where there is a dissolution of the semiquavers by the persistent rhythmic cell. Smith[30] observes the parallel here with the end of the first movement of Beethoven's *Piano Sonata in D minor* op 31/2.

The third étude of op 39 is entitled *Scherzo diabolico* and is the most concise of the single études of op 39, being only fourteen pages long and Alkan indicates a very fast tempo of dotted minim = 132. Op 39/3 is mysterious, dramatic and formally conventional. Alkan does not apply the symbolic signal of the tritone to indicate devilment, instead the Neapolitan is applied at the first right hand entry after some menacing left hand chromatic descents. The repetition of this right hand entry leans on the submediant minor key and the closing section introduces diabolus tritones contained within the locked octave figuration. The trio provides a total contrast to the scherzo: dense chords at a slightly slower tempo introducing sustained augmented and added sixth harmonies. But the cross rhythmic patterns, the circling of the tritones and the low register dissolution of the texture towards the end are most impressive features about op 39/3.

Etudes four to seven of op 39 form the *Symphonie*, the most consistently successful of all the op 39 group études in melody, harmony, rhythm, form and texture. Moreover, the *Symphonie* is unified by a motivic transformation. Diagram 4.1 illustrates this motivic relationship.

The first movement of the *Symphonie* op 39 is an expansive C minor allegro moderato which sets out the first subject in syncopated left hand octaves against a pulsating right hand accompaniment: Alkan may have derived overall inspiration for this from the opening of Beethoven's *Eroica Symphony*. The ensuing appoggiatura effect is repetitive, but this repetition is alleviated by a finely drawn melodic contour and quickly moving harmonies pinpointing the diminished seventh at strategic phrasal climaxes. The transition to the second subject is magically handled with 'sordamente' repeated diminished sevenths without resolution in low and high registers as an antecedent and consequent with an overall motivic ascent akin to the first subject. The second subject group is very artfully drawn with melodic transformations of the overall motive and involves a now familiar process of the generation of new harmony by a chromatic melodic rise. Tonal instability thus invoked is resolved by a freely flowing Mendelssohnian espressivo melody which leads naturally into a more generously felt lyrical group with turbulent left hand broken chord texture. These elements of the second subject are closely integrated and promote easy access to the closing section.

Given the vast scale of the development compared with the exposition of the *Symphonie* it is absolutely necessary to play the exposition repeat to balance the sonata-type structure. The development itself is one of the most satisfying in any of Alkan's large-scale works and transformation of previous material plus new material are wonderfully amalgamated. The darker submediant key is now the favoured springboard for the development of the motive. Tonally, after transference to the right hand, there is a sense of D flat major/D flat minor duality. At one stage A major is invoked which leads rapidly to C major, the tonic major of the movement. An impressively full use of orchestral sonority with Wagnerian-like tremolandos is intriguingly set with rhythmic displacement. The chromatic side-slip to B minor yields another variant of the motive of the movement, this time accompanied by full left hand tremolando chords interrupted by canonic left hand imitation.

Études 65

Diagram 4.1 Motivic unity in the *Symphonie* op 39 (adapted from Sitsky (1974)

a

I: Allegro Moderato

b

II: March Funèbre

c

Trio

d

III: Menuet

e

Trio

f

IV: Finale (Presto)

Through an unresolved dominant seventh chromatically moving up the semitone, the relative major is invoked which almost acts as a false recapitulation but instead leads to a break in the ad hoc ostinato figuration and into a chordal section which has a harmonic chromaticism which antedates Franck. Here, harmonic movement, phrase shape and dynamic control are perfectly as one. With the return of the tremolando figuration the real false recapitulation is signalled, and the downward chromatic descent passage (employed in the coda section even more brilliantly) is announced. The recapitulation presents a much shortened version of the exposition as the formally awkward transition between the first and second subject groups show. The Mendelssohnian elements of the second subject group are now omitted and the block chords are extended in a three-fold manner to give a nineteenth-century type of harmonic parallelism.

The coda employs octave tremolandos at the low bass register and leads into a chordal outline of the motive with a canonic overlap. The dramatic apex of the whole movement is the conversion of the innocent Mendelssohnian second subject element into a most powerful B major pulsating chordal passage and then a transference back via ever quietening diminished seventh harmonies to the corresponding C minor home key version of this subject. The movement ends peacefully with a series of chords outlining the elements of the motive. A final ironic twist is the conversion of the C major Picardy third back to the minor.

The grave second movement, a funeral march, is beautifully controlled in pathos and mood. Its character relates to the slow movement of Beethoven's *Piano Sonata* op 2/2 rather than either of the funeral marches by Beethoven or Chopin. The textural balance is admirable between the dry staccato chord accompaniment and the sustained tenor cantus firmus melody. Additionally, the onward rhythmic direction and the melodic contour are beautifully controlled. The next section perhaps looks back to the unforgettable dropping fourths of the Chopin *Fantasy* op 49, but Alkan is more directly sequential than Chopin. But the success of the first part of this second movement is attributable to a stable rhythmic pulse and a variation of textural density. To disrupt this rhythmic tread, more chordally smooth descents in chorale style appear, first in the tonic minor, F minor, and then these are converted to the tonic major to launch the trio section. This results in a release from the concentrated anxiety of the funeral march but the trio still retains some rhythmic motivic links (notably dotted quaver/semiquaver) with the opening of the movement. Despite the sustained line there are ample surprises in the shape of sudden jolts of dynamics and key changes between blocks such as the chromatic slip downwards from F major to E major. Timbral inflections in the movement are wide ranging too: the coda itself of this movement imitates muted drum rolls and beats, almost fading away totally before a brief affirmation of the trio chorale and the desolate final plagal cadence.

Ex. 4.5   *Symphonie* op 39/1, bars 206–220

The third movement, to quote Lewenthal, is 'a real Hexen minuet complete with broomsticks'. The irregular rhythmic scansion of the opening is arresting and the large leaps, irregular phrase lengths, and the highly dramatic use of opening octaves are all controlled within a structured framework of dynamics. Undoubtedly enhancing the drive of this minuet is the ascending series of melodic cells which traverse the interval of thirds to sixths and these provide the strongest linkages possible with the final movement. Motivic unity and formal musical logic are mirrored in the second half of the minuet. There is some tranquillity promised at the 'dolce e sostenuto' section with its more confined melodic range but, very quickly, the minuet theme returns strengthened by its presentation in the left hand with some gruff bass appoggiaturas.

As befits the powerful forward momentum in this movement, the increase of volume, range and texture is greatest towards the end of this minuet. The trio in the submediant key itself is one of Alkan's finest creations being beautifully contoured melodically, euphonious harmonically with its gently moving harmonies over light pedal points, and, on repetition, has a most carefully chromatically coloured melodic variant which provides a most delicate introduction to the bell-like sonorities of the remaining trio section. At the reprise, the repeat of the minuet is regular, apart from some impressively static dominant/tonic passages which hold up the dynamic movement before the trio is marginally reaffirmed and the whole texture finally vaporizes in an upward B flat major arpeggiated decoration.

The final movement of the *Symphonie* is an extraordinarily fast presto at semibreve = 96. Its nature, musical and technical, has been aptly described by Lewenthal as 'more like a wild ride in hell rather than to it'.[31] Notionally at least with the ascending motive there is a link with the minuet. Texturally, too, the octave similarity is striking. Rapidity of harmonic rhythm and short breathed phrasing also are factors which contribute to the dizzily headlong progress through time. Even more breathtakingly brilliant is the quaver motive, first with two repeated harmonies per bar, then even faster with four harmonic changes per bar. Alkan lifts the tonality from E flat minor through to E major then through to F major. The bravura of this section reaches a climax with a simultaneous counterpointing of the opening motive and quaver motive of the movement before expiring to a chordal resting point harking back to the first movement, but this time with a most unusual unresolved diminished seventh. To add even more furious pace to the movement Alkan resorts to a type of bi-rhythmic procedure with chromatic 'slides' in the left hand which pick up the chordal theme then reject the bi-rhythmic process to leave the pungent clarity of root chords, with a German sixth for chromatic flavouring to complete this most magnificent *Symphonie*.

The *Concerto* (nos. 8, 9, 10) of op 39 is the most extended work by any nineteenth-century composer for piano solo[32] and surpasses the *Symphonie* in scale and intricacy of constructional unification. The first movement alone of the *Concerto* consists of some seventy pages compared with eighteen for the *Symphonie*'s first movement since in the *Concerto* there is the grandest possible extension of block structures. Diagram 4.2 shows the double motivic links throughout all three movements. The first subject of op 39/8 is immediately arresting because of its dramatically terse material in powerful brass style and potent use of silence and simple root chords. An extended orchestral tutti continues with colourful orchestral textures, contrapuntal and phrase expansion techniques and Neapolitan-related harmonies. The second subject is poised and lyrical and featuring a mordent motive derived from the initial theme. This subject is one of Alkan's finest melodic creations and it is supported by placid accompanimental texture and root-directed harmony.

After several sequential dominant pedal points, a third theme is presented employing the opening motive. This leads to a tutti variant of the initial theme and thereby a dissolution of texture. Rather than restate the full theme, Alkan, after a thoughtful and meandering scalic passage, introduces a wayward cantabile melody in which the mordent motive is internalized. Marked 'quasi solo' it gives a hint of the extemporized solo in the manner of the Chopinesque concerto. But the rhythmic energy of the opening soon returns with renewed energy set against a derived version of the mordent motive in dominant seventh harmony and the occasional Neapolitan excursion. In the next section there is a much freer use of mobile tonality which ultimately gives rise to the expression of the lyrical second subject group, this time as a solo. Alkan's romantic melodic gifts are seen here at their finest. The closing section is powerfully introduced by a surprise B major ff chord. Construction in this *Concerto* is firmly delineated aurally by such punctuation points, visually by strong double bars, and rhythmically by the introduction of a brilliant 'alla polacca' motive and bravura writing. Even within the passage-work the descending fourth of the opening theme is still evident. The closing section is terminated by a brilliant tutti statement in B major truncated by an inactive seven bars which effectively lay the tonal foundation for a Schumannesque-type outpouring. This passage modulates in Schubertian fashion by thirds. Eventually, the tonality stabilizes to A flat minor/ enharmonic G sharp minor the overall tonality. Present here is the locked chord figuration beloved by Alkan.

Diagram 4.2   Motivic links in *The Concerto* op 39 (adapted from Starr (1985) 29–30)

a

First movement, first subject

b

First movement, second subject

c

Second movement, main theme

d

Third movement, main theme

Ex. 4.6   *Concerto* op 39/1, bars 635–640

The development section makes an austere contrast by interval, tonality, texture and direction, but still contains the fourth descending motive. This bleakness is only disrupted by a tumultuous C minor statement of the opening theme. Possibly the most intriguing part of the development section is the G sharp minor pedal point which persists for some sixty-six bars. This is truly a remarkable static given the duality of the tonality. This opposition reaches its peak with the tritone dissonance. Bravura sections follow in the style of the skyscraping arpeggios of *Quasi-Faust* and lead to a truncated recapitulation with an alternation of tutti and solo entries with the lyrical second subject in G sharp major. The presence of a fragmented chorale impedes the recapitulation before a coda of some two hundred bars of incredible repeated note virtuosity marked 'quasi tamburo', where the lyrical second subject is subjected to this powerful rhythmic treatment but still in the G sharp major key. The triumph of the simpler enharmonic key of A flat major clinches the final tutti which is stately in virtuosity.

Most of the dramatic argument has been borne by this first movement, so clearly the final two movements are of lesser weight and character. Intensely emotional and of elegiac beauty is the central adagio of the *Concerto* which, after a mellow gathering together of the motives introduces a Chopinesque C sharp minor melody with a four-note descending motive derived from its first movement counterpart and is lightly punctuated with a persistent triplet in the left hand. This motive is also present in the tenderly romantic C sharp major section. Alkan also resorts to a baroque recitative passage with the four-note motive now openly exposed in appoggiatura fashion which develops into some passionately exciting canonic interplay. Funereal aspects occur next before the return of the second theme, and then the recapitulation follows which is decked out with murmuring sextolet semiquavers. Extracts from the opening of the movement and the funereal elements flash by quickly before a cadential dissolution firmly finalized by the now typical Alkan chordal punctuation. In this movement Alkan once more approaches the expressive and structurally balanced world of Chopin.

The tonal shift up a semitone for the third movement establishes an initial tonality of D major after which the tonality stabilizes to F sharp minor for this allegretto polonaise-like movement. The next solo passage is discursive in melodic outpouring and rhythmic elegance, and makes the fullest use of the piano keyboard. Although the thematic material is primitive and highly disconnected, motivic and formal elements are very carefully calculated. Written out trills on the upbeat contain the four-note motive. The idea of semitonal raising is developed intervalically to provide a most abrasive end to a development section. The recapitulation also investigates this semitonal D/C sharp interplay before a more evident display of polonaise rhythm and a pentatonic descending glide to complete this *Concerto*. Unique amongst Alkan's large-scale works, it is this movement which most reveals Alkan's Jewish roots since much of the material has cantor-like and klezmer auras.

Placed after rather than before the *Symphonie* and *Concerto*, the *Overture* op 39/11 is the most substantial of all the self-contained études. The pulsating opening texture at once imitating orchestral strings and displays Alkan's massed style of pianism. Harmonically in op 39/11, simple and chromatic chords are well balanced.

Equally the evolved chordal density is answered by an ascending, questing dotted note figure which provides a thrust forwards to the dominant relaunching the dominant minor of the opening measures. On reappearance, transposed up a tone, this dotted note figure is extended and involves the rapidly moving dominant seventh shifts characteristic of Alkan. This eventually blends with the semiquaver rhythmic motto and merges cadentially into the second main section which is essentially a lyrical 6/8 meandering theme, but it is punctuated too with quickly moving dominant sevenths. This theme is subjected to some exquisite filigree-type decoration giving contrast to the opening section. The tonality is pushed up a semitone to introduce a characteristic Gallic march with typical Alkanian chromatic side-slips, first quietly moving then splendidly erupting. Alkan demonstrates an almost Berliozian grandeur although some elements verge almost towards the banal. The working out of these ideas in the sonata structure is somewhat academic with an over-reliance on the rhythmic figures, but the four-note motive is retained from the second subject group in the relative major suitably lightened in texture and more stable in range. The closing section, however, is unfortunately limited to pianistic pyrotechnics.

After this excessive virtuosity the development introduces a new theme, anxious in its pathos, which is worked up rather earnestly to provide a magnificently bold statement set against an extended version of the previous rhythmic cell now in rhythmic counterpoint. The rest of the development is concerned with some rather tedious bravura patterns in double thirds resulting in dominant seventh/tonic excess. At the recapitulation the B minor march theme returns arrayed with octave counterpoint. The recapitulation compared with the exposition is severely curtailed to permit only the main theme to emerge sotto voce as a pedal point. It is to be regretted that Alkan added an extensive hunting-style coda to this *Overture*. Given the rhythmic élan of the persistent dotted figure and its variants, this coda contains too many barren clichés of anonymous nineteenth-century style such as broken octaves, split octaves and densely chordal passages. The *Overture*, then, is the weakest musically of the op 39 études, more backward looking in style than the other works in the op 39 cycle.

Finally, to complete his monumental op 39 *Études in the minor keys*, Alkan produced a set of variations, twenty five in all, entitled *Le Festin d'Ésope*. This is certainly the most approachable of all Alkan's works and is a brilliant concise étude consisting of a memorable theme and highly original set of variations with coda. The theme itself is absolutely disciplined, marked 'senza licenza quanlunque': this instruction might also apply to the majority of the variations with the exception of the lyrical ninth tonic major one. The derivation of the theme has been likened to the Hasidic melody, *Utso Etso*, with the similarities of the rising fourth cells, but a comparison with the minuet from *Mozart's G minor Symphony K550* is more meaningful.[33] The theme is remarkably potent for variational possibilities given its terse harmony, its rhythmic drive and unpredictable modulation by unresolved dominant sevenths.

Ex. 4.7   *Le Festin d'Ésope* op 39/12, theme

In variation 1 the left hand simply takes up the rhythmic directness – a bass version of the theme of brutal power. Variation 2 has an interestingly notated sustained sextolet accompaniment to the theme. In variation 3 Smith perceptively notes 'the malicious glee with which he will keep the listener harmonically poised on one leg'.[34] This is mainly caused by the denial of home tonality in contrast with the first two variations and the low double drum taps which emphasize the remoter submediant rather than the tonic. Variation 4 explores Alkan's penchant for contrasts of parts with wide spacings and bare fourths and fifths in quasi-march rhythms which lead without any affectation into the real march-like variations 6 and 7, the former complete with heavy triplet octaves and the latter, as a complement, in higher register and initially in the submediant before a bombastic octave return to the tonic. Variation 7 extends the idea of the left hand statement of the theme of variation 2, but this time includes cascading scalic cells which stabilize as a shuddering trill in the left hand of variation 8 with only the harmonic skeleton extant to emphasize the awkwardness of diminished and chromatic harmonies. Lewenthal amusingly likens this variation to a 'torpid hippopotamus wallowing in hot mud and twitching off flies with her almost non existent tail'. Animal-like images may be applied to several of the later variations also.

The ninth variation is in the warm tonic major key and leads directly into the tenth which extends the textural bell-like sonority of the op 16/1 étude described earlier. In variation 10 the indication 'scampanatino' might suggest a music box plus a musette-like French clock. This directly links to variation 11 which implies a horn call and the slithery use of thirds and sixths in the right hand might suggest a very elusive pair of foxes. Variation 12 expresses the graceful elegance of swans across the glassiest of water which is only gently undulating. Variation 13 is the most directly pictorial representation of the whole set with unequivocally pesky fleas musically portrayed by light, extremely wide ranging pp awkwardly itchy chords. Variations 14 and 15 are more chordally regal.

Variation 16, marked p and 'preghevole' is somewhat more reticent and offers a welcome respite from the furore of previous variations. This variation renews the concept of delayed dominant sevenths. The next two variations (numbers 17 and 18) exhibit extreme fingerwork virtuosity, and are the most étude-like of all of this variation set. Both are not merely virtuosic however, since they complement variations 5 and 6 in the E minor/C major tonal polarity. The nineteenth variation contains some of the most deliberate dissonances before Schoenberg. Howling, lamenting animals are evoked in broken, blind bitonality and chromatic octaves: indeed Stravinsky is anticipated in *The Rite of Spring* 'stamping' chord. Dissonance is enhanced by Alkan's decision to specify the sustaining pedal throughout the whole variation.

Ex. 4.8 *Le Festin d'Ésope* op 39, variation 19, bars 1–4

The twentieth variation is marked 'impavide' so perhaps this is the leonine variation. (Alkan is very non-specific except in variation 22). The full strength of powerful hammered chords in variation 20 is certainly referential to this particular animal.

Pictorialism continues with the hunt being evoked in variation 21 which again turns to the major. The figuration is retained in the right hand despite the wonderful evocation of noisy dogs marked 'abbajante' which becomes quite chaotic. Alkan here experiments with mobile rhythmic blocks to provide two dimensional levels.

Variations 23 and 24 form a coherent pair, both involving an extremely novel use of tremolando effects, the former more specifically close packed, the latter more conventional in an Alberti-type figure. The whole set converges towards the final twenty-fifth variation which has the power of the fifth variation, the fifteenth variation and the directness of chordal dryness of variation 20. This variation is the only one to be stretched and developed to reconcile both minor and major. All previous variations have eight bar structures and appear to be grouped in multiples of five. The coda reduces the texture of the theme to a fragment but then builds climaxes magnificently. Indeed, the last two pages represent the pilgrimage of a continuous crescendo concentrating the massed effects of Alkan's middle compositional period. There is the final abbreviation of the theme, an expertly inbuilt dissolution and also the most abrupt chordal slapshot imaginable to end this most notable of variation sets by Alkan. In *Le Festin d'Ésope* there is a satisfying union of the referential and abstract in musical terms.

'Scarcely anything more is to be attained in the field of mechanical combinations beyond what modern virtuosos have already reached.'[35] Thus spoke Schumann when reviewing Kullak's *Two Concert Studies* op 2. This quotation might easily be applied to Alkan's op 76, op 35 and op 39 sets of studies. Bravura, lyricism, simplicity, orderly form and development have also been achieved by Alkan in his studies and therefore they can be placed alongside the masterpieces of Chopin and Liszt. At the risk of generalizing, it is true to say that Alkan's first set of op 35 études most resemble the Chopin études in the pursuit of the single technical and musical idea, whereas the second set of the op 35 *Études* excepting op 35/12 more resembles the Liszt *Transcendental Études* in their symphonic and programmatic content. Alkan's op 39 *Études* follow the Lisztian model also. The conservative étude world was not ready for an Alkan, Liszt or a Chopin. The latter's études were vilified in a contemporary periodical as suited to 'players with dislocated fingers may be able to end their misfortune by practising these études'.[36] Nowadays, of course, the Chopin études are a cornerstone of the étude repertoire[37] and their main technical innovations can be compared with the études of Alkan's op 35.

The first of the Alkan op 35 set can be superficially likened to the first three finger activity of Chopin's op 10/6 although the Chopin étude is much more intense in key and layout: alternate right hand and left hand parts can be observed as well. Some comparison can also be drawn between the Alkan tremolando *Étude* op 35/3 and the Chopin op 10/7 but the Chopin is much more dissonant harmonically although both are highly mobile and virtuoso études. Octaves and thirds are investigated in the Alkan op 35/9 étude in a mainly diatonic way but the Chopin octave *Étude* op 25/10, and the thirds *Étude*, op 25/6, are more technique-centred but more chromatic and forward looking. The Alkan octave *Étude* which most resembles the Chopin concept in op 25/10 is the op 35/12. The op 35 set contain varied, symphonic elements and Alkan, in the extended op 35/5 and op 35/10 études and in his vast op 39 set, relates strongly to the étude attitude of Liszt in his *Transcendental Études*.

Both composers' études are extremely difficult to perform. Dale comments that 'the very look of [Liszt études] on the printed page may well strike terror to all but the boldest sight readers'.[38] This comment might well be applied to the Alkan op 39 set: both composers marked a distinctive break between the performing skills of the professional and the amateur. The alliance of Liszt with Alkan was observed by Busoni who described them as 'ranking Liszt with the greatest post Beethoven composers for the piano, Chopin, Schumann, Alkan and Brahms'.[39] This comparison with Liszt may also be made with Alkan's earlier études and the works which most closely resemble those of Liszt's *Transcendental Études* are firstly the astonishing étude-like op 13/1, Alkan's *Andante Romantique*, and Liszt's *Mazeppa* which both have mobile chromatic blocks. Alkan's parallel octave bravura étude, op 35/5 is more similar to the Lisztian extroversion in *Eroica* than any of the Chopin octave études. The breadth of melodic span of Alkan's op 35/10 although similar to the Chopin *Prelude in E flat major* op 28 has a restlessness more reflected in Liszt's *Wilde Jagd*.

Alkan's remarkable op 39 *Études* far exceed in length and grandeur the *Transcendental Études* of Liszt: the massed style of the op 39 set in say the pulsating texture of the *Overture* op 39/11 is as impressive in keyboard layout as Liszt's evocative *Harmonie du soir*. Both composers achieved an orchestral power in their understanding of the étude genre where texture and sonority reign supreme, but Alkan's op 39 is unrivalled by any other composer of études in the nineteenth century.

Chapter 5

Sonata Types for Piano

Both the *Grande Sonata* op 33 and the *Sonatine* op 61 although very different in scale and gesture are, along with the *Études* op 39 amongst the most important of Alkan's larger works. The paucity of sonatas in Alkan's output compared with études and miniatures is indicative of the general reluctance of French composers to be as enthusiastic about the sonata genre as their German compatriots. Newman[1] in his seminal study of the sonata has convincingly argued that the romantic sonata belongs to the German romantic composers. As well as quoting examples from major composers, German theorists and philosophers writing about music tended to regard the sonata as their own invention. This 'German hegemony' (Newman's term) implied scepticism towards any non-German sonata composer. In France, attitudes towards sonatas or instrumental music generally were summed up by Rousseau who in 1755, made some of the most important statements on the meaning of the sonata in France. Rousseau's remarks reveal the low status of instrumental music compared with vocal music: 'instrumental music enhances the singing and adds to its expression, but it does not replace it'.[2] To clarify the meaning of all this jumble of sonatas that overwhelms us, one would have to do as the inept painter did who had to write below his figures, 'this is a tree', 'this is a man', 'this is a horse'. I shall never forget the quip of the celebrated Fontanelle, who, finding himself worn out with these eternal instrumental pieces, exclaimed aloud in a fit of impatience, 'Sonata, what do you want of me?'

Many French composers including Alkan in his op 33 have propounded the meaning and personal significance of the sonata. Indeed contemporary French composers are still questioning. For example, Boulez[3] wrote an article à propos his *Third Sonata* in 1964 based on Fontanelle's remark which continues the Alkanian search for the meaning of the sonata. Several recent writers[4] on French instrumental music have stressed the importance of the sonata in France for piano aware of German sonata hegemony as 'that [form] which was of the greatest significance in advancing progress'. Momigny, a significant writer of a French piano method added, 'a piano sonata was completely independent ... two, three, four, five ... or eight or nine parts'.[5] The completely autonomous nature of the piano to 'express a whole range of sounds and colours is observed by the same author noting that 'a piano is a whole orchestra'.This portrays the very nature and function of the piano strongly as the complete instrument of Romantic music. Alkan sought to express completeness of this kind in his *Les Quatres Ages Sonata* op 33 in a work of remarkable progress, independence and orchestral variety.

The French eighteenth-century piano sonata was rather different. Piano sonatas required 'artistry of the first order ... and the most beautifully elegant phrases with poetic descriptions or animated dramatic dialogues'.[6] These eighteenth-century aesthetics were often extended to composers of the nineteenth century in France. There existed a plethora of miniaturist composers whose attempts at sonata writing were lamentable in creating sonata structures with any degree of force, strong motivic and structural cohesion. Prowess at opera composition or skill in orchestration did not ensure success in constructing sonatas. Momigny again realized that 'ariette producers and orchestral noise makers would be unsuccessful at writing sonatas'.[7] Operatic zeitgeist initially attracted Alkan but after an early flirtation with the operatic aria and variation form, Alkan turned to larger works of which the op 33 sonata is the most original of his sonata oeuvre.

To understand Alkan's opus we need to review something of the background to his sonata predecessors and contemporaries in France. As implied in the historical introduction, Alkan had a thorough training in all aspects of musicianship. In his piano studies at the conservatoire he would be familiar with the contemporary French and earlier sonata repertory as well as the sonata literature of Haydn, Mozart and Beethoven. The latter composer was an important influence for Alkan and it is well documented[8] that Beethoven's titanic impact hung over any potentially serious writer of sonatas in France. Alkan's *Les Quatres Ages* sonata is his reply to Beethoven's *Hammerklavier* op 106. Very few other examples of sonatas of this scale exist in France.

Nevertheless there are many stylistically French aspects in Alkan's sonata types which derive from earlier French composers. For example, certain features of the style of piano music as demonstrated in the sonatas of Edelmann[9] are also found in the sonatas of Alkan. These include a persistent tendency to section off the main divisions of the movements with double bars which may reflect the persistence of the clavecin tradition in France as demonstrated in the keyboard music of Rameau. Another similarity between the sonatas of Edelmann and Alkan is their extravagant use of dynamic and tempi expressions. In Edelmann one also finds indications for example 'avec tristesse, volupteusement'. Also, Edelmann and Alkan both share a Gluck-like tragic quality in their works. But Gluck was a major influence[10] on all serious French composers in the nineteenth century, until his eclipse by Rossini whose operas promoted a general Italianization of French music. Berlioz and Alkan however, remained rather sceptical about the rather superficial nature of Italianate melodic writing and, after a flirtation with Italianate style in the early variation sets, Alkan returned to a more classical approach in his sonatas. An equally classical style of piano sonata writing is found in the works of the German composer Hüllmandel.[11]

A fellow countryman of Alkan's was Méhul,[12] whose sonatas give a clear indication of the late eighteenth-century form at its most lucid with Gluck again as an important influence. This severity of style is copied in Alkan. Less impressive is Méhul's use of rather vapid tremulo figures perhaps as a quasi-orchestral device. This was adopted by Alkan in the last movement of his op 33 sonata. Both composers derived much of their dramatic style from Beethoven.[13] Post-Beethoven composers in France often experimented with more distant keys. A distinctive Parisian musical figure, Jadin,[14] showed a likeness for far major and minor keys, a factor which was considerably expanded by Alkan in *Quasi Faust* op 33 which is in D sharp minor. Jadin's works were not however approved of in Germany,[15] and once again in instrumental music throughout the nineteenth century, France had to battle against Germanic prejudice and lack of sympathy. Schumann's own reviews on Alkan's piano compositions are witness to this fact,[16] although he did not review Alkan's own sonatas. Schumann's lack of empathy with Chopin's *Sonata Funèbre* would surely have been extended to Alkan's *Les Quatres Ages*.

The French sonata post-1815 naturally has most direct relevance to the works of Alkan. Preceding Alkan's sonatas are several sonatas by Adam, Boieldieu, Steibelt and Kalkbrenner. The change in musical taste around 1830 discussed in the historical introduction triggered a growth of composers of piano sonatas who were charlatans of the first order. Correspondingly, it is disappointing that many of the most distinguished composers such as Auber, Berlioz, Bizet, Gounod and Meyerbeer took no interest whatsoever in the piano sonata. Inordinately few of these nineteenth-century composers took much notice of the German theorists and lexicographers who had placed German sonata writers as pre-eminent. The sonata masterpieces of Haydn and Mozart were rarely performed in France in public and it was left to virtuosi such as Liszt to perform the late sonatas of Beethoven.[17] In the abstract medium of the sonata, French composers had to struggle against unsympathetic audience response as well as Germanic domination. French composers' senses of frustration were noted by Fétis;[18] 'nature struggled in vain to give birth to a Haydn or Beethoven in France'. Sonatas were not regarded as suitable public fare, mainly because of the unsophisticated and lowly taste of the audience. Alkan only performed sonatas as far as can be ascertained at the end of his career[19] and his own sonatas were unplayed during his lifetime. During Alkan's lifetime the Fontanelle issue dominated. It asked 'Sonata what do you want of me?' This now increasingly became altered to 'Sonata, what use do you have for me?' Composers of sonatas in France therefore rejected German sonata aesthetics and incorporated more popular elements into their sonatas.

One of the early nineteenth-century French piano sonata composers who has been studied extensively is Boieldieu,[20] whose early sonatas were published between 1795 and 1803. Following his appointment to an academic post at the Paris Conservatoire, Boieldieu specialized in light Italianate operatic style inappropriate for the medium of sonatas. Alkan, c1830, also used Italianate airs for lightweight rondos (for example, *Un p'tit homme* op 2), but he ultimately rejected operatic style for sonata material. Alkan may have felt the same desperation as Beethoven who wrote in 1822: 'The solo pieces [ie sonatas]: they went out of fashion long ago, and here fashion is everything.'[21] Indeed, the spread of the fashionable Italian style of operatic aria plus variation in France may have delayed Alkan's sonata writing since his first fully fledged essay in the sonata, *Les Quatres Ages* op 33, was not published until 1847. This is a much more distinguished work than any of Boieldieu's sonatas where thinning of pianistic textures, reliance on weak melodic material, domination of scalic thirds and sixths and repetitive dotted patterns are all pervasive. French enthusiasm for their own sonatas which verged on chauvinism was not shared by other Europeans. Boieldieu's sonatas were cursorily treated in a German review which described them as 'too long, lacking in consequential slow music and unexceptional'.[22]

The French composer, Ladurner,[23] wrote fifteen piano sonatas after the turn of the century. In his sonatas there is much brilliant but intense passage work influenced by Clementi's *Gradus ad Parnassum*. This type of intense scalic writing influenced Alkan and all his sonatas abound with brilliant passages. Ladurner's sonatas also contain programmatic elements found in Alkan. A famous example is *Le Seigneur* in the *Quasi Faust* movement of his op 33 sonata. Ladurner, in keeping with the spirit of the times, wrote battle finales. This degree of mimetic illustration was rejected by Alkan for the abstract medium of the sonata. Battle effects were more appropriately reserved for more obviously referential works such as his *Capriccio alla soldatesca* op 50/1.

The more facile of French sonata writers in the mid-nineteenth century were overindulgent in sonata composition. Of all French composers easily the most prolific was Steibelt[24] whose sonata output surpassed even Haydn in number. Of Steibelt's one hundred and fifty sonatas, sixty are for solo piano. Unlike Alkan, Steibelt courted bourgeois popularity by often writing two movements with rondo finales. His harmonic plan is very basic and his melodic style is quite deliberately simple. He resorts to very mechanical transpositions of the main thematic material unlike Alkan who is much more sophisticated in thematic development. Kalkbrenner,[25] another significant piano sonata composer working in Paris whose output included thirteen piano sonatas, was mainly known by his lucid and slightly old-fashioned piano playing.[26] In this respect his playing was similar to that of Alkan. Compositionally, Kalkbrenner has been dismissed as the salon composer of pot-pourris and fantasias of dubious merit, but his sonatas were positively received by Schumann[27] who mentioned the 'first, lively, truly musical sonatas' of Kalkbrenner's early years.

Kalkbrenner, like Alkan, had a thorough academic training, although in expressive style, Kalkbrenner in his sonatas shows a more Chopinesque cantabile and ornamentation of the melody. Alkan, however, has a much surer sense of architectural design in the op 33 sonata and the op 61 sonatine. French composers have usually had a preference for the formal Czernian approach to sonata design and Alkan's late example in the sonatine op 61 adheres much more rigidly to Czerny's ideal than the earlier example of op 33. Alkan and Chopin are the two outstanding examples of composers moreover who follow Schumann's sentiments regarding form: 'I no longer think about form when I compose, I create it.'[28] In other words, these composers modified the boundaries of sonata form according to their own creative desires. Titles sometimes gave a clue to the nature of these desires. To emphasize the importance of the sonata one writer[29] coined the term *Grande sonate*. 'Grande' then became attached to many piano compositions of varying degrees of merit. 'Grande' accurately describes the piano sonata *Les Quatre Ages* of Alkan which is his largest essay in sonata structures and gives full rein to his subjectivity and creativity. Nevertheless nineteenth-century French criticism regarding the sonata was led by Fétis, that doyen of nineteenth-century lexicographers. Although he cannot invariably be relied on to give factually accurate accounts of musical history, but he does, however, state with remarkable acuity that 'in the last several years the sonata has fallen into discredit. A certain futility of taste which has contaminated music has replaced the serious forms of this sort with kinds of lighter works called fantasias, air variés, caprices.'[30] Fétis wrote this in 1830, and particularly at this time, all manner of serious composers were composing mass audience music.

Alkan did not attempt more serious forms until the composition of the *Duo concertant* in 1840. Perhaps he reflected on the problems of sonata composition so clearly expounded by Schumann. Between 1839 and 1851 Schumann raised some related issues: 'there is no worthier form by which [composers] might introduce and ingratiate themselves in the eyes of the finer critics. But ... most sonatas can be considered only as a kind of testing ground as studies in form'.[31] This type of formal academicism is totally absent in Alkan's op 33 and op 61. Furthermore, Schumann realized that the sonata was unpopular with audiences. He regretted that: 'the sonata is but smiled on with pity in France and scarcely more than tolerated in Germany'.[32] Following Schumann's remarks a French reviewer noted that 'the sonata had been unpopular in France for thirty years'.[33] In 1855 too a French critic insisted that 'the sonata has died with the eighteenth century that produced it so abundantly'.[34] Much later in 1901 another writer pronounced the end of the sonata describing it as an 'admirable, vanished species'.[35] All these commentators had an essentially conservative view of the sonata, only considering them to be worthy if written in pseudo-eighteenth-century style. French commentators and critics do not seem until recently to have accepted Schumann's creative approach to form. Alkan's epoch-making op 33 with its freer sonata boundaries seems to have been totally neglected by them in Alkan's lifetime. It still suffers neglect by pianists, audiences and critics.

For Alkan then the sonata presented a technical and musical challenge. He was specific about the need to expand its classical structure yet he was fully aware of the sonata as a personal utterance. In the introduction to the op 33 work Alkan required that a sonata should not be mere routine but possess some originality. In the same introduction he stressed that 'each of the four movements corresponds in my mind with a given moment of existence, to a particular category of thought or imagination'. The conventional four-movement format was retained by Alkan. He did not compress the structure as did Liszt, but the op 33 sonata demonstrated many facets of musical Romanticism including referential allusions.

The most favourable period for piano sonata composition in France was after 1850 when a classical revival took place. Newman[36] has carried out a statistical analysis of sonata distribution in France during the early, middle and late Romantic periods, and on conversion to a percentage basis it is found that respectively 22%, 28% and 50% of French sonatas were composed during the aforementioned periods which overlap somewhat, but Newman's sample is large enough to be meaningful statistically. In France during the late romantic period there existed the *Société Nationale de Musique* which was started by Saint-Saëns in 1871 to promote sonata and chamber music as a means of expression. Alkan's own promotion of the sonata was confined to the programmes of the Petit Concerts where the handbill of the 1875 series[37] shows Alkan's classical preoccupation with the sonatas of Mozart and Beethoven, as well as the romantically stormy *Funeral March* sonata of Chopin, as well as an extract from his own *Symphonie* op 39 (the minuet). Correctly he realized that the public were not ready for the experimental op 33 sonata which far transcends any romantic sonata in aesthetic scale by Chopin, Schumann, Liszt or Brahms. In essence Alkan's work is only paralleled in vastness by Richard Strauss's *Ein Heldenleben* of 1897–1898. It is now to a description of op 33 that we turn.

Grande Sonate op 33 Les Quatre Ages (1847)

The ethos of the op 33 *Grande Sonate* is that of realism in the first and third movement and symbolism in the second and fourth movements conveying the main mythical elements of Faust and Prometheus. The individual movements correspond to the four ages of Hindu man from twenty to fifty years. As well as a programmatic study in outwards habits displayed by these life stages, Alkan provides a personal psychological study. Lewenthal has enthusiastically described op 33 as 'a cosmic event in its composer's development and in the history of piano music. Nothing in Alkan's previous output leads one to expect anything of such magnitude'.[38] Certain aspects of Alkan's massed style such as the magnitude of the movements, the chordal density of the writing and the extreme severity of the virtuosic writing are cosmically developed in the *Grande Sonate* from the lineage of the op 76 *Études* and the op 26 and op 27 marches. The composer himself recognized a path of personal development within his *Grande Sonate* through the observation that: 'each of [the four movements] corresponds in my soul with a specific moment of existence to a particular way of thinking or imagining'.[39] Appropriately then, the first movement of op 33 is a fleet-footed scherzo relating back to Alkan's energetically driven études of 1838, and this movement is titled 'at twenty years'. At first glance this first movement appears to be a simple ternary structured scherzo influenced by the magnificent example of Chopin's *Scherzo in B minor* op 20 which had been published in 1835. Undoubtedly there is a similarity in cross accents in both pieces.

Ex. 5.1a   Chopin – *Scherzo in B minor* op 20, bars 10–15

Ex. 5.1b   *Grande Sonate* op 33, first movement, bars 1–4

Harmonically the Chopin example is much more stable tonally at the outset but the Alkan movement opens outlining mediant relationships and binary cross-rhythmic figurations. In the Alkan first movement, compared with the Chopin *Scherzo* the harmonic emergence of B minor is frustrated by persistent V^7/I fluctuations and, also by Alkan's favourite device of chromatic sideslips in this case from C double sharp to D sharp minor, a tonal precursor of the key of the second movement of the *Grande Sonate*. At the reprise of scherzo Alkan provides a sudden unprepared statement of the opening which now climaxes in the flattened submediant of the relative major of B minor. The third of this chord functions as the enharmonic to launch F sharp major and thence back to this dominant pedal to launch the trio by a very artful dissipation of texture. The trio show an impressive confidence in its move towards the impassioned 'amoureusement'. In the 'toujours lié' section following, the emphasis is on symmetrical phrase structure and diatonic harmony spiked with the tritone being traversed chromatically.

Ex. 5.2   *Grande Sonate* op 33, first movement, bars 197–216

This trio shows a strong resemblance in rhythmic values, melodic line and texture to the Chopin's *Scherzo in E major* op 54 which was published in 1843. The reprise of the Alkan scherzo is regular, but there is now an expansive transformation of the trio's main theme stated fortissimo and with full voiced texture. Further reliance on the Chopin *Scherzo* model is indicated in Alkan's bravura coda with, firstly, its similarity in heavily accented chordal passages and, secondly, the similarity of the flattened plagal cadences. Several other points of contact with the Chopin *Scherzo* have been recorded by François-Sappey.[40]

The next movement of the *Grande Sonate*, entitled *Quasi-Faust*, as well as providing a peak in Alkan's densely chordal style, is moreover one of the most remarkable displays of purely virtuosic piano compositions of the nineteenth century, even eclipsing the *Transcendental Études* of Liszt. Lewenthal provides an admirable introduction to *Quasi Faust*:

> [it] is actually a tone poem within a tone poem ... it forms the apex of the sonata and it is the longest and most difficult movement. It stands very well by itself and no one performing it without the other movements need fear being criticised for serving up a bleeding chunk.[41]

From the outset of '*Quasi-Faust* the power of the Faust motif appearing transposed another twice is truly satanic. The futility of this motive is swept away temporarily by a derived rhythmic variant set in the low piano register.

Ex. 5.3 *Grande Sonate* op 33, second movement, bars 265–267

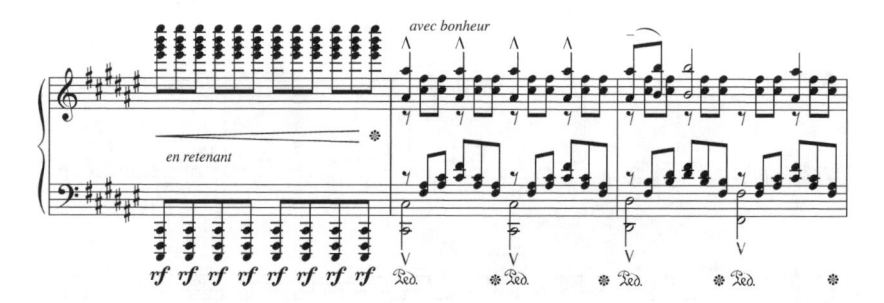

François-Sappey and Smith[42] compare this with the Liszt *Sonata in B minor* of 1853, but the likeness to the Alkan is mainly rhetorical. There follows a freely brillante improvisation passage based on the ascending and descending fourth of the rhythmic variant leading to quite incredibly virtuosic arpeggios after which 'Le Diable' motto is starkly presented. Interestingly, this is an inversion of the Faust motto theme thereby presenting a binary divide. The rhythmic variant is soon transformed into a lyrical Marguerite theme of considerable beauty which despite a four square structure is delicately accompanied by gently chromatic harmony. After a development of this in an impassioned manner with finely controlled pianistic textures, and a recall of the first subject initially on the Neapolitan relationship of A major, the second subject next blazes forth in the passionate major with full Lisztian glory, but whereas Liszt might have written swashbuckling left hand textures, Alkan chooses much drier, but equally effective, left hand textures.

The closing section passage is very effective in its canonic interplay and by diminishing the energy of the previous measures a convergence is achieved. At the start of the development section the Faust motto theme is reheard at tempo, making the fullest use of the extremes of the piano. Texturally, this part of the development is one of the most massed in style amongst all Alkan's works, and certainly is the summit of textural density in the middle period works. This section displays the most orchestral of sonorities yet, paradoxically, it would be destroyed by orchestration. The lyrical second subject somehow emerges amidst this tempestuous development, but Alkan's instructions: 'suppliant, avec désepoir, déchirant' Satie-like in their vividness of supplication, despair and fearing apart. These indicate the frustration of the second subject's lyricism. The recapitulation bursts in with a real sense of diabolical frenzy describing the Faustian drama being overcome with the vanquishing octaves. Alkan wisely removes any reference to the second subject which had many transformations in the development section. Densely massed style effects abound just before the final fugal section over a tremendously sonorous pedal point on the dominant with the chromatic semitones melodically gap filling the interval of the fourth. This is really an augmentation of the previous second subject group.

This dominant pedal reaches the fullest expansion in the heaven reaching arpeggios covering over five octaves and encloses the cancrizans of the fugal redemption motto theme. This is a truly impressive moment in *Quasi-Faust*. The ensuing textural contrast could not be greater. The sparse nature of fugue's subject adds an infinite modal mystery from which this single fugal subject grows inevitably towards six real parts in invertible counterpoint then three doublings and two extra voices are further added. *Le Seigneur* theme then bursts in as a release from this complex counterpoint at fff level in glorious homophony with a fragment of the fugal answer in the left hand. The focus of the whole of the *Quasi-Faust* movement is revealed in the combination of the Marguerite lyrical second subject and *Le Seigneur* motto in counterpoint.

Ex. 5.4 *Grande Sonate* op 33, second movement, bars 1–5

The coda of *Quasi-Faust* is a magnificent example of Alkan's application of the cycle principle muting the Devil motto and endlessly repeating *Le Seigneur* motto theme, and in the last two bars the most elemental interval of the fourth emerges triumphant. There is no comparable work in the whole of instrumental musical literature which deals with semantic fusion of motives through thematic superimposition.

The third movement of the *Grande Sonate* is titled 'at forty years'. The performance instruction: 'très lié ... avec tendresse et quiétude' (very binding ... with tenderness and quietude) gives some idea of the calm of fulfilment on reaching the age of forty. Subtitled 'un heureux ménage' (a happy family) this movement provides a peaceful reflection after *Quasi-Faust*. This third movement, like the first movement of op 33, is of ternary design and employs at its outset a Mendelssohnian melodic simplicity contrasted by a low bass accompaniment which flows into a surprisingly unsymmetrical seven bar structure. Harmonically, the unpredictable modulation scheme from the G major tonic of the opening of the third movement via the flattened submediant shows a Schubertian influence. The middle section of 'un heureux ménage' represents in music the energy of three children. Marked 'les enfans' (a curious mis-spelling!) Alkan employs three flowing independent parts mainly operating with diatonic sweetness, but occasionally rising to some chromatic squabbling.

Ex. 5.5   *Grande Sonate* op 33, third movement, bars 74–79

The opening section of this movement on recapitulation is delicately changed texturally and is now more mellow and perhaps more comfortable in melodic line. Not even the subtle move to the mediant major with the designation 'dix heures' (presumably bedtime) with the ten-fold chime on a single note disturbs the final prayer which is at first hymn-like then secondly is presented with the children's motto. Elements of the hymn-like prayer, the opening figure float towards a finally gently suspended cadence. François-Sappey[43] has commented on the affinity between this work and Liszt's *Benediction de dieu dans la Solitude*.

The final movement is titled 'at fifty years' and subtitled *Prométhée Enchaine*. The seven-line preface from Aeschylus's tragedy outlines the suffering of Prometheus and his puzzlement over the various tortures he endured. From the historical background it is recalled that Alkan craved recognition of his artistic talents and the last movement of the *Grand Sonate* is a pessimistic projection of his own personal life at the age of fifty. Set in pseudo-rondo form, it has a primitivism comparable with the slow movement of Beethoven's *Fourth Piano Concerto*. In the Alkan Prometheus movement, after a desolate opening, the Faust motto re-appears in the low piano register in hymn style and with smoothed out rhythmic values.

Ex. 5.6   *Grande Sonate*, op 33, fourth movement, bars 9–15

This is explosively swept away by a funereal theme for five bars with a dotted rhythm based on the funeral march from Beethoven's *Eroica Symphony*. After a reappearance of the hymn-style figure transposed down the semitone, a variant of the Faustian motto theme now seems to describe in musical terms the very nadir of melancholy. The energy of the Faust motto theme also has been swept away in smooth octave sextolets. After further downward transpositions of previous material, the movement and the whole sonata reaches an ascent through a piano range of three and a half octaves. The compound interval of the fourth, and representative of *Le Seigneur* from *Quasi-Faust*, still triumphs through the desiccated texture and the whole sonata ends convincingly with a IV/V/I cadence but with unusual duality of dynamics and register. In short, Alkan's *Grande Sonate* carries colossal internal and external semantic and programmatic meaning and Sorabji's[44] judgement of the *Grande Sonate* as a 'clever piece of musico psychological characterisation' is astute. As the previous remarks show, the *Grande Sonate* is remarkable in concept and massed style and requires a performer of the greatest ability to project the widest range of emotions. In expressive and technical requirements it certainly reminds one of 'Berlioz, particularly Berlioz of the *Symphonie Fantastique*' but the *Grande Sonate* is conceived in pianistic terms for piano, not orchestral performance.

The scale of the *Grande Sonate* and other works had been mentioned in a letter from Alkan to Fétis.[45] This letter also includes remarks about an overture for piano and studies[46] and a large scale scherzo. The latter is the *Scherzo focoso* op 34, published in 1847. This work is of much lesser calibre than the *Grande Sonate* and seems to revert to an earlier style, although the op 34 work is far more fiery as the title implies. Sonata principles inflect op 34. It is grander in concept than the early *Scherzi* op 16 and also more virtuosic than the scherzo movement from the *Grande Sonate*. Smith's conjecture[47] that the *Scherzo focoso* existed originally as the opening piece for the *Études* op 39 is plausible given the date of op 34 and stylistic unity with the op 39 *Études*. Both op 34 and the overture to op 39 moreover share the same key of B minor. Alkan was correct to discard op 34 as the opening to op 39 since the overture is the finer work. The *Scherzo focoso* is propelled by the rhythmic motive of three quavers followed by four semiquavers and a quaver as an antecedent followed by a group of hurtling semiquavers as the consequent. This very simple construction of phrases gives a very square phrase structure.

The first trio itself is not without imperious energy but its attempt at dynamism seems rather empty. The second trio is even more four square and does not have the energy of the former trio. This second trio is usurped by a recapitulation of the first trio, before a return to the gymnastics of the scherzo now, enhanced with octave bravura and a short coda. Alkan's scherzo/double trio structure shows the composer experimenting with larger form building applying some of the concepts of sonata principles to a work of only variable standard.

The sonata compressed: the *Sonatine* op 61 (1861)

There is no fluctuation whatsoever in musical inspiration in Alkan's next sonata-type composition. This is the *Sonatine* op 61 published in 1861 and along with the *Symphonie* op 39 is the finest work for piano by Alkan. The *Sonatine* is no sonatina in scale or weight: op 61 runs to some forty-seven pages of intensely developed musical argument. Moving away from the miniature approach in many of the post op 39 works, Alkan produced in op 61 a highly compressed and convincing essay without resorting to massed effects. It is a significant contribution to nineteenth-century piano sonata literature and anticipates in crystalline coherence and controlled bravura the example of Ravel's *Sonatine* of some forty years later. The combination of Beethovenian drive with Berliozian romanticism was observed by Sorabji who described op 61 as 'vehement, droll ... childlike and naïve in turn almost as though Berlioz had written a Beethoven sonata'.[48] The first movement of op 61, an A minor 6/8 allegro vivace is generated from a memorable rhythmic and melodic motive.

Ex. 5.7   *Sonatine* op 61/1, bars 1-9

Block harmonic movement upwards to the relative major follows immediately with the inverted fourth being gap filled. This expressive device is expanded at intervals then subjected to a four-note rise reflecting the opening bars. A hemiola plus the augmented sixth and a dramatic silence launch the transition passage characterized by circular semiquaver texture. The second subject is unified directionally to the first subject, but the former is accompanied by a charmingly gruff but springy left hand part with a measured use of the diminished seventh. The closing section darkens the mood with minor turns to the harmony, the reappearance of the hemiola and an exact two to one rhythmic relationship between right and left hands. Thereafter, within some seventy-seven bars, Alkan has produced a concise yet perfectly balanced formal unity. It is his most compact and convincing sonata exposition.

The development section continues in dark tonality with fleeting minor key touches but there is more than a degree of harmonic restlessness with non-functional use of dominant sevenths coupled up with melodic gap filling culled from the first subject. A plateau of stability is reached with the warm cantabile left hand 'cello type melody but this is soon interrupted by a three-note point of imitation climaxing in discordant diminished sevenths and a three-fold restatement of the second subject each ascending by tones. Even the following pedal point texture has a well organized sense of direction with canonic imitations towards the augmented sixth which is enharmonically converted to the dominant seventh and thereby to the recapitulation. This reprise is not exact but has applied decorative suspensions in the accompaniment. The transitional and second subjects of the *Sonatine*'s first movement behave regularly, but the closing section is extended considerably and progresses with total conviction and a depth to the virtuosity worthy of Brahms. The coda itself is a reminder of the opening four bars and reduces the material to skeletal outlines with the minimum of virtuosity. The spirit of classicism is very much evident in this first movement from the relationships of musical sections to the eighteenth-century attitude to scale and musical devices.

The second movement is a quite delightful allegramente to be played in a 'peaceful and sustained fashion' (Alkan's own performance instructions). The texture here is varied in its independent voicing. Again, in common with the first movement, the block harmonic structure shifts up the third. The first episode in D minor opens with a two bar unit which relates back to the opening of the movement and despite its repeated note insistence, it soon is presented as a more tortured and chromatically restless version and then introduces the reprise of the rondo theme in a fourth related key. This neatly uses E flat major as the Neapolitan relationship for the next episode in a peaceful dotted rhythm. This generates much harmonic and melodic invention but a constant right hand ostinato is the main outcome which combines this element with a reprise of the opening theme, first in the tenor voice then, very smoothly, in the soprano register before a return to the opening texture. Harmonically interesting points are the unresolved seventh appoggiatura-type chords applied five times. A sober reference back to the opening of the movement in the lowest register much truncated terminates the movement and the final coup de foudre is the Alkanian explosive chordal punctuation.

The brilliant scalic French étude influenced the next movement of op 61. Extremely virtuosic, the third movement of the *Sonatine* is also unique in the history of nineteenth-century music in combining a minuet with a scherzo. In this case the delicacy of the left hand represents the minuet whilst the right hand gives the character of the scherzo with its hurtling semiquaver movement. Thematic and motivic unification in the *Sonatine* is further exemplified by much harmonic reliance on the tonic pedal, a feature found also in the preceding movement. Alkan shortens the symmetry of the phrase in order to accelerate the harmonic rhythm which also causes the rapidly modulating dominant sevenths in the second half of the movement. The ability to achieve longer formal unification is further realized by the rhythmic augmentation of the opening left hand three-note ascending melodic motive. This example shows the extreme contrast of texture, movement and temperament of the trio with the scherzo. This three-note motive is retained later for a most fascinating and texturally sparse section which heralds a long dominant preparation of the varied scherzo minuetto reprise before a brief reiteration of the trio. This is soon transferred to the tonic major with a fortissimo restatement of the all important ascending three-note cell.

The finale dispels any possible doubt regarding the weight of the *Sonatine*, given its fiery, impassioned and grimly determined A minor opening. Alkan's bell effects now are increased to a fullness hitherto unrealized.

Ex. 5.8   *Sonatine* op 61/4, bars 1–8

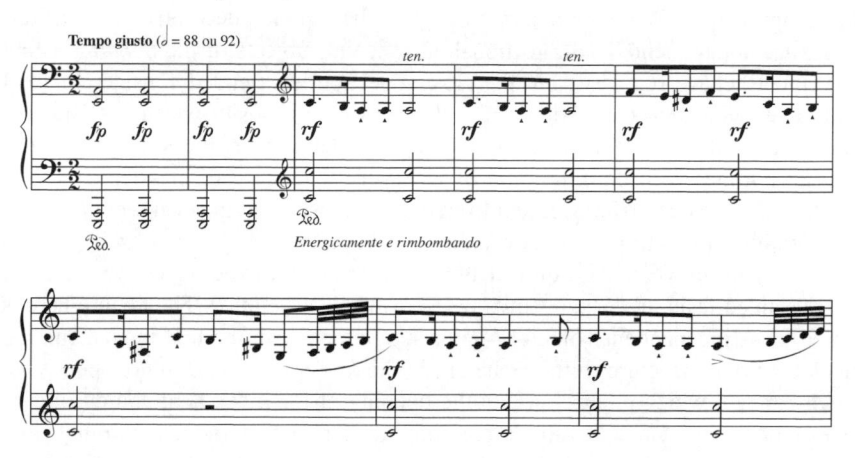

The transitional material consists of a flurry of parallel semiquavers with a repeated octave hammer blow to effect the modulation gradually encompassing the characteristic right hand rhythmic cell of the opening, then alternating right and left hand semiquavers and rhythmic cells. The second subject of the finale of the *Sonatine* is as graceful as any in Alkan's output and provides a full release after the onward drive of previous material and diminished seventh preceding bars. This second subject is subjected to varying degrees of syncopation, but towards the end of the second subject group there occurs an augmented sixth modulation to the key of C minor which appears at first sight to reactivate a reprise of the opening of the movement. This version, however, is rather unstable harmonically and proves to be only a false reprise. The *Sonatine* has several other excellent features. For example Alkan makes splendid use of dramatic silence throughout and perhaps the finest individual example of this is the link into the development section which starts with a transference of the second subject to A flat major in a succession of third related modulations from A minor, the tonic key. Then, the power of the rhythmic cell of the opening subject is fully exploited imitatively.

When the recapitulation returns it is more fully scored and canonically compressed as is the second subject material first in the Neapolitan key of B flat major then wrenched back to A major, the tonic major. This is especially effective at the pianissimo dynamic. The coda of the *Sonatine* is one of Alkan's most brilliant yet concise efforts and it gathers up the previous allusions to Neapolitan relationships as well as including highly extended pedal points and a powerful use of bass octaves. As a measure of Alkan's perfectly controlled virtuosity, the final three lines of op 61 are extremely convincing and transcend mere surface brilliance found in earlier works.

In essence, the piano sonata types of Alkan are more uneven in quality than those of Chopin, but Alkan's examples are much more extreme in character. The *Grande Sonate* op 33 looks forward to the era of the tone poem of Richard Strauss whereas the *Sonatine* op 61 is an affectionate tribute to the already extinct classical world which Alkan valued for clarity of expression and form. The *Sonatine* op 61 retains the four movement classical structure and is an inspired expression of Alkan as classical form builder. This expertise also inflects the *Scherzo focoso* op 34. Like Chopin however, Alkan reserved his finest effort in large-scale sonata structuring for the violoncello sonata op 47 which will be discussed in Chapter 10.

Chapter 6

Morceaux Caracteristiques

The polar opposite to the massed style works such as the *Grande Sonata* op 33 and the *Études* op 39 is found in Alkan's miniatures or more accurately his character pieces (*morceaux caracteristiques*). In the middle of the nineteenth century this French term referred to a descriptive, realistic or pictorial short work most often for piano although the term was first applied by Brendel to elements of the works of Berlioz.[1]

The derivation of the French Romantic character piece is found in the clavecin school. The general aesthetic of the seventeenth/eighteenth century was that music should be imitative. As a miniaturist[2] Alkan may indeed be thought of as occupying a place between Chambonnières to Poulenc. In the tradition of the French clavecin composers, Alkan copies Couperin's *Un petit rien* by composing a similar example in his *Preludes* op 31. Alkan's *Les Soupirs* from the *Esquisses* op 63/11 also might owe its title from the exquisite same named composition from Rameau's *Pièces de clavecin* of 1724. Miniatures in France were very strongly influenced by opera and ballet from the seventeenth to the nineteenth century. This can be instanced by Alkan's transcription of the gavotte from Gluck's *Orphée*. The later bombastic operatic style of Meyerbeer was brilliantly parodied in Alkan's *L'Opéra* from *Les Mois*. The other important influence on the Alkan miniature is the ordres of the French clavecin composers. These composers influenced many of the dance-type miniatures in Alkan's *Esquisses*. The *Rigaudon* op 63/27 is an example of this clavecin tradition filtered through Alkan's own harmonic proclivities.

Reflecting the state of political unrest in France in the eighteenth century, miniatures depicting battles were topical. In France probably the first eighteenth-century example is Corrette's *Divertissements pour le clavecin ou le pianoforte*, published in 1780 which attempts to portray a naval battle. Many tombeaux and battle pieces were composed during the 1789 revolution. Alkan's miniature battle pieces, the op 50 *Capriccios* were published in 1859 and are a musical expression of the 1848 revolution in France.

The prelude was a less referential type of miniature and the originator of this form in France was Louis Couperin whose *Préludes non mesurés* are a landmark in improvisation. At this stage the form was very free: the preludes were short and of slight thematic interest. By the end of the eighteenth century the form was more structured as seen by Beauvarlet-Charpentier's[3] *Recueil de sept préludes* op 17, published in 1785. The nineteenth-century trend to write preludes in many or all keys was started by Viguerie[4] who composed twelve preludes in the most used keys published in 1815. Chopin's later *Preludes* op 28 display a masterful variety of mood, texture and other parameters. Alkan's *Preludes* op 31 are more uneven in compositional value but they are still interesting musically and the finest of the Alkan set, particularly *La chanson de la folle au bord de la mer* (no. 8) and the *J'étais endormie ...* (no. 13), can easily stand comparison with any of the reflective examples in Chopin's op 28. Alongside the prelude the caprice most captured the improvisatory mood of the times for the French romanticist. Momigny in 1818 defined it as 'a piece full of liveliness and originality'.[5] Significant contributions to this miniature form were made by Hérold[6] in his *Neuf Caprices en trois Suites* ops 4, 6 and 7 (published posthumously) and by Boëly[7] in his *Caprice* op 7 (published 1843).

Alkan's Caprices however, published earlier in 1837 comprised pieces as diversified as improvisations, andante romantiques, morceaux and scherzi. In these caprices the most significant formal feature was the replacement of a traditional sonata-allegro design with a type of moment form often with elements of song form to enhance a lyrical approach. As a set *Les Mois* op 74 is the most typical of Alkan's early miniature style, and all the pieces demonstrate a concentrated motivic approach, a pungent atmosphere, a wide range of tonal freedom for the date of composition, a general reluctance to indulge in virtuosity for its own sake and the fullest use of resources in register, dynamics and the use of the pedals. All of *Les Mois* are motivated by a French compositional characteristic that is, the principal idea (*l'idée principale*) which can portray a musical instrument. Bell-type pieces were popular with the French miniaturists and an Alkan example is *Les Cloches* from the *Esquisses* op 63/4. Many composers attempted to imitate a wide range of instruments on the piano by specific rhythmic and melodic patterns as well as the use of actual melodic fragments associated with these instruments. Some miniatures by Alkan are more crudely referential. Several of these exist in the final period of composition, for example the op 53 *Quasi-caccia*, the op 55 *Une fusée* and the op 60 *Ma chère servitude* all published in 1859. But Alkan is at his best as a miniaturist when groups of pieces are collected into what might be called the character-piece suite. His *Esquisses* op 63 can be categorized thus as can the ordres of Couperin and works such as *Carnaval* op 61 by Widor and the *En Languedoc* by Sèverac.

Composers in nineteenth-century France did not have to start ab initio to create the various types of musical expression. Morellet[8] produced a handbook in which was explained the manner of all the various phenomena or processes in nature. Alkan's *Le grillon* op 60 bis follows the procedure outlines in Morellet as does the heavenly *Le ciel vous soit toujours prospère* from the *Esquisses* op 63 with its celestial depiction of nature. *Les Diablotins* op 63/45 with its non functional harmonies or clusters accurately represents satanic emotion. Often, fluctuating tempi also tends to move music away from the absolute plane to that of the expressive indicating extra-musical content. Chief amongst the examples of this in the *Esquisses* is *Héraclite et Démocrite* op 63/39 which, towards the end, by adjacent demonstration of tempo and texture precisely reflects the mood of the two philosophers.

An emotive type where music embraces the world of sentiments and the arousal of types of emotions is well instanced by *Les Soupirs* op 63/11, which adopts melodic contour and non-functional harmony to give a sharp portrait of emotion in music. Suggestive types in the French miniature are exemplified by *L'homme aux sabots* op 63/23 where the accents suggest the heaviness of the footwear. This is a directly descriptive piece. An important distinction was made between imitative and descriptive music. Goblot states that 'imitative music reproduces artificially the sounds of nature ... descriptive music suggests the idea of visible objects ...'.[9] The early étude *Le Vent* is imitative of the various aspects of winds and storms. This piece can be placed in context in French piano literature with Dupont's[10] *La Chanson du vent* (from *Les Heures dolentes* composed 1903–1905) but directly imitative pieces generally declined in Alkan's output and also generally in the history of French piano music as the century progressed. A subdivision of the descriptive category might be named 'evocative types' which were particularly favoured by French miniaturist composers. Prunières has provided a possible explanation: 'French musicians are peculiarly impressionable to the charms of nature, and their music is replete with sonorous tableaux of most various sorts signed by Berlioz, d'Indy, Debussy, Ravel, Ibert ... not to mention Jannequin or Rameau.'[11] Alkan's early set of miniatures *Les Mois* contain two superb examples of evocative nature depictions in the *Nuit d'Hiver* and *Nuit d'Été* and fit into the lineage of French nature scenes continued by Chabrier's *Paysage* (from the *Pièces Pittoresques* published 1881) and Poulenc's *Trois Pastorales* published 1918. But as Ellis observes,[12] there is in the French miniature a special 'X factor' which is indefinable and contributes to the natural charm variously stemming from the first idea, the principal idea or the first melodic inspiration omnipresent in the finest of Alkan's miniatures. The range of these miniatures is quite astonishing from clavecin type pieces to works which strongly anticipate the twentieth century.

Character pieces to 1846

To construct the miniature Alkan turned first to the medium of fugue or more precisely fugally inspired miniatures, namely *Jean qui pleure* and its complement *Jean qui rit*. Subtitled 'due fugue da camera' the estimated date of composition of both pieces is *c*1840. The fugue subject of *Jean qui pleure* is suitably neo-baroque but has an Alkanian melodic tang to its outline.

Ex. 6.1   *Jean qui pleure*, bars 1–4

These fugues are both chamber fugues although the second, the *Jean qui rit* is more weighty with the subject based on the famous theme from Mozart's's drinking song from the first act of the opera. Probably the best known setting is Liszt's monumental *Réminiscences de Don Juan* composed in 1841. Liszt's version consists of a grave introduction, the *Là ci darem duetto*, with two large variations on this theme before a presto version of the drinking song. Alkan's version is more primitive, archaic and much less conspicuously virtuosic by comparison. An unusual and refreshing variant of fugal technique is the announcement of the subject of *Jean qui pleure*, then a combination of both subjects in parallel to provide a fine climax to this pair of chamber fugues.

Also descriptive is *Le Preux* (the valiant knight) op 17 which is a concert work of considerable weight and grandeur and stands alongside Liszt's *Ab Irato* as an example of this genre. Alkan's opening theme is rather four-square perhaps, but perfectly conveys the momentum of the referential title of op 17. The regular phrase sequences and the chordal punctuations on the last beats of every bar express the mood of this composition. Alkan employs an amazing variety of bravura textures and *Le Preux*, even more than earlier works demonstrates an exuberant use of octaves, chords, broken chord figurations and hand crossings. His locked chord figuration with 'les deux mains bien liées entr'elles' gives rise to an implied melody emerging from the chordal contour. Most interestingly the final section marked 'grandement fff et ped: du bras jusqu'a la fin' implies an early use of arm technique which is usually solely credited to Liszt particularly in the *First Concerto in E flat major*.

In sharp contrast with this bravura piece is the *Premier Nocturne* op 22, the first of a set of four pieces published in 1844. The others are the *Saltarelle* op 23, the *Gigue et Air de Ballet dans le style ancien* op 24, and the *Alleluia* op 25. The op 22 work represents a newly expressive lyrical style in Alkan miniature writing undoubtedly inspired by the more well known example in the same key by Chopin because of similarities in melodic contour, chromatic auxiliary notes and melody resting points. Alkan's example is also influenced by John Field particularly with respect to melodic range and uninflated emotional span. The middle section of his op 22 is more diatonic and has an attractive undulating melodic shape, a direct phrase length and a colourful use of seventh and ninth chords. Perhaps the finest section is the discreet combination of melodies of the opening and middle sections which provides a satisfying coda to this shapely nocturne.

Alkan returned to the baroque dance for his next two miniatures. The *Saltarelle* op 23 was one of the most popular of his middle period étude-type pieces but op 23 is stylistically regressive and seems closer to the spirit of the earlier op 12 and op 16 études. Nonetheless, a perceptive twentieth-century writer on Alkan thinks that the op 23 is 'thoroughly delightful ... and abounds in skips of really difficult character'.[13] Undoubtedly the opening measures of the *Saltarelle* are naïvely delightful with its bracing rhythmic pulse, symmetrical melodic rise and fall and a lightly punctuated chordal accompaniment. This accompaniment is occasionally reinforced by a gruppeti drumbeat, a feature which looks forward to the intense *Marche funèbre* op 26. There is some harmonic interest in op 23 however. Particularly striking are the shifts of the thematic material into the tonic major key and the locked chord compressions of the opening measures. The piece really impresses also by Alkan's tight control of harmonic block structures and large-scale form. Although this is the most extroverted of Alkan's middle style pieces, it is a landmark in technical innovations, particularly in the use of repeated notes with special fingerings by the composer, extended skips and melodic chromaticisms. Texturally, too, the wide spacing of the left hand chords from the brilliant right hand figuration builds on the foundations established in the earlier études.

The next sets of miniatures op 24, op 25, op 26 and op 27 shows Alkan's interest in baroque form and massed style. The *Gigue* op 24 is the most intellectual of all the mid-period works. It is the most concise being only thirty-four bars long with an asymmetric 14–20 binary bar subdivision. The influence of Mozart's extraordinary *Gigue K574* with its quirky imitative style may be observed but the influence of the chromatically descending melodic motive of Bach's *Fugue in E minor* (Book

1/10 of the 48 *Preludes and Fugues*) is more important. In the Alkan example some extreme dissonances occur almost by contrapuntal design. An interesting harmonic variant is Alkan's use of the submediant rather than the relative major for the second half of the *Gigue*. The craggy uncompromising style of the *Gigue* contrasts sharply with its companion piece, the *Air de Ballet* (op 24) which is less inspired. Here the model is the opéra ballet of Rameau, thus illustrating Alkan's subtitle to this piece 'dans le style ancien'. This 'ancient style' in Alkan's op 24 is exemplified by square harmonic modular phrase structure, a quasi chanson rhythm and a persistent use of the Dorian mode with its characteristic flattened seventh and an omission of the third of the chord at cadences thus blurring the major/minor tonality. All these factors combine with Alkan's characteristic use of the five bar phrase, his liking for tonic-centred melodies and a romantic reinforcing of the lower bass octaves. Despite the length of the piece (207 bars) which contains much simple repetition of ideas, op 24 has considerable charm from the direct opening D minor rondeau theme in pungent octaves designated 'très carrément' to the delicacy of the first couplet with its soprano tenor delicate texture. A delightful harmonic surprise is the sudden move to B minor via a D major [V^7 of VI] and an inner use of melodic chromaticism.

*

This couplet theme is picked out as part of the triplet melodic variant. After a reprise of the rondeau theme, Alkan announces the second couplet in the dominant key which in its heavy use of tonic/dominant harmony, self-contained sequences and incessant use of right hand octaves is more reminiscent of his early style. His dense use of chordal and heavy left hand octave textures indicates a move towards a more uncompromising massed style. This approach is more fully developed in the *Alleluia* op 25 where the structure of the piece is determined by massed textures which increase in density through the piece towards an impressive climax on the tonic F major augmented sixth chord acting non functionally. Indeed in op 25, melody has almost been superseded by texture: parallel harmony abounds and rhythmic novelties are presented within a basic compound quadruple metre. A subdivision into six quaver units means that the mid-division of op 25 has a divided bar. It is the non-resolved augmented triads which looks forward to the quartal harmony of *Skryabin*. In the context of Alkan's own piano music, op 25 most anticipates the quieter but equally joyful 'J'étais endormie mais mon coeur veillait' from the *Preludes* op 31 with its similarities in repeated chords and displaced harmonies.

*

Further important examples of Alkan's massed style in the miniatures are in the two marches, the Marche funèbre op 26 and the Marche triomphale op 27 both composed in 1844 but published in 1846. The impetus for writing these pieces may have emanated from Berlioz's Grande Symphonie Funèbre et Triomphale which was first performed during the tenth anniversary of the 1830 Revolution on the 28 July 1840. The reception by critics was very positive and the beauty of these marches was much extolled. The post-publication critical review of op 26 compared Alkan's funeral march with that in Beethoven's Eroica Symphony: 'that famous composer's plan is not that of Alkan's; [in Beethoven] there is all the majesty of the hero ... [in Alkan] there is the deep sadness ... its sentiment is true and profound'.[14] This 'deep sadness' is immediately apparent in the opening page of op 26: a low, care-ridden melodic fragment moves inexorably to its lowest point at the end of a twelve bar sentence. This procedure is evocative of Morte op 15/3; that remarkable earlier example of Alkan's massed style. The pianissimo quasi-trombone melody in op 26 is supported by an incessant bass drumbeat.

*

Alkan's avoidance of a defined tonality and his control of block structures and the movement of the opening melody to the alto register are all confidently handled. This section finally converges towards a fine full orchestral chordal theme again, like the opening, in a twelve bar sentence. Adding to the vitality here are the parallelisms in textures and seventh- and ninth-type harmonies. After a return to the opening paragraphs the orchestral chordal theme is sequentially extended with modulations by thirds and then a descent with a special use of a resting point trill undoubtedly influenced by Chopin's *Funeral March*. The special charm of this passage is the fleeting non-resolved harmonies which briefly stabilizes before a fragmentary return to the opening desolate trombone melody. This gives way to a new episode in the tonic major with a bell-like melody revolving around a central note in true Alkanian style. Not for Alkan is the melodiousness of Chopin in the trio of his *Funeral March* sonata. Alkan increases the static centricity of this episode by employing pedal notes and an ostinato-like peal of bells in the alto part. This accompaniment is in the spirit of the 'campane' example in the earlier *Étude* op 16/1. The textural interest of this passage in op 26 is enhanced by Alkan's directive: 'en laissant bien vibrer le son' and, later, 'en gardant toujours la même pédale'. Both these instructions give an exotic sheen to this episode which looks forward to the eastern sonorities of a Debussy. There is a fuller textured repeat of the chordal theme, a return of the opening desolate theme and a truncated version of the bell-like theme providing a very satisfying conclusion to the piece. The excellence of op 26 is well summed up by the contemporary review:

> This not very extended piece is notable for feeling as well as understanding of the subject matter ... it is precisely the alternation of a religious respect and tragedy which moves the heart ... these sentiments are so well conveyed by M. Alkan ... that I consider this composition to be individually perfect.[15]

The companion work, the *Marche triomphale* op 27 is a more bravura work. The description in a contemporary review is an excellent summary: '[op 27] concerns triumph and the most dazzling display of worldly vanities. There is a great deal of energy throughout, although the originality of thought is less remarkable than in the preceding work [op 26]'.[16] The manifestation of more obvious genre virtuosity is clear from the opening with a harmonic block in B major matched by its exact repeat in the dominant key. Rather too stereotyped is the imitation of orchestral brass in the left hand as are the obvious rhythms and melodic chromaticisms which, however, do not disturb the strongly tonal harmony. The massed effect of the final page fully exploits the upper and lower registers of the developing piano. The review of the *Marche triomphale* also points out 'the splendour of radiant sonority and the brilliant tramp of proudly victorious rhythm'.[17] This review made much of the op 27 work being destined for success in the concert hall and op 26 being more suited to private performance.

*

Alkan composed several descriptive portraits of mechanical vehicles. An early example was Les Omnibus variations op 2. Le Chemin de Fer also designated as op 27 and published in 1844 is one of Alkan's most curious descriptive works. Perhaps the total length of this étude of some 509 bars may derive from the composer's wish to portray a long train journey from one place to another. An obvious comparison is Honegger's more famous Pacific 231 composed in 1923 but as Beck has observed, Alkan was 'the first to have expressed the exaltation of speed and the poetry of the machine'.[18] Op 27 in fact operates as a referential tone poem with the opening scalic figuration continuously varied over a 'choo choo' train bass ostinato which functions as a pedal with only one harmonic change during the first 52 bars. The first episode is more abstract in patterning before the opening figuration returning followed by a train whistle motive and braking motive vividly portrayed. There are repetitions and variations of previous material to provide a coherent structure. Alkan diminutes motives to produce an exciting coda. As a perpetuum mobile Le Chemin de Fer is in the tradition of Alkan's obsessively fast études. Companion pieces to Le Chemin de Fer are obviously Le Vent op 15/2 and Comme le Vent op 39/1.

Amongst the middle period miniatures the *Bourrée d'Auvergne* op 29 published in 1846 is the most consistent in compositional quality. The uncompromising opening of op 29 casts one back to the early op 16/2 *Étude* with similarly stark textures and motoric rhythms which progressively diminute and measure off the square phrase structure. The most arresting part of op 29 is the bagpipe episode, influenced perhaps by a passage in Beethoven's *Bagatelle* op 126/4 to which Alkan adds acciaccaturas and wide left hand leaps prophetic of Bartok.

Ex. 6.2   *Bourrée d'Auvergne* op 29, bars 88–96

Harmonically powerful dissonances result by Alkan's bass chromatic chordal movement which characteristically mismatches the triumphant right hand chordal melody. Unfortunately the coda of op 29 suffers from an excess use of double octaves and a rather too heavy reliance on density of piano texture.

Preludes op 31

Vintage Alkan does exist in the next set of miniatures in the 25 *Preludes* op 31. These preludes were written for piano (or organ) and published in 1847 and are one of the best collections to sample the stylistic variety of the composer. At least one prelude *Dans le Style Fugue* [sic] (no. 10) has strongly organistic figuration but Alkan adds the instruction 'pieds et mains' implying that neither piano nor organ is specified. The preferred medium might have been the pédalier but during the 1840s this instrument was regarded as rather too esoteric for the general public. Alkan's publishers (Brandus) may have suggested therefore that piano or organ would be more appropriate. On inspection, only nos. 1, 3, 4, 5, 6, 9, 15, 19, 21 and 25 are really suited to pédalier or organ performance. As a set the obvious comparison for Alkan's op 31 is Chopin's 24 *Preludes* composed 1836–1839 but whereas the Chopin collection contains pieces of transcendental virtuosity (for example no. 16 in B flat minor), Alkan's set as a whole is more reflective, introverted and more diffuse.

Fétis in a very full review of op 31 concurred:

> We must not expect to find in this artist's volume of preludes a flurry of fast notes by means of which certain pianists presage the skill before the performance of a piece. Alkan is a person of heart and mind; his preludes are dream-like which conceal a very calculated and finished art form.[19]

Alkan's plan of his 25 *Preludes*, unlike that of Chopin's 24 is to complete his set with C major (the key of his first) thus providing a satisfying cyclic whole. Unlike Chopin, whose key structure is built upon majors and their relative minors, Alkan's progressive tonality moves through a cycle of rising fourths and falling thirds. These op 31 preludes have a mixture of concentration of meditation, simplicity and objectivity. In these miniatures Alkan achieves a finesse and naïve intensity not hitherto discovered. The beauty and peace of the first in C major is immediately apparent with its inner melody, its emphasis on floating second inversion chords, its control of dynamics and its neatness of chromatic movement matching the crescendo in the penultimate bar. For op 31/1 the influence of Schubert the miniaturist may be somewhere in the background particularly of his *Moment Musical in C major D780*. The second prelude in F minor combines a song of an extremity of bleakness in the tenor with an accompaniment giving a feeling of a skeletal march which burgeons forth as an obsessional march which has the Alkan melodic centricity. Op 31/2 serves as an introduction to the more finely developed example in the late period music such as *Héraclite et Démocrite* op 63/39 where two opposing ideas are sharply differentiated and yet paradoxically well integrated. Op 31/3 *Dans le genre ancien* harks back to the atmosphere of the *Air de ballet* in baroque style again with a quasi chanson rhythm used persistently as a head motive. Alongside the deceptively simple contrapuntal flow, there is daring use of chromatic harmonic movement.

Preludes nos. 4–6 demonstrate the Hebraic aspect of Alkan's temperament and these three preludes can be considered as a coherent group. No. 4, entitled *Prière du soir*, is the most intensely devotional of all the preludes in its simplicity. The purity and calming effect of its repetitive incantation is magical. Fétis judged it to be the 'prayer of a suffering and restless soul'.[20] It is admirably suited to the sustained qualities of the organ despite Fétis judging that 'the organ, essentially calm and majestic, is not at all appropriate'.Prelude no. 5 is an instrumental setting of *Psalm 150* and wonderfully reflects the universality of praise to the Lord with all manner of instruments: 'trumpet, psaltery, harp, stringed instruments and organ, plus loud cymbals and high sounding cymbals'.[21] This is expressed musically by a Charpentier-like trumpet fanfare followed by the use of heavy massed textures in the flattened mediant key representing the idea of universality of praise. This musically and spiritually is a continuation of the massed style from the earlier *Alleluia* op 25 published in 1844. The most directly Hebraic of this set is no. 6 which is entitled *Ancienne Mélodie de la Synagogue*. This prelude is undoubtedly derived from a Hasidic dance named Rikud.[22]

Ex. 6.3a   *Prelude* op 31/6, opening and cadential extract

Ex. 6.3b   *Rikud* extract

Alkan's transcription is plentifully enriched by performance instructions mirroring the cantors' declamation: 'doux et suppliant ... et largement'. The warmth of harmony and texture is stripped away towards the end in several recitative-like passages with rhythmic freedom, frequent pauses and several antiphonal effects. No. 7 acts as an antidote to the severity of nos. 4–6 and although its musical content is rather thin it is in the words of Fétis 'an excellent study in nimbleness'. More exactly, it is an essay in wrist technique, sixths, and two note phrasings. The harmonic link back to no. 5 is the Alkanian device of mediant-related keys this time providing an E flat/G major/E flat cadence at the end.

One of the most evocative of the preludes is no. 8, *La Chanson de la folle au bord de la mer* is the most original work of op 31. Immediately striking is its widely spaced texture with densely menacing left hand chords in a hypnotically potent rhythm separated by a spare right hand melody with simple plagal cadences punctuating phrase ends. This piece is superbly organized reaching an impassioned climax without any textural change before a decay of the original material. It looks forward to the rugged melancholy of Mussorgsky and the *The Old Castle* from *Pictures at an Exhibition* (1874). With no. 9 *Placiditas* we return to much more ordinary four-square melodic phrases with elegant Mozartian triple appoggiaturas at the cadence points. Indeed the whole nature of this piece is an unassuming eighteenth-century gavotte. *Dans le style fugué* (no. 10) returns to the chamber style fugues of *Jean qui pleure et Jean qui rit* of 1839/1940 but also looks forward to the toccata style of the *Toccatina* op 75 (published c1872). But op 31 no. 10 reflects back in the agility of its figuration to the étude op 76/3 discussed earlier. This prelude however has a wider variety of texture and because of the vitality of the head motive. It has a fine sense of direction culminating in a triumphant statement of the motive in the 'pieds et mains' climax near the end. Fétis judges no. 11 entitled *Un petit rien* as an abandoning to 'dreamy, melancholy ways'. Given its precise clavecin style and tempo indication assez vite, this judgement seems strange. The energy of this prelude derives from motivic impulses and the undulating accompaniment. *Le temps qui n'est plus* (no. 12) is wistful in its expressive melodic line and persistent repeated notes. Most of the charm of this piece derives from a surprise shift to the tonic major in Schubertian manner. At the climax an internally descending variant of the four-note motive from the beginning is stated before a Chopinesque delayed cadence. A parallel with the Chopin *Prelude no. 2 in A minor* can be seen.

Along with *La chanson de folle au bord de la mer* another high point in the *Preludes* op 31 is no. 13 *J'étais endormie, mais mon coeur veillait*. As Fétis states 'this music can only be played from the heart'. Drawn from *The Song of Songs* 5:2 the prelude symbolically translates the citation into two groups of five quavers. The success of this prelude can be attributed to the sustained repeated chords, the quintuplet metrical characteristic, the length of the smoothly undulating melodic line and, not least, the subtle use of Neapolitan harmonies sequentially which moves towards the mediant major. All these parameters are contained within an overall closed binary structure. The final magical touch is the suspension of the harmony over dominant and tonic pedals resulting in a dissolution in the final bars to an unresolved 6/3 chord. The next prelude, no. 14, returns to the clavecin-type prelude but is notable for its massed style middle section in the tonic major, and compounding these two ideas brings this prelude to a satisfying conclusion.

Continuing his exploration of pre-classical style in the prelude, Alkan's pre-baroque techniques permeates no. 15 entitled *Dans le style gothique*. Fétis found the duality of meaning of gothic style and the real nature of the piece (really in gavotte style) difficult to reconcile, particularly given the performance instruction of 'rather fast, gracefully, very sweetly and very sustained'. It is the mixture of Bach/Rameau influences and the romantically sustained melodic line which gives the prelude its special charm. Like no. 8 and no. 13, no. 16 is amongst the most successful preludes compositionally. Two contrasting ideas, firstly a sparsely imitative opening, secondly a swaying passage in 6/3 harmonies, are presented alternately. *Rêve d'amour* no. 17 starts rather unpromisingly with an over-reliance on mundane V^7/I harmonies but the section marked 'en augmentant' shows an imaginative chromatic harmonic ascent. In the spirit of the *Rêve d'amour* is the section marked 'délicieusement' over a dominant pedal which leads to an impassioned diminished seventh climax with a fragmentary reminder of the 'en augmentant' section. No. 18 is intriguing because of its similarity melodically to Schubert's *Serenade*, although Alkan's melody is much narrower in range. Fétis decided that no. 19, *Prière du Matin*, 'does not have the peace and calm which one might think one ought to discover within it; it has a certain agitation'. It is strongly primitive in the repeated bass ostinati and interesting in its alternation of three bar phrase lengths and four bar lengths in the second section.

For the next prelude no. 20 Alkan experiments with modal rather than scalic units. As an octave study in Dorian mode, no. 20 serves as an introduction to the superbly developed allegro barbaresca of Alkan's op 35 *Études*. On the other hand no. 21 looks forward to the simplicity and white note harmony of Poulenc and is effectively propelled by a swinging 6/8 rhythm enhanced by octave leaps in the left hand. The next prelude no. 21 entitled *Anniversaire* has a persistent dotted note figure which aggregates towards a determined rhythmic counterpoint. Fétis described no. 22 as 'an anniversary of a funeral at once sad and resigned in nature'. In complete contrast is no. 23 which again reflects the *Rêve d'amour* and the later *Quasi-Faust* love theme from op 33. Although Fétis rates no. 23 as having 'a graceful melody of remarkable elegance', Alkan's tends to be repetitive. Alkan most relates to Chopin in the next prelude of his op 31 prompted by the extreme brilliance of the B flat minor *Prelude* op 28/16. Alkan's op 31/24 also relates back to his virtuosic approach in the earlier op 76/3 étude discussed previously, and forward to the *Toccatina* op 75 of c1872. Despite the severe admonition of Fétis regarding op 31/24 as a 'debauchery of the composer's talent', he nevertheless acknowledged its brilliance. This prelude provides a balance to the rather introverted nature of the op 31 set. Alkan's nostalgia for the eighteenth century is present in op 31 and was noted by Blanchard.[23] On that occasion Alkan had played: *Un petit rien, Le Temps qui n'est plus, J'étais endormie mais mon coeur veillait* and *Dans le genre gothique*, which were adjudged to be 'delightful in form, style and colour'. Introspection completes the *Preludes* op 31 with a simple prière which is touching and effective in its simple root chord harmony, and the instruction 'très soutenu constamment' means practically that it is also well suited to the organ. In summary, op 31 represents Alkan as a sensitive miniaturist and op 31 is a valuable addition to the cycles of preludes in piano literature.

Impromptus op 32

In both sets of *Impromptus* op 32 the intimate style of the *Preludes* op 31 is continued and the first piece of the *Impromptus* op 32/1 is a melodic and perhaps textural tribute to the B minor prelude of Chopin op 28/10. Alkan's impromptu is entitled *Vaghezza* (longing) and this nature is manifested by an impassioned V^7/I in the remote D sharp minor key. The second of op 32/1, *L'amitié* is a soul-stirring marching hymn marked 'avec ampleur'. The most interesting area of *L'amitié* is the sudden switch of key via a type of augmented sixth relationship to the dominant which is followed by a fast series of V^7/I relationships. The next in the first series of *Impromptus* is named *Fantasietta alla Moresca*. Its simple block chord harmonies and the resulting primitive effects give an effective moorish North African characterization and its modal effects look forward to Bartok's *Rumanian Dance no. 1*. The last piece in op 32/1 is *La foi (The Creed)* which suffers from rather four square phrase structure is only redeemed by the varied texture of the middle section with its static melody, striding left hand octaves and triplet inner ostinato.

The second set of op 32 represents the rhythmic influence of the zorzico. The first three pieces of op 32/2 are in five time with an acceleration of pace from the first (andantino) to the second (allegretto) through to the third (vivace). Yet all these pieces represent a continuation of the miniaturist and intimate style of the *Preludes* op 31. The first is a plaintive binary air with a persistent rhythmic figure and simple modulations, the second a more interesting vigorous five beat rumba employing a drum bass in ternary form. Easily the most radical of all the *Impromptus* op 32 is the final piece, an air in seven time. Here the evocative world of Satie is present with simple melancholy fragmentary melodies, angular non functional harmonies and, above all, a cyclic incantation-like atmosphere.

Return to revolution: the op 37 *Marches*

The op 37 *Trois Marches quasi da cavalleria* are in direct lineage from the *Allegro marziale* op 12/3 étude, *Le Preux* op 17 and the *Marche triomphale* op 27. If there is a model on which Alkan built his op 37/1 in A minor it is likely to be the *Novellette* op 21/1 by Schumann where the bass texture, the short breathed phrases and the motoric rhythm show similarities. Op 37/1 has a simplicity with its strongly closed bipartite structure and its monorhythmic impulse. This march nevertheless is not free of military bombast. However one of the most interesting features of this march is its quizzical trio with a farewell motive included within the semiquaver activity and strongly contrasted by chordal punctuations much beloved by Alkan. The delicate decoration of the wistful trio melody is especially memorable.

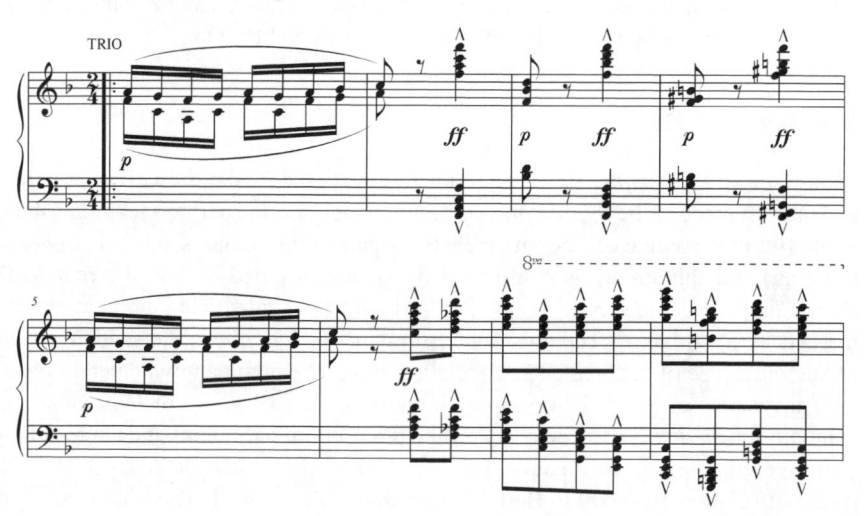

Ex. 6.4   *Trois Marches* op 37/1, bars 111–118

The second march of op 37 is slower in tempo and is of much less interest than op 37/1 texturally. It is much more mundane also in harmonic interest as well as being very highly repetitive. Yet the trio of op 37/2 employs some highly original layout which may relate back to Alkan's admiration of baroque keyboard music[24] which often involves frequent hand interlocking[25] as at the start of the trio of op 37/2 which also contains an excellent example of contrasting blocks – differentiated by texture, dynamics and range. Unlike op 37/1, the recapitulation of this march is unvaried apart from some added drumbeats and the coda unfortunately harks back to the earliest style of Alkan in relying on contemporary virtuosic formulae.

The third march is a 6/8 C minor work with a high degree of motivic and rhythmic similarity between march and trio sections. This march combines eighteenth-century elegance and Berliozian airiness which appealed to Beck who described it as having 'a lightness more like a scherzo'.[26] There is a fine preparation of the reprise of the first idea just before the trio, where chromatic harmony is balanced against diatonic harmony both contained within the rhythmic motive. The trio itself of op 37/3 is rather more extended than those of the other op 37 marches and moreover maintains the rhythmic momentum with Alkan's favoured Neapolitan tonal excursion within the repeat sign. As in op 37/1 on its reprise, op 37/3 explores the very lowest parts of the contemporary piano but the coda of the latter disappoints in the same manner as op 37/2 in its statement of rather too typical virtuosic clichés.

Mendelssohnian influences: the *Chants* op 38

In complete contrast to these dynamic marches, two volumes of chants were published in 1857. Both volumes were given the op 38 designation and may have been prompted by the more famous *Songs without words* of Mendelssohn. It is the example of Mendelssohn that Alkan reflects especially in the first volume of chants. Not only does Alkan follow the Mendelssohnian key scheme of E major, A minor, A major, F sharp minor and G minor, but the idiom and tempo of the individual chants resemble the corresponding Mendelssohn pieces very closely. de Bertha,[27] moreover, considered that the Alkan *Chants* were merely slavish imitation of the Mendelssohn *Songs without words*. But this is a superficial judgement as close analysis shows radical differences between the two sets of pieces. For example, Alkan's op 38/1 compared with Mendelssohn's *Songs without words* op 19/1 shows Alkan's piece to be more inspired melodically, more full blooded romantically and showing a generally higher level of musical creativity.

Ex. 6.5a Mendelssohn – *Songs without words* op 19/1, bars 1–7

Ex. 6.5b Chants op 38/1, bars 1–5

The middle section of the Alkan op 38/1 is more agitated than Mendelssohn in the sharp mediant key of G sharp minor and gives rise to some delightful minor/major shifts. An characteristic feature of op 38/1 is its stretto compression of fast dominant to tonic shifts before a compact coda strongly based on the tonic. Then a bass descending figure which marks out a motivic cell of six notes complements the opening figure. Alkan's op 38/2, entitled *Sérénade*, is less pious than Mendelssohn's op 19/2 but the latter's style model dependence is certainly quite apparent. However, Alkan's op 38/2 is ultimately more clearly differentiated texturally with an almost orchestral representation of an oboe and bassoon wind duo whereas Mendelssohn's is definitely truly pianistic. With respect to the well-ordered modulation and ornamentation of the melodic line, however, Alkan is firmly rooted in eighteenth-century classical style. A graceful switch to the tonic major and a prolonged supertonic with a crescendo swell through its three bars duration halts the activity at the final cadence.

The third piece of op 38 is named *Choeur* and is very similar in outline to Mendelssohn's op 19/3. Perhaps the voicing and the insistence of dotted chordal textures are the parallels most obvious but Alkan as always is quirky harmonically, forcibly led by melodic chromatic descents. Equally unpredictable are Alkan's sudden virtuosic scalic outbursts. The most vital part of *Choeur* is the final two pages where Alkan's massed style, cross rhythmic features and chordal punctuation for piece termination are all strongly characterized. But it is op 38/4 *L'Offrande* shows the closest possible melodic link with Mendelssohn. Both composers' introductions are exactly the same length but Alkan's sliding harmonic chromaticisms are far removed from the Mendelssohn harmonic spectrum as are Alkan's wider textural differentiations. As with many of Alkan's most tightly organized miniatures the structure of this piece is propelled by a rhythmic cell, in this case the motive quaver four quavers. The next piece of the op 38 *Chants* op 38/5 is labelled *Agitatissimo*. Given its rhythmically divided left and right hand parts and melodically organized chromaticisms it may have been influenced by the Chopin *Étude in F minor* op25/2. This Alkan chant also has a similar ceaseless flow, but it is rather less subtle chromatically and in symmetrical bar structure. Constructionally the alternation of left and right hand melodies delineates the overall structure. Smith[28] points out that the profundity of the E/E sharp dissonance in the supremely magisterial adagio from Beethoven's *Hammerklavier Sonata* may have influenced Alkan's *Agitatissimo*. But the Chopin *Prelude in F sharp minor* from op 28 may have had a stronger compositional bearing.

The coda as is often the case in Alkan's works is particularly successful with a reminder of the descending opening chromaticism in rhythmic augmentation before that special Alkan thumbprint of the major/minor shift. The final piece in the *Chants* op 38, book 1, is an attractive *Barcarolle* with a more interesting use of detail, unprepared harmonic, melodic and dynamic contrasts than the corresponding work in Mendelssohn's *Songs without words* op 19. Particularly Gallic are the dissonant touches and minor ninths as are the Satie-anticipating outbursts. Neatly effective also in this barcarolle are the semiquaver undulations leading back into the main reprise. This is undoubtedly a most successful miniature, its final bars being perfectly controlled in their pessimistic juxtaposition of modal and tonal shifts. This final chant of op 38, book 1, would make a perfect short lyrical encore.

The second book of the *Chants* op 38 is less inspired than book 1. This volume of chants shows compositional haste and over-reliance on Mendelssohn's example. The opening piece of book 2 is the *Hymne* which is modelled on the pious Mendelssohnian four-part style yet the German composer would not have written such Gallically ornamented supporting figuration with such remote enharmonics. The middle section continues the mood of the *Vaghezza* op 32/1 with its Chopin *B minor Prelude*-inspired left hand. However, the real curiosity of this set of chants is to be found in the next piece, the allegretto, subtitled *Fa*. This implies that an 'F' might be all pervasive. Precedents for repeated ostinatos are certainly not new for

Alkan but exceptional here is the manner in which the repeated note shapes the form and tonality of the work. Despite the repetitions of the single F there is a sense of cadence either by dominant tonic real or implied progressions. Worthy of mention here is the block-like structure of key centres with frequent rondo-like reference to the initial phrase. The final bars of the work fade out to leave the note F just suspended above an A major key centre giving a curiously satisfactory finality. This is one of the most interesting miniatures of the nineteenth century.

Ex. 6.6   Chants op 38(2)/2, bars 126–141

Chant de guerre is surprisingly peaceful with the atmosphere of a Mendelssohnian 6/8 hunting song, although there are several harmonic eccentricities such as severely applied diminished sevenths before returning to the more typically chordally bound Mendelssohn-like model. This chant also includes a fugato leading to a magnificently vanquishing climax with brilliant figuration and coloured by Neapolitan harmony. Texturally too it prefaces an effect in the *Festin d'Esope* op 39 in its use of locked hand figurations. Next is the *Procession-Nocturne*, the fourth of this volume of chants, a highly compressed miniature suggesting perhaps two clarinets against plucked double basses with closed phrasing and sectional construction alternating direct and highly diffused cadences. This chant is characterized by an ubiquitous rhythmic motive.

The *Andantino* continues the plucked string accompaniment idea but with fragmentary melodic material at the start which gives rise to a swaying tune and accompaniment with a Fauré-like elegance. Included are some interesting submediant enharmonic mediant experiments, but the persistent working out of the hymn-like sustained middle section over some three pages is ultimately rather tedious. The last piece named *Barcarolle en choeur* starts promisingly with a floated dominant related harmony and a novel wave-like texture but settles down to a rather solid chordal dotted rhythmic pattern. The melodic span in this chant is rather narrow and there is rather too much use of German sixths. In summary, the second volume of the op 38 *Chants* is more uneven inspirationally with the exception of the amazing *Fa* piece.

The desire for an expansion of chamber music sonorities may have been inspired by Alkan's own transcriptions of classics from the chamber baroque and classical repertoire. His interest in this medium started with the 1847 set of transcriptions and terminated in the 1861 and 1869 sets. Study of the classics helped Alkan toward greater precision of expression and concision of structure in the next set of miniatures.

Petites fantasies op 41

The *Trois Petites Fantasies* op 41 of 1847 are the first of the concentrated miniatures of the final period works. In many ways these contain the quintessence of vintage Alkan – distillation of ideas, direction, rhythmic drive, novel sonorities and an idiosyncratic sense of dry musical humour. Many features in these works relating to sonority, texture and rhythm look forward to twentieth century composers but it is to the romantics and Alkan's relationship to Schumann of the *Nachstücke* that is most immediately striking in op 41/1, an *Assez Gravement in A minor*. The exact symmetry of the phrasing, the precisely placed sf and the tonal shift of the second four bars up a third are Alkan stylistic hallmarks. The rhythmic drive of this opening is interrupted by a cascading sforzato but unlike earlier style periods this now has a more confined economical function. Lightness is continued by a quasi-scherzando symmetrical figure with voice paralleling between soprano and tenor. This neatly merges into a version in the major key with the included quasi-scherzando rhythmic motive. Before the reprise of the opening there is an interesting case of non-resolved diminished seventh harmony. Aurally the coda is perhaps the most remarkable section of op 41/1. It is superficially akin to Debussy in texture, and the sonority in the 'quasi vibrazione' is easily relatable to the Debussian instruction of 'laissez vibrer'. Alkan's parallelisms of harmony anticipate Debussy as do the non-functional unresolved dominant sevenths secretly located within the context of drooping thirds.

The second *Fantaisie* of op 41 is viewed by Smith[29] as influenced by the opening measures of Beethoven's *Piano Sonata in G major* op 31/1 but the relationship is rather elliptical: only the dryness of the accompaniment and gentle playfulness of the respective works are really similar. The rhythmic downbeat is artfully displaced in op 41/2, and strongly tonic-centred harmony is applied as ostinati which controls the occasional rhythmic fluster and chromaticisms. Harmonically there is the now familiar shifting of the sectional block up a tone. Some of this op 41/2 *Fantaisie* is étude-like: the parallel semiquavers an octave apart hark back to the op 76/3 étude but here the effect is much less overtly virtuosic and more demonic. Perhaps the Beethoven influence alluded to earlier is more observable in the reprise with its syncopated left hand, but the leaping octaves are more prophetic of Prokofiev, in that op 41/1 flows forward to an intriguing blend of controlled lyricism and rhythmic zest. Elements of étude-like semiquavers return before a full blooded version of the opening measures with only a touch of the broken octaves so beloved of Alkan from earlier style periods. As a tripartite structure, formally this work is satisfyingly symmetrical. The tightly constructed three note motive is employed in the cantabile coda against a suitably rhythmically active left hand before the briefest of referrals to the opening measures.

Op 41's third *Fantaisie* is the most retrospective of all of the op 41 set with its stark drumbeat opening and its reminiscence of earlier features, including the solid octave style of the *Air de ballet*. This is a reminder of Alkan's predilection for baroque styles. That said, the minimalism of melodic material in op 41/3 is progressive as is the wry exploration of the bass register and the level of dissonance. The twentieth-century composer evoked again is Prokofiev. As in the other *Fantaisies*, the melodic components are finely disciplined and formal boundaries well marked. Resembling Prokofiev also are the toccata-like left hand octaves against whirling semiquavers conjoining to produce some grinding sevenths. Alkan cannot resist the temptation to be lengthy in this discourse (some five pages of unadulterated semiquaver figuration) but this passagework is blended with the drumbeat figure of the opening before a return of the cantabile lyrical section and then, rather out of character with the rest of this *Fantaisie*, the time signature is altered to 6/8 with over-indulgent semiquaver passagework and bravura octaves. This excess is counteracted by the drumbeat return and a coda where virtuosity is kept in control by a masterly use of syncopation. Without doubt this final *Fantaisie* represents most obviously the battle within the composer to expunge virtuosic excesses.

Referential and baroque-derived miniatures op 42–op 60

After the fairly substantial scale of the *Fantaisies* Alkan, in the mid-1850s, continued his exploration of the smaller scaled miniature. *Réconciliation* op 42 (published in 1857) is one of the most interesting of the mid-fifties series and the full title of op 42 is *Petit caprice, réconciliation*. Of special intrigue is that op 42 includes a 5/4 *Zorzico dance* as an episode. This piece is well worth exploring for its harmonic adventurousness with mobility of harmony above pedal points. A very neglected work of this period is *Salut, cendre du pauvre* op 45 which is designated by Alkan as a paraphrase for piano and continues the chamber music style of op 41. It is a noble and dignified composition as befits the subject matter. The opening page wonderfully places low arpeggiated soft trombone-like funereal chords against a simple sequentially organized melody and accompaniment.

Ex. 6.7   *Salut, cendre du pauvre* op 45, bars 1–6

The *Minuetto alla tedesca* op 46 is the nineteenth-century translation of a tragic Mozartian minuet in its direct manner and its off beat accented chords. Op 46 is constructed by a six-note rhythmic/melodic cell which seems all pervasive. This is subjected to great development firstly against a compact right hand melody then secondly in sequential two-bar octaves and terminating in a twenty-four-bar dominant pedal. Smith points out[30] that this minuet is prophetic of the tragic scherzo of Mahler's *Sixth Symphony* where the tragic insistence on ostinati are very similar. Alkan's op 46 can be related also to the gigantic *Scherzo/Trio* of the Bruckner/Mahler tradition since formally the second half of the minuet of op 46 is hugely expanded. Whereas the minuet is grimly determined, the trio is delicate and light by dint of its airy texture, its octave leaps and its fine contrast of staccato and legato touches. The trio also maintains the two-note ostinato motive from the dominant pedal of the scherzo. The reprise of the scherzo is exact with an extension of the trio section added on in an attractive inversion of right and left parts and a scalic ascent with fourth spaced left hand octaves which is a really novel harmonic touch.

Alkan's devotion to the *ancien régime* was all encompassing and his opposition to the Second Empire profound: its military vulgarity may have triggered his withdrawal from public concerts. His next two published compositions are his two finest essays in military satirization. Entitled *Capriccio alla soldatesca* op 50/1 and *Le tambour bat aux champs* op 50/2, these pieces may be played separately but they are complementary stylistically. A wide range of military images represented in music are present in both op 50 works. In op 50/1 drumbeats via gruppetti and arpeggiated chords dominate the *Capriccio*. These are the only wisps of melody and direct harmonies within the square block-like sections. Military bombast becomes more apparent at the 'quasi trombata' which contains some startling tonal juxtapositions. This rhythmic cell leads to further bugle calls and military-type rhythms before a deliberately sentimental melody filled with pleading slurs is stated.

This is brushed aside brutally to admit a vulgar one-step march marked 'crânement' (swaggering) but Alkan manages to transform this material into something more weighty before the return to the opening drumbeats. A long pedal-point build-up is constructed from a simple three-note sequential motive as preparation for more bugle calls. Then a victorious C major march bursts forth resplendent in texture, rhythm and pianistic verve. Later Alkan allows some bravura tremolando figuration to celebrate the victory. There is a brief reminiscence of the sentimental melody, a snatch of the return of the C major march, a desiccated version of the bravura figuration rhythmic motive then the coda reinforces the drumbeats in minimalist form. A decorated plagal Amen brings op 50/1 to its conclusion. The *Capriccio* follows the sequence of events outline in *Zedlita* – Nimmersatt's ballad *Die nächtliche Heerschau*.

The complementary work of op 50, *Le Tambour* is more impressive than the *Capriccio* being less openly referential and also more compressed. Lewenthal observes that 'Alkan was extremely fond of marches of all kinds, a penchant which he shares with Mahler'.[31] In concentration and variety of idioms this is Alkan's finest march. The opening of *Le Tambour* is quite magnificent in representing drumbeats for the dead as the title suggests. Alkan's realism however is never crudely imitative: arpeggiated chords often marked staccato plus frequent acciaccaturas portray accurately but not over-realistically the sound of drumbeats and the representation of continuous gunfire is sustained within the musical texture. Alkan may be likened to Mahler in naïve nostalgia sentiment in the central E minor section replete with off beat accents. This is a temporary situation since this lyricism is swept away by swirling diminished sevenths acting as a parody of bugle calls, then the hypnotic automatism of the march finally triumphs with an assertion of the tonic major.

The sharpest possible contrast with the two military pieces of op 50 is offered by the *Trois minuets* op 51 in which Alkan adopts an almost Viennese ländler-like Schubertian approach to this 3/4 dance. Compared with the more virtuosic *Minuetto alla tedesca* op 46, these minuets are smaller in scale and more chamber-like in sonority but as a set they are quite concentrated in invention and are filled with unpredictables. From the start of op 51/1 in E flat major within the regularity of the sixteen bar framework there is the harmonic delight of an 8-7 suspension on a strong downbeat alongside the symmetrical repetition of the swaying minim crotchet rhythm and the cambiata effect of the cadence. Attractive too, is the close canonic imitation of all four voices in string quartet fashion at the opening of the second half of the binary structure in the Schubertian mediant key. The minuet concludes with a reference back to the controlled astringency of the dissonance in the first sixteen bars, making a cyclically reasoned musical entity. The trio maintains the minim crotchet rhythm and modulation by a third but in compressed form. After some harmonic rhythmic quickening, the Neapolitan key arrives by Alkan's favoured process of chromatic side-slipping and this is reversed to promote entry back to E flat major. On repetition the minuet is fitted out with controlled octaves and the symmetrical restatement of the minuet terminates with the rhythmic stamp minim crotchet, convincingly presented in the final bar in full voiced cadence.

The second minuet continues the mediant investigation. Here desolation stems from the high frequency of single, double and triple appoggiaturas as well as low voiced syncopations in stark octaves. Also here the Neapolitan relationship near the cadence is enhanced by a time delay. The key scheme of the second half of the minuet makes use of the chromatic side slip to G flat to trigger some harmonic adventures. The trio of op 51/2 is direct and texturally interesting with the high register emphasized by some expert high right hand figuration which, on repetition, precedes an unassumingly dissonant descending two voice passage. In the coda op 51/2, the pp reference within the flowing Schubertian melody and accompaniment becomes part of an ostinato background.

Despite the persistence of the rhythmic motive, op 51/3 is the most elusive of the set of op 51 minuets. Carried over from op 51/2 is the presence of wide leaps which wander in a very unprepared way into the flat leading note tonality. An inspired part of op 51/3 is the energetic tension building before the trio where sf accents, low ff registers and pauses all feature, but of most interest is the G/F# juxtaposition over a wide range, a feature perhaps borrowed from the scherzo of Beethoven's *Hammerklavier Sonata* op 106. These bell-like effects are transferred to the trio and alleviate its severe two-part style.

Alkan's Jewishness imbues much of his music but a particularly intense period of religious studies during the 1850s resulted in translation into French of selected Old Testament passages.[32] *Psalm 137* (By the waters of Babylon) yielded up a very beautiful musical setting for solo piano which follows the pictorial imagery of the text most movingly. The opening, a recitativo-like adagio consists of a doleful G minor Hebraic melody with diminished harmonies, the lamenting and weeping of the waters. When the text refers to the remembrance of Zion and the hanging up of the harps, Alkan appropriately invokes a throbbing harp-like accompaniment with a 'molto espressivo' contoured melody. When the text poses the question of how to sing the Lord's song in a strange land, there is reference to this remoteness by subtle harmonic changes. A vivacissimo 12/8 C minor section with harsh dissonant leaps, marks out the Psalmist's frustration before an 'allegro feroce' finale with powerfully primitive harmony and very powerful rhythmic impetus. Indeed in this setting of *Psalm 137* text and music are admirably fused. Here is an excellent example of Alkan's unforced paraphrase style akin to the 1861 and 1869 set of transcriptions.

Rather less admirable is the hunting style *Quasi caccia* op 53 of 1859 which suffers from an over-obsession with a rhythmic hunting motive which is emphasized by single note centricity and harmonic monotony. Smith[33] speculates that this piece might have been intended for the third volume of *Chants*. There is much that is Mendelssohnian about this work such as the scurrying imitative semiquavers and fluent bravura. Within its seventeen pages of rather vacuous virtuosity only the fragmentation and chromaticizing of a diatonic melodic line provides interest.

Another imitative piece this time portraying a rocket is *Une fusée* op 55 later subtitled *introduction et impromptu*. Published in 1859 it has a most appealing introduction with a swirling B flat major figure complemented by a simple but effective rhythmic motive. The systematic nature of the repetitions reminds one of Satie. Op 55 is in Alkan's toccata style being an incredibly light rocket propelled presto with an obsessive rhythmic head motive.

1859 was the year when Alkan returned to composing nocturnes some fifteen years after the publication of his first *Nocturne* op 22. In the first of the 1859 published nocturnes actually designated *Deuxième Nocturne* op 57/1 Alkan adopts a more concentrated plangent approach which antedates early Fauré in rapid melodic chromaticisms.

Ex. 6.8   *Deuxième Nocturne* op 57/1, bars 1–9

Also Fauré-like are the ever increasing melodic skips and angular chromatic tonality near the end of the first section. The middle cantabile section is less memorable but the dominant ninth and bell-like link to a restatement (and development) of the cantabile melody are vintage Alkan. Unusually in this section Alkan gives the performer some degree of interpretative freedom. Just before the recapitulation, there is an extended stretch of structured Neapolitan harmony. The *Troisième Nocturne* in the romantically mellifluous key of F sharp major is unusually fast in pace at dotted minim = 72. Despite its melodic centricity, the impassioned line and delicate triplet accompaniment and the deft chromatic modulations anticipate Fauré. Smith[34] judges the trio section of this nocturne rather harshly, stating that 'despite some characteristic piquancies [it] remains earth bound'. In texture it is rather similar to Chopin's *Nocturne in G minor* (trio section) in its simple root chordal layout although Alkan utilizes once again his favourite rhythmic motive. A cross-phrasing section terminates in the tonic minor accessing the tonal centre of the nocturne. There is then some canonic dialogue of melodic fragments and a rather stark recitative-like octave statement before a snatch of the trio section is transposed to the bass register.

An example of Alkan's composing binary opposites in the miniatures is to be found in the op 60 pieces published in 1859. There is little evidence musically given the highly repetitive textures and rhythmically square phrase structures and a general dearth of any melodic distinction in either piece that 1859 is a likely composition date. A comparison of the maturity of the opening of op 60/1 with that wonderful op 31/13 prelude *J'étais endormie* ... reveals the primitivism of the former. In op 60/1 there is a rather coy use of quickly modulating dominant sevenths which suggests a date of the early 1840s. The quasi-scherzando middle section remains very earth bound in its banal over repetitive rhythmic motive and melodic centricity which extends over some thirty bars without rhythmic variation. On reprise, the opening melody of *Ma chère liberté* is treated to some elementary broken and split octaves of the earliest stylistic period of Alkan (a comparison with *Les Omnibus* op 2 is quite revealing) and the Schubertian right hand accompaniment in the final page of op 60/1 is also regressive for the 1859 date of publication. The companion piece to *Ma chère liberté* is *Ma chère servitude* op 60/2 which is rather more concise but the tonic/dominant harmonization of the squarest of melodies in thirds outstays its welcome. Again the piece only makes some impression by its startling applied dissonances. The middle cantabile section contains very short breathed phrases perhaps a contradiction in terms of the cantabile direction but there is more than a passing resemblance to the sparse texture of Liszt's *Mal du pays*. On reprise this sparse texture is extended to give a much more luxuriant sustained effect and builds to a fine climax based on fully scored dominant sevenths then a brief reference to the all pervasive rhythmic cell of op 60/1 draws the piece to a logical conclusion.

In drawing on nature for inspiration for his miniatures Alkan is continuing the tradition established by Couperin le Grand and other clavecin composers. *Le Grillon* is given the op 60 bis number and is the final and the most characteristic of all the nocturnes. The cricket noise is portrayed by a third hand part in the highest piano register unvarying except when the harmonic direction demands it. The naïvity of *Le Grillon* is quite delightful, its tonality hardly disturbed and its stability maintained by the monorhythmic figure. The middle section marked 'quasi tremante e poco più mosso' is also rather monorhythmic and explorative of the bass register.

The *Chants* op 65, op 67, op 70 and a baroque postscript

Turning again to the world of the 'Lieder ohne wörte' in French garb we arrive at the third book of the *Chants* op 65, published *c*1866. This is certainly the most interesting in varying styles and also the least uneven of the sets of chants. The *Chants* op 65 are rather more sophisticated technically and none of these works are overwritten. The opening piece of the third book is not given a descriptive title but it is simply marked 'vivante'. The character of this chant is expressed by its ambivalent key centre, its centricity around a small range and quick silver left hand triplet accompaniment. As usual with Alkan the sense of romanticism is never sentimental but always controlled and here even the sense of rubato is inbuilt. A very freely ranging key scheme moves from the tonic to the leading note major which effects a reversed Neapolitan harmonic area and a reprise of the opening strains. The individual melodic line is then combined in duet to give an open textured effect. The closing measures reflect once again Alkan's fondness for suspended harmonies over bell-like pedal points.

The next piece, *Esprits follets* (goblins) is one of Alkan's fleet footed miniatures with Scarlatti-like virtuosic gestures at the beginning which recur throughout. This gesture is answered by a rapid semiquaver Alberti bass pattern underpinning a melodic line which is a close relative to the opening theme of the *Sonatine* op 61. This semiquaver pattern persists increasing the delicacy of the piece, and although this chant is strictly limited in range, it is extremely successful in portraying a Mendelssohnian fairy-like image. It presses onward to an ethereal ending which is tinged with a touch of influence from the scherzo of Chopin's *B minor Piano Sonata* op 58.

The *Canon* op 65/4 is an academically strict canon of the octave, introduced and concluded by a sequentially lyrical tune and accompaniment. The canon itself is deceptively simple and introduced by a dramatic pause before the 6/8 metre takes over launching the canon at the octave between soprano and tenor voices at one bar's distance. This results in very Fauré-like added seventh and ninth harmonies although the melodic shape is very strongly related to the Mendelssohn *Songs without words* op 19/4. Just before the end the series of suspended dominant sevenths gives a magnificently sensual effect.

The tempo giusto op 65/4 piece has veiled references to the Chopin *A major Polonaise* op 40/1 but this Alkan chant is lighter and less virtuosic. Perhaps the most overt reference to the Chopin polonaise is the ascending scalic passage, but how different is Alkan's middle section with its flat submediant relationship to the tonic, its tonic added ninth harmonies and the subtle touches of melodic chromaticisms.

The fifth chant of op 65 is entitled *Horace et Lydie*. Alkan takes inspiration form-wise from the stanza form of the author Horace in which the dialogue increases in intensity but is of equal length. In the case of op 65 this means eight bar phrases. The first two stanzas are set in the Dorian mode and involve a tenor and soprano recitative with a feeling of circular monotones which look forward to the static neutral world of Satie and his *Socrate*. This is reinforced by a regularly fragmented accompaniment. In keeping with the fourth stanza which expostulates the burning for Calais, Alkan writes in parallel inversions which gives a grave chordal density. This builds to a fitting climax, involving fully filled in chords of a more functional type.

The final piece in op 65 is the best known and the finest of the barcarolles of all the chants. It is a masterpiece of invention and economy in its plaintive G minor, its easy third related and minor-major modulations and not least its gently melodic chromatic decoration. It is a superb conclusion to the third book of chants, certainly the most consistently inventive of the set of *Chants*.

Chronologically the fourth book of *Chants* op 67 followed after a gap of two years and was published in 1868. Like all volumes of the chants, book four ends with a barcarolle and also contains a mixture of referential and abstract pieces.

The op 67 set opens with an apparently neutral piece marked *Neige et Lave* with the performance indication 'tranquillement con indifferenza'. This piece is reckoned by Smith to 'contrast a pallid andante with a fast middle section, fierce in manner but thin in substance'.[35] The opening andante has a special charm with its soothing Mozartian elegance and its cryptic way of avoiding the dominant at the end of the symmetrical eight bar structure. The dissolution of the principal motive just before the fiery middle section is organized with its decay of the symmetrical figure until only a two-note motive remains which acts as the main activator for this middle section. There is a delightfully gauche seventh dissonance – perhaps a rare example of an uncorrected proof or is it an example of Alkan's wry humour? Just before the reprise of the opening section the two-note motive over a German sixth of the dominant pedal is employed as a pivot to an arpeggiation of the German sixth itself.

The *Chanson de la Bonne Vieille* (song of nanny) is devastatingly acidic and starkly presented at a slow tempo with folk like crushed notes and octave doubling between soprano and bass at frequent places. Its simple phrase structure is punctuated by Neapolitan colouring at the cadence. Cadential decorations by means of fast chromatic gap filling, are similar to those in *Héraclite et Démocrite* op 63/39. The middle section of this chant marked 'quasi-rimenbranza', is a major version of the opening and its smooth contour conceals its asymmetrical structure. Since this chant ends curiously with a 6/3 chord, the piece is perhaps intended to lead without pause into the third piece of op 67 which is named 'bravement'. The four equivalent dominant sevenths spaced well over the piano range introduce a rather ordinary left hand characteristic 'hunting' dotted 6/8 rhythm which is relentlessly followed throughout. The repetitive nature of this rhythmic figure is subjected to rather academic imitation. Also, the paucity of harmonic invention in op 67/3 might indicate a much earlier composition date than $c1872$, since the fifth book of *Chants* op 70, published simultaneously with book four of the chants, is much more advanced harmonically. The coda of op 67/3 reaches back to a rather barren virtuosic style with contrived scalic passages.

Doucement op 67/4 is of vintage quality in contrast with op 67/3. There is an affectionate tribute to his compatriot, Chopin, in the shape of a quotation from the latter's *Nocturne in D flat major* op 27/2. Alkan's work settles down to a graceful use of lightly sprung rhythm with a particularly well organized harmonic scheme with some pungent dissonances applied at higher tensional points. A brief return in a more chromatic manner of the opening Chopin tribute is introduced near the end before a return to the sprung rhythmic figure and a very peaceful ending.

The *Appassionato* op 67/5 is akin in textural outline and rhetoric to Chopin's *Prelude in F sharp minor* op 28/8 but Alkan's composition is a pale shadow of the Chopin work being over-sequential and repetitious. Alkan furthermore attempts to alleviate the problem of the short breathed phrase structure by avoiding the traditional use of the dominant at the end of each eight-bar structure. The *Reminiscenzia* section is simple and hymn-like combating the excessive energy of the fiery outer sections. Again, as in op 67/3, the coda relies on well worn virtuosic formulae with a touch of Neapolitan harmony at the end and the work ends rather unconvincingly with two second inversions chords.

The final piece of op 67 is a G minor barcarolle. This is not as immediately appealing as that of op 65/6 or as gaunt as the one to be discussed in op 70, but op 67/6 with its hypnotic inevitability is very musically satisfying. This barcarolle harmonically tends to be modal in mid phrase and harmonic at the cadence and this exoticism extends into the more melismatic development section. The middle section of op 67/6 is of special interest. A gentle 6/8 French baroque dance with a persistent tenor right hand melody arises and is coupled up with some harmonic quirkiness over a pedal point which is transferred to a sepulchral left hand tremolando. The final bars of this chant with the interruption on the dominant seventh, the parallel 6/3 chords and the recapitulation of the major section rather than the reprise of the opening section are strikingly innovative.

The final volume of the *Chants* op 70 published around 1872 leans on the Mendelssohn op 19 *Songs without words* which Alkan had followed in his own first volume of chants. The op 70 set is the most concentrated of all Alkan's sets of chants and opens with a prelude which relates to Mendelssohn's *E minor Prelude* op 35/1 but Alkan's piece is much more indebted to the French tradition, stemming back to the unmeasured preludes of Louis Couperin. This opening *Duettino* is deemed the 'least compelling' by Smith,[36] but the continual efflorescing passagework with a tenor range melody and excellent clarity of texture is most effective. Also in its chromatic approach to cadences as well as its seventh related harmonies op 70/1 looks forward to Fauré.

Ex. 6.9 *Chants* op 70/1, bars 7–9

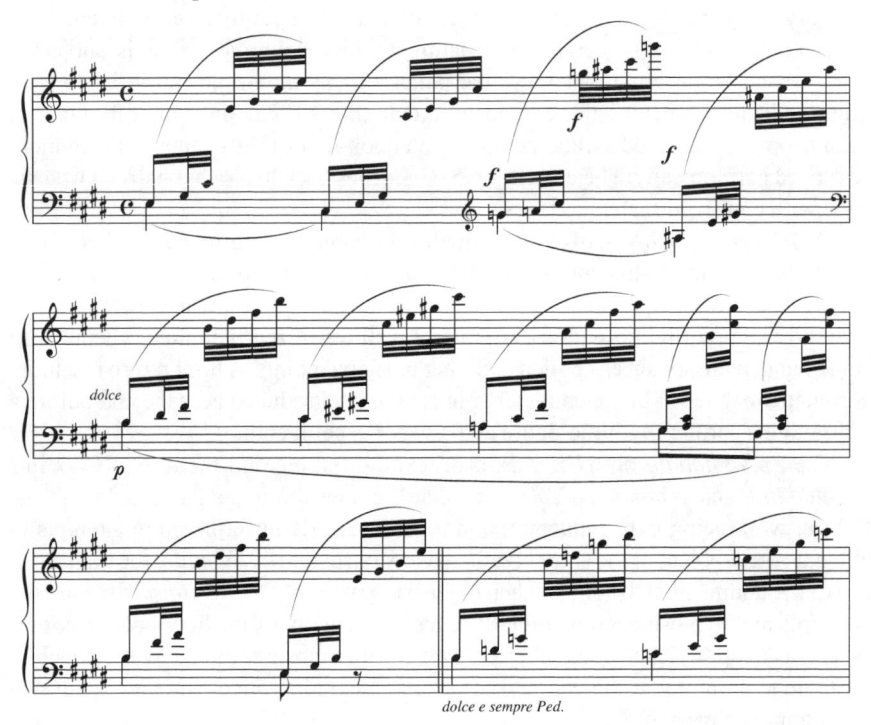

The piece ends convincingly with parallelism in chords of an abstracted melody and a suggestion of the arpeggiated texture and the fifth of the tonic remains to remind one of the opening of the piece. The second chant of op 70 is one of Alkan's tough and concentrated miniatures in the tradition of the obsessively perpetuum mobiles such as *Le chemin de fer* op 27. This op 70/2 piece is merely titled *Andantinetto* and it is an essay in bi-rhythmic metre with a plain quality in the tonic/dominant harmonization and a circular quality to the melody and harmony. The next in the set, the *Allegro vivace* op 70/3 is one of the best constructed of chants with clearly defined sectional themes with contrasted textures. The militarily-based fanfares and trills are later developed into a more cavalry-type rhythm with a heaviness of left hand octave which looks back to the *Marche triomphale* op 27. This is offset by a gruff left hand propelled figure with an idiosyncratic rhythmic motive which is combined with the fanfare of the opening to provide an admirable display of controlled virtuosity. The rhythmic figure becomes more scalic to yield a compressed lyrical middle section, a reprise of the cavalry-type rhythm, then a coda of appropriate brilliance which is entirely in equilibrium with the component scale of the piece. Smith judges this Chant to be 'highly original, dramatically exciting and pianistically hair raising'.[37]

The next of the *Chants* op 70 is very different indeed. *La voix de l'instrument*, the fourth of the op 70 set, is the most referential of the op 70 *Chants*, being concerned with the unfolding of a short phrased melody in the tenor range, closed by pizzicato type chords much in the manner of the second prelude of the op 31 set. Modulations in op 70/4 are smoothly achieved to the dominant and its relative minor. Just before the varied recapitulation there is a freely moving single left hand line culminating in the transference of the main melody to the soprano register, closely imitated by the original tenor melody and the end of the work features a starry re-exposition of the opening melody high up in the piano register. There is a natural progression of piano range in this piece and this contributes to the success of the piece.

More dance-like is the *Scherzo-coro* op 70/5, Alkan's return to the style of the op 16 scherzos but compared with the early op 16 works there is now a much more concentrated use of melodic harmonic and textural parameters. There is occasional recourse to some oscillating harmony, but in general the harmonic schemata is remarkably simple but effective in its hunting horn open harmonic density. The relentless rhythmic progression is extended to the con bravura left hand restatement of the opening melody which leads to a varied reprise of this melody with an opened out hunting horn accompaniment. The trio is ingratiatingly simple in the tonic major but the repetitive trochaic rhythm is disrupted by an asymmetrical phrase structure. By far the most interesting section harmonically follows with obsessively unresolved seventh harmonies with applied appoggiaturas resulting in a German sixth just before the espressivo. This harmonic adventurousness is increased by a judicious use of contrasting dynamics and range. The recapitulation of the scherzo is varied by the addition of a compounded scherzo and trio figures with locked chord bravura until only the trochaic rhythm is left to complete the final cadence.

To complete the set of *Chants* op 70 Alkan opts for a most interesting solution. As in the famous finale of Beethoven's *Ninth Symphony* where the main themes of each movement are reviewed quickly, Alkan chooses also to briefly quote from the preceding chants of op 70. This section is described as 'récapitulation, en guise de transition, ou introduction, pour le numéro suivant'. Like Beethoven Alkan presents the extracts in a bleak and gruff manner with the main melody of op 70/5 transformed in tritones, and a long range chromatic shift from F sharp minor to G minor (with dominant preparation) which admirably sets the scene for the final barcarolle, the last of all the series of barcarolles. In breaking free of the Mendelssohn model and in its anticipation of Fauré's masterly set of barcarolles, it is the finest of all the series. Marked 'andante flebile', it is highly varied in melodic line and type of accompaniment together with an inspired harmonic palette including non functional sevenths and fluctuating minor-major tonal centres. Rather than switch to the major for the central section as in the barcarolle of the third book of *Chants*, Alkan employs a progressive type of long-range tonality disguised by the suspended use of the dominant then elements of this to reform the original tonality. The late arrival of G major, the major tonicization, gives rise to one of the finest of Alkan's melodic inspirations in its balance of controlled freedom, chromaticisms and voicings.

Toccatina op 75: a final return to the baroque

Alkan's last published composition is characteristically a neo-baroque toccatina which appeared around 1872. It is a summary of all the Alkanian stylistic tendencies of his final period: a directness and concentration of approach, a reaching back to the baroque period for virtuosity, coupled up with pre-twentieth-century attitude towards dissonance in the lean two-part writing. In sustained intensity at the quietest level, only interrupted by a brief excursion into contrary movement forte semiquavers. This last work is a fascinating glimpse of twentieth-century French piano music and, as such, it is a fitting conclusion to his magnificent contribution to the piano repertoire of the nineteenth century.

Alkan's miniatures as with all his other compositions demonstrate the widest range of musical stylistics. Many of these works are rather uneven in inspiration and the weakest of these may be dismissed as contemporary pièces d'occasion. The finest of these pieces such as several of the *Preludes*, *Chants*, *Fantaisies* and *Nocturnes* can stand comparison with the finest examples of other Romantic piano compositions. But for fully sustained inspiration within the format of the miniature we need to turn to one of Alkan's real masterpieces, the *Esquisses* op 63.

Chapter 7

The *Esquisses*

Alkan's art in miniature writing is found at its zenith in his set of *Esquisses* op 63 of which there are forty-eight short pieces classified as shown in Diagram 7.1. They represent Alkan's style in a most potent manner yet some are only one page long. The publication date of 1861 is, as often in the final period of Alkan's output, deceptive. Smith[1] produces evidence to demonstrate that some of these miniatures such as *Délire*[2] (no. 29) may have been formulated as early as 1847. The composition and revision of these miniatures therefore ranged over about fourteen years, but for final publication in 1861 Alkan organized them into a logical key sequence similar to the order in the *Preludes* op 31. The *Esquisses* op 63 however move through all the major and minor keys twice like the 48 *Preludes and Fugues* of J.S. Bach, but Alkan in his first twenty-four, moves through rising fourths and falling thirds then a complementary twenty-four in falling fourths and rising fifths. The final forty-eighth *Esquisse* moves back to the opening key of *La Vision* (no 1) completing the cyclical unity from C major to C major. The chronological range of Alkan's op 63 is legendary. Gorer[3] discusses these works as 'standing like some musical pithecanthropus as a link between the clavecinists and the impressionists of the early years of the twentieth century'. In the esquisses compared with his other miniatures the range of expression is even wider and includes aspects of the pre-baroque, the eighteenth-century Austro-Germanic school and the post-impressionists. Lewenthal as always when writing about Alkan is enthusiastic. His comments about op 63 are eloquent.

> He [Alkan] allows his effulgent imagination to run rampant and indulges in the most outlandish experiments. Even the titles are enchanting and, while the style remains distinctly his own, one is reminded of the old clavecinists and the whimsical extravagances of Erik Satie. These homunculi of Alkan's are the microcosms of his art and show facets – a tenderness and poetry and a pixyish humour – that one might not expect from the composer of works of such terrifying grandeur as the *Symphonie* and *Quasi-Faust*.[4]

In Lewenthal's Alkan collection eleven of the finest of op 63 are selected. Even given the lofty heights of the aforementioned large scale works, the esquisses have a special claim to be Alkan's finest composition because of a constant level of inspiration, an integration of all styles, an incredible prefacing to twentieth-century harmonic tendencies and a confidence in form building.

Of the pre-baroque-type of esquisses many modal colourings are featured. Of touching simplicity is the *Petit Air* (*genre ancien*) (no 26). Its plaintive completeness delicately tinged by the use of the Phrygian mode consists of the simple repetition of a melodic rhythmic cell, cryptic harmonizations with rapid minor/major shifts and sequential blocks. No. 26 is a microcosm of Alkan's stylistic world. This purity is also reflected in *Odi profanum vulgus et arceo: favete linguis* (I hate and dismiss the profane rabble) (No. 34) with its simple plain chant melody, personalized by Alkan's favourite dotted rhythm within a Dorian modal context. The invocational nature of the middle section with its sawtooth melodic line and its frequent recourse to neutral mediant harmonies generates an incantatory effect. Reflecting Alkan's reclusive state of mind, this is his anti-Philistine statement.

Ex. 7.1   *Odi profanum* op 63/34, bars 1–10

Most profound of all the pre-baroque esquisses is the final *Laus Deo* which is truly devotional in its invention. This esquisse is characterized by bell effects in treble and bass register but parallel fourths are used in the former register thus regenerating a medieval-type organum. The obsessive cross-phrasing and accents add to the power of externally determined praise in quintuple meter with a cyclic melodic cell against a Dresden-type Amen. There then follows an unfolding of a Parisian-type antiphon with frequent chorale-type pauses before a mirror image of the quintuple meter and the final peal of bells, making *Laus Deo* the perfect example of denominational unity.

Alkan is equally convincing compositionally in the baroque-influenced esquisses. Affectionate tributes to the clavecin school of Couperin and Rameau are shown by the *Rigaudon* (no. 27). Within the stylistic restrictions of this period Alkan combines the tension of diminished sevenths within a purely diatonic approach. Not for Alkan was the floating chromaticism of a Wagner. The approach to the cadence is expertly handled with smooth melodic chromaticism aligned against an unexpected contrary movement in the right hand.

The *Fuguette* (no. 6) is the most formally baroque of all the esquisses. Its subject has a fine balance between accentuation and wedge-shape melodic movement and the answer bears more than a passing resemblance to *And with his stripes* from Handel's *Messiah*. The tonal spectrum of this *Fuguette* is wide-ranging with a German sixth just before the stretto with concomitantal harmonic density. The formal atmosphere of the French baroque also appealed to Alkan. A good example of his reminiscent French baroque species is the *Ressouvenir* (no. 13) which is marked andante flebile.

Ex. 7.2   *Rigaudon* op 63/27, bars 25–33

The statement of its opening melodic utterance is sublimely Hasidic. On repetition it is deftly harmonized with individualized harmonizations of each note. In the middle section an augmentation of rhythmic values and Schubertian modulation by thirds place the opening melody into relief. Towards the end, the return of the opening melody is transferred peacefully to the bass register. A substantial *Esquisse* reflecting another aspect of the French baroque is the *Tutti di concerto (dans le genre ancien)*. This is a warm-hearted tribute to the baroque concerto grosso of the Handelian rather than the Bachian type. Alkan adds a piquant interest to this *Esquisse* op 63/15 by a persistent flattening of the seventh degree of the scale by the Neapolitan colouring of harmony at cadences and also by applied diminished seventh harmony. The most energetic part of this miniature is the rapid alternation of soloistic filigree answered by a triumphant chordal tutti which shows a similarity to the same point in Mendelsshon's *G minor Piano Concerto*. Much more of a descriptive work but still relating back to French baroque elegance is the esquisse named *Grâces* (no.19) where a delicate F sharp minor melody is underpinned by a persistent drumbeat. This piece is harmonically simply organized with momentary use of the subdominant major adding an unusual touch. In simple ternary form the middle section of *Grâces* explores the major tonality implications of the opening melody with a more trenchant texture before a repeat of the opening and a coda which recalls the opening.

The *Esquisses* as with much of Alkan's output may mix conventional form or idiom with radical attitudes in musical parameters. One of the most curious of op 63 is *La Poursuite* (no. 25). Nominally in allemande style with quietly flowing semiquavers it is however marked prestissimo. Its tonal centre is rather fleeting after the subdominant modulation in the second half. This esquisse effectively is a legato toccata with elements of a two part invention. Perhaps Alkan was proposing no. 25 as an addition to traditional types of suite movements. Another radical piece is the *Duettino* (no. 14) which is a fascinating mixture of idioms. At a first glance the opening appears to be in minuet rhythm with typical baroque chordal progressions, but soon a truncation of the standard two-bar phrase, cross-bar phrasing and crossing of parts add a quizzical complexity. Less mixed in idiom is the *Inflexibilité* (no. 28) which is of the fugally decorative type but contains a few Alkanian quirkinesses at harmonic points near cadences with a tendency towards elliptical modulations. Uncharacteristic of baroque style is the tremolando figuration which complete the piece. Perhaps string figuration of the baroque era also inspired the *Toccatina* (no. 36). Also no. 36 is more related to the form of the string concerto grosso than a keyboard toccata. But the *Toccatina* is rather weak harmonically, relying on regular functional harmony reaching a faster harmonic rhythm well before the cadence. A pseudo-canon is attempted near the end. This *Toccatina* therefore does not challenge musically or indeed supersede the marvellous *Toccatina* op 75.

Several of Alkan's *Esquisses* are influenced by classicism in texture, form and idiom. For example a direct imitation of eighteenth-century string trio writing is to be found in the *Petit Prelude à Trois* (no. 17) where the performance instruction 'legatissimo quasi col arco' indicates pianistic imitation of string medium. The diminished seventh harmonies hark back to the controlled tension of Mozart as do the expressive sighs, but the uneven phrase lengths and the deliberately gauche double cadential trills are very much in line with Alkan's own quirky stylistic tendencies.

A tribute to classical string quartet style is found in no. 31 which is entitled *Début de Quatuor*. Here the emphasis is on the upper voice rather in imitation of first violin bias, but the persistence of imitation and the extremes of contrast and range point more strongly to the milieu of late Beethoven quartets. Dance idioms feature in the classically influenced esquisses. One of Alkan's favourite forms is the minuet and this is found in the *Minuettino* (no. 32). Based on *Vedrai carino* of Mozart's *Don Giovanni* this is a very faithful transcription. An unusual aspect of this *Minuettino* is the 2/8 trio which arrives twice and is considerably more animated and more pianistically idiosyncratic than Alkan's previous 2/8 excursion in the *Étude* op 16/3.

Most of the *Esquisses* op 63 are firmly rooted in the nineteenth century harmonically and texturally. The lyrical pieces in the esquisses like the chants lean on the Mendelssohn *Songs without words* model. As Smith[5] notes, there is a strong indebtedness of the *Notturnino inamorato* (unloved little nocturne) (no.43) to Mendelssohn's op 30/6 *Songs without words* in that both pieces have similarities in melody and accompaniment formats but a closer comparison serves to illustrate how much more interesting is the Alkan example which dispenses with Mendelssohn's vapidity and only employs a minimalist two-note cell. An examination of the two composers' accompaniments serves to illustrate Alkan's more cryptic, less powerful, dominant-tonic downbeat.

Ex. 7.3a   *Notturnino-inamorato* op 63/43, bars 1–12

Ex. 7.3b Mendelssohn – *Songs without words* op 30/6, bars 1–10

A perfect example of the lyrical miniature is *Fais Dodo* (no. 33). Its twenty-six bars pays tribute to the Schubert's exquisite *A flat Moment Musical* whilst maintaining a harmonic potency of its own. Much of its special quality emanates from momentary surprises such as a harmonic flattening of the seventh and the fifth often at structurally and dynamically significant climaxes. The hypnotically repetitive rhythmic motive, strong pedal basses, the plangently self contained melody and the approach to the final cadence all provide a stable background for the extraordinary harmonic twists. Perhaps the harmonic vocabulary of Schubert influences *Le premier billet doux* (no. 46). But other features certainly mark it out as one of the most inventive of the series of *Esquisses*. From the outset one is struck by the boldness of the Neapolitan sixth structural upbeat, its endlessly inventive melodic style and the perfect utilization of material.

Ex. 7.4 *Le premier billet doux* op 63/46, bars 1–11

Lewenthal rightly claims that the 'sophistication of this morceau would indicate that this was neither the first love letter received nor sent, and that the beguiling young lady ... is nothing less than an outlandish flirt'.[6] *En Songe* (no. 48) with the unusual time signature of 9/16 is a slumber song. Rather unsoporific is Alkan's continuously applied sixth harmony, widely spaced melody dissonant sevenths between parts and chromatic sixth flattening in the melody. In the second half a harmonic sharpening serves only to frustrate a modulation to the relative minor. Its linear function is again sixth flattening implying decorative not a structural use of harmony. At the end Alkan terminates the peaceful nature of this *Esquisse* by a sudden fortissimo jolt.

Many of the titles of the esquisses give a strong indication of their contents and several of the esquisses conjure up a specific programme. The first of op 63 is entitled *La Vision* and is colourfully described by Lewenthal:[7] ' ... on a dark stage a white Giselle-like creature appears, moves about slowly and sadly, and in a few seconds the wraith dissolves before our very eyes. The orchestra plays a few quiet solemn chords – the curtain falls'. The charm of this perfect little miniature rests in its daringly wide spacing between the melody and accompaniment, its pseudo-naive Satie-esque plain chordal accompaniment (recalling the *Gymnopédies*) and not least by the direct simplicity of the melodic phrasing without any sophisticated melodic rubato. Alkan's fondness for unresolved dominant sevenths occurs again as does canonic imitation of the op 61 *Sonatine*. On reprise the opening melody is subjected to the simplest of decoration and Alkan very precisely builds the rhythmic rubato into the melodic line. The opening melody is partially recapitulated and this *Esquisse* closes with solemn chords, their low register perfectly complementing the opening of the piece. Pairing of opposite characteristics is a feature of the second and third pieces of op 63 which are respectively titled *Le Staccatissimo* and *Le Legatissimo*. The former has a brilliant finger staccato technique with some cross hand effects and the Alkanian predilection for the Neapolitan and augmented sixth harmonic colouring. The latter is characterized by extremes of legato enhanced by cross-bar phrasing, closely worked textures and sliding chromaticisms.

Another perfected crafted miniature is *Les cloches* (no. 4), another of Alkan's essays in bell sonorities with an asymmetrical two-note chime which dictates the overlay of harmony. A magical effect of seventh flattening slowly causes this miniature to fade out. Images of the country are not neglected either in the esquisses. For example *Petite Marche Villageoise* (no. 20) is suitably rustic in its simplicity with chordal textures, its modal scale system and some deliberately awkward modulations. Fanfares and decorations of the melodic line do not disrupt the charm of this miniature. Equally rural is the *L'homme aux sabots* (no. 23), its heavy accents marking out the regular clanking of this mode of footwear. Unresolved dominant sevenths again occur before the termination of the miniature in the lowest register.

A group of esquisses display a considerable range of sensibilité in music. The most interesting of this group is the remarkable *Héraclite et Démocrite* (no. 39), a marvellous essay in duality of moods.[8] There are many examples of Alkan's notion of duality expressed in contrasting pieces, exemplified by *Jean qui pleure* and *Jean qui rit*, also *Ma chère liberté* and *Ma chère servitude*. In the third book of *Chants*, published *c*1869, duality exists within a single piece in *Horace et Lydie* and similar duality exists in the fourth book of the *Chants* with *Neige et lave*, published *c*1872. The *Héraclite et Démocrite* piece is the finest of all of them and certainly the most concise. Héraclitus is portrayed by the first D minor section with heavy second quaver beat chords; also characteristic of the dark mood is the emptiness and despair of the open fifth intervals. Harmonically simply treated, the emphasis is thrown on to the isolation of the mournful melody. In the second section of the Héraclitus episode, however Alkan's favourite chromatic side-slip results in a series of non-functional dominant sevenths and thereby to an altered augmented chord which leads back to the tonic after an inserted two-bar repetition. Démocritus is given the sunnier related key of A major which bears a fifth harmonic relationship to the melodic fifth cell of the opening of the piece. This faster section is marked to be played twice and its melody is treated sequentially. Cluster effects of bitonal G major/F sharp give a delightfully piquant flavour to the harmony. Perhaps the most innovative part of this miniature is the very close juxtaposition of the *Héraclite et Démocrite* duality near the end of the piece. Rhythmically this section anticipates Stravinsky's varied rhythmic blocks.[9]

Mood painting is also powerfully apparent in several other of these op 63 miniatures. *Le frisson* is motivic in conception: the rising third permeates the whole piece usually accompanied by a minimalist broken arpeggio but the smooth chordal answer does not alleviate the overall uncertainty. Modulations through the mediant major enharmonically give B flat major and thereby yield the relative minor with mood darkening before the Alkanian chromatic side slipping to F sharp minor. The pessimism of this section presumably is that part referred to by Smith as a 'Mahlerian fantasy haunted by funeral drums'.[10] There is here also a darkening of texture and a tension producing effect by use of unresolved diminished sevenths. A good example of Alkan's ability to portray the simplest but perhaps an ironically simple state in music is *Pseudo-naiveté* (no. 8) which is an artless ternary structure with a very repetitive rhythmic and melodic cell and phrase structures being much reiterated. The only degree of sophistication here is the Neapolitan colouring just before the reprise. *Increpatio* (no. 10) which is defined rhythmically by its aggressively strummed arpeggios answered by swirling quintuplets. This rhythmic power is increased by positive bass harmonies and the sharpened seventh within the arpeggios. The quintuplet figure persists in the piece, boiling up to a superbly dissonant climax.

The tension-ridden diminished seventh harmony has the final word in this *Esquisse*. As potent in mood setting as *Héracrite et Démocrite* is *Les Soupirs* (no. 11), a quite extraordinary portrayal of sighs and the mood evoked is magnificently hypnotic. Lewenthal[11] sums up no. 11 as follows: 'delicious sighs waft over the years that bridge the gap between Schumann and Debussy'. This esquisse however looks forward to the language of Debussy with its unresolved harmonies and arpeggiated phrase contours. The most daring harmonic bitonalities occur in this miniature, notably the enharmonic dominant seventh with the B minor/C minor upwards resolving appoggiatura in the left hand.

The *Barcarollette* (no. 12) is a remarkable miniaturing of the standard barcarolle but Alkan employs the unusual time signature of 18/8 rather than the usual 6/8 or 12/8 of the standard barcarolle. Alkan's portrayal is light years away from those of Offenbach, Chopin or Mendelssohn, being only fifteen bars in length. The ostinato pattern in the right hand is continuous, complemented by a left hand circular pattern with a dotted note figure which includes an echo effect. There is a slight Neapolitan turn then the miniature finishes in the tonic major. If the *Barcarollette* is a truncated affectionate tribute to Mendelssohn the *Fantaisie* (no. 16) is a whimsical pastiche of the Schubert *A flat Impromptu D 899* with its cascading semiquavers. The *Liedchen* (no. 18) is romantic in outline with more than a hint of the Schumann inner voice in its constitution and its expressive phrase ends. Of equal inner calm is *Innocenzia* (no. 22) in its simple tonic dominant harmony, smooth third-based textures and gliding double appoggiaturas. The emotional temperature of the esquisses is raised by *Délire* (no. 29) which as already mentioned is a re-working of the earlier esquisse, *Délire* dated 9 October 1847. This is the only example at present we have in Alkan's pianistic output of a revision. The main differences between the versions are firstly the transposition up a tone to E major to avoid a too direct comparison with the *D major Novelleten* op 21 of Schumann which has a similar textural energy.

Secondly to mark off *Délire* from the Schumann work, Alkan adds rhythmic lengthening to both melody and accompaniment, and his miniature is really a study in right hand triplet agility and left hand octave leaps. Harmonically and melodically, the piece is simply treated, only including some diminished seventh colouring near the conclusion. *Le Ciel vous soit toujours prospère* is an affectionate and amiable miniature in G major with a gently pianissimo minor version of the opening strain and a harmonic rhythmic quickening at the first section cadence. The opening melody is transferred to the tenor register with an untroubled continuation of the overall phrase contours which gives a charmingly rustic atmosphere. Also, the diminished seventh and altered scale system at the final cadence give a bracing, outdoor aura. The *Scherzettino* (no. 37) is a Berliozian flighty scherzo miniature in C minor and 3/8 time. Within the broken octave figuration there is a sensation of macabre nature with the sharpened sevenths. This atmosphere is heightened by widely spaced right hand tenths punctuated by the lightest of dotted rhythms in left hand octaves. The long range tonality in this esquisse is well structured. Also, Neapolitan colouring before the reprise adds interest but this miniature really coheres because of the melodic outline of the minor ninth first found at the opening of the piece. The finest of the dance pieces in the *Esquisses* is the *Scherzetto* (no. 47). Set in presto tempo, it is propelled by decorative triplets in thirds with rhythmic syncopation, and the triplet rhythmic cell is subjected to imitation then contrary movement. The second section includes imitative devices between the right hand and left hand semiquavers and a rhythmic augmentation of the rhythmic cell. There is a very neat linkage between the scherzetto and trioletto sections – the rhythmic cell is maintained but transferred by chromatic side slip up the semitone to the major key of B major.

The most exciting esquisses are those which directly anticipate twentieth-century idioms. Mention has already been made of the fragments of a Stravinsky aesthetic in the *Duettino* (no. 14) with its asymmetry and *Héraclite et Démocrite* (no. 39) in which there is juxtaposition of two tempi blocks. *Musique militaire* (no. 35) is far removed from the homely world of the Schubert *Marches militaires*. Deliberate banality in the Alkan piece is not eschewed but manipulated. Smith shrewdly observes that 'Alkan reveals a rare mastery of the most jejune material: a blank, four note oscillation, a handful of detained chords and a triplet twiddle'.[12] this very adequately explains the activity of the opening page, but although Smith hints at Prokofiev as a parallel, it can be stated that the factors which antedate Prokofiev are the relentless automaton nature of the rhythm, the strait-jacketed thirds and bare octaves, widely spaced texture, and the hard-driven chordal sonorities.

Les enharmoniques (no. 41) is a fantastic exercise in chromaticism which might be regarded as a parody of the Wagnerian sickness referred to by Alkan.[13] Indeed the opening of no. 41 with its expressively applied harmonies and altered chromaticisms mocks the *Tristan und Isolde* prelude. To make its full impact this work demands exact compliance with the composer's performance instructions. Chromaticism verges on Schoenbergian atonality at certain points in no. 41 and this atonality is all the more pronounced by its juxtaposition alongside highly diatonic harmony, and even the 'subterranean rumbles', so appropriately designated by Smith[14] as the ending of this esquisse, have a distinctly atonal quality to the cadential decoration. *Les Diablotins* is also astonishing, with its note clusters looking forward to Cowell and Ives. Nominally set in E flat major, this tonality is immediately disrupted by single, double and triple appoggiaturas which cause a clusters noise effect, and the skill with which Alkan builds these complements the massed chordal density – in the latter aspect there is a return to textural tendencies of Alkan's middle period. The middle section contains more extraordinary textural innovations at a very low piano range. Marked *très etouffé*, the aim is to produce a muted or stifling touch to this part. Harmonically, this piece is a minefield of interest and the only harmonically neutral areas are the two hymn-like sections, each of four-bar length and pious beauty, but these are swept away by renewed vengeance ending in a tremendous downward scalic cadence.

Of all Alkan's compositions for piano the esquisses show the composer at his most endlessly creative. The range of canonic awareness is phenomenal and the inventiveness more consistent than many of his other collections. The esquisses deserve a place in any adventurous pianist's repertoire. They are equally rewarding for performance and listener.

1.	Le Vision	4a	25.	La Poursuite	1
2.	Le Staccatissimo	4a	26.	Petit Air	0
3.	Le Legatissimo	4a	27.	Rigaudon	1
4.	Les Cloches	4a	28.	Inflexibilitié	1
5.	Quasi-coro	5	29.	Délire	4b
6.	Fuguette	1	30.	Petit air dolent	4b
7.	Le Frisson	4b	31.	Début de Quatuor	2
8.	Pseudo-Naiveté	4a	32.	Minuetino	2
9.	Confidence	4b	33.	Fais Dodo	3
10.	Increpatio	4b	34.	Odo profanum	0
11.	Les Soupirs	6	35.	Musique militaire	6
12.	Barcarollette	5	36.	Toccatino	1
13.	Ressouvenir	1	37.	Scherzettino	5
14.	Duettino	6	38.	Le Ciel vous soit toujours prospéré	4b
15.	Tutti di concerto	1	39.	Héraclite et Démocrite	4a
16.	Fantaisie	4b	40.	Attendez-moi son l'orme	5
17.	Petite Prelude à Trois	2	41.	Les enharmoniques	6
18.	Liebschen	4b	42.	Petit air à 5 voix	0
19.	Grâces	1	43.	Nocturnino-inamorato	3
20.	Petite Marche Villageoise	4a	44.	Transports	4b
21.	Moriturite salutant	4b	45.	Diablotins	6
22.	Innocenzia	4b	46.	Le premier billet doux	3
23.	L'homme aux sabots	4a	47.	Scherzetto	5
24.	Contradanse	5	48.	En Songe	3

```
0 = pre-baroque type        4a = descriptive type
1 = baroque type            4b = mood-painting type
2 = 18th century type       5 = dance type
3 = song type               6 = 20th century precursor type
```

Diagram 7.1   Classification of the *Esquisses*

Chapter 8

Arrangements and Cadenzas

The titles of Alkan's first two sets of arrangements, the *Souvenirs des Concerts du Conservatoire*, published in 1847 and 1861 and the third set of arrangements, the *Souvenirs de Musique de Chambre* published c1866 are only partially helpful in discovering the real nature of these pieces. The 1847 set and the succeeding 1861 and c1870 series are additionally subtitled *transcriptions de concert pour piano seul*. So, Alkan evidently intended these works to be concert works. But all these arrangements are reductions of the original orchestral/vocal/chamber scores. Like many romantic composers Alkan was fascinated by the ability of the piano to telescope a full orchestral score into a meaningful keyboard format. Unlike several romantic composers such as Liszt, he was anxious to maintain the spirit and letter of the original baroque, classical and romantic works selected. But what exactly *is* an arrangement?

Riemann writing in 1882 gives a pithy definition of an arrangement as 'the adaptation of a composition for instruments other than those for which it was originally written'.[1] Riemann's example infers that adaptation means a piano reduction. Other writers such as Keller have expounded on the validity of arrangements saying that:

> arrangements are not amiss musicologically and perhaps we should trust our musical instincts more and other objective factors less ... The progressive artistic insecurity of our age ... has gradually turned our search for authenticity into a compulsion: the less you know instinctively what's good both in creation and in interpretation the more frantically you depend on extraneous historical scientific evidence.[2]

In the light of both Riemann's strict piano reduction definition and Keller's freer creative approach, Alkan's skills as transcriber are particularly successful.

*

Alkan's own aims for the art of transcription are laid out in the preface to the first series of transcriptions. This preface is dated 30 March 1847 and this volume was published in the same year. A full translation is provided in Smith[3] but we need only summarize Alkan's main points here. These are:

1. Alkan intended the transcription to fit the developing piano and the technique of the modern virtuoso.
2. Previous arrangements simplified the work in order to be manageable by all levels of pianists.
3. 'Arrangers' often over-decorated and 'improved' the masters [Alkan was almost certainly referring to Marmontel].

4. Alkan is sensitive to the textural layout of the original. In 'transcribing' Alkan insists on making everything heard knowing which parts to bring out and deciding how the parts should be accompanied.
5. Only a few extracts from the operatic or symphonic repertoire are, according to Alkan suitable for 'transcription' because of the difficulty of reproducing orchestral sonorities on the piano.

These procedures are consistently followed in all three sets of 'transcriptions.'

Souvenirs des Concerts du Conservatoire

Partitions pour piano seul (1847)

The minuet from Mozart's *Symphony in G minor K550* from this 1847 series is an excellent example of Alkan's art of the transcription. The tragic nature of the work is very much in tune with the musical world of mid-nineteenth-century Paris. Fétis critically describes it as 'having a melancholy colour with invention and impassioned expression'.[4] The minuet is ideally suited to Alkan's own similar temperament. His arrangement of this symphonic minuet maintains the melancholy, inventiveness and expression of the original with no compromise made whatsoever to ease of piano performance. In Alkan's arrangement no decorations or improvements are made to Mozart, but sensitive voicings are required by pianists to bring out the honesty of Alkan's version. There is only one deviation from Mozart's original, the omission of doubling of the flute at the octave with the oboe at the end of the first half of the minuet, but conversely Alkan maintains this doubling at the conclusion of the second half. There are some concessions to nineteenth-century inexactitudes however, including the arpeggiations of some chords and the misunderstanding of mezzo staccato dashes, but the musicality of Alkan's version is impressive.

Other pieces in the 1847 *Souvenirs* series include equally severe but truthful transcriptions of several interesting more récherché baroque and classical masterworks. Inspired perhaps by the publication in 1841 in Paris of Benedetto Marcello's complete psalm settings (with piano accompaniments), Alkan set the eighteenth psalm *I cieli immensi narrano*. One of the most important composers who influenced French Romantic composers was Gluck, and Alkan's tribute to him includes *Jamais dans ces beaux lieux* from *Armide* where the colourful orchestration is reflected in the subtle arrangement and the *Choeur des Scythes* from *Iphigénie en Tauride*. Just as Gluck's *Tauride* had the greatest success, Alkan's adaptation of the chorus was one of his most popular works performed in the first of the 1872 Petits Concerts. Haydn's *Thirty-sixth Symphony* is represented by Alkan's arrangement of the andante. All these classical works were strongly commended by the *RGM* critic Blanchard who described them as 'models of how our old scores can be paraphrased'.[5] The other work included in this first *Souvenirs* set is *La Garde passe*, a chorus from Grétry's *Deux Avares* which was immensely popular in Paris because of the fashion for pseudo-orientalism and also because of Grétry's usual gifts of truth, realism and simplicity, qualities very close to Alkan's own musical cosmos.

Souvenirs des Concerts du Conservatoire

Partitions pour piano (2me serie) (1861)

The format of this second set of *Souvenirs* is similar to the first series, that is a baroque preface followed by five classical pieces. The baroque 'transcription' here is of Handel's *Choeur des prêtres de Dagon* from his oratorio *Samson*. This extract illustrates Alkan's Jewish roots since Dagon was a West Semitic god of fertility who was second only in importance to El. Alkan's transcription is splendidly faithful in orchestral character to the original version which is scored for trumpets, oboes and timpani, as well as the usual strings and choral parts. He differentiates orchestral parts and choral parts by the use of accents for vocal entries and attempts to separate con ripieno parts from senza ripieno parts by transposition of the former down the octave. Interesting alterations to the original include omissions of trumpet, oboe and timpani parts according to the exigencies of piano texture. Some chordal and octave doublings are applied in the 'transcription' but never in a bombastic manner. Notationally too, part writing and chordal voicing are clearly indicated.

Equally, Alkan's transcription of Gluck's *Gavotte* from his opera *Orphée*, like *Iphigénie en Aulide*, was produced in Paris in 1774 and by adding extra dance movements to the earlier *Orfeo* Gluck ensured personal success with the Parisian public. The *Gavotte* is placed near the end of act three. Alkan's knowledge of Gluck's score was probably based upon the Berlioz *Orphée* of 1859 which later became the standard French version of Gluck's opera. Alkan's transcription is a compact reduction of Gluck's orchestral score. Sustaining wind instruments are given prominence by tenuto marks. All other agogic marks are accurately copied from the original score. The à 4-string texture is particularly well suited for piano reduction as the following section shows.

Ex. 8.1   Gluck/Alkan – *Orphée*, bars 1–6

The finale of Haydn's *Thirty-eighth Quartet* [op 64/5] inspired another superbly idiomatic transcription. The toccata style of this finale is ideally suited to Alkan's precise keyboard approach as in the late *Toccatina* op 75. Alkan, however, does not hesitate here to move away from a literal reduction in order to lighten the bass texture of the piano. He is also pragmatic in providing piano fingering for the parallel thirds in the upper string parts and for the repeated string figures. As in Alkan's other transcriptions, bass doubling is sparingly applied and there is some compromise in textural arrangement because of the limitations of the pianist's hands. The exuberance of the Haydn quartet is perfectly captured and the ending of the Alkan version balances fidelity to the original text with Alkan's own pianistic verve.

A much greater challenge to the transcriber exists in the motet *Ne pulvis et Cinis* from Mozart's *Thamos König in Agypten K345*. The Mozart setting of the heroic drama of von Gebler is demonic and majestic. Mozart's music looks forward to the drama of his *D minor Piano Concerto K466* and the opera *Don Giovanni*. The dramatic heldentenor in the motet is highlighted in Alkan's transcription by accents and sometimes with octave doublings. Mozart's tremolandos are quickened in the Alkan version and much of the figuration has the appearance of the extended ostinati of works such as the *Concerto* op 39. The Mozart-Alkan alliance here is powerfully intense.

Ex. 8.2   Mozart/Alkan – *Thamos König in Agypten*, bars 1–5

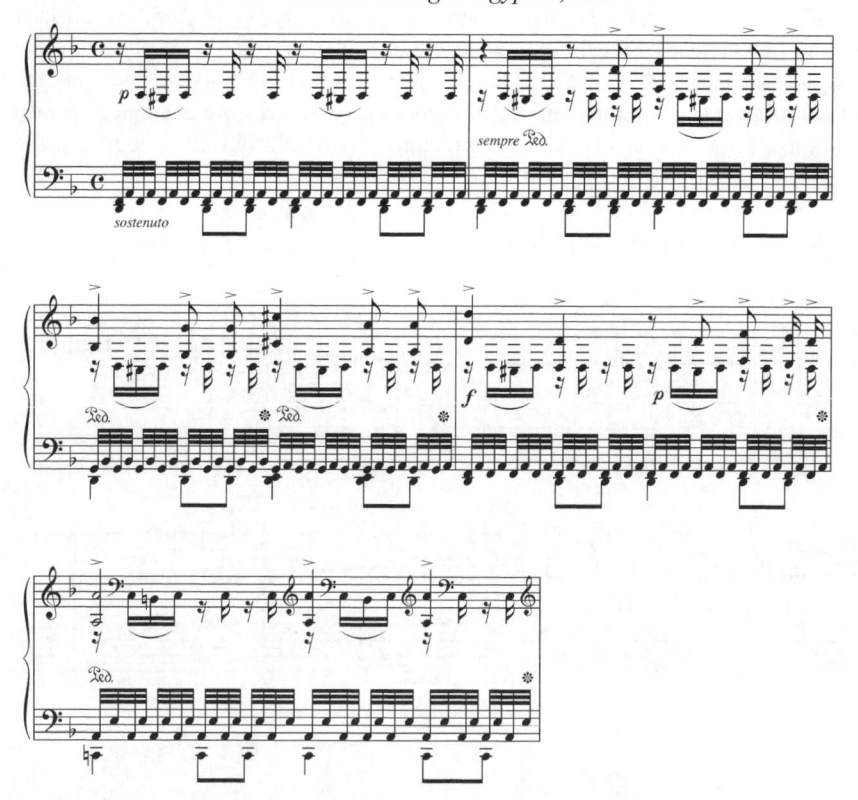

Conversely, the divine triple time section *Höchste Gottheit, milde Sonne* is simply and nobly arranged by Alkan. This is one of Alkan's most skilled exercises as a transcriber where he fulfils all of his five criteria mentioned earlier.

A Beethoven rarity, the *Bundeslied* op 122 is next in the 1861 series of Alkan's transcriptions. Beethoven employs tenor and bass soloists, male choir and wind instruments for his setting of Goethe's text. The *Bundeslied, In allen guten Studen* is a convivial unsophisticated text which receives suitably Teutonic musical swagger in Beethoven's hands. In Alkan's piano version also, the spirit of the original is superbly maintained with accurate octave and chordal reductions and precise replication of all other performance instructions. As in the Mozart transcription Alkan allows himself some virtuosic latitude and a much freer version results in the last page.

Ex. 8.3   Beethoven/Alkan – *Bundeslied* op 122, bars 8–?

The final piece in the 1861 series is an arrangement of the *Choeur des filles de la mer* from the finale of the second act of Weber's opera *Oberon*. The elegant cantilena of Weber's original is masterfully preserved by Alkan. His piano transcription retains the omission of the tonic in the final chord thus maintaining[6] a 'strange effect of dramatic suspense'. This Weber chorus provides a gentle coda to the whole 1861 series.

Souvenirs de Musique de Chambre

The final set of arrangements published *c*1866 are contemporaneous with the third book of *Chants* op 65 and the *Onze grands preludes* op 66. As the title of the final set suggests, Alkan draws exclusively now on chamber music for these arrangements.

As in the other series Alkan organizes the six works into chronological compositional order from the baroque to the romantic era. This series opens with an affectionate and literal transcription of the *Rigaudons des petits violons de Louis XIV*. Equally effective is the next piece a transcription of the slow siciliano movement from the *Bach Flute Sonata in E flat BWV 1032* in which the elegiac nature of the original version is maintained throughout. Very little of Bach's original text is altered: Alkan merely transposes some passages down to obtain smoother voice leading.

Ex. 8.4   Bach/Alkan – *Sonata in E flat major* BWV 1031 (Adagio), bars 1–7

The three middle transcriptions of the c1866 chamber music series are of quartet movements by Haydn, Mozart and Beethoven. The Haydn work chosen is the bucolic minuet from his *String Quartet in D minor* op 76/2. A few rearrangements and omissions are applied by Alkan for reasons of pianistic facility. But those minor transcription rule transgressions apart, the direct tense style of this Haydn minuet is ideally suited to Alkan's musical sensibilities. The trio section seems especially stylish.

Because of its sustained line the exquisite andante from the Mozart *A major String Quartet K464* is less suited to piano arrangement. Yet in the hands of a master transcriber such as Alkan, much of the original slow movement's intensity is preserved. Only minor alterations are made to the original such as some bass transpositions up the octave for the sake of pianistic clarity, although Alkan, despite his transcription pronouncements, cannot resist adding bass octaves near the end of the movement.

In Paris c1850 the *Société Maurin-Chevillard* started playing Beethoven's late quartets. To further promote the exceptional quality of these quartets to a wider audience Alkan transcribed the famous adagio *Cavatine* of the op 130 B flat major quartet. Kerman[7] in his classic studies of the Beethoven quartets points out the importance of vocal transcription in this movement and this is accurately mirrored in Alkan's version. As in the Mozart quartet transcription only minimal alterations,

Arrangements and Cadenzas 137

transpositions and rearrangements are made. Arpeggiations are sparingly used and original voicings are preserved as the following extract shows.

Ex. 8.5 Beethoven/Alkan – *String Quartet* op 130 (Adagio), bars 36–45

For the final piece in the c1866 series Alkan selects a less well known example of chamber music. The vivacious scherzo of Weber's *Trio in G minor J259* for flute, violoncello and piano (c1819) harks back to the energy of Alkan's own *Études de bravoure* op 12. The clear texture of Weber's *Scherzo* is wonderfully reflected in Alkan's transcription. The parallel thirds and sixths (flute/piano) are well suited to piano transcription and, overall, this *Scherzo* is a fitting conclusion to Alkan's transcription art where the essence of the original format is always respected and pianistic virtuosity minimized.

Other orchestral transcriptions and cadenzas

Meyerbeer's overture to *Le Prophète* was transcribed by Alkan and published c1849. *Le Prophète* was received with enormous acclaim in April 1849. What attracted Alkan towards this overture? The answer lies in Meyerbeer's heroic style, his instrumental realism and his unexpected combinations of sonorities. Alkan also had the real possibility of a good fee for the transcription of this piece. By the mid 1840's Alkan had himself expanded the role of piano sonorities in works such as *Les Quatres Ages Sonata* op 33. Alkan's transcription of *Le Prophète* continues this sound world expansion.

The most interesting piano transcriptions of all are those piano cadenzas which Alkan furnished for the Mozart *Piano Concerto in D minor K466* (outer movements) published in 1861 and for the Beethoven *Piano Concerto in C minor* op 37 published 1860. All three movements of the Mozart but only one movement of the Beethoven are arranged for solo piano by Alkan.

*

The Mozart concerto is bereft of the composer's own cadenzas. The Alkan cadenza may be tested against the various 'rules' of a contemporary theorist Türk[8] who set out recommendations for potential cadenza writers in his Klavierschüle of 1789. A brief summary of these ten 'rules' follow.

1. The cadenza ... should present the most important parts of the composition in the form of a brief summary ...
2. The cadenza ... must consist not so much of intentionally added difficulties as of such thoughts which are most scrupulously suited to the main character of the composition.
3. Cadenzas should not be too long, especially in compositions of a melancholy character.
4. Modulations into other keys particularly to those which are far removed either do not take place at all – for example in short cadenzas – or they must be used with much insight and, as it were, only in passing. In no case should one modulate to a key which the composer himself has not used in the composition.
5. Just as unity is required for a well ordered whole, so also is variety necessary if the attention of the listener is to be held. Therefore as much of the unexpected and the surprising as can possibly be added should be used in the cadenza.
6. No thought should be often repeated in the same key or in another no matter how beautiful it may be.
7. Every dissonance which has been included, even in single voiced cadenzas, must be properly resolved.
8. A cadenza does not have to be erudite but novelty, wit, and abundance of ideas and the like are so much more its indispensable requirements.
9. The same tempo and metre should not be maintained throughout the cadenza: its individual fragments ... must be skilfully joined to one another. For the whole cadenza should be more like a fantasia which has been fashioned out of an abundance of feeling, rather than a methodically constructed composition.
10. A cadenza ... should be performed as if it were invented on the spur of the moment consisting of a choice of ideas indiscriminately thrown together which had just occurred to the players.

Alkan's cadenza to the first movement of *K466* is highly original but only partially fulfils the requirements of Türk. Unlike the transcriptions, Alkan in writing cadenzas inhabits the world of the nineteenth-century composer/pianist. Hence the full range of the nineteenth-century contemporary piano is used in the Alkan cadenza with a scalic passage leading back to the reprise based on the Beethoven cadenza model.

Alkan in his cadenza concentrates on the initial material of the first movement which leads by rather abrupt modulations to a statement of the opening theme from the *Jupiter Symphony* (first movement).

Ex. 8.6   Mozart/Alkan – *Piano Concerto K466* (first movement), Alkan cadenza, bars 25–32

Alkan realized the confluence of the triplet accompaniment figure in both *K466* and the *Jupiter Symphony*. In his cadenza there is rather excess redevelopment of this material. Mozart's second subject is presented in the remote key of B major by Alkan (also Beethoven), but Alkan, as might be expected, is more florid in piano figuration. Both composers break the Türk modulation dictum. Interlocking chords as found in the first movements of Alkan's own *Concerto* op 39 with resulting dissonances leads to the scalic passage already described. Alkan's cadenza to the third movement of *K466* is even more inventive if rather too long in Türk's terms. The finale cadenzas attempts to present themes from all the movements of *K466*. A rondo episode from the finale is then subjected to a retrograde relationship with the opening of the concerto. The third movement does indeed carry out Türk's unity requirements in that its final pages provide a cyclic relationship to the opening section of the cadenza.

Inspection of the plate numbers of Alkan's transcription of the Beethoven *C minor concerto* op 37 suggests a publication date of 1860. Alkan's cadenza to the first movement is even more massive than the one he provided for the first movement of Mozart's *K466*. The Alkan-Beethoven cadenza was the subject of a perceptive article by Roger Smalley.[9] He points out that two modes of cadenza writing exist, firstly the 'authentic' stylistic cadenza (the Badura-Skoda/Mozart type) and secondly the re-interpretative type (the Alkan/Medtner approach). The latter of course stays well outside of the Türk model. The creative approach to cadenza writing suits the Beethoven concerto rather better than the Mozart because of Beethoven's own bolder attitude to scale length and range of modulations seen in his own cadenza to his *C minor Concerto*, and earlier also in the large third cadenza to his *C major Concerto* op 15. The Alkan cadenza extends this process to stupendous ends resulting in a cadenza constructed in eight sections marked off clearly with double bars. Although the Alkan cadenza runs to almost two hundred bars there is a strong feeling of unity (*pace* Türk) through the descending fifth motive.

Ex. 8.7   Beethoven/Alkan – *Piano Concerto in C minor* op 37 (first movement), bars 112–126

A few diagrammatic comments on each of the eight sections and their tonal region follow as shown in Diagram 8.1. Alkan's frequent use of unresolved dominant and diminished sevenths (breaking Türk's seventh rule) is an obvious feature of the harmonic vocabulary of his cadenza. More importantly, Alkan's subtle underlining of the C minor – E major – C minor tonal framework of the whole concerto is implied in the E major and related dominant region within the cadenza particularly in Section 6. In short, the Alkan cadenza broadly acquiesces to some of the established Türk-like procedures in artful tonal unity and apparent improvisation. But through remaining true to his own compositional inventiveness, Alkan's concerto cadenzas are honourable additions to the creation of mid-nineteenth-century styles in cadenza writing: Busoni (see Diagram 8.2) championed the Alkan cadenza in his performance of this concerto in Berlin 1906.

Section 1 bars 1–18	Piano scales in octaves, thirds and sixths	C min (V) – dim 7 – E min
Section 2 bars 19–61	Mainly concerned with ur motive in inverted and original forms	E min – f min – chromatic – E maj – C min
Section 3 bars 62–72	Quasi – trombe	D flat maj
Section 4 bars 73–115	Canonic use of ur motive with internal V pedal	F min – modulating dim 7
Section 5 bars 116–137	Extended statement of finale theme of Beethoven 5th Symphony, against C min Concerto 1st subject theme	C maj – dim 7 – A maj (V)
Section 6 bars 138–145	Pedal to link with section 5 to Concerto 2nd subject theme	A maj – B min – dim 7
Section 7 bars 146–173	Statement of Concerto 2nd theme internally chromatically harmonised	C maj – G maj (V7) – F min – C maj – (V7)
Section 8 bars 174–196	Trill and tremolo passages with rhythmically displaced Concerto 2nd subject theme	(V) pedal

Diagram 8.1

Konzertdirektion Hermann Wolff.

Berliner Konzerte 1906.
Rudolph Ganz.

1) 6. Okt. Beethovensaal, m. d. philharm. Orchester
   a) Liszt: Konzert in Es-dur
   b) Paur: Konzert in B-moll (z. 1. Male)
   c) Liszt: Konzert in A-dur.
   Herr Emil Paur wird sein Werk persönlich dirigieren.

2) 18. Okt. Bechsteinsaal: Recital. Compositionen von Brahms, Chopin, Grieg, Alkan, Ravel, Debussy, Liszt.

3) 3. Nov. Beethovensaal, m. d. philharm. Orchester
   a) Tschaikowsky: Konzert in B-moll
   b) Vincent d'Indy: Symphonie montagnarde (z. 2. Male)
   c) Brahms: Konzert in D-moll
   Herr Vincent d'Indy wird sein Werk persönlich dirigieren.

4) 6. Nov. Beethovensaal: Modernes Orchester-Konzert, veranstaltet v. F. Busoni.
   a) Debussy: Zwei Tänze für Piano und Streichorchester (z. 1. Male)
   b) Beethoven: Konzert in C-moll, erster Satz. mit Cadenz von Alkan (zum 1. Male).
   Herr Busoni wird beide Werke dirigieren.

Konzertflügel: Bechstein.

Diagram 8.2

Chapter 9

Organ and Pédalier Music

Together with the chamber music, Alkan's organ and pédalier music are the least explored of all his compositions. Very few organists have felt inclined to investigate the richly varied Alkan organ repertoire which ranges from the simplicity of the 25 *Preludes* op 31 (1847) and the spirituality of the *Petits preludes sur les huit gammes du plain-chant* (1859) to the more extended 11 *Pièces dans le style religieux* op 72 (1867). This last work also includes a transcription of *Messiah*. Moreover, there are the astonishing pedagogical studies for pedal board along with the 12 *Études d'orgue ou de piano à pédales pour les pieds seulement* (1866) which is of the greatest technical importance.

Many of the works discussed in this chapter as seen in Diagram 9.1 may be performed on pédalier, organ or, in the case of the op 72 pieces, harmonium. This of course gives greater flexibility of performance practice but as will be seen, certain technical characteristics of each composition governs a final preference for pédalier, organ or harmonium. It is appropriate at this point to outline some of the features of interest of each instrument and its importance for the writings and music of Alkan. The pédalier launched by Erard in 1855 in the universal exhibition in Paris was effectively a grand piano with a pedal board attached (range of the pedals bottom A to E above middle C). In a letter to Fétis Alkan justifies the use of the pédalier as follows: 'The services that (this instrument) could render to the organ in our country and to music in general are immense and incontestable.'[1]

Alkan states that French organists are little concerned with the clarity of performance of baroque music, particularly Bach. The pédalier would enhance this clarity and might make Bach's music and other baroque music more popular with audiences. Alkan also considered that because of the clarity associated with the pédalier, composers and performers might revive part writing in their composition instead of over abusing the sustaining pedal and over indulging in arpeggio writing. The pédalier's limitation conversely was its inability even with the most skilled pedal technique to achieve smoothness comparable with manual legato. This instrument however did open up baroque organ music to Parisian audiences and critics who admired the instrument's virtuosic exponents. For example Alkan's brilliant pédalier performance of the Bach *Toccata in F major* was much praised by Cavaille–Coll.[2] Alkan included this work in several of his Petits Concerts and received much critical acclaim for his exceptional pédalier skill.

Diagram 9.1 Suggested instrument for performance

		Piano à 3 mains	organ	pedalier	harmonium
op 31	25 Preludes (1847)				✓
op 54	Benedictus (1859)	✓	✓	✓	
op 64	13 Prières (1866)		✓	✓	
op 66	11 Grands Preludes (1866)			✓	
op 69	Impromptu sur le choral de Luther (1866)			✓	
op 72	11 Pièces dans le style religieux et 1 transcription du Messie de Haendel (1867)		✓		✓
	Praeludium composed 1850		✓		
	Petits preludes sur les 8 gammes du plainchant		✓		
	12 Études (c1866)		✓		
	Bombardon Carillon (c1872)		✓	✓	

These skills were of course developed by his prowess as an 'organist', winning a premier prix in 1834 at the age of nineteen. His teacher François Benoist (1794–1878) was according to Saint-Saëns[3] a poor organist but a brilliant teacher and improviser. Benoist is chiefly known today for his monumental *Bibliothèque de l'organiste, ou suites de pièces* (1841–1861). This comprehensive collection was timely given the many improvements and innovations carried out to the French organ in the nineteenth century. These included improved bellows, voicing, overblowing stops and application of the Barker mechanical pneumatic action. Indeed this latter 'improvement' was later extended by Moitessier in 1845 to give full tubular pneumatic action. As Smith notes[4] Alkan's friendship with leading contemporary French organists such as Franck and Lefébure-Wely probably provided him with access to the finest French romantic organs in Paris. Consequently Franck made a judicious selection from Alkan's *Prières* op 64 and two of the *Grands Preludes* op 72 and this selection was published in 1889 and will be discussed later.

The harmonium, now perhaps considered a curiosity as an instrument was popular in France in the nineteenth century. First manufactured in France by Alexandre Debain its expressive power was enhanced by Mustel's improvements in 1854, which comprised double expression, forte expressif and the large éolienne stop. Alkan's 11 *Pieces* op 72 may be included in the small but important repertoire for this instrument.

Turning now to the organ/pédalier/harmonium music itself, the first most important composition by Alkan in this category is the *Benedictus* op 54 (1859) a magnificent work and although some parts are texturally organistic, it is best suited to performance on the pedal piano because of its mainly highly pianistic figurations. Roger Smalley[5] has made a fine transcription of op 54 and the op 69 *Impromptu* for two pianos – both works should be in the repertoire of duo-pianists. Additionally this op 54 work could be played as three hands on one keyboard with some modifications. Op 54 is a remarkably extended example of Alkan's massed style works continuing the concept of redemption from darkness into light as is *Quasi Faust* op 33. The musical inspiration of *Benedictus* arises from the liturgical idea of 'blessed is he who goes in the name of the Lord'. In op 54 Alkan takes a personal approach to thematic metamorphosis. Three themes are involved in op 54 to this aim.

Ex. 9.1a *Benedictus* op 54, bars 5–8

Ex. 9.1b   *Benedictus* op 54, bars 21–26

Ex. 9.1c   *Benedictus* op 54, bars 97–100

The work is structured by the omnipresence of the fourth motive in all of the themes and the transformation of the first theme from a struggling D minor to powerful D major – a typical romantic movement from minor key tension to major key enlightenment. The second theme – a heavenly A major is more contoured than the first theme and perhaps represents the celestial world. This has much contrapuntal influence on the first theme. A heroic march-like third theme directed upward in a fourth-based motive leads to a development section. The first theme is then reprised providing an impressive cyclic unity to the work.

The op 64 *Prières* are most conveniently approached in the selection Franck made from Alkan's set of thirteen. Franck deemed nos 1, 2, 5, 6, 8, 9 and 11 as most suited to organ performance and additionally added nos 3 and 7 from the *Grands Preludes* to his selection. The first of op 64 is redolent of the spiritual atmosphere of the quieter *Preludes* op 31 and evolves through a repetition of the rhythmic motive with a melodic swelling towards the end of each four-bar unit. These units are delicately harmonized with some parallelism offset by a more contemplative two-bar recitative-like unit. The tonal ambiguity of the opening page with its third related modulation settles down to an extended plagal relationship and finally a triumphant assertion of the tonic harmony with the opening rhythmic cell but Alkan's triple pedalling needs to be modified!

The second *Prière in A major* is in Mendelssohn *Songs without words* vein with a smoothly flowing lyrical melody spiced up by some chromaticisms, a harmonically interesting middle section and a pedal musette effect. Op 64/5 playable on either the pédalier or organ is amongst the most profoundly serene of the prières: a freely given recitative with typical Alkanian note centricity as the *idée fixe* finally gives way to a more pianistically arpeggiated version. The sixth prière starts with very unpromising material, with a circularly centred melody and an incessant tonic dominant harmonization. The middle section is nonetheless undeniably brilliant and breaks free of the weak opening by dint of some strikingly virtuosic texture.

Ex. 9.2   *Prière* op 64/6, bars 25–26

Subtitled *Dieu des armées* (*Lord of hosts*) the eighth prière is a jubilant B flat major celebration where the simplicity of the chordal material and the basicity of the harmony demand the attack of the pedal piano. Smith[5] amusingly comments that on the organ it can 'become debased into fairground jollity'. The opening measures with the head motive triply reinforce the need for the pedal piano. The ninth prière has something of the contrapuntal clarity of a Bach organ trio sonata with its precision of movement and highly active pedal parts but the harmonic language with third-related modulations upwards and downwards is very much Alkan's own. The middle section includes a more defined rhythmic motive and is more parallel in nature, being harmonized in thirds. This is then combined with the opening flow in a coda of ineffable tranquillity.

Ex. 9.3   *Prière* op 64/9, bars 80–86

The eleventh prière is a tranquil pastoral siciliano in E major with delicately organized texture, equally suited to the organ or pedal piano. This leads to an even more serene 'nobilimente' which is aligned in stretto with the opening siciliano melody to provide a supremely satisfying conclusion. The *Prières* op 64 contain much music which is vintage Alkan but despite the judicious rearrangements of Franck one longs to hear the complete set on pedal piano. A brief study of Franck's alterations has been made by Sabatier[6] but given op 64's repeated staccato chords, double octaves and other pianistic textures the pedal piano is the only instrument to fulfil Alkan's compositional intentions. The energy and textural interest of the original pedal piano version of op 64/9 most especially has been quite emasculated in Franck's organ compromise version.

Ex. 9.4   *Prière* op 64/11, bars 54–55

Rather more daring technically and musically, the *Onze grandes Préludes* op 66, published *c*1867, were written with the pedal piano in mind and da Motta arranged nine of these preludes for piano duet. Op 66 is as important to the final period of Alkan's compositional output as the *Preludes* op 31 were to his mid-period work. Dedicated to Franck, they are arranged in order of major and relative minor keys starting from F major and terminating with a transcription of no. 26 and no. 27 from Handel's *Messiah* in increasing order of flats. These preludes represent a culmination of Alkan's brilliantly controlled virtuosity and this lyricism is worthy of the finest examples of the chants. Alkan's knowledge of Bach's *Toccata in F major* may have inspired the textural layout of op 66/1 which is an example of neo-romantic baroque revival. The interest in this prelude centres around pedal virtuosity although keyboard virtuosity is by no means neglected with parallel third passages and unison figurations to test the agility of any performer. The nature of the prelude is nevertheless a warm up exercise rather in the manner of the opening prelude of Liszt's *Transcendental Studies*. The second of the *Preludes* op 66 is an exercise in grace notes underpinned in the left hand at the outset by the obsessive rhythmic motive of Alkan. The directness of this rhythm is enhanced by the phrase structure in a symmetrical two-bar unit terminating each time on either the tonic or the third of the scale. Melodic elements are consumed by the energy of the rhythmic figuration. The texture then thickens and alternating block chords between hands triggers the triplet figuration in the pedal part. The grace notes of the opening become transformed into a continuous tremolando before a coda which amalgamates all these elements. The piece ends with an amazingly brilliant sextolet scale.

Ex. 9.5   *Onze grandes preludes* op 66/2, bars 58–61

The third prelude harks back to the plaintive world of the *Preludes* op 31 (the F minor op 31/2 in particular) but here the melodic line is even more fragmented and recitative-like. Alkan experiments with independent harmonic blocks, the first being in B flat major the second being more ambiguously centred around the dominant of the relative minor and the relative minor itself. This self contained tenor register left hand reflects back to the chordal layout of the A flat *Étude* op 35/8. The next part of this prelude is a beautifully sustained treble melody with a rippling accompaniment tonally restless and modulates Schubert-style in thirds to F sharp major before being subjected to some rhythmic alteration. The enharmonic is then invoked to reintroduce the B flat major tonality and then the recitative, chordal and melody elements are united, climaxing in a finely graded crescendo and this prelude ends with the recitative restated in triumphant octaves.

The fourth of Alkan's op 66 is a ponderous 'moderatamente' piece, heavily chordal and martially monorhythmic. This repetitive rhythm is built into a unit which shapes the overall form of the piece. In contrast to this is a deceptively lyrical middle section, surely influenced by the similar portion of the previous prelude but with more turbulence in the left hand with shifting six and four groupings and wide-ranging tonal regions. The return of the martial section provides Alkan with a glimpse of the virtuosity of the *Festin d'Esope* passagework type, before an imposing coda unites the martial figure and the lyrical element. The fifth prelude is a mellow ternary quasi adagio. With a nobility and hymn-like quality all of its own and its three-fold melodic sequence, it remains firmly in the tonic before being subjected to dominant seventh modulations. The rhythmic character is preserved in the next section with skeletal textures before an impressive use of measured chordal tremolando, Lisztian in attitude but much stricter in layout. A return of the skeletal texture, a repeat of the hymn-like section and extended plagal cadence provide the conclusion to op 66/5.

The next prelude, the sixth, is interesting harmonically involving floating chromaticism. With a freely applied concept of sonata principle a hypnotic atmosphere is engendered by repetitive rhythmic head motives and more extended phrase structures. A staccatissimo parallel chord section increases the macabre nature of the piece and drives the prelude on to a massed style climax with muted tonality before a return of the staccatissimo section. The seventh prelude evokes the world of Jewish chant. Marked 'alla guidesca', it imitates a cantor's vocal decoration for its first twenty-nine bars. Thereafter the chant is treated to sentimental harmonization. There is moreover, some awkward padding plus a thickening of the chant's texture both of which really do not convince. However musical inventiveness returns in the eighth prelude with a strongly harmonic part in both hands complemented by a powerfully rhythmic motive in the pedals. This is followed by a chromatic sideslip to yield up a cantabile melody in octaves surrounded by a harmonically mobile left hand part. The most interesting section of this prelude is the duality of the opening melody in the outer parts surrounded by strongly accented triplet appoggiatura chords. The coda employs this melody with some non-functional dominant and diminished sevenths chords before a rhetorically chordal ending. As Wells points out[7] op 66/9 needs to be performed on a French romantic organ with good reeds and a broad selection of colours to sustain its peacefulness. Op 66/9 is marked to be played 'langsam', and the nature of this work has been commented on by Smith as sharing 'with some of Bruckner's great adagios a spacious inevitability that links both composers to Beethoven's final period'.[8] In

Alkan's own terms, op 66/9 relates back to the glorious *J'étais endormie* (*Preludes* op 31/13) in its sustained intensity, its slower rate of harmonic change. In op 66 Alkan employs a greater use of surprise modulations and non-functional dominant sevenths.

Ex. 9.6   *Onze grandes preludes* op 66/9, bars 10–18

There is a whole middle section built around Neapolitan harmony which leads via its dominant seventh to its enharmonic German sixth, back to the D flat major tonic and the final bars are attractively tinged with unresolved D flat-7 tonality. Of great keyboard difficulty the tenth prelude of op 66 is a bewitching Cossack 2/8 dance in ternary form. Over an ostinato bass the melodic material is very limited in range, the modulations are very minimal and the formal structure is well defined by Alkan's punctuated bars. The melodic figure of the opening is subjected to invertible counterpoint. A sighing basic two-note motive lightly accompanied by chords is treated in the middle to two variation before the opening section return. This prelude is concluded by a fragmented chordally enlarged version of the opening section. Op 16/11, the penultimate prelude employs baroque but recitative in a manner in which the unresolved nature of the opening is melodically and harmonically questioning. The Alkanian chromatic shift is applied before another semitonal notch upwards.

Ex. 9.7   *Onze grandes preludes* op 66/11, bars 23–26

The chromaticisms are vapourized into appoggiaturas and a great song of praise emerges culminating in the most assured version imaginable of the opening recitative, now in the triumphant key of F sharp major. This is another fine example of Alkan's identification with the concept of darkness into light in musical transformation. The final prelude of op 66 is a literal transcription of 'Thy rebuke hath broken his heart' and 'Behold and see', the tenor recitative and arioso from Handel's *Messiah*. The recitative and arioso are transposed down a semitone to conform with the key order organized by Alkan for op 66. Accordingly these are very faithful versions with only some octave doubling of the continuo part and the original vocal part is placed in the pedal piano's tenor register. Although the op 66 were written with the pedal piano in mind most may be adapted for the organ except the really pianistic no 6 and no 10.

Dedicated to Alkan's organ teacher Benoist the *Impromptu sur le chorale du Luther* op 69 published in 1866 is a colossal work running to some 421 measures. Because of its range (a–1 to e bemol 6) pédalier performance is necessary. The model for Alkan's use of the chorale in his op 69 possibly derives from Mendelssohn's chorale treatment in his *Six Organ Sonatas* and/or the tradition established by Boëly in his op 15 *Quatorze préludes sur des cantiques de Denizot* of employing Lutheran chorales.[9] Boëly was the most important figure in establishing the Bach organ music revival in France. For the organ at St German-l'Auxerois, Boëly adopted a German type pedal board and appropriate stops to permit more authentic versions of the organ music of Bach. Alkan like Boëly was interested in independent contrapuntal organ music. Alkan's op 69 is therefore highly inventive contrapuntally with the chorale theme (*Ein Feste Burg*) being employed as a passacaglia in the bass (variations 1–8) in the tenor (variations 9–10) and in the alto (variation 11) and in the soprano (variation 12) for the first movement. The first four variations use a baroque 'divisioning' technique but variations five to eleven employ the same ostinato figuration with variation eleven presenting the six phrases of the chorale. The final variation twelve uses the latter part of the chorale with a cantus firmus in longer notes.

The second section of op 69 functions as a scherzo movement. Here the gigue-like dotted theme is surrounded by swirling broken chords figures as has been noted[10] in Chopin's *Third Scherzo*. The second half of Alkan's second movement of op 69 is based on a thematic rhythmic augmentation in the pedal part with canonic diminutions consequents in the manual part. The third movement in reflective slow mode maintains rigorously contrapuntal approach. After a highly chromatic harmonization of the first half of the chorale, there is much technical brilliance – firstly a canon at the fifth, then an imitative variation, then a development section with extraordinarily bold harmonization of the chorale accompanied by chromatic decorations in the pedal part. The final section of op 69 is a fugue structured with alto subject, soprano answer, tenor answer and bass subject entries. For episode material Alkan draws on the initial head motive of the chorale melody. After a Lisztian stretto trill pedal passage the chorale emerges for the final time with Alkan's characteristic massed chords. Like many nineteenth century compositions op 69 finishes quietly. The first section of the chorale is peacefully reprised giving a most spiritual conclusion to the work. The importance of op 69 to the organ literature cannot be overestimated. As well as being superbly written for organ, there are many interesting and innovative touches. Sabatier[11] observes polytonalism (at m 158) daring contrapuntal superimpositions (at m 17) and a harmonic language (at m 41) more akin to Dupré than Saint-Saëns.

The last of Alkan's compositions, the *Onze pièces dans le style religieux* op 72, published 1867, are designed for organ, harmonium or piano without pedal board. Dedicated to Simon Richault,[12] they are a delightful set of miniatures in the lineage of the spiritual examples in the *Preludes* op 31 and the *Esquisses* op 63. Less defined is the instrumental medium of op 72: nos 1 and 5 are most suited to the medium of organ (or harmonium) given their sustained textures whilst nos 3, 4, 7, 8, 10 with their rapid figurations are better suited to a more articulated attack of the piano. Nos 2, 6, 9 and 11 are possible on either organ, harmonium or piano. But the twelfth pièce, a transcription of the *Pastoral Symphony* from Handel's *Messiah* is best suited to the organ. In short, any of op 72 would make ideal voluntaries and interludes in church services.

The *Onze pièces* are very different from the *Onze grands Préludes* op 66 being much less extended and much less virtuosic. The first of op 72 is a carillon type piece built over an ostinato type ground bass. Gradually, Alkan's obsessive rhythmic motive emerges and thereafter the opening theme is firmly maintained in the right hand. Formally the piece is simply organized as a rondo type with the final full-blooded version of the theme being reserved for the triumphant end. The strongly harmonic style can be traced back to the directness of Louis Couperin and the French baroque organ tradition. The second *pièce* is a peaceful A major andantino in 3/4 time in sarabande style with emphasis on the second beat of the bar. Alkan's eighteenth-century gracefulness is exemplified by elegant two-note slurring but the innocent turn to the minor and whimsical decoration in the lengthy melodic middle section belongs to Alkan's own stylistic world. All elements are briefly recounted near the end of the piece which has Alkan's usual expertise in its conclusion. Op 72/3 is a D minor 'quasi-adagio' and is a strongly imitative and almost fugal miniature with a recurring rhythmic head motive. Over basically dominant pedal harmony, added chromatics provide an acidity to this most mellifluous of pieces.

The fourth of the *Onze pièces* is a plaintive 'assez doucement' in Rameau Mozartian style with French neatness and Austrian expressive 'sighs' but as often with Alkan there is a delicious harmonic surprise. The addition of several 'foreign' scalic notes produces a delightful effect. The piece fluctuates easily between major and minor and is only marred by a rather pompous middle section. There is further evidence of the influence of the French high baroque in no. 5's chordal sonorous textures and dotted rhythms but modified harmonically by Alkan to provide another example of his characteristic use of diminished seventh, augmented sixth, dominant ninth and Neapolitan harmonies. Both minor and major sections are fully developed and the final page is a fine example of the clear texture employed by Alkan. The ninth pièce opens with a plagal cadence reminding one of the slow movement of Beethoven's *Appassionata sonata*, but op 72/9 has also something of the atmosphere of a funeral march. There is a reminder of the headstrong octave passagework of the *Étude* op 35/5 in op 72/10, but now the virtuosity is thoroughly controlled. Like the op 35/5 *Étude* this pièce is modally inflected. The sheer impact of minimal material in the middle section is quite startling. An obsessive rhythmic figure is set against a truncated right hand octave figure then this is employed to full harmonic potency in the fortissimo climax of the dominant ninth sequences. A notable experimentation in this work is the juxtaposition (as in *Héraclite et Démocrite*) of block structures with contrasting textures and dynamics and time signatures.

Ex. 9.8 *Onze pieces* op 72/5, bars 97–106

Op 72/6 is in truly French majestic style with downward scalic passages and earnest left hand quaver figuration, but in harmonic unexpectedness and romantic melodic swirls, it could only be an Alkan composition. The seventh *pièce* is a moderate tempo F major miniature in 6/8 time. It has some flavour of the wonderful Beethoven *G major Bagatelle* op 126/5, since in melodic ascent op 72/7 has some similarity, but the flirtations with major and minor sections and the use of the Neapolitan for an extended part are very much Alkan's own harmonic world. Op 72/8 is a grimly determined miniature with an agitated semiquaver pulsating accompaniment which is offset by a curvaceous tonic major middle section with an augmented sixth link between the two sections. Some intriguing enharmonic elisions occur just before the cadence.

The final *pièce* is rather sentimental in which an encircling accompaniment, sharpened fourths and sevenths and a whimsical tendency to halt on a single note at the end of each two-bar phrase is noted. A C major barcarolle section follows which strikes a resemblance to those in the chants, then a return of the opening gives way to a chordal essay in quintuple metre. The opening melody and the barcarolle section are combined, there is a texturally lighter reprise of the quintuplet metre section and then a ghostly version of the opening completes Alkan's op 72 except for an added appendix as in the op 66 *Grands Preludes* of an excerpt from Handel's *Messiah*. In the op 72 set the setting of the *Pastoral Symphony* is beautifully direct and is as fine as the Handel transcriptions at the end of the op 66 set. In summary, op 72 represents the austere but strongly characterized side of Alkan's musical nature. Any of the op 72 would make ideal sacred voluntaries and many are eminently accessible technically to non-virtuoso organists.

More minimalist are the plainchant preludes of 1859 possibly inspired by Boëly's *Versets d'orgue en plain chant à 4 parties*. Written for an organ of the proportions of that in the synagogue in rue Notre Dame de Nazareth these exquisite preludes distil the essence of Alkan's mysticism. The preludes traverse all eight Gregorian modes and these are an antidote to Alkan's more extroverted organ works.

Finally the *Bombardo-Carillon* for pedal board (two players) dedicated to Delaborde is extreme in technical demands as are the *12 Études* for pedal board of c1866. These extraordinary études are dedicated to Lefébure-Wely and capitalize on the pedal board virtuosity of such players as Jaak Nikolaus Lemmens who inaugurated the organ at St Vincent de Paul in January 1852. These études survey the widest stylistic field from the baroque violoncello-like no. 1 to a three voice fugue in no. 3 and a ground bass in the last two études. Technically the difficulties are legendary. In the second chords of three or four voices are found: in the fourth a legato right foot technique is required set against a left foot staccato. The final étude demands the player to be fluent in arpeggios, three and four voice chords, parallel thirds and hazardous pedal leaps. There is no other nineteenth-century organ composition to rival these Alkan études in difficulty. As Sabatier observes,[13] one has to look to the post-war twentieth-century compositions of Demessieux, Dupré and Langlais to find comparable complexities in organ writing. Alkan as in the *Esquisses* op 63 has cast an arrow into modern times.

Chapter 10

Piano and Strings

French music journals and catalogues of the early part of the nineteenth century carried many advertisements for the latest duo sonatas, trios or larger ensemble works by French and foreign composers. This popularity of chamber music may be attributed to the enhancing of instrumental standards by Baillot whose 1814 public chamber-music concerts won considerable acclaim from middle class audiences. Baillot's repertoire for these concerts was however exclusively Austro-Germanic-Italianate (Haydn, Mozart, Beethoven and Boccherini). By 1838 *La France Musicale* reported over six hundred concerts of classical chamber music. That other leading French journal, the *Revue et Gazette Musicale* encouraged an equally severely classical diet. Its leading voice Fetis deemed romantic music to be a 'crisis of taste in music'.[1] Fétis was not to alter this critical stance until mid-century. Given this hostile atmosphere to the articulation of romanticism there is until the arrival of Alkan very little French chamber music to rival that of Mendelssohn, Schubert or Schumann.

This chapter will show that Alkan's finest chamber music can easily stand comparison with that of these three German masters. The *Grand Duo for piano and violin* op 21 published in 1840 as Alkan's earliest chamber work is the first really balanced romantic violin and piano sonata of the French romantic era. Prior to this work the violin sonata in France was essentially a violin 'concerto' with piano accompaniment. Once again the academicism and conservatism of several Paris Conservatoire composers must be called to account for this imbalance of roles in duo sonatas. In Rode, Kreutzer and Baillot's *Méthode de violin adoptée par le conservatoire*' the insignificant role of keyboard parts in chamber sonatas is apparent. Baillot's own sonata op 32 for violin and piano of 1820 is an example of this imbalance in that there is little attempt to write a keyboard part in dialogue with the violin part. At the other balance extreme several composers essayed 'accompanied' piano sonatas. These composers' works encouraged a better balance between violin and piano. Notable composers in this category include Edelmann who penned piano and violin sonatas with less soloistic violin parts. Hullmandel wrote finely balanced duo sonatas with real motivic interchange between keyboard and the string instrument. But probably the most influential figure for Alkan's chamber music was Adam who studied with Edelmann. In his chamber sonatas Adam's keyboard writing anticipates those of Alkan in rhetorical gesture, passagework and pyrotechnics and Adam's rejection of the harpsichord and championing of the piano made the accompanied chamber music of Alkan possible.

As well as the *Duo Concertant* op 21 written in 1840 Alkan composed a trio for piano, violin and violoncello which was published in 1841. His crowning achievement is the *Sonate de concert* op 47 published in 1857. All Alkan's chamber works are substantial ones with demanding piano and string parts and should be in the repertoire of all imaginative chamber musicians. More chamber works may still exist since Alkan announced[2] to Fétis in 1847 several more chamber works which may have been intended for publication release at a later date. Possibly Alkan considered that the contemporary concert-going public was not ready for these works. Three years earlier Alkan had also mentioned[3] quintets and string sextets of his own composition to d'Orfigue but these have not yet surfaced.[4]

Turning to the *Duo Concertant* op 21, the first movement is one of the most concise yet austere sonata principle movements of all Alkan's sonatas. There is something of the eighteenth-century 'sturm und drang' in the opening paragraph of op 21 with an astute feeling for harmonic rhythm and a natural sense of counterpoint. The role of the piano is prominent in the Edelmann/Adam mould. Maybe in chordal energy and piano figuration there is a tendency towards overstatement but this is counteracted by the compression of motives (a), (b) and (c) of the second subject.

Ex. 10.1   *Duo Concertant* op 21, first movement, bars 45–?

The closing section is more lyrical with its extended violin melody against a Mendelssohnian figurative piano part. The development section maintains this momentum with derived versions of the main theme in subdominant and Neapolitan tonal regions with powerful piano broken octaves in the piano and dramatic octaves from the violin. The temporary harmonic stability of G flat major (the enharmonic of the tonal centre of this movement) is upset by a reference to the second subject marked 'with exaltation'. Smith[5] considers the recapitulation starts after the double bar but is the tonality here not too unstable? The recapitulation is more convincingly placed with the return of the first group fff with octave doubling and virtuosic piano right hand passage work à la *Festin d'Esope*.

The second movement of op 21 entitled *L'Enfer* (*Hell*) is innovative in many ways. It explores the dark but clear registers of the contemporary French piano. Its chordal density anticipates Messiaen and its freely mobile internal chromatics look forward to Fauré. Did Franck know this slow movement when he composed his violin sonata?

Ex. 10.2 *Duo Concertant* op 21, second movement, bars 8–29

This ethereal mood is exquisitely deepened in the central core section where the 'angelic' motive is developed by the violin with shimmering piano accompaniment. This blissful state is broken by a return of the rhetorical opening now resplendent with increased chordal densities before a final descent to the underworld.

The final movement of op 21 is substantial and end weights the sonata with its perpetuum mobile nature. In rhythmic activity Alkan's movement is akin to Schumann's whirlwind sonata finales but Schumann never ventured into such rhythmic dislocation. The strict opening of op 21/5 finale opening leads to a French toccata-like first group in F sharp major for the piano with simple violin accompaniment and frequent doublings. More homophonic is the second part of the first group. After a Fauré-like transition with freely moving chromatic passages, the lightness of texture of the second group in the dominant is very appealing. The toccata pattern is re-absorbed into the second group's tonality and the closing group concentrates on the first group's second part. The development consists of a thorough investigation of the second group in invertible counterpoint before some non-functional dominant sevenths lead to long dominant pedals heralding the start of the recapitulation. A new transition passage appears marked by a military dotted note figure with a Neapolitan relation to F sharp. There is now scant reference to the second subject. Then the coda with full voiced textures in both instruments derived from the first group, second part, neatly incorporates fragments of the opening of the movement and powerfully re asserts F sharp major. This sonata's finale is overall a long-range tonal search for the tonic key of the work in the same manner as the finale of the *Symphonie* op 39.

Piano trios were popular with early-nineteenth-century Parisian audiences. An example of this is the rapturous reception[6] for a trio concert in 1837 of the dedicatte of Alkan's op 21 *Grand Duo* given by Liszt, the violoncellist Batta and Urhan. For Fetisian success a chamber work had to be fundamentally classical in mood and form. Alkan's next work was stylistically acceptable for Fétis since this trio for piano, violin and violoncello in G minor op 30 is the most severely classical of all Alkan's chamber works. It is influenced by the classical periodic phrase construction of Haydn yet as an early romantic work it nevertheless deserves to take its place in the repertoire alongside the more familiar trios of Mendelssohn which have similarly brilliant piano parts.

The work is completely centred round the tonal pole of G minor/G major with the trio of the second movement providing submediant release. As with the *Grand Duo* the first movement of op 30 (marked 'assez largement') at first sight has the energy of an allegro con brio, but the gravitas of op 30 is considerable so a slower performance speed seems preferable to bring out its full character. On closer inspection many classical stylistic markers are present. In the first movement for example, antecedent-consequent phrases (with some degree or irregularity in the phrase structures) are reinforced by unison octave writing. The piano/strings balance here veers towards the Edelmann/Adam model rather than the Baillot, in that the piano is very much in the foreground for the first group. The transition passage is, as in many classical trios minimal and a Mendelssohnian second group soon appears with several attractive melodic duets between occupying a subservient role. The development section in the first movement of op 30 is concerned with the contrapuntal potential of the first group. Thereafter the recapitulation omits the first group and proceeds to the lyrical second group. This permits the foreground of the coda to be more dramatic texturally, motivically and tonally. This coda has a submediant link to the trio of the next movement.

In this movement one is aware of dominant pedal relationships, asymmetrical phrases and the velocity of the piano figuration mainly in sixths and thirds. The latter gives a Mendelssohnian gossamer-like scherzando feeling which nevertheless gains tonal strength and leads to powerful tonic assertion. The trio conversely is an admixture of quasi-fugal treatment plus a lilting Schubertian melody with Alkanian twists which are treated sequentially and are passed from violin to violoncello to piano. The return of the scherzo is regular with a coda harking back to a fragment of the trio transposed down a semitone before a tranquil ending.

The slow movement of the trio is one of Alkan's most extraordinary creations. Its severe binary contrasts far transcend the obvious model of the slow movement of Beethoven's *G major Piano Concerto*. The sustained string writing and intense piano interruptions point the way forward to Ives' *Unanswered Question*. But there is also certainly something of the calm of Beethoven's op 57 slow movement in the opening of the Alkan trio's slow movement.

Ex. 10.3   *Piano Trio* op 30, slow movement

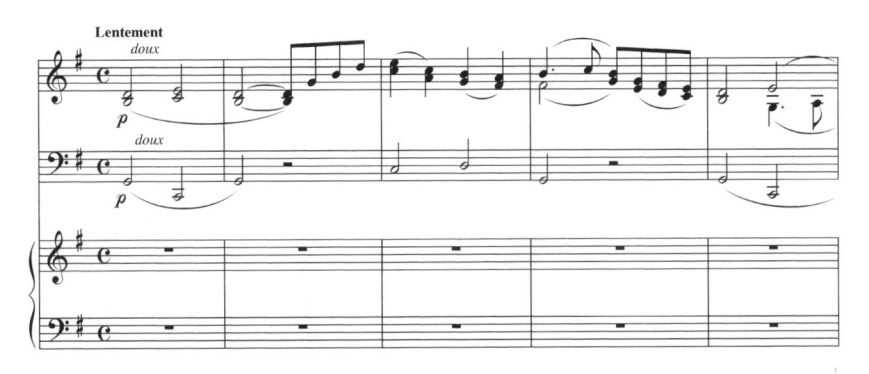

In the piano's recitative there is tremendous almost Lisztian rhetoric mixed with Jewish modality. Halbreich[7] enumerates seven separate sections in this movement with forty bars for strings in duo, thirty-nine for piano solo and only twenty for all three instruments. The movement is finely proportioned and appears to be composed in a single statement.

Less inspired is the finale of op 30 which is a conventional piano virtuoso movement. The surface brilliance here emanates from the model of the scherzo of the Mendelssohn *D minor Trio*. This Alkan movement is a large sonata structure piece such as op 21 which despite its vapid nature does successfully end weight the trio as a whole. The strings' role until the coda is essentially supportive but the obsessive nature of the piano part in the manner of the *Saltarella* op 23 is the main point of this finale. Undoubtedly this figuration is exciting but on careful inspection one notices many square phrase structures and rather uninspired sequences. All the thematic material is closely linked by a falling third motive. The coda in this finale reverses the solo and accompaniment pattern of the rest of the movement and renders a triumphant conclusion to the movement.

The *Trio* op 30 is the shortest of Alkan's three main chamber works. The finest of all Alkan's chamber works is the *Violoncello sonata* op 47 which is the grandest and longest of all his chamber essays. Weight and scale apart, op 47 is a highly integrated work much more so than op 21 or op 30. In the violoncello sonata one can trace distinctive ur-motives between the movements and within the movements. The distinctive character of each of the movements in op 47 is not compromised either. In this respect Alkan's achievement parallels that of Chopin in his *Violoncello sonata* op 65.[8] Interestingly, the violoncellist Franchomme's personal copy of op 47 dated 23 March 1857 shows several manuscript annotations by Alkan. Chopin left many sketches[9] of op 65 but we can only speculate about the manner in which Alkan composed his op 47. Compared with both the *Duo concertant* and the *Trio* there is a much more significant part for the solo instrument and there is much better integration now of the solo and piano part. From its inherent limpid lyricism it is possible that Alkan sketched the violoncello part and then allowed the piano part to evolve. Even more than Chopin, Alkan had to restrain his natural but extravagant sense of piano bravura. So his op 47 still demands considerable pianistic skills but its virtuosity compared with similar sections in op 21 and op 30 is more appropriate for the needs of chamber music.

Samson[10] has written perceptively on Chopin's op 65 sonata pointing out his ability to learn 'new skills' in his autumnal years. Alkan in 1857 had many more compositional years ahead of him, but the thematic constructive experience of the *Symphonie* op 39 seems to be the work from which Alkan was most to benefit in the composition of his op 47. Like the *Symphonie* op 39 Alkan is structurally convincing in all of its four movements and like the *Symphonie* op 39, op 47 employs intermovemental progressive tonality returning to the tonic minor.

E major – Ab/G# major – C major – E minor

Compared with op 21 and op 30 Alkan takes a much more expansive attitude to form. In the first two movements of op 47 the dramatic and sensual components respectively are fully investigated. Equally in the last two movements there is much discourse on the divine and on the satanic. In at least two of the movements the spirit of Schubert is evoked that is *Der Fischermadschen* in the slow movement and *Tod und der Madschen* in the finale.[11]

The first movement of op 47 is a powerful allegro molto confidently propelled by distinctive interchanges between violoncello and piano and by much textural variety. Much of the cohesion of this movement derives from a characteristic ur-motive first displayed in the first group material. Alkan's first movement, like its Chopin counterpart is extremely economical in motivic usage. Indeed in the Alkan as in the Chopin this ur-motive may be said to dominate the whole surface of the music. Lining up various sections of the first movement of op 47 is instructive.

Ex. 10.4 *Cello Sonata* op 42, motives in first movement

The first group then proceeds scalically on the piano with trill-like commentary on the violoncello, a third related sequence and brief transition to the second group at bar 26, the first element of this second group being saturated with the falling ur-motive. As with many romantic sonata principle movements the second group is discursive and lengthy. In the case of op 47 a third related sequence is applied to this first element of the second group before introducing a second element with the falling second now opened up to the falling third. Forward direction is produced by unforced use of sequential movement and colourful but not excessively over-written piano figuration. The sturdiness and contrapuntal confidence of the third element of the second group is impressive and this vertical sonority is enlarged in the closing section replete with dramatic octaves, Brahmsian triplets and a surprise Schubert third-related modulation before closing in the expected dominant. It is essential to perform the exposition repeat since material in the first time bar relates back to the ur-motive.

The development section of op 47's first movement is a model of balance between existing material from the exposition and new material. Alkan applies classical discipline here and there is no trace of the aimlessness or prolixity of the development sections as in some of the other chamber works. There is a real sense of Beethovenian drama in the alternation at the outset of the development of staccato/pizzicato octave leaps and a menacing tremolando figure which acts as an accompaniment for a darkly coloured upwardly mobile violoncello new theme although directionally relatable to the second group third element. The atmosphere generated here looks forward to Brahms.

Much of the next part of the development is concerned with the exploration of triplet imitation with the accompaniment of the rising second from the violoncello. Bravura passages from the violoncello are not absent. The con-fuoco scales are integrated with the triplet figure from the piano in downward descending tonal groups concealing a reference back at (m 117) to the three-note opening motive and this is the subject of much violoncello/piano dialogue before a brief reminiscence of the second group's first element. The most tonally adventurous part of the development is illogically modulating to the isolated key of G minor. The falling second motive triggers some fine romantic rhetoric and sequential modulations but the tonality remains in G minor. By successive chromatic side slips Alkan moves to G# major, the mediant of the movement. By pushing the tonality upwards again Alkan appears to start the recapitulation in the subdominant A major. This is no Haydnesque false recapitulation though. The opening theme is treated to an intensive series of interchanges between instruments compressing elements of all the thematic and motivic material already heard. This distillation allows the most beautiful 'dolce' dialogue between violoncello and piano to take place over a dominant pedal with perfect timing and consummate shaping. Then the recapitulation starts dolcissimo with piano and violoncello now lyrically combined. Tremolandos lead to non-resolving harmonies before the second group reappears. The closing section material is tonally transported to usher in brilliant coda with closely derived ur-motive passages. Alkan's bravura is again restrained in the final page of this movement.

The second movement of op 47 is a very gentle barcarolle-like siciliano in A flat major. This movement has an intermezzo function between the large scale first movement and the weight and gravity of the adagio third movement. The tempo of the movement and allegrettino (dotted crotchet = 80) encourages performers to take an unsentimental view of the music. This tempo allows disjunct intervals and melodic chromaticisms of the opening theme to be absorbed into the musical fabric and flow.

Formally simple, this siciliano movement is in ternary design with a coda. This tripartite nature is reinforced by the overall major – minor – major tonality. Easily transposable to the dominant the opening theme is subjected to third-related modulation processes à la Schubert and given a barcarolle-type accompaniment. Throughout, the dialogue between violoncello and piano is refined and restrained in the best Gallic manner. A more upward moving violoncello theme is then presented with a rhythmic relationship to the first theme. This rhythmic figure is echoed by the piano before some thematic restatements of the opening theme including one in the dominant of the submediant which leads to the more impassioned but cantabile middle section integrated to the opening section by two-note rhythmic cells and fluid accompaniment patterns. This section contains some curious but typical Alkanian enharmonics. On reprise the violoncello is now permitted to sing the full version of the opening melody in its most resonant register. The second main theme is then presented in the tonic minor and proceeds regularly, but instead of concluding conventionally, offers a fragment of the opening theme then a series of unresolved dominant sevenths – ascending in fourths from B flat^7 to Gb^7 slipping chromatically back to E flat[7] to usher in the magical coda. Exquisitely scored for piano (low bass texture and clear treble textures) and violoncello (fragments of the opening theme piquant decorations and sustained barcarolle figures) this coda is a fitting conclusion to a most beautiful movement.

The mood of the slow movement adagio of the op 47 sonata is indicated by a quotation from the Old Testament prophet Micah 5.7: '... as dew from the Lord, as showers upon the grass that tarrieth not for man ...'. If there are musical agents for the Lord and man respectively they are seen in the low violoncello statement and piano shimmering melody/accompaniment in the opening pages. These represent the theme A and first episode B of the movement's rondo structure. The second episode C has a related ethos to theme A yet contains contour resemblances to theme B.

Ex. 10.5   Themes A, B, C, *Cello Sonata* op 42, slow movement

The crystalline quality of theme B in the piano in F major contrasted with the violoncello's tendency to pizzicato monotones is made complex by rhythmic irregularities in the manner of Messiaen's rhythmic modes. As in the *Symphonie* op 39 slow movement a chromatic slide-slip downwards yields the reprise of theme A in E major which is shortened. On reappearance theme B now in A minor contains further rhythmic complexities thereby increasing the tension of this section. There follows theme C on the dominant side of C major. The tremolandos in the piano part continued from the previous section are contrasted with staccato chords and single notes harking back to the pizzicati in the violoncello. Stretto devices are applied to the piano and violoncello parts before a legato sequential falling ur-motive gives way to a molto espressivo passage enlivened by descending chromaticisms in the piano part. The rhythmic complexities have now ceased and the tremolandi are confined to the violoncello and piano left hand. Theme A reappears now accompanied by tremolandos in the piano part with a sustained bass line but the peacefulness is momentarily disturbed by a diminished seventh before a coda reprise of A in bar 95 now doubled by violoncello and piano. The theme now vanishes reflecting the nature of the quotation and the movement achieves its rest in violoncello pizzicati and piano pianissimo shimmerings.

The finale, although the most brilliant of the movements of op 47, is the most stereotypical inhabiting as it does a Mendelssohnian/Hellerian saltarella world. The fourth ur-motive is shamelessly exposed in the opening theme of this sonata rondo movement. Minor tonality prevails throughout the narration of the rondo theme (except for its second appearance) but it is the transformation of the ur-motive which organizes the long-range structure. The episodes of this saltarella movement offer (a) a chordal/triplet dialogue between violoncello and piano with continuity of triplet figures from the rondo theme with the ur-motive concealed at the phrase end and (b) non-thematic tonally unstable areas with rhythmic motivic recall of the theme. This is subjected to several more interesting operations firstly up a semitone and then in augmentation in the piano part dislocated by appoggiatura chords. One of the remarkable passages in the finale is the textural dissolution area marked 'stanco' (exhausted) where the 12/8 pulse effectively becomes transmuted to 6/4 but the oscillation of the saltarella still exists here. After a return of the first episode the coda follows making much of the Neapolitan 6th – V^7 – 1 formula and extremes of piano virtuosity with the finale exposure of the ur-motive.

In comparison with his piano output Alkan's works for piano and strings seem less significant. But these works show him as a composer who is willing to modify the German sonata hegemony to create music of immense intensity and inventiveness. The finest and grandest of Alkan's chamber output is unquestionably the *Violoncello sonata* op 47. Like Chopin's companion work it deserves an equal place in a violoncello repertoire dominated by German composers. There is in op 47 within its Olympian scale an economy of material and an integration of movements through the ur-motive. In both respects it is the chamber equivalent of the *Symphonie* op 39.

Chapter 11

Miscellaneous Compositions

This chapter surveys Alkan's remaining compositions. Several of these compositions are either still in manuscript or are still to be located. It is convenient to divide all these works into vocal music and instrumental music.

Vocal music

Like Chopin, Alkan's vocal music is much less significant then his instrumental music. Nevertheless two extended vocal works exist in manuscript. These vocal settings were entries for the Prix de Rome competitions in 1832 and 1834. The 1832 *Cantata* is a setting of Pastoret's *Hermann et Ketty* for soprano, tenor and small orchestra (double woodwind, two horns and strings). This cantata, like Alkan's first *Concerto di Camera* (also of 1832) displays superb technical security and much youthful compositional confidence although Alkan was strongly influenced by the melodic model of Rossini and the orchestral precision of Mendelssohn. It is not surprising then that it won second prize in the 1832 competition. (The winner of the Prix de Rome that year was Ambroise Thomas.) The 1834 work *L'entrée en loge[s]* to a text by Gail for tenor and orchestra is a much less inspired work and was not awarded a prize. The winner of the 1834 Prix de Rome prize was Antoine Elwart, a music theorist historian and composer who taught harmony at the Paris Conservatoire from 1840–1871.

Alkan's song output is minimal. A solo song the *Romance du phare d'Eddystone* was premiered in 1 March 1845 by a British singer Elizabeth Masson and Alkan himself. The popularity of romances in France has already been stated. The Eddystone lighthouse was subjected to many vicissitudes so it was an ideal subject for romance. First swept away by the great storm of 1703 the lighthouse was rebuilt in 1708 but was destroyed by fire in 1755. The third lighthouse constructed in 1756–1759 remained until its replacement in 1882. The lighthouse inspired countless folk ballads and seamen's tales and Alkan's setting (now lost) was according to the review[1] 'an attractive and modest floral melody'. Turning from the secular to the sacred, Alkan's tribute to Protestant baroque vocal music is his fair copy of the Bach chorale *Wie schön leuchtet der Morgenstern*. Dedicated to a Mme Zina de Mansouroff, it is scored for soprano and piano. The manuscript is dated 11 October 1855. Mme Mansouroff again was the dedicattee of a setting of the *41st Psalm* composed in the same year. Here the manuscript gives the date as 19 May 1855.

A short choral piece, the *Stances de Millevoye* for female voices (SSA) with piano accompaniment was published in 1859. This secular vocal work is typical of mature Alkan being both macabre and plaintive. It has a vocal refrain in parallel concords and piano links with fragmented harmony between the refrain repeats.

Published also in 1859 is the extraordinary *Marcia funèbre sulla morte d'un Pappagallo* (*Funeral march on the death of a parrot*). This curious piece shows Alkan at his most grotesque and funereal. Its natural precursor are works such as Gossec's *Marche lugubre* of 1790 and Berlioz's *Symphonie funèbre et triomphale* of 1846. The full title of Alkan's composition is *Marcia funèbre sulla morte d'un Pappagallo, per due Soprani, Tenore, Basso, contre Oboi e Fagotto: Parole e Musica del Cittadino C° V^{mo} Alkan (primogenito). Orgue expressif (jeu d'anches) à defaut des quatre instruments à vent.* (Scored therefore for two sopranos, tenor, bass with three oboes and bassoon words and music by Alkan. Harmonium [reed stops] could substitute for the wind instruments.) One clue to Alkan's inspiration for this work is given in the composer's explanatory note at the beginning of the main vocal section: 'it is due to a fortuitous rapprochement purely ornithological that this reminiscence is due. Admirers of *La Gazza Ladra* please therefore should not attribute any impertinent attention to the commemorator of the defunct parrot!' The instrumental introduction of Alkan's *Marcia funèbre* is exceptionally bleak in its sparse texture, Mahler-like high oboe timbre and its chromatic tension and restricted bass figuration.

Ex. 11.1   *Marcia funèbre sulla morte d'un Pappagallo*, bars 27–37

After a mock Baroque tenor-bass recitative interchange the sombre march commences with an insistent rhythmic *idée fixe* permeating the musical fabric, the squareness of phrase structure being reinforced by terraced dynamics. A temporary calm is provided by a submediant homophonic section before a return of the opening vocal section now decorated with grotesque chromatic contrary and parallel scales. The first episode provides a contrast with paired voices and the lightest of accompaniments. Here, Alkan's musical language is that of the eighteenth-century operatic ensemble with short periodic-balanced articulated phrases. Is Alkan symbolizing in music the death of his beloved *ancien régime*? After a repeat of the main section with the accompaniment now enhanced with chromatic scales the second episode is constructed around a four voice fugue with several 'normal' elements such as countersubjects, stretti and pedal section before a triumphant return of the main section employing the fugue subject as part of the accompaniment. The soprano voices unaccompanied are isolated in the final page before a brief reprise of the bassoon accompaniment. This funereal but curiously effective work concludes with an optimistic tierce de picardie.

Two brief choral settings of Jewish chant show Alkan's involvement with Judaism and music in Paris.[2] As indicated in the biographical chapter, traditional Jewish customs were overturned by greater rapport between liberal and orthodox factions. In order to reflect this rapport in music the Consistoire (the consultative board for all Jewish religious matters in Paris) sought advice from Alkan and Halévy as to the most suitable cantor. They selected Samuel Naumbourg (1815–1880), author of many distinguished collections including the *Zemîrôt yiserael chants religieux des Israelites, contenant la liturgie complète de la synagogue, des temps les plus reculés jusqu'à nos jours*. Many of Naumbourg's settings follow the euphonious Biedermeir melos of the Austro-Germanic romantic composers such as Schubert.

Alkan contributed two settings for Naumbourg's collection for the first volume. Published in Paris during 1847 he provided the *Etz chajjim hi* (*The Tree of Life* no 93) set for four voices. Traditionally this chant was a vigorous statement of the sanctity of life inspired by the text from Proverbs 3.17,18 and Lamentation 5.21: '[wisdom] is a tree of life to those who embrace her; those who lay hold of her will be blessed. Restore us to yourself O Lord that we may return; renew our days as of old[3] ...'. Alkan's setting is heartfelt and positive and spiritual.

Ex. 11.2   *Etz chajjim hi* bars 1–11

Scored for SATB with optional piano or organ accompaniment, the *Hallelujah*, Alkan's setting of verses from *Psalm 150* for Naumbourg's third volume was published in Paris ten years later in 1857. The text reads: 'praise him with the harp and lyre ... let everything that has breath praise the Lord. Praise the Lord'. This is closely related to the Austro-Germanic parameters of *Etz chajjim hi* but as befits the text the style here is much more celebratory and triumphant. After a characteristic rhythmic head motive rising through all the voices the *Hallelujah* is thereafter an almost exclusively homophonic setting. The final praise section is closely related to the world of Italianate operatic ensemble with dense textures, transcendent soprano voices and Verdian turns to the harmony.

Instrumental music

The extant miscellaneous instrumental music of Alkan comprises works of mainly short duration. The large-scale symphony is unfortunately lost but the existence of an enthusiastic contemporary review as discussed below leads one to hope for a rapid rediscovery of this substantial piece.

The earliest of these miscellaneous instrumental works is the *pas-redoublé* (literally double quick time). The manuscript is dated 1 October 1840 and this work is scored for military band. The title page states that this is 'no. 1' so several other pas-redoublés may have been planned. It is probable that this piece was performed after suggestions by a military band specialist since there are many alterations made to the manuscript. The *pas-redoublé* is one of Alkan's happiest and succinct compositions set in march militaire style with relative minor and tonic minor episodes and a brilliant coda.

As mentioned above the loss of Alkan's symphony severely restricts an evaluation of his large-scale compositions. This orchestral work does exist since *La France Musicale*[4] in late 1844 stated that Alkan intended to launch his 'Symphonie pour grand orchestra' but there is no review of any performance in the Parisian musical press. The *Symphonie* is not located[5] within the thirty-six manuscripts bequeathed to Alkan's brother Napoléon. Smith[6] mentions that Napoléon's great grandson Cyril Ray believes that several documents and manuscripts by Alkan were deposited with his grandmother Emma Christina (1879–1954) who was Napoléon's wife. Macdonald[7] considers that Emma may have hidden the manuscript of this symphony and other works during the invasion of France in 1940. Kreutzer's enthusiastic review[8] of 1846 is sufficiently tantalizing to wish that the *Symphonie* might reappear.

According to Kreutzer it would appear that Alkan's *Symphonie* was a four movement work with a moderate allegro first movement in four time. The B minor opening motif is 'all pervasive' (perhaps in the manner of Beethoven's *Fifth Symphony*). The second (slow) movement apparently had an extremely interesting, perhaps bizarre effect where flutes, clarinets and bassoons remain on a held note while various strings play the theme, interrupting one another. The trio in Alkan's symphony seems (again according to Kreutzer) to have found inspiration from Mozart's *Symphony no. 39* since 'the clarinet phrase which forms the trio is accompanied by strings (alternately viola and 'cello)'. The mood of Kreutzer, a leading *RGM* critic, reflects that of current practice in *c*1850 France that is of promoting and favouring Beethoven as a yardstick for composers. Kreutzer chides Alkan therefore for not employing Beethoven's 'fantastic orchestral effects'. In Kreutzer's view Alkan seems to have had melodic inventiveness problems for the finale although his technical skill in the development is never in doubt.

Even on this slender information the loss of Alkan's symphony must be regretted and its absence means an incomplete picture of the history of the symphony in France in the nineteenth century.[9] From the limited review provided by Kreutzer Alkan's symphony may be the natural successor to the symphonies of Gossec and Méhul which are also strongly structured and colourfully orchestrated. So Alkan's symphony seems to be firmly centred in the classical *ancien régime* era rather than the self-expressive, romantic Berliozian world of post-1830s France.

The remaining instrumental music discussed here includes a fragment of a string quartet and a recently discovered piano work. The report of other chamber works such as quintets and sextets for strings by Ortigue[10] in 1847 is frustrating since none of these works have as yet come to light. It is likely these manuscripts are located alongside the *Symphonie*. But the fragment of just six bars of a string quartet signed to his colleague P Cavallo 12 June 1846 gives sufficient impression of a composer well skilled in string sonorities, textures and motivic dynamism.

Finally, Alkan's most individual features such as intense and evocative impressions, melancholy yet touching melodies and pungent yet surprising harmonic turns are to be found in a work only discovered[11] in 1991. Dedicated to a Mme Louise, the manuscript is dated 7 July 1854. 1854 was a rather fallow year for Alkan's compositional activity but this work for piano solo *Les Regrets de la Nonnette* (*the regrets of the young nun*) is classic mature Alkan and looks forward to techniques in the esquisses (1861). There is similar subtle voicing in thirds and sixths, piquant false harmonic relations, neatly turned modulations and a brilliant tonic major coda which turns towards the tonic minor for a most delicate ending. Although bell effects feature in many of his other piano works, in *Les Regrets* the imitations are perfectly integrated into the piece's ternary structure. *Les Regrets* inhabits the subtle rhythmic and modal world of Chopin's mazurkas. From the marking 'dolce flebile' at the start of the piece it might be deduced that Alkan's quasi-mazurka might invoke the ballrooms which the young girl of the title abandoned for the monastic life. Overall, *Les Regrets* is exquisite, vintage Alkan and would make an ideal encore work to an all-Alkan recital or indeed any piano recital.

Chapter 12

Reception

Any study nowadays of Alkan as composer and pianist would be incomplete without an analysis of the critical response to his music and performances. The reception area will be mainly centred around the nineteenth century although the case study of the *Concerto* op 39 will serve to survey the reception shift during the twentieth century of a representative Alkanian work.

Broadly speaking, Alkan's compositions and performances of other composers and his own music have evoked the widest range of reception from the highly negative to the enthusiastic in France and elsewhere. Most nineteenth-century critical writing about Alkan tends to centre around the genre compositions: the op 15 *Morceaux* (by Schumann and Liszt and Blanchard) and the op 31 *Preludes* (by Fétis). The works considered today to be the high points in Alkan's output namely the op 33 *Quatre Ages Sonata*, the op 35 and op 39 *Études*, the op 76 *Études*, the op 47 *Violoncello Sonata*, the op 61 *Sonatine* and the op 63 *Esquisses* received scant attention by critics in the nineteenth century. But we turn first to two major composers' views of an Alkan work.

The composer's approach: reception of Alkan's op 15

Schumann and Liszt's reception of these pieces are especially valuable since their writings represent the only evaluation of Alkan by major romantic composer-critics. The reception by these two composers could not differ more strongly: Schumann's critique is terse, general and dismissive whereas that of Liszt is lengthy, detailed and approving. After a jibe at the limitations of Gallic culture Schumann proceeds:

> … one is startled by such false, unnatural art. Liszt caricatures intellectually; in spite of his occasional aberrations, Berlioz has a human heart; he is a voluptuary full of strength and daring; but here we find little more than weakness and unimaginative triviality.[1]

So in placing Alkan below Liszt and Berlioz (two of Schumann's least favourite composers) Schumann effectively rates Alkan as worthless. Furthermore, Schumann is puzzled by the lack of any performance directions in the score of op 15. Realizing the importance of imitation in music in France in op 15/1 *Aime- moi* Schumann accuses Alkan of irrelevance to the title. Also, Schumann dislikes Alkan's borrowing of a chromatic idea of Beethoven's *Seventh Symphony* for Le Vent (op 15/2): unlike Blanchard[2] Schumann dismissed the directly mimetic value of *Le Vent*. Schumann in reviewing op 15 displays a lack of understanding of Alkan's musical aims: everything Alkan represents through the op 15 set is *ipso facto* bereft of talent.

The Lisztian approach is much more sympathetic in its understanding of Alkan's 'wirkung' (effect). The musical processes in op 15 are also much more carefully considered through a positive and imaginative approach. After a rather rambling introduction in romantic nature/wanderer/isolation mode, Liszt seems impressed by 'this mark of sympathy from an artist of both soul and intelligence'.[3] In complete contrast to the strictural vacuity of Schumann's remarks, the op 15 pieces according to Liszt were:

> ... read and re-read many a time since the day when they brought me such great joy. These are compositions which could not be more distinguished and, all friendly prejudice aside, are likely to excite the deep interest of musicians.

Liszt debates whether the three pieces of op 15 are connected pointing to the reprise of a fragment of op 15/1 at the end of op 15/3 as evidence. Alkan's op 15 are technically skilled too: 'taken singly, each one of them forms a complete whole in which the principal motive skilfully managed developed with wisdom always dominates the abundant subsidiary melodies'.

Liszt unlike Schumann is detailed on modulations and harmonies quoting verbatim pages and bar numbers. Liszt is indeed most eloquent on the 'wirkung' element in op 15/2 and op 15/3. Temperamentally the wild romanticism of *Le Vent* op 15/2 is very much to his taste and Liszt finds in it rather more eloquent effects than either Schumann's complaint about artifice or Blanchard's 'whistling of the wind' imitation. Liszt continues:

> ... We do not know whether M. Alkan has intentionally omitted to emphasise the main notes which form the melody ... or whether this is a simple copyist's error ...

Liszt in fact was fond of indicating main melody notes with emphasis and/or longer notes (see chromatic passages in his second *Ballade* for example) but the overall notational criticism is certainly constructive. In short, Liszt's review of op 15/3 (*Morte*) is filled with phrases of critical empathy. Like his reviews of the other pieces the review of *Morte* is quite detailed and technical in its approach:

> Op15/3 opens with the plainsong of the *Dies Irae* ... followed by some lines of recitative 'pathétique'. Next comes a gloomy and lugubrious song low down in the bass accompanied a little more distantly by the triplet chords in the left hand and by the repeated Bs in the right hand which toll like the knell of the dying. These three pages, in the same way as the following ones in which the new theme is presented in octaves by the left hand are in some way the introduction to the presto finale whose plan is like that of many finales of sonatas with the exception of the last two pages in which the second half of the *Dies Irae* and several bars of the first caprice return.

Liszt does not however approve of Alkan's op 15 unreservedly. Unlike Schumann who scatters destructive criticism everywhere, Liszt delays censure until the end of his review:

> [*Morte*] contains very beautiful things but it seemed to me that M. Alkan was too unconcerned with detail. The transition passages thrown as bridge from one idea to

another (p 45 lines 3, 4, 5 and pages 46 and 47 lines 6, 7 etc) are a bit careless. One sees that the author considers them as being of minor importance ...

Liszt's final criticism (noted also by Schumann) is Alkan's omission of signs for speeds, nuances and expression.

In essence, Liszt's challenge to the contemporary reader is surprisingly formalistic through his discussion albeit brief of elements and structure. Schumann, on the other hand, remains lodged in a world of imitation, antipathy and stylistic dislocation. With the exception of the views of Fétis on Alkan's op 31, most of the reception writings are rather less intensively considered.

Without doubt French critical writing on Alkan revolves around *La France Musicale* (*LFM*) and *Revue et Gazette Musicale* (*RGM*) in the early part of the century and, almost exclusively, around the *RGM* in the second half of the century. Both journals reflect the audience expectation of an artist and both aim to provide general musical instruction. It would be tedious however to catalogue every minor journalistic review of Alkan's compositions or pianistic style so an overview will be undertaken here. Neutrally enlightened data collection has limitations. But with the popular 'pièce d'occasion' piano works of Alkan reception history can point up larger social issues around these works and, additionally, can trace where the compositions themselves may vanish. This seems to be the process involved in the 1830's: 'audience-centred' works rather than in the 1860's 'composer-centred' music. A good starting point then in reception history for Alkan is precisely this shift in musical repertoire and performance through the contemporary literature from the 1830's to the 1860's.

Journal reception of Alkan the pianist and composer

As alluded to earlier, indubitably Alkan's most popular piano work up to the mid century was the *Saltarelle* op 23. In rapid 6/8 time and étude-like in its brilliant fingerwork it was premiered in 1844. It is canonic with Mendelssohn's example in his 'Italian' symphony. At the première of op 23 Alkan was obliged by public demand to repeat the piece. Described as the 'most poetic and original composition'[4] several other pianists took up this piece including Josephine Martin whose brilliant performance of op 23 was 'interrupted at each reprise with frantic applause'.[5] Journalistic criticism therefore mirrored audience evaluation but perhaps nowadays we view op 23 as rather superficial and not at all original or poetic!

The earliest source of French critical opinion on Alkan is to be found in the *Revue Musicale* (1827–1835). Fétis, its chief editor, contributed several important reviews about Alkan's music. Earliest amongst these is his review of a concert rondo by Alkan (possibly op 4). Alkan's musical precocity was observed:

... one noticed in particular a concert rondo for piano with orchestra composed and performed by the young bénéficiare with an energy and perfection ... there are many fine things in his rondo and one did not suspect that this was the work of a child.[6]

In Alkan's early reviews the fusion of composer-pianist or pianist-composer is always noted. But the *Revue* was highly critical of mere Gallic brilliance:

> in a brilliant rondo [op 3] ... Alkan showed that his fingers are also strong, brilliant and agile, but that is all ... of style or expression, nothing. Perhaps this will come later: let us wait until his heart speaks.

This is a typical reaction of Fétis to the young pianist-composer. Unlike Chopin whose inherent expression was commented upon by all the French critics including those in the *RGM*, Alkan was never credited with Chopin's 'sensuous distinctiveness', Rose Subotnik's memorable later phrase. It is now well established that several French composers were marginalized at the expense of others: this is the case with Alkan. Compared to Chopin, Alkan represented even at this stage a straightforward brilliant child virtuoso. The ideal of the romantic poetic-hero was not easily projected on to him. Furthermore, Alkan's early performance and enthusiasm for Austro-Germanic music such as his performance in November 1833 of the Beethoven *Triple Concerto* was seen subtextually by the French critic as a capitulation to Germanic hegemony.[7]

Taking his lead from Fétis and his antipathy towards Beethoven, Blanchard, another leading critic of the *RGM*, understandably was dubious about Alkan's transcription (for eight hands) of the Andante from Beethoven's *Seventh Symphony*. By his focus on the problem of transferring the melodic violoncello line to the piano Blanchard projects the ideologically unsuitable nature of Beethoven for the French ideal of elegance, style and refinement. Imitation particularly of nature was always acceptable to the French critic-aesthetician though. In discussing Alkan's *Le Vent* [op 15/2] Blanchard is lyrical about its mimesis, usefulness and value:

> [*Le Vent*] is a delicious conception of descriptive music ... all the whistling of the wind is infinitely varied in the most pleasant way by M. Alkan. The piece is a first class study for the agility of the right hand and, as a composition, it combines unity of thought and harmonic richness.[8]

After 1838 Alkan abandoned the life of the piano virtuoso and devoted himself to composition. The *RGM* is silent on this subject but the *LFM* in 1844 attempted to portray an image of Alkan as a reclusive but brilliant romantic artist-hero. By denying Alkan's apprentice period *LFM* enlarges this mystique:[9] '[Alkan] who has so far refused to appear in public is fully the equal of others in performance and composition.' Reflecting audiences' taste for bravura works the journal approves the *Saltarella* [op 23] as having 'purity, nobility, melodic grace and energy'. These qualities of course are present in the dance music of the French baroque. Therefore Alkan is praised equally for maintaining a similar canonic discourse in his *Air de ballet dans le style ancien* [op 24]. The post revolutionary fervour of the *Marche funèbre* op 26/1 and *Marche héroique* op 26/1 caught the attention of the *LFM* critic also. A tribute was paid to Alkan the virtuoso for his 'power and relentless energy' and to Alkan the composer for beauty of writing which would 'satisfy the most exacting of composers'.[10]

By 1844 the *RGM* returned to comment on Alkan the pianist and the composer.[11] Unlike the *LFM*, the *RGM*'s criticism centred around Alkan's elitist non-populist stance. By blaming him for being regressive, 'finicky' and choosing too 'academic a programme for a public concert', Alkan's preservation of the glories of French baroque music was acknowledged but his originality was questioned. The *RGM* in short demanded originality and mass popularity, modernism, romanticism and overt expressiveness. Alkan's performance of the Viennese classics according to the *RGM* contained the necessary classicism but did not have the requisite feeling. Equally the unconventional form-building structures and the introverted macabre nature of the *Trois Morceaux* op 15 left the reviewer baffled. Liszt and Schumann presented very different opinions on op 15 but their views are clearly and forcefully expressed. The *LFM* journal seemed equally attracted to classicism. In 1846 *LFM* announced with some delight that Alkan had composed several chamber compositions in classical form.[12] These included sextets, quintets and a trio. The latter would be a second trio, the first being the op 30 piano trio published in 1841. The journal also remarked on the existence of a symphony: this we may presume to be the *Symphony for orchestra* of 1844 now lost, but Kreutzer's outline is discussed in Chapter 11.

By mid-century therefore the critics of both the *RGM* and *LFM* made considerable objective judgements on the composer and aesthetic opinions on his work were powerfully stated. Recent reception theorists such as Feyerabend draw clear distinctions between objectivist and relativist views: the relativist does not need to arbitrate say between the views of the *RGM* and *LFM*. The *RGM* in 1846 considers the relativist view of the isolated artist and the problems of the public eager for novelty.

The period 1838 to 1847 marked a significant reception shift in the evaluation of Alkan by the *RGM*. By 1847 the *RGM* is considerable more relativist in its reception of the op 26 and op 27 *Marches*. In the light of the 1844 comments, the *LFM*'s reception of these marches now is aesthetics-based: 'in [op 26] the colours were sombre and sounds painfully solemn'. [Op 27] had a 'radiant sonority and a brilliant tread of a proud victorious rhythm.' Alkan, now according to the *RGM* in 1847, showed greatness of pianism and originality and intelligence in composition.[13] This originality was manifested of course in the op 33 *Sonata* and 12 *Études* op 35 published in 1847 but not reviewed in either the *RGM* or *LFM*.

Alkan's artistry had been reinforced by Kreutzer's long article in the *RGM* in 1846. This is an extremely important landmark in the reception of Alkan's attitudes, playing, compositions and choice of repertoire. Kreutzer maintains that artists such as Alkan: 'became rather disgusted with a public ... [obsessed] ... with the banal and the stereotype [but] they continue none the less to perfect their own works ...'.[14] Yet the pursuit of reclusivity in order to intensify their compositions might lead to too much restraint. Kreutzer links this tendency to Alkan's 'fondness for the old piano school, noble majestic and strict'. Alkan had written an extensive preface regarding the revival of baroque masters in piano transcription in the *Souvenirs des Concerts du Conservatoire* in 1847. Kreutzer chides Alkan for austerity:

... a Bach fugue is a wonder of genius to an educated artist, but the uninitiated find nothing in it but an inextricable network of patterns ... M. Alkan ought therefore to be exceedingly circumspect in deciding which pieces to play in concerts ... .

Kreutzer goes on to suggest to Alkan that he might play the Bach *Le départ d'un ami*. The concert-going public would presumably be more receptive to its mimetic nature.

But Kreutzer seems well pleased with the op 21 *Duo Concertante* composed in 1840. 'Wirkung' elements are emphasized in the review:

The allegro is treated in a severe and grandiose manner. The adagio bears the title 'L'Enfer'. It begins with a series of chords, low down on the piano, strange chords which, by the introduction of an inner pedal seem to float amidst unknown and mysterious tonalities. Shortly after, the violin has a melody both plaintive and impassioned which is the sad cry of a desolate, wandering soul.

Kreutzer thinks that Alkan had been inspired by the Scheffer painting of the same title in the Louvre. He continues: 'the rondo finale of the sonata abounds in piquant effects and varied rhythms'. Kreutzer's overall judgement of this work is positive and enthusiastic.

Another most important article on the reception history of Alkan is the 1847 Fétis *RGM* critical review[15] of the *Preludes* op 31 which poses a reader response criticism and also attempts an overview of the affective stylistics of the music. Fétis is methodical in the latter carefully dissecting each prelude. This discussion is preceded by a learned, if rather conservative, discussion about Alkan's audacity in using unprepared dissonances. But throughout his writing on the *Preludes* Fétis praises Alkan's 'thought and feeling'. The suitability of medium of performance (piano or organ) is considered in relation to each piece's character. Many of Fétis's comments relate to Alkan's dreaminess and melancholic nature (the letter was particularly evident in nos 16, 17 and 18). He especially commends the originality of no. 7, the *Song of the Mad Woman on the Shore* and the heartfelt intensity of no. 13 the *Song of Songs*. Fétis reveals himself to have fixed ideas on what a prelude should be and only Alkan's no. 11 (in fugal style) seems to fulfil his criteria. Moreover Alkan's miniature forms irritate Fétis despite the composer's ingenuity and originality. It is surprising therefore that the *RGM* neglected to review Alkan's op 33 *Sonata* or op 35 *Études* both published in 1847. Both works are highly original but are beyond the pianistic capabilities of most of the *RGM*'s readers.

Two years later in 1849 the *RGM*'s critic Blanchard supported and encouraged Alkan. Blanchard praised Alkan's progressive attitude as an artist and also affirmed his compositional discipline: '[Alkan] maintains the strict rules of the art of writing music.' This systematic academicism was Blanchard's response to Alkan's retiral from the concert platform from 5 May 1849 at the Salle Erard. This was an auspicious occasion where the audience included several distinguished artists such as Meyerbeer and Delacroix. Blanchard is a most important reception figure of Parisian musical life and from 1849 to 1858 he was the *RGM*'s chief critic of nineteenth-century music. From a general reading of Blanchard's reviews it is clear that his musical sympathies were more progressive than previous *RGM* critics. For

Blanchard however the *sine qua non* was a thorough grounding in musical technique based on the classics. Hence he naturally praised Alkan's faithful transcription and performance of several excerpts from the symphonies of Haydn and Mozart and the *Chorus of Scythians* from Gluck's *Iphigenia en Tauride*.

In the same concert Alkan also played a baroque concerto, the allegro [first movement] from J.S. Bach's *D minor Concerto* accompanied by some distinguished Parisian string players Alard, Armingaud, Casimir, Ney and Chevillard. Alkan was singled out by Blanchard for having 'energy ... delicacy and gradation of sound ... to the highest degree in ... fullness, volume and sensitivity ... that rare gift based on the art of singing and of stirring the emotions on this instrument'. From other Blanchard reviews of the period one gathers that he valued the expression of emotion within a classical structure when judging a composition or a performer. Yet Blanchard was not averse to novelties of timbre in contemporary music and/or instruments. Alkan's *Air à cinque temps* and the *Marche Triomphal* op 27 were praised for presenting 'all the splendours of rich and grandiose harmony, plus all the effects and contrasts of the most brilliant sonority of an Erard piano'.[16]

By 1852 the *RGM* had broadened its musical scope to include some polemical articles by Alkan on the subject of irregular rhythms.[17] The *RGM* as also discussed earlier reflected Wagnermania in France and reaction to this composer.[18] During the 1850's there were no reviews of Alkan's important larger scale works. His retirement from the concert platform in 1849 probably resulted from his confrontations with Marmontel, the low standard of musical taste and political instabilities in general. The *RGM* neglected Alkan's talents as composer and pianist during this era.

When Botte replaced Blanchard in 1862 as concert reviewer of the *RGM* an encouraging note was sounded: 'two pianists C.V. Alkan and Henri Ravina have for a long time unfortunately renounced the acclaim of the public'.[19] Ravina was also a student of Zimmermann but like Alkan was unsympathetic to the mid-century music ethos in France. The *RGM* from 1862 to 1873 was silent on the subject of Alkan, and during this period as noted earlier Alkan busied himself with an intense correspondence with Hiller and, of course with composition and teaching.

The *RGM* broke its silence[20] on information about Alkan in 1873 with the news about his return to the concert life with the start of the series of Petits Concerts. The tone of the *RGM* towards Alkan at this point is full of respect and gravitas, as by this point he was regarded as a composer-pianist (not a pianist-composer) of the greatest talent, learning, accuracy and restraint.[21] Reception for Alkan was restricted to an exclusive group of fellow artists. He was now ranked as an artist for connoisseurs who thirty years ago had shunned the sentimental and the popular in music.[22] The *RGM* now applauded Alkan's championing of first class-music and looked forward to receiving more music of the highest standard.

The enthusiastic reception of Alkan's own music and his pianistic insights increased over the series of Petits Concerts and from the reviews from 1873 to 1880 there is a marked trend for ever-growing respect for this most aristocratic of French composers and pianists. We now need to investigate the type of repertoire and performance approach to his chosen repertoire which brought him this acclaim.

Repertoire choice in the Petits Concerts

First we are restricted in an analysis of repertoire reception by the lack of a complete documentation of Alkan's concert life. Press notices rarely included full details of every Petits Concert from their inception in 1873 to their conclusion in 1880, and, in many cases, the notices are woefully incomplete as to details of works performed.

Nevertheless, several broad trends emerge regarding Alkan's repertoire choice in the Petits Concerts. Each concert contained at least one substantial baroque work (of French or German origin) and a classical work of substantial proportions. The rest of the programme comprised favoured romantic composers particularly Schubert, Schumann and Mendelssohn. Liszt and Brahms were significantly excluded. Several of Alkan's own compositions were played but not complete performances of the étude set or sonatas. The historic first concert[23] of the 1875 season significantly contained a phenomenal range of piano music including works by Couperin, Scarlatti, Rameau, Handel, J.S. Bach, W.F. Bach, Clementi, Mozart, Moscheles, Field, Weber, Czerny, Schubert, Mendelssohn, Chopin and Schumann. The *RGM* critic was clearly impressed by the stylistic performance of this wide range of composers: 'all the pieces were played with profound intuition ... with a constant awareness of style ...'.[24] A later review in the *RGM* in 1875 points to Alkan's ability to penetrate a composer's thought without performer exaggeration.[25] Alkan's performances were deemed to be recreations of the original score. This special quality had been commented upon earlier by Blanchard who after hearing Alkan's transcription of Gluck's *Jamais de ses beaux lieux* from Armide declared: '[this is] a model of how our ancient scores can be paraphrased'.[26] Reviews of Alkan's performances of other works were less definitive, but a very broad picture of his repertoire, his performance of this repertoire and the critical response from his early concert life to the Petits Concerts can emerge. This is summarized by the statement in 1877 where the critic of the *RGM* was moved to write: '[this is] the history of piano music reinvented under the digits of M. Alkan of the most characteristic of all the eras and masters from Couperin to Schumann'.[27]

Baroque repertoire and reception

Alkan did not rediscover and perform French clavecin music until the initiation of the Petits Concerts. The opening concert of the first series in 1873 contained works by Rameau and the historic opening concert of the 1875 series included Couperin's *La Fine Madelon* and Rameau's *Les Sauvages*. Equally, Alkan's enthusiasm for the tradition of French tragédie-lyrique is shown by his excellent transcriptions of Gluck's *Jamais dans ces beaux lieux* (*Armide*) and the *Choeur des Scythes* (*Iphigenie en Tauride*). The former transcription's merit has already been mentioned. The *Tauride* item was picked out for special mention by the *RGM* critic in Alkan's first concert of the 1874 series[28] and this work was equally popular with audiences since it was encored at the 1875 second concert[29] and it excited the audience to vigorous applause at the first of the 1877 series.[30] The Gluck transcriptions had the 'greatest effect' at the first of his final 1880 concerts. Other baroque composers performed, although somewhat less frequently, were Scarlatti and Handel. Scarlatti features of course in the historic opening 1875 concert[31] in the shape of a vivace and also in the second of the 1874 concerts as 'various pieces'.[32] Handel is represented by Alkan's version of a minuet and passacaglia in the last of the 1873 and 1877 concerts. The vigorous *Choeur des prêtres de Dagon* from *Samson* was performed at the fifth of the 1877 series and the more esoteric medium of Handel's fugue and passacaglia were presented at the 1880 series (last concert).[33]

Of all baroque composers Bach was Alkan's chief passion. In mid-century Alkan tended to perform the concertos or chamber sonatas reserving the solo works for the Petits Concerts. So for example we find the D minor keyboard concerto being performed with string quintet in 1849[34] and in 1853 the Bach triple keyboard concerto was played.[35] Also the Petits Concerts abound with examples of Bach's solo keyboard or organ transcribed pédalier works. Alkan's performance repertory included the [48 Book 1?] C minor fugue at the 1873 series second concert.[36] The pédalier offered Alkan the chance to make the organ music more widely known to French audiences. Chorales feature at the 1874 second concert[37] and at the 1877 concerts[38,39] (5th and 6th concert). Named chorales performed included the *Schumücke dich* and *L'étoile du matin* in the last of the 1875 series[40] and the *Pleure ô morte* chorale in the very last concert in 1880.[41] But organ (pédalier) fugues dominate Alkan's performances of Bach. In 1877 the *RGM* remarked on Alkan's performance of the Bach D minor fugue [BWV 565?] as having 'a vigorous and exact performance style and M. Alkan produced a great impression'.[42] An examination of the 1875 series shows this D minor fugue and the G minor fugue [BWV 542?] being performed. The latter fugue was repeated in performance in the first of the 1878 series[43] and provided the contrapuntal energy in the final of the 1880 series.[44]

Classical repertoire and reception

Of the three major classical keyboard composers Haydn, Mozart and Beethoven, Haydn was the composer least performed. The low status accorded to Haydn's piano music in nineteenth-century France is reflected by the omission of the details of the Haydn keyboard works played by Alkan at the fifth concert of the 1873 series.[45] Equally in the 1875 historic series Haydn merely features as last item in the fifth concert as an andante [presumably a pedal piano transcription from the 1847 *Souvenirs* series]. Mozart's piano music was much more extensively featured in the Petits Concerts. Before this concert series Alkan had performed the *Andante of the C major sonata* [K521?] for four hands[46] in 1845. Piano duet music of Mozart continued to interest Alkan for the 1873 series since he performed[47] the Mozart *Fantasie* with Saint-Saëns, and in 1875 (sixth concert) a duet sonata [unspecified] took pride of place as the opening work in the programme. As for the solo works of Mozart, Alkan was most attracted to the dramatic *A minor sonata K310* playing two movements from this sonata at the fifth 1873 concert[48] and the first movement of the same sonata at the opening concert of the 1875 series. As a composer Alkan probably saw this piece on its own terms. His interpretation was likely then to be intelligent, rigorous and thoughtful. The *RGM* reviewer was respectful but somewhat reserved in his admiration for Alkan's interpretation:

> ... may we dare to search out a little problem with M. Alkan over his interpretation of the first movement of the Mozart A minor Sonata? He has perhaps dramatized and modernized it rather much. The development does contain several really dramatic effects ... but the effect of this section would be greater if the theme was played more simply and if the feeling was more restrained up to this point ...[49]

The reviewer clearly had a more conservative eighteenth-century view of Mozartian interpretation. But one has the impression that the first movement of *K310* inspired Alkan's dramatic style in such works as the *Sonatine* op 61. Himmelfarb[50] also points out a resonant relationship between these two works.

As briefly discussed earlier Beethoven's music had mixed reception in France: Ellis's recent work has enlarged the early but magisterial study of Beethoven in France by Schrade.[51] Alkan's public repertoire of Beethoven's piano music was not extensive. Performances of the largest sonatas were very rare indeed. An exception was the complete performance by Liszt of the *Hammerklavier Sonata* in Paris in 1836 which drew the following reactions from Berlioz writing in the *Gazette Musicale*: 'Liszt, in thus making comprehensible a work not yet comprehended has proved that he is the pianist of the future.'[52] So Liszt's position was that of a radical: Alkan's position at least in the 1840's was more conservative and he obviously was unwilling to court public unpopularity by performing a whole Beethoven sonata. But in 1844 Parisian audiences would accept classical rondos and variations, therefore Alkan could perform[53] a rondo from Beethoven op 31 *Sonatas* [probably op 31/1] with the confidence of audience comprehension of this work. He reserved the greater listening and understanding demands of the slow movement from the op 10/3 *Sonata* for the more rarefied audience of artists for the 1875 Petits Concerts (second concert). His performance drew much praise for artistry from the *RGM* critic.[54] The same work was performed at the first 1877 concert series. The *RGM* critic again especially commended Alkan's exquisite interpretation of this work.

Some Beethoven sonatas were performed complete at the Petits Concerts. Unlike Liszt, Alkan favoured the op 109 and op 110 sonatas rather than the *Hammerklavier*. The gentle op 110 sonata was part of the opening and closing concerts of the 1873 season.[55,56] In the third and fifth concerts of the 1875 series Alkan played both the op 109 and op 110 sonatas which according to the critic 'without exaggeration was a real recreation'.[57] In the fourth concert of 1877 Alkan again performed op 110 to critical acclaim. His interpretation had 'a nobility of style and real feeling known to us from this eminent artist'.[58] The same sonata featured in the final 1880 series first concert[59] and his performance was again commended for its impressive stylistic awareness. One of the op 2 sonatas was played at the first of the 1874 series.[60] A smaller Beethoven piano work the op 77 *Fantasie* was played twice at the Petits Concerts, at the second 1875 concert[61] 'played with real originality' and at the fourth of the 1877 concerts.[62] In short compared with his public romantic repertoire, the range of Beethoven works played by Alkan is very restricted.

Romantic repertoire and reception

As might be expected from an examination of the *RGM* programmes and reviews it is romantic works which proliferate in Alkan's public repertoire. But the composer was highly selective in his choice. He programmed the more concert-like études of Heller, Clementi, Schmitt, and Mendelssohn and Moscheles in the 1873 season. But Alkan's austerity in romantic repertoire met critical disfavour. On programming a minuet by Schubert and a fugue by Mendelssohn in 1844 Alkan was accused of being rather 'finicky and old fashioned in style'.[63] Critical reception obviously mirrored audience reception in considering these works to be 'too dryly academic for a public concert'. Schubert and Mendelssohn along with Hummel, Field, Weber, Schumann and Chopin were Alkan's favourite romantic composers. In his later concerts, given the reception shift for all these composers, all Alkan's performances of these composers were warmly applauded by the critics. But as we shall see there is still a little critical bemusement at some of the more esoteric of these romantic piano works in the 1873–1880 concerts.

Of all the German romantic sonatas played in the Petits Concerts the 1875 performance of Schubert's *G major Sonata D894* [op 78] attracted Alkan most. Perhaps he had taken cognisance of Schumann's view that this is Schubert's 'most perfect sonata in form and spirit with everything organic although the finale should be avoided by those without the imagination to solve riddles'.[64] Newman reminds us that nearly half of Schubert's sonatas were available in Richault's 'collection complète'.[65] Alkan's decision to play all of *D894* at the second of the 1875 series provoked incomprehension from the *RGM* critic regarding its proportions:

> [Alkan's] programme [started] with the sonata op 78 of Schubert which is rarely played because of its length – the first movement, very much developed, behaves like an orchestral not a piano work and the entire sonata lasts for not less than half an hour.[66]

In complete contrast is Alkan's choice of Schubert's *Variations for piano duet* op 35 [*D813*] 'which are concise and more amenable to audience reception'. These were performed with Mlle Massart at the fifth concert of the 1873 season.[67] Various Schubert pieces were performed during the 1874 series (second concert) and during the survey first concert[68] of 1875. This included a 'Pensée musicale' [presumably a moment musicale]. During the 1877 season third concert[69] Alkan devoted the whole of the first part to Schubert's music. Perhaps he took heed of the uncongenial 1875 review of *D894* because on this occasion he only performed movements from the *Sonata*, along with the ubiquitous *Marche Militaire* in D major transcribed by Alkan for pédalier. Some Schubert lieder were performed by Mme Hamon including *Thekla* and one of the *Schöne Mullerin* songs, both presumably sung in French. Interestingly the *D984* sonata extracts were passed over for criticism but the March was 'warmly applauded'. The *RGM* continues:

> ... the really original (!) march for four hands in D which M. Alkan played ... on the pedal piano. Berlioz who cannot support four handed piano music because he says, two pianists can never be perfectly together, would doubtlessly be satisfied with this adaptation which M. Alkan played in a manner which conquered the greatest difficulties.

The model for Alkan's set of *Chants* was, as has been stated, Mendelssohn's *Lied ohne Worte*. Several other [unnamed] Mendelssohn piano pieces featured in the fourth concert[70] of 1873 and the first of 1874.[71] For the 1875 historic concert[72] Alkan chose a Mendelssohn *Étude in F minor* [1836] and for the second concert[73] in 1875 a *Fantasie in A minor* [op 16/1]. In concert six[74] of 1875 Mendelssohn was performed in both halves of the concert. The more demanding fifth prelude and fugue [in F minor] was played in the first half, a more relaxed 'romance sans paroles' in the second. A Mendelssohn fugue [possibly in F minor] was played in the second[75] of the 1877 series. The 1878 series only featured Mendelssohn in the first concert[76] but the final series of 1880 included a Presto scherzando in F sharp minor [op 26] in the second concert and a fugue in the final one.

Alkan's interest in Hummel seems to have been restricted to the B minor concerto. This work was performed[77] from the 1830's right up to the Petits Concerts of the 1875 season (the complete 1875 programme). Field's piano music also found some favour with Alkan. He performed pieces by Field in the first concert[78] of 1878, Field's *Romance in B flat minor* was selected for the 1875 first programme, and the C minor nocturne for the 1874 sixth concert.[79] Alkan's musical acuity towards this music was well expressed in an 1878 *RGM* review: 'at the piano M. Alkan maintains an exquisite style: in the manner of phrasing, a certain delicacy of touch which is difficult to express'.[80]

Weber's piano music was an important ingredient of many romantic pianists' recitals. Often single movements were selected by Alkan such as the finale of the C major sonata performed in the April concert of 1844. This clearly would have demonstrated Alkan's virtuosity in passage work and scales. But the rather bolder more classical-like scherzo of the *A flat Sonata* was performed in the first[81] 1875 concert. The same [?] scherzo and a polonaise [*Polacca brillante* 1819?] was played in the 1874 season [second concert].[82] The *Polonaise* in E flat major featured in the second[83] of the 1875 concerts, in a performance in which Alkan rediscovered 'a momentum often distorted [by other players]'. The very effective *Filles de la mer* chorus from Oberon transcribed for pédalier, the polonaise in E flat major, the minuet [scherzo] of the second sonata and the rondo of the E flat major concerto in the Bülow piano solo version were the substantial items in the fourth Petit Concert of 1877 devoted to Beethoven and Weber. The reviewer found Alkan's performances virtually flawless praising his rhythmic accuracy especially in the polonaise:

> ... the Oberon chorus effectively and simply transcribed gave great pleasure. We like rather less the caprice in the minuetto of the second sonata, but that is a matter of taste and does not need further discussion. As for the E flat major polonaise we are delighted to hear a virtuoso performing the second note in every reappearance of the theme with the value given to it by the composer ... .[84]

Finally, it is instructive to examine the repertory of Schumann and Chopin chosen by Alkan in his recitals and the reception of Alkan's performances of these chosen pieces. Schumann's pedal piano pieces featured in the fourth concert[85] of 1873. The medium of performance and Alkan's expertise in pedal piano performance was praised:

Several of the fine works of Schumann suit the pédalier or were written especially for it. Is it not desirable that more pianists should devote themselves to this type of work? ... Alkan's authority [on the pédalier] is that of a master ... .

No large-scale Schumann works were performed complete by Alkan in any of his concerts: perhaps he was concerned about the critical reaction to the length of Schumann's larger piano works particularly after the reception of the *D894* sonata. At the second concert of 1875 therefore only the opening piece of *Kreisleriana* was performed along with the brief *Romance* [op 28]. At the final concert of 1873 the *Esquisses* [*Sketch* op 58] was performed on the pedal piano and the reviewer complemented[86] Alkan for bringing to his notice a wide range of pedal piano compositions including those by Schumann. One of the *Fantasie* op 111 pieces was included in the 1875 first concert[87] and the pedal piano featured again in the Schumann canon [op 56] played at the fifth concert[88] of the 1875 season.

Alkan reserved a large part of 1877's last concert for Schumann's solo and chamber music performing the *A minor violin sonata* [op 105] pieces for clarinet and viola [*Märchenerzählungen* op 132?] and two sketches for pedal piano [op 58]. The other pieces of various titles were played 'with a great deal of charm'.[89] The reviewer had slight reservations about the performance, of the violin sonata which was taken a 'little too slowly'. More pédalier pieces from op 56 by Schumann were performed at the third[90] 1878 concert. Schumann also featured in the very last season of the Petits Concerts in 1880. Various unnamed Schumann works were performed in the first 1880 concert and some Schumann canons for pedal piano were part of the final[91] concert.

Along with his interpretation of Schumann's music Alkan's insights into Chopin's piano music receive much critical attention. His relationship with Chopin and his stylistic indebtedness to him has been mentioned elsewhere. From the recital handbills and press reviews we can make some insightful remarks regarding Alkan's choice of repertoire and his mode of interpretation. On surveying the Petits Concerts we find this pattern:

1873 – first concert[92]	Études
1873 – fourth concert[93]	Fantasie [op 49]
1873 – final concert[94]	Sonata op 35 (Largo)
1874 – first concert[95]	Three preludes
1875 – first concert[96]	Polonaise op 26
1875 – third concert[97]	Nocturne in C minor [handbill]
	Two preludes [review]
1875 – fourth concert[98]	Second Sonata [op 35] [handbill]
	Mazurka and first Ballade [handbill]
1875 – sixth concert[99]	Mazurka (F minor)
	Third Ballade
1877 – first concert[100]	Nocturne in C minor op 48/1
1877 – third concert[101]	Third Ballade
	Second Sonata [presumably complete]

1877 – fifth concert[102]	Second Sonata [Largo only]
	Fantasie op 49
	First Ballade
1878 – third concert[103]	Allegro de concert op 46
1880 – second concert[104]	Mazurka [F minor?]
	Third Ballade
1880 – final concert[105]	Mazurka [F minor?]
	Fourth Ballade

There are some discrepancies between the works advertised on the 1875 handbill and the works reviewed in 1875, but overall Alkan's choice of Chopin shows a marked tendency towards large structures such as sonatas, fantasies, ballades and the allegro de concert of which the latter is effectively a compressed solo concerto. From similar evidence of reviews and handbills smaller works feature much less prominently and there are no salon works (for example, waltzes) programmed. What was said about Alkan's interpretation of Chopin? The general statement made in the 1873 fourth concert about Alkan's interpretation was applied to his Chopin performances: 'Alkan's playing was mainly remarkable for its qualities of style.' Later in 1873 at the final concert Alkan's Chopin interpretation was characterized by 'sobre style and nobility'. And similarly in 1875, praise continued: '[everything] was played with a profound intuition for the mind of the masters with that high and constant feeling for style ...'.[106] Generally, the critics realized that Alkan had a special affinity with the world of Chopin: 'one knows that M. Alkan interprets this composer like no one else: it probably follows that [Alkan] is very close to a real and living tradition'.[107]

Undoubtedly Alkan made the Petits Concerts' audiences aware of the masterpieces of Chopin despite the fact that in 1875 some of the larger works were still thought to be inaccessible: 'the third ballade op 47 is a very difficult work which is never or hardly ever played in public. M. Alkan approached it for the first time ... the imagination of the executant was added to the imagination of the composition ...'.[108]

Alkan's interpretative ideas on this ballade provoked a detailed if minor criticism two years later: 'we have however one cavil about [Alkan's] rhythmic manner in the first bar of the ballade op 47 where the 6/8 bar was transformed by means of accents on certain notes into a four beat bar ...'.[109] Alkan's performances of Chopin otherwise evoked the highest praise: 'the largo of the second sonata, the *Fantasie* op 49 and the first ballade were played with the greatest feeling and stylistic delicacy as is always the case with M. Alkan'.[110] No other romantic composer clearly drew such unstinting commendation. One only wishes that Alkan might have produced a critical edition of Chopin's works with a commentary on interpretation.

Chamber music reception

Throughout his lifetime as a pianist Alkan placed chamber music high in priority in every recital. A trend evident however from the 1830's to 1880 is the phasing out of chamber music by genre composers in favour of music by classical and romantic masters. Another factor common to Alkan's chamber repertoire is the preponderance of string-based music. Thus we find in his first concert[111] in 1821 a performance by Alkan as violinist of the *Rode Air and variations*. Alongside solo pieces in the 1829 concert[112] in the Salle Favart, Alkan participated as accompanist in extracts from Weber's *Der Freischütz* (the overture, a vocal duet and a sextet). Four years later Alkan joined the Société Académique des Enfants d'Apollon and he retained membership of this organization until at least 1836.[113] Genre composers represented at this concert were Ries, Spohr, Moscheles and Mayseder. The latter composer's second piano trio was a popular choice of work for Alkan and he programmed it in 1835 and 1836.

As well as small ensemble chamber performances Alkan in his early virtuoso years sometimes performed concertos with chamber accompaniment. His performance of the Beethoven *Triple Concerto* in 1833 was praised for its purity and perfection of performance although Alkan's interpretation was considered to be 'a little cold'.[114] Reviewers in early-nineteenth-century French journals favoured a more romantic approach to interpretation. The virtuosity of Alkan's playing in the second Mayseder trio was much appreciated by the critic when reviewing the Urhan-Chevillard-Alkan performance in 1835: 'Alkan acquitted himself with perfection: [he makes] ... the piano sing delightfully, and it would be difficult to find more vigour, more clarity and more brilliance in which a myriad of notes fall like enchanted showers of pearls and diamonds.'[115] A second performance of the Mayreder second trio was given in the salon Pape in 1838 this time with Ernst and Batta. Blanchard of the *RGM* merely commented that the trio of players gave a 'worthy performance'.[116]

Alkan's retirement from the concert platform between 1838 and 1844 was accompanied by the composition of two of his chamber works, the op 21 *Duo Concert* in 1840 dedicated to Urhan and the op 30 *Trio* in 1841. When Alkan did emerge as concert pianist again in 1844 his choice of work[117] was the Hummel *Concerto in B minor*, a favourite work of romantic artists and this concerto remained in Alkan's repertoire right up to the Petits Concerts (see the handbill of the 1875 series fifth concert). On the other hand the allegretto movement of the Beethoven's *Seventh Symphony* for two pianos, eight hands, with Zimmerman, Pixis and Napoléon Alkan was dropped for the Petit Concert series. Alkan's performance of this work in 1845 was judged to be 'sincere and precise but lacking in musical feeling'.[118]

After 1845 baroque chamber music begins to feature in Alkan's programmes as a result of his general rediscovery of Bach prior to Pasdeloup's first Paris performance of the *St Matthew Passion* in 1868. Paris mid-century saw a rise of interest in chamber music following the direction given by Alard and Franchomme in 1835 who in 1848 founded the Quartette Alard-Franchomme. Chevillard also was an important influence in the performances of chamber music forming the Société Maurin Chevillard. Alkan in 1849 selected Alard, Chevillard as well as Armingand and Casimir Ney to provide the string accompaniment to his chamber performance of Bach's *D minor Keyboard Concerto*. Critical reception was now enthusiastic for Alkan's baroque playing, and there were no negative remarks about coldness or lack of feeling. Blanchard writes that Alkan's own playing was filled with: 'energy, delicacy [and] the gradation of sound which he possesses to the highest degree in its fullness, volume and sensitivity that rare talent on which is based the art of singing and stirring the emotions'.[119]

During the period 1849 to 1852, Alkan retreated from concert life and devoted most of his life to composition and attacks on Marmontel. On return to chamber concert life in 1853 Bach's *Concerto for three keyboards* was performed with Hiller and Tellefsen and string quintet accompaniment. The critical comment 'old fashioned in style' was again applied to this performance.[120] However, his performance later in 1853 of Beethoven's *Archduke Trio* prompted much enthusiasm.[121]

Between 1856 and 1873 there is very little information regarding Alkan's concert career: most of his time was spent on teaching and composition. His return to the concert platform for the Petits Concerts in 1873 was heralded by a statement which implied the pianist's inclusion of chamber music: 'classical music for solo piano ... or along with other instruments'.[122] The chamber works in the first concert included an unidentified allegro [first movement?] of a Handel [keyboard] concerto and the Schubert op 70 *Introduction and Rondo*. The general tone of the review is also pertinent to the chamber music performances: 'the audience, consisting mainly of artists gave the composer and virtuoso one of those warm, respectful receptions that one never forgets'.[123]

For the second programme[124] of 1873 Alkan played extracts from the two concertos by J.S. Bach for three keyboards. The other players were Delaborde and Mlle Clauzz Szarvedy. For 1873's fourth concert a Mozart *Fantasy for piano* duet was played with Saint-Saëns and the *Trio* (op 7) of Hiller along with Léonard and Franchomme. Despite the feeling that the trio was musically of 'secondary interest', Alkan's performances were adjudged to be 'remarkable for their stylistic quality'.[125] The fifth programme[126] of 1873 contained chamber music by Schubert – the *Variations for four hands* op 35 (with Mme Massart) and the last concert of the year included the Spohr *Wind Quintet*. According to the reviewer 'this is a major work but the compositional qualities in it are quite remarkable'.[127]

Surveying the 'Petits Concert' series of 1874 one finds some romantic chamber music – the extracts from the *Mährchenerzählungen* of Schumann with Grisez and Mas in the first[128] of the 1874 concerts and the Mozart Wind Quintet in the last[129] concert of this year. Schumann (the *Fantasy Pieces* op 73) featured in the second of the 1874 concerts. The performances of these pieces for clarinet and piano drew special mention: 'M. Grisez was partnered by M. Alkan ... they performed the Schumann fantasies with perfect taste and very delicate nuances.'[130]

Throughout the Petits Concert series one finds the same critical response to Alkan's chamber music performances. The third concert of the 1875 series included Hummel's piano duet *Sonata* [op 51 or op 92?] and received praise for its intimate and recreative interpretation.[131] 1875's fifth concert[132] contained a delicate performance of the andante from the Bach *Second Violin Sonata* with Alard. For the last 1877 recital Alkan returned to Schumann, one of his favourite romantic composers. The players included Alard, Mas and Grisez, and the works were the A minor violin sonata and two pieces for clarinet, viola and piano. The reviewer commented that: 'the evening made an excellent impression and the audience by a flattering demonstration gave great appreciation to the personality and art of M. Alkan ...'.[133]

For 1878 Alkan continued his chamber music policy of programming Schubert piano duets. At the second recital[134] he performed the A flat variations with Fissot and at the third two marches (also with Fissot). Fissot seems to have been an excellent duo partner playing his parts 'with precision and brio ...'.[135]

In the 1880 series Alkan seems to have abandoned playing chamber music concentrating now on solo piano music by highly selected composers as discussed earlier and a survey of his own solo and pedal-piano works. It is to the reception of these that we now turn.

Reception of his own performances and music in the Petit Concerts

Returning to a point made in the introduction to this chapter it is interesting that nineteenth-century detailed reception of Alkan's own piano music has been confined to op 15. In the next section we will take an overview of the reception of op 39 but this evaluation is mainly twentieth century. Are there any indications in the journalistic literature of the 1870s–1880s to form an end of century reception value?

Firstly, one notices an absence of former warhorses like the op 23 *Saltarella*, but the *Marches* op 26 and op 27 are retained for the Petits Concerts, and extracts from sets of pieces are also included. Secondly, compared with the 1840's, reception of Alkan's music was now mostly positive. In the review of the opening Petit Concert in 1873 for example Alkan's own compositions were now found to be 'remarkable in every way'.[136] For this recital Alkan selected three representative works, the lyrical Mendelssohnian *Chants* op 38/1, a vigorous *March* from the op 40 set and the spiritual *Deus Sabboath* (*Prières* op 64/8). The second recital[137] of 1873 repeated the chant (which was encored) and additionally Alkan performed the *Nuit d'Eté* from *Les Mois* and the op 13/2 *Étude*. During the 1873 series many of Alkan's pieces were deemed to be delightful or charming. For the fourth concert[138] Alkan performed more of these morceaux characteristiques including the *Hymne* from *Chants* Book 2 and the F sharp major *Impromptu* op 32. Alkan also premièred three pieces from the hitherto unpublished fourth volume of chants, the *Barcarolle, Allegro con bravura* and the op 67/2 *Le chanson de la bonne vielle*. Not every concert was stylistically consistent. The relative value of Alkan's piano music is now exemplified by an interesting aside given by the reviewer of the last concert of 1873:

> We regret a little the concert for seven trumpets and timpani by Altenburg ... we would rather have substituted this bizarre creation for some compositions by Alkan which are more charming: nos 10–15 of the 25 *Preludes* (op 31) pieces of quite modest proportions but in which one feels the hand of the poet and master [for example] part of the brilliant minor étude (op 39/8) ... and the first étude of the major key studies [op 35] of delightful character.[139]

Alkan's own standard of performance throughout the whole of the 1873 series is summed up by the reviewer of the first concert: 'his great talent has remained unaltered – restrained, learned and accurate although he appears to have lost his technical skills to a slight extent'.[140]

For the 1874 concerts Alkan introduced excerpts from larger works into the programme including the adagio and saltarello from the op 47 *Violoncello Sonata* which were 'two works of great merit in which his original and profound talent made a great impression'.[141] The third and fourth concert of the 1874 Petits Concerts included the first *Étude* of op 35, the first movement of the second *Concerto de Camera*, the *Ancienne mélodie de la synagogue* [*Preludes* op 31/6], several chants, prières and the popular op 26 and op 27 *Marches*. The *RGM* reviewer continued the 1873 praise for Alkan the composer: 'all [his] compositions [are] of high value appreciated by both us and the audience'.[142] For the last concert of the 1874 season Alkan included the whole of the op 21 *Duo* (with Léonard). The 1875 series follows this trend with performances of the same work and three movements from the op 47 *Violoncello Sonata* (the second movement was excluded). Extracts from the *Symphonie* op 39 (the funeral march and minuet) were also performed.

For the next season of Petits Concerts Alkan also declined to perform any of his larger compositions with the exception of the op 21 violin and piano duo. The 1875 handbill for example yields an interesting mixture of solo piano works and pedalier pieces as well as repeat performances of op 21 and the 'shortened' version of op 47 as detailed on the programme, replacing op 21 on the handbill. Of the shorter works the op 38/1 *Chant* particularly 'roused the applause of a large audience which had gathered to pay their respect and admiration to the master'.[143] Similar sentiments were provoked by the *Deus Sabbaoth* [*Prières* op 64/8]. Alkan's own music in the third and fourth concert (rather different from that on the handbill) included the same chant and *Deus Sabboath* but also the *Barcarollette Esquisses* op 63/12] and the *Chanson de la bonne vielle* [op 67/2]. The reviewer enthused:

> M. Alkan is, moreover, a creator in the literal sense of the word: his compositions are original and of fine and elevated sentiment ... the audience enthusiastically applauded the first of book one of the *Chants*, the *Barcarollette*, the *Deus Sabboath*, the *Chanson de la bonne vielle*, and the *Étude* op 13 with double quartet when the muted strings gave the ensemble a really poetic sonority.[144]

During the 1875 season – the middle period of the Petits Concerts, Alkan considered that his audience was prepared for the greater concentration demands of larger works. Thus we find that in the last concert of 1875 instead of performing the op 21 *Violin Sonata* Alkan substituted the larger op 47 *Violoncello Sonata* performed with Jacquard. But the review comments only on the abundant melody and the great difficulty of the finale. However, the whole performance was 'justly and warmly applauded'.[145]

By 1877 Alkan's pianistic reputation was such that he repeated his first concert in the Salle Pleyel in the Salle Erard. His success was now 'sincere and marked. The valiant artist received [much] encouragement which proved that the audience follows him and is attached to his work'.[146] Substantial pieces were again performed in 1877: in the second[147] the op 21 *Violin Sonata* and in the fourth the first movement of the *Concerto* op 39. The reader was reminded that this was an examination piece for the Conservatoire Concours of 1874. The op 39 first movement was now described as 'one of the most substantial and brilliant works ever written for the piano'.[148] Alkan's piano music now attracted the attention of other pianists Mlle Marie Poitevin (a student of Delaborde's) who performed the Alkan *Symphonie* op 39 in March 1877 at the Salle Erard.[149] Now in fact the op 39 *Études* were quite frequently performed in the 1877 season. At the 1877 fifth concert[149] Alkan performed the funeral march and minuet from op 39. Smaller works were also performed in the 1877 series. For example Alkan repeated some of his most popular works in 1877 from the 1875 series including the first *Chant* [op 38] at the first concert[150] and the *Barcarollette* at the fifth concert[151] as well as the op 21 *Duo* at the second concert.[152]

The later years of the Petits Concerts show Alkan performing less melodic, more austere repertoire. In 1878 for example at the first concert,[153] he played the *Minuetto alla tedesca*, and the *Voix de instrument* [*Chants* op 70/4]. At the second recital he included the octave canon from the third book of *Chants*, the *Chant de guerre* and returning to the Jewish liturgy the *Ancien melodie de synagogue* and the *Super flumina* psalm. In 1880 Alkan reduced the number of Petits Concerts to three. Although the critical reviews for these concerts are brief mostly are glowing in respectful praise for Alkan. The first concert[154] included some extracts from the *Chants* and the ninth of the *Grands Preludes*. The only reported compositions by Alkan performed at the third concert[155] were the 'canon' (presumably the *Canon à l'octave* as in the 1878 series), the *Air de ballet* and a prière. For the second concert[156] Alkan dared to perform his complete *Symphonie* op 39. Despite the reviewer's slightly negative opinion about the length of the first movement the rest of the work gained approval. Both the music and the performer were again applauded.

Throughout the Petits Concerts' series Alkan maintained the very highest standards of music and performing style. By performing a personal if rather quirky repertoire he gained immense respect for uncompromising standards. The Petits Concerts along with Alkan's teaching repertoire discussed in the last chapter are the best practical indicators of his tastes as composer and pianist. Alkan's rejection of much of his early virtuoso works for the Petits Concerts' repertoire is very apparent as is his revival of the French baroque/classical idioms through the medium of transcriptions. His audience and critics now applauded him for this focus. As for the larger works, with the exception of the *Symphonie* op 39, reception evaluation had to wait until the twentieth century. Despite José Vianna da Motta's championing of the first movement of the *Concerto* op 39 in Berlin in 1899 (probably its first performance outside France) the review studiously neglects to mention this key work.[157] Twentieth-century critics on the other hand have reacted to this colossus of romantic piano music in many different ways.

The *op 39 Concerto*: a case study in reception

After da Motta's performance of op 39 in Berlin 1899 there followed in 1900 a review by the same individual of the work in a minor journal *Der Klavier-Lehrer*. The link here between the work's reception and its value is obvious:

> In this work, Alkan has revealed all of his musical characteristics, brought here to brilliant heights. The thematic sensitivity, the gigantic dimensions, the simplicity and unity of the form, the richness of the polyphony, the unusual treatment of piano technique, and the biting harmonies – all of these elements stamp this work as one of the most beautiful and most powerful compositions that exist in the literature for the piano.

At first, one is astounded by the first movement's extraordinary length: 72 pages. However, then one is amazed that the musical interest never wanes. Every page brings a surprise. No phrase is ever repeated. The transformations of themes are inexhaustible. The construction of this movement is, to us, clearly that of the first movement of a piano concerto. Despite a wealth of details, the characteristics of the individual parts are so clear that Alkan's overview of the whole is never covered over ... .

Technically, the work is of the highest interest to pianists. In addition to passages with unusual acrobatics, Alkan makes much use of chords and octaves ... not only for virtuoso effects, but also for reasons that are musically justified. In matters of sonority and digital dexterity, he poses new problems, with highly felicitous results. Alkan uses no typical repeating formulas in his figurations. In every movement, he appears new and original. His piano writing is rich in colour, and it always finds the right means to express his ideas.[158]

And also in 1901 the technical skill and pianistic value of op 39 is emphasized:

To characterize his writing for the pianoforte, one must note that Alkan possesses a real technique that is all his own. He has studied the instrument in depth, and he knows well its technique and its sonorities. In both of these matters, Alkan offers the pianist great challenges that are both fascinating and very fruitful ... for example, a very interesting extended passage for repeated notes can be found in [the coda of the first movement, op 39] the *Concerto for solo piano*.[159]

The latter review was written curiously one year later in 1901 in the much more important journal the *Allgemeine Musik Zeitung* which boasted such distinguished former contributors as Robert Schumann. But da Motta's advocacy is less analytical and much more general. Within these reviews da Motta attempts to build a canonic status for Alkan alongside other titanic masters of the romantic piano literature and the *Concerto* op 39 is deemed also by many writers from da Motta onwards to be *the* most important of all. One might say that such writers are forming indirectly an Alkan foundation to promote his cause in order to raise Alkan's position in the romantic canon of piano composers. Alongside these early-twentieth-century writers stand piano rolls by such distinguished artists as von Zadora, Bauer and Petri (details in discography appendix) which brought an admittedly narrow range of Alkan's piano music to an international audience.

The problem of programming the larger works in concerts was as suggested earlier a real dilemma for Alkan. Hence reception of the gigantic *Concerto* op 39 is dominated by considerations of its genre. Like Schumann's *Third Piano Sonata* op 39 the so-called *Concerto without Orchestra* there is no simple performance context within a conventional piano recital: its length, scale, and transcendental nature are such that it has an extraordinarily dominant status. Bolte's 1913 review summarizes this problem:

Alkan's masterpieces: the *Concerto pour piano seul* and the *Symphony for piano*, both part of the *Études* op 39, a work with a modest title. These two compositions are the most difficult and the most beautiful he ever created.

The three-movement piano concerto, because of its immense difficulties, is hardly ever enjoyed. After an hour and a quarter of reading through its 120 pages, one is left speechless. This mass of tones is overwhelming ... .[160]

By 1932 Sorabji in a distinguished collection of essays entitled *Around Music* demoted the question of length and concentrates on its originality:

One has no hesitation in saying that this is one of the most remarkable and original piano concertos in existence ... Its astonishing freshness, the absolute independence and individuality impressed on every bar, the splendid richness, variety and brilliance of the keyboard writing, the prodigious vitality and energy of the work, make its neglect a matter of mystery – indeed one suspects that not one pianist in a hundred even knows of its existence.[161]

British critical reception in the 1930s varied between the uncomprehending conservatism of W.R. Henderson:

I got, in one long session with the undauntable Mr Petri, at Alkan. It was the so-called *Concerto* of op 39 – a session timed for 50 minutes, but mercifully got through in 45. The first movement tags out to 24 minutes, and has the most desperately hurdy gurdy end you ever prayed for long before its time. The composer was bedevilled (as so often) by his invincible triviality of idea and feeble power of consecution, coupled with a passion for stagy rambling. There is a pleasant harmless adagio, and a finale that, amusing enough in its notion of 'barbaresca', allows the work to end in the pure futility of a boredom truly shriek-worthy.[162]

and the broader perception of the London-based Viennese critic Mosco Carner:

Alkan witnessed those discoveries of new orchestral colours which Berlioz, Meyerbeer, Liszt and Wagner were making, and in these works he successfully imitated the orchestral style on the piano in such a way that one can mentally hear the scoring for the different instruments of the orchestra. Nevertheless, Alkan's music is genuine keyboard music and offers the pianist a wide scope in every direction.

In certain pieces, he seems to have forestalled points in modern music. For instance, the third movement of the *Concerto* is an allegretto alla barbaresca, written long before Stravinsky and Bartok introduced 'Eastern barbarism' into the music of our times.[163]

This type of reception is further explored by several American writers. Joseph Bloch's 1941 Harvard dissertation set the tone of liberal canonic discourse. As a conservative canonbuster he fully realizes the lineage of the *Concerto* op 39 and its concerto grosso structure:

The solo part resembles that of a Chopin, Moscheles, Hummel or Weber Concerto, with emphasis on delicate filigree patterns and brilliance of a light sort (le jeu perlé) – in other words, the solo piano is the 'ornamenting' factor. The orchestral part is represented by the massive chords of which Alkan is so fond, by the characteristic orchestral trills and tremolos, and by a variety of brass and timpani effects. Also, the orchestral part reveals a constant interweaving of separate lines, whereas the solo piano is almost entirely homophonic.[164]

The op 39 *Concerto* remained unobserved by writers for another twenty years or so until the American virtuoso Raymond Lewenthal, that most enthusiastic of Alkan writers, described the chief virtue of his style as found in this concerto:

> One should look to the 12 *Études* in the minor keys (which include a solo concerto, a symphony and a set of variations called *Aesop's Feast*), the *Grande Sonate*, the *Impromptu* on *Ein fest Burg*, the 48 *Esquisses* and the *Chants* to savour the true Alkan – that is, if you can find the music.
>
> ... His music sounds like no one else's. It was wilfully and aggressively modern when it appeared, and it contains none of the Italianisms which formed for the opera adoring public of the time the bridge from terra cognita to terra incognita in the music of Chopin and Liszt, and which makes themselves felt even in Wagner.[165]

Lewenthal's 1960's recordings were indeed pioneering but the *Concerto* op 39 was not recorded complete until 1969 by John Ogdon and in 1970 by Ronald Smith. The latter's recording prompted an enthusiastic review of the work and its essential innovations:

> The first movement, allegro assai, is an extraordinarily lengthy piece, and I don't doubt the claim in Ronald Smith's excellent sleeve notes that it is the longest first movement in classical form (my score runs into 72 pages) ... [Some cuts] ... are discreetly done, but I cannot help a feeling of regret that for the sake of a very few minutes, we are denied the complete masterpiece – for masterpiece this incredible study is ... Even so, this movement is immensely satisfying, with its blurred whirling images of previous composers – the orchestral Beethoven (in the final two pages), Liszt (particularly the *B minor Sonata*) – and some hints of things to come, most noticeably the highly effective quasi tamburo marking heralding the immense coda, which Saint-Saëns used in his *Fifth Piano Concerto* nearly 40 years later, as well as Sibelius and Brahms.
>
> The slow movement, Adagio, is a lament with 'sober, unsensuous cantilena' ...
>
> The finale, allegretto alla barbaresca, is a tour de force which Smith plays with bewildering brilliance. The opening few bars are reminiscent of the *Rakoczy March*, though distorted and phantasmagorical, whilst the second page unbelievably recalls music inextricably associated with belly dancers! The movement continues to explore higher flights of fancies than Liszt ever imagined, and proves the claim that Alkan must have been a virtuoso of frightening gifts.[166]

Also in 1970 the British musicologist Stanley Sadie crystallized many of the unconventional aspects of this work:

> A curious mixture of extreme severity and profound passion characterizes this music. What of the actual style? It is not easy to describe, still less easy to compare with others. The tutti sections are tough, severe, dramatic music, utterly unlike anyone else's ... Possibly the most remarkable passage comes in the first movement's development section, with cold, granitic textures and austere harmonies, the music is poised and motionless. The *Concerto* has an adagio that starts quite conventionally, but constantly devolves to the keyboard's extremes, with the left hand suggesting funereal drum beats. And there is a finale of demonic energy, music of extraordinary dark power and fiendish difficulty.[167]

These pioneering recordings of the *Concerto* were possible the most important influences on favourable reception of the work. The early 1970s afforded insightful reviews from both sides of the Atlantic. Eric Salzman (USA) points out the virtues and formal problems associated with the *Concerto* when he writes in 1972:

> Mad Alkan was well worth reviving, and his *Concerto for Piano Solo* is a heroic work that would do credit to Liszt. The first of these 'études' lasts almost 27 minutes – even at Ogdon's furious tempos – and never, but never flags. The adagio and finale, a mere 22 minutes between them, are scarcely less impressive, the former a kind of funeral march, the latter something like a cross between a polonaise and a bolero. The combination of imagination, skill, craft, and virtuosity – performer's and composer's – is simply staggering, and the quality of invention and fantasy is high. I don't find Alkan's formal sense convincing – he sprawls all over the place – but then, of the middle and late Romantics, only Brahms is entirely successful at making large-scale instrumental pieces. Missing also is the final touch of stylistic coherence. But Alkan's eclecticism hardly need bother us much more than Mahler's, and this music, furious and demented, is not lacking in character.
>
> The mind boggles. The technical demands of this 50 minute hour crammed full of music are staggering ... I know of no other nineteenth-century work that makes such extensive and continuous musical and technical demands upon the performer ... .[168]

The British musicologist Ates Orga takes a stylistic overview of the piece and includes the essential Jewish temperament of the work:

> The *Concerto* was described by Fétis as a 'musical epic', and this remark is as true of its stature and content as of its length. The G sharp minor first movement is no less than 72 pages long, and combines relentless virtuosity with a powerful symphonic argument. Particularly fascinating is the layout of the tutti and solo passages. Such textural detail is also evident in the central adagio (in C sharp minor) with its opening violoncello imitations and the recitatives and the string-like tremolos of the middle section – which, of course, have clearly traceable antecedents in the concertos by Moscheles, Chopin and Liszt. The finale, an allegro barbaro in F sharp minor, is a compulsive fusion of oriental and western elements in which Alkan's delineation of the Jewish soul and temperament is particularly prominent. Technically, the exploration of new piano sonorities (the widespread left and right hand parts, the textural distribution of chords, and so on), the range of the harmonic dissonance, and the kind of key relationships with which Alkan experiments, are seldom anything less than uniquely original for their time. No doubt there are some who find Alkan a rather long winded, overblown figure, but for several years now, I have become increasingly fascinated by the character and style of his thinking. He shows in a work like this *Concerto* a gift for continuity, development and emotional climax denied to men of, say, Liszt's calibre.[169]

Reception for the *Concerto* in the late 1970s illustrates the aesthetic idea of 'kairos', that is its reception was sensitive and precise to the nature of the work. Chief amongst writers on op 39 were Ronald Smith and Hugh Macdonald. Ronald Smith in 1977 as a supreme Alkan interpreter takes a more performer-centre viewpoint:

> The *Concerto* for solo piano, has been described as the nineteenth-century's answer to Bach's *Italian Concerto*. In both works, a single player is invited to imitate the impression of solo and massed forces. But the Alkan is on a massive scale; and while it has been

known to make an immediate and overwhelming impact, its underlying depths and subtleties, especially those relating to the overall tonality of its first movement, only become apparent after repeated hearings.[170]

Hugh Macdonald in 1978 balances aesthetics and tonality observations:

> It is time to stop thinking of Alkan only as a grotesque and a virtuoso. There are many layers of poetry in this music ... The warmth and exaltation of the *Concerto*'s first movement have never emerged so strongly. Furthermore, Alkan's tonal grasp in this movement (nearly half an hour long) is as strong as in the much shorter finale of the *Symphony*, itself a remarkable movement. The polarity of major and minor modes is particularly significant in a series of pieces purportedly all in the minor, for Alkan continually uses the major for touching dramatic effect ... .[171]

Ronald Smith's complete recording of op 39 provoked two other outstanding French music scholars to write extremely meaningful stylistic points on the op 39 *Concerto*. First, Martin Cooper:

> Probably the most impressive single study in the set [that is, the *Douze études dans les tons mineurs*, op 39] is No. 8, the first movement of the Concerto, original in form as well as in much of its content. The introduction of a lyrical episode, and one of high quality, as a kind of afterthought before the development section, and of a distant, as it were, 'visionary' chorale fragment later in the movement, both point perhaps to some undisclosed 'programme'. But there is nothing necessarily programmatic in the strange thematic grouping of the development section (anticipating, as Smith suggests, similar passages in Sibelius) or in the brilliantly imaginative coda, where Alkan's use of repeated notes foreshadows Ravel's in *Scarbo*. It is characteristic of Alkan in all of these pieces to 'trump his own ace' in the coda of a piece, not only building to an emotional climax, but adding yet another technical difficulty to stun the connoisseur. These feats, however, are very seldom simply digital or manual; they almost always introduce a new dimension, or a new shade of colour. Their very 'bigness' – the suggestion of a multiple orchestra by a single player – is a legitimate quality of its own.[172]

Equally Wilfred Mellers realizes the supreme craftsmanship of the *Concerto* and its marvellous musical contents:

> ... the slightly monstrous *Concerto for solo piano* has three movements which rise sequentially from G sharp to F sharp minor. The solo and tutti sections are clearly defined, and the pianist's task is formidably taxing, in that he has to cope with the orchestra as well as with the soloist's hair-raising bravura. This technical problem is, however, only the superfices of a structural complexity that creates a first movement which lasts 25 minutes but never runs to fat. Smith's notes draw attention to the chilling ostinato passage – prophetic of Sibelius's *Symphony No. 4* – in the development, and to the traumatic chorales that creep into the coda.
>
> The adagio is structurally simpler, yet hardly less prophetic – a funeral march that links apocalyptic Berlioz with Mahler. The finale starts like a cross between a Chopin polonaise and the butterfly pianism of the nineteenth-century salon, only to grow progressively

more 'barbarous'. The coda is indeed 'carried through with a fiendish single-mindedness that rides roughshod over all obstacles' (these words are Smith's, at whose performance imagination and ears boggle together).[173]

In 1980 Hugh Macdonald contributed the Alkan entry to the *New Grove* dictionary. He points out two less well researched ideas in the *Concerto* that extreme technical rigour and the touching simplicity of the work:

> Alkan's structures sometimes run to epic length; the largest is the first movement of the *Concerto*, which lasts nearly 30 minutes ...

> A surprising aspect of Alkan's style is its technical rigour, for he wrote not as a pianist with a keyboard before him, but with the cerebral exactness of someone for whom the notation is more important than the sound. He refused to spell enharmonically and facilitate reading, with the result that at least twice he was compelled to use [in the allegretto alla barbaresca] a notation for a triple sharp. He was scrupulous in his part writing. The same obstinacy is to be seen in his harmonic writing, in which, for example, he used pedal points or ostinatos against theoretically incompatible counterpoints.

> At a period when the piano was undergoing universal exploitation for new and more dazzling sonorities, Alkan made a positive contribution to virtuoso technique. His music can be exacting beyond the capacity of any but the most powerful players in technique, dynamic demands and stamina. It can also be disarmingly simple.[174]

Eighties reception of the Smith recording of the *Concerto* concentrated on psychological aspects of the expressionistic kind by Rothstein:

> The recording of the *Concerto* is a major accomplishment, its sweet lyricism mixing with flourishes of orchestral tutti impulses, its long-range structure becoming something of an over-wrought epic of a troubled soul ...

> Much of this music can not only rank with anything by Liszt, it also has a more disturbing power. Other music of this period continually invoked Mephistophelian passions, dream sensations, suggestions of desire – all matters lying outside the rational social order. The nineteenth-century virtuoso, in fact, was thought to embody such forces; he also succeeded in controlling and displaying them. Alkan, in some ways, was an extreme personification of the nineteenth-century virtuoso ... While Chopin gave expressions of dream and desire an aristocratically polished surface, Alkan's passions break through without any pretence of elegance or control.[175]

Without explicit analysis Rapoport points out the sheer variety of moods displayed:

> I do not hesitate to call [the *Concerto*] one of the greatest works for the piano of all time. On first hearing, it may seem disjointed, even empty in places. But listen again and you will hear just the opposite. The superhuman pyrotechnics of the work are essential to its message of transcendental struggle. The incredible variety of music in the colossal first movement is essential to its power and scope, its grandeur and intensity, its pathos,

brooding, bitterness, irony, tenderness, violence, madness, and much more. There are real emotional wars being fought here. The attentive and receptive listener will be caught up in them as in no other music.[176]

Mid-eighties reception for the *Concerto* was dominated by Mark Starr's remarkable orchestration and commentary in 1985[177] and more specifically by Smith's monograph on Alkan's music. The uniqueness, necessity and virtuosity are all admirable summed up by Smith:

> [The *Concerto* is] an isolated masterpiece which cannot be sensibly compared with any other work. The impact of a public performance, an understandably rare occurrence, is immediate and overwhelming.
>
> ... In their totality, Alkan's 24 studies in all the major and minor keys op 35 and op 39 embody the fullest realization imaginable of a lifetime of lonely musical and technical exploration by one of the greatest, but also most isolated keyboard giants of all time ... Certainly, within their 370 or so pages is engraved the most complete evidence of what must have been an almost frightening keyboard command ... a wizardry that once led Liszt to declare that Alkan possessed the biggest technique known to him. Indeed, several of these works stand on the very threshold of possibility and are only rescued from freakishness by their unfailing expertise. Berlioz has demonstrated [in his *Grand traité d'instrumentation*] how it is quite possible to invent impossible piano writing. Everything in Alkan is possible; he simply calls for unrivalled speed in finger techniques, keyboard freedom unaccommodated by rhythmic licence and, in op 39, a physical and mental staying power unparalleled by any of his contemporaries.[178]

Finally, in France, during 1991, after over a century of the grossest neglect, François-Sappey edited a volume of essays on various aspects of Alkan's life and music. The editor contributed an important article which concentrated on motivic aspects and more completely on symbolical elements:

> ... more than in any other Alkan work there is a musical metaphor of the errant Jew. The common cyclic cell behind the generated themes could symbolize the original persona of the hero, the modulating progressions his itinerary followed unceasingly ... The *Concerto* op 39 represents the limit of excessive tendencies – polymorphic and symbolic – of Alkan.[179]

Modern analysis and postmodern aesthetics permits us today to accommodate such excesses in a romantic composer.

Chapter 13

Performance Practice

Essential to any study of performance practice in Alkan is the understanding that many of his technical developments in performance practice resulted from the advances of piano construction in France. An overview of the history of the piano in France and the concomitant application to examples in the Alkan literature follows.

The development of the piano in France

We return briefly to the eighteenth century to learn that as far back as 1758 Stein[1] invited Eckhardt[2] to Paris. The latter published a set of sonatas in 1763 for 'forte e piano'. Later in 1759 a journal announced:

> A harpsichord of new invention called piano e forte, having a round pithy harmony imitating the harp or the lute in the bass, the flute in the treble as well as the quality of bells ... When the full sound is let out, it is louder and more pleasing than an ordinary harpsichord ... This instrument is very easy to play and to maintain.[3]

From Alkan's earliest piano works the wide dynamic range of this developing instrument was fully utilized as was the imitative potential of such an instrument later employed with bell-like treble sonorities in the *Étude de bravoure* op 16/1. Despite conservatism in French culture, life epitomized the preference for the harpsichord over the piano. By the 1780s the piano invaded the rarefied atmosphere of the Concerts Spirituels, the centre of Parisian instrumental musical life. In 1786, eleven different pianists played solo pieces in one of these concerts which established the piano as a solo instrument. The developing piano was additionally very popular with female amateur pianists in Paris and Abbé Vogler reported in 1783 that 'there are not a few ladies who can compete with any keyboard professor in the playing of a difficult sonata, perhaps even a sonata of his own composition'.[4] The popularity of the piano with women continued into the 1840s. An example of this era of piano playing was instanced by the brilliant performance of Alkan's virtuosic *Saltarelle* op 23 by Josephine Martin.[5]

Who were the most important figures in the development of pianos in France? The first manufacturer of pianos in France of note was Sébastien Erard who produced a clavecin mécanique, that is a harpsichord with several registers with leather plectra and quills which could be shifted and combined by means of a pedal mechanism. Erard was fortunate to secure a full licence by Louis XVI to allow him to manufacture the first early pianos. These were essentially modelled on Zumpe's square pianos without escapement mechanism with five-octave range and manufactured to much higher standard than Zumpe's. Perhaps because of this technical quality, the piano became a serious rival to the harpsichord.

Academic status was then conferred on the piano by the appointment of piano professors at the Conservatoire from 1795, but according to Pierre,[6] prizes were only awarded for piano competitions in 1800. Several early-nineteenth-century pianists were sceptical about the qualities of the early instruments but the election of the distinguished pianist and composer Louis Adam to a professorship of piano was the single most important event to advance the cause of the early French piano. Thereafter Erard set about experimenting with methods of improving piano action to make it more touch-sensitive, to widen dynamic contrasts and to rid the piano action from the inbuilt slowness of the early 'pushing action' (Stossmechanik). Erard's first piano with repetition action (méchanisme à l'étrier) was produced in 1808, with advancement to the 'simple escapement' in 1816, and the 'double escapement' in 1821. This should be more accurately termed as 'compound escapement'[7] and was used in a modified form by other leading manufacturers including Steinway, Bechstein, Pleyel, Collard and Broadwood.

Erard's invention was spurred on by a combination of the 'bouncing action' (prellmechanik) with the aforementioned 'pushing action' giving respectively lightness with power in the action and also an ease and precision of note repetitions. Many virtuosi-composers including Alkan exploited this invention. His *Les Omnibus variation* is a composer's response to this escapement invention. After Erard's innovation therefore, piano touch was revolutionized.[8] Prior to the compound escapement invention pianistic touch was somewhat detached and non-legato in nature, but increasingly sophisticated French piano actions after 1800 resulted in a greater possibility of legato touch. Moscheles[9] noted that Erard pianos after 1830 particularly had a sustained mellow fullness of tone.

Other technological improvements such as the development of stringing led to a further advance of resonant piano tone. Historically, all strings for pianos up to 1820 were made from small-gauged iron or brass. Broadwood,[10] however, was the first manufacturer in 1815 who used heavier string in his pianos with English action and in 1826 Henri Pape was granted a special French patent for the use of tempered steel wire strings. Bass strings coiled with copper appeared in the 1820s but overspun strings were not generally used until the 1820s when metal bracing began to be applied. In addition to improvements in stringing and bracing, a most significant invention in piano construction in France occurred in 1808 when Erard invented the agraffe which was a blade, one to each note, which was perforated with as many holes as the note had unison strings. These agraffes were fitted into the rear edge of the wrest plank behind the tuning pins. Essentially the agraffes formed an upward bearing for the strings and prevented the hammer blows from bending them.

The last important stringing invention before 1830 occurred in France in 1828 when Pape devised the system of cross-stringing[11] which increased the volume of tone. Also French virtuosi demanded a greater dynamic range in piano sound. Given the upward extension of the treble range and the raising of standard pitch, extra strain was placed on the primitive frame so, logically, the inclusion of metal to support the tension followed. Modern tension resistance really dates from 1825 when Babcock[12] produced the first one-piece iron frame, which included hitchpin plate, wrest-plank and tension bars. Soundboards were not scientifically constructed in the early-nineteenth century and judging from an 1828 patent,[13] the only specification was that it be thicker in the treble than in the bass. Other changes to pianos in early-nineteenth-century France included improvements to hammer heads. Until 1826 most hammer heads were leather covered which produced a rather dry, harpsichord-like tone. In 1826 however, Pape devised felt coverings for the hammer heads which were more durable than leather and also gave a more mellow tone compared with leather because of the 'development of vibrations more slowly along the entire length, thus encouraging the formation of stronger lower harmonics on which a richer quality of sound depends'.[14] With this brief survey of the development of the early French pianos in mind we turn to the essential features and differences between the Erard and Pleyel pianos, the instruments favoured by most nineteenth-century virtuosi including Alkan.

Alkan's choice of pianos: Pape, Erard and Pleyel

For his début recital in 1826 in the Salle Pape, Alkan used neither an Erard nor a Pleyel but a Pape piano.[15] These pianos were popular in France: Cherubini composed at an 1817 Pape square piano and leading contemporary pianists and composers such as Moscheles, Boieldieu and Auber purchased Pape's instruments. Pape is best known for many inventions such as the use of tempered steel strings and felt coverings alluded to earlier but it is likely that for his début recital, Alkan chose the down-striking Pape grand piano. This type of action avoided the displacing effect of the strings of the up-striking type and solved the issue of lack of strength across the action gap. After the 1838 concert in the Salle Pape,[16] again presumably using a Pape piano, Alkan changed his recital venue to the Salle Erard from 1849 and used Erard pianos.[17] Towards the end of his concerts in the Petits Concerts series he sometimes previewed recitals in the Salle Pleyel using Pleyel pianos.[18]

It is rare nowadays for pianists to shift allegiance. But in the nineteenth century, pianos by different manufacturers had distinctive and varied tone colours. Chopin for example contrasted the different sounds of the Erard and Pleyel pianos and expressed preferences according to his emotional state: 'When I feel out of sorts I play on an Erard piano where I easily find a ready-made tone. But when I feel in good form and strong enough to find my own individual sound, then I need a Pleyel piano.'[19] Chopin considered that his Pleyel piano was capable of the most subtle nuances. Pleyels were favoured by several other famous pianist-composers of the times including Kalkbrenner and Hiller. Although Liszt and Alkan preferred Erard's, Liszt did not stint in praise for the qualities of the Pleyel piano particularly when played by Chopin: 'it permitted him to draw sounds that might recall one of those harmonics of which romantic Germany held the monopoly'.[20]

In order to decide on the most suitable piano for the contrasting styles in the Alkan repertoire we need to understand the construction differences between Erard and Pleyel pianos of the mid-nineteenth century. A full size Erard grand was about 253 cm long and a Pleyel grand about 200–230 cm in length. The Pleyel bass strings were about 25–50 cm shorter giving much less resonance and power. Hence the Pleyel was a more intimate chamber instrument and was chosen by Alkan for previewing his last Petits Concerts before the main recital on the Erard piano. Frame tension on the Pleyel grand was about 40% less than on the Erard. Erard specialized in the widest variety of tone colour from soft to loud, and because of the striking point in the bass of 9½ to 10, the most brilliant bass power was possible and employed to great advantage by many composers including Alkan in the final section of the *Quasi-Faust* movement of the op 33 *Sonata*.

Ex. 13.1   *Grande Sonate* op 33, second movement, bars 223–236

In the treble register the Erard piano has a maximum striking ration of 11 compared with 14 on the Pleyel, so the Erard piano is ideally suited to the brilliante passage work in the following variation from *Le Festin d'Esope* op 39/12.

Other factors such as multilayered hammers on the Erard calculated to emphasize the fundamental rather than upper partials and the Erard underdamping system to suppress tone immediately compared with Pleyel's light gravity-based over dampers were important factors in the choice of instrument for an artist. For the orchestral sonorities of Alkan's largest piano works the Erards of the late 1870s are ideal with a range of 90 notes G^3 to C^5. These pianos have immense clarity, power and dynamic range. A surviving mid-century Erard instrument is of the greatest interest.[21] The Paris Conservatoire has in its museum Alkan's own pédalier no 24598 built by Erard in the 1850s and this instrument demonstrates all the aforementioned qualities. Excellent performances by Ronald Smith of several of Alkan's miniatures on an Erard piano of c1855 make the strongest case for authentic instruments in this repertory.

Ex. 13.2 *Le Festin d'Esope* op 39, variation, bars 5–8

The Alkan tradition in performance practice

When reconstructing Alkanian tradition a good starting point is Lewenthal's remark 'when a performer is faced with a completely unfamiliar work by a completely unfamiliar composer, how can he know how it is to be played? The answer if quite simple. He cannot'.[22] Reconstructing an authentic style for Alkan on the other hand is free from various performing traditions[23] and variant editions as found in Chopin scholarship. A possible starting point for a preparation of any of Alkan's compositions for performance is to examine the reports of Alkan's own playing.

'Effortless, light, brilliant and rapid'[24] were the adjectives applied to Alkan's early pianistic style. One is reminded of the Leschetizsky comment that 'French pianists ... fly lightly up into the clouds'.[25] Alkan's own playing appeared to be 'lacking in feeling and cold'.[26] In classical piano repertoire Alkan's performance style was criticized as 'a little old fashioned'.[27] As we will see later, Alkan's classical discipline was reflected in his choice of repertoire for teaching material and for his own performances in the Petits Concerts. Alkan did benefit from the improvements in piano sonority in post-1800 French pianos in cultivating a lyrical quality making 'the piano sing delightfully'[28] and also 'he possessed to the highest degree ... sensitivity ... that rare gift on which is based the art of singing and of stirring the emotions on this instrument'.[29] To reconstruct an 'authentic' Alkan interpretation it is necessary to strive for this French lyricism of the chaste rather than sensual type. Lewenthal describes[30] the search for the correct legato sound as 'a lively dryness ... of Piper-Heidsieck Brut'.[31]

As well as a search for this type of French piano sound, successful performances of Alkan's more virtuosic works requires much pianistic stamina. A totally developed sense of athletic form is needed to negotiate Alkan's bravura passage work. His playing was, in fact, characterized by 'power and relentless energy'.[32] To recreate this pianistic strength Lewenthal practically suggests[33] much repetition of difficult movements with metronomic discipline. A total sense of control seems to have been an essential feature of Alkan's own playing which was described in 1873 as 'restrained, intellectual and precise'.[34] D'Indy summarized Alkan's pianistic style as 'technically less skilled than Liszt although more personal and humanly moving'.[35] As a composer-pianist Alkan apparently had a characteristically personal approach 'neither resembling Thalberg, Chopin, Liszt, Prudent nor Döhler'.[36] The pianistic method adopted by Alkan was probably based on a finger technique derived from the French clavecin system. This school relies on key proximity and immaculate finish. Even given the ample tone of Alkan's preference for Erard pianos the resultant volume was probably of smaller dimensions than the Liszt arm-weight approach. An example from Alkan's *Le Preux* op 17 exemplifies this rather rare use of arm-weight: 'du bras' is added as a performance instruction.

Despite Alkan's brilliant early career, his eminence as a composer and teacher and the respect he gained from musicians for his classic performances in the Petits Concerts, there is no evidence of an Alkan 'school' of piano playing. Had Alkan accepted the offer of a post at the Geneva Conservatoire in 1836 we might have reports from students about his pedagogic approach. Only the lesson notes of a private student Marie Aucoc[37] discussed in the next section give evidence of Alkan's teaching style and performing practice.

Alkan's lack of academic conservatoire-based status perhaps denied him many really talented students. In contrast, his chief rival, Marmontel, as head of the Paris Conservatoire piano school was highly influential in establishing the next generation of master composers and pianists in France including Bizet, Debussy, d'Indy, Planté, Diémer and Marguerite Long. When Diémer succeeded Marmontel in 1888 he taught many of the great twentieth-century French pianists including Risler, Dupré, Schmitz, Casadesus and Cortot. All these pianists represent the French school of piano playing characterized by fluency, purity, elegance and classical taste.[38] These are all qualities found in Alkan's piano playing and are essential features for the recreation of authentic performances of his works. Since Alkan collaborated with Saint-Saëns in the classical duet repertoire in the Petits Concerts we may surmise that he respected Saint-Saëns' performances. Stevenson[39] has researched the latter's precision in the classical repertoire particularly in Mozart. We are reminded that Saint-Saëns accused Reinecke for an excessive use of a sustained touch in Mozart[40] 'legato, molto legato and sempre legato which is the very opposite of what the composer intended'. We have Alkan's own opinion of the equally false school of Mozart playing promoted by Marmontel referred to in Chapter 1.[41] Reception of Alkan's performances of the classical repertoire point to, as we have seen, a purer, more classical approach.

For an authentic recreation of the late works of Alkan and especially the *Chants* which are precursors of Fauré's *Nocturnes* and *Barcarolles*, we might apply Long's requirements for fine performances of these works: 'depth of sound in the suppleness of the attacks, the even lightness of the attacks, the even lightness of the fingers (that famous gliding over the keyboard) the rapid winged action ...'.[42] Long's summary of French pianism at its best is a guideline for the successful performances of Alkan's compositions. All French pianism possesses grace, elegance, clarity and suppleness and depth of inner feeling.[43] More specific insights into Alkan's performance practice of other composers may be discovered by examining briefly the contents of the lessons he gave to Marie Aucoc.

Alkan's teaching repertoire and his comments on performance practice

Marie Aucoc (1861–1945) started her piano studies with Alkan in 1877. According to her son Jacques Lagrenée[44] Alkan was famous for understanding the aesthetics of music and he was also able to transmit the meaning of a work in the most admirable manner. On Wednesdays and Thursdays from 3–5 pm he played Bach, Mendelssohn and Schumann on the piano and pédalier always by heart. In fact Alkan's teaching repertoire centred around these composers with the addition of Beethoven and Chopin. The impression of Alkan's teaching methods from the lesson notes is that he was not especially voluble during lessons, he played infrequently to students and he was naturally shy. For those students he accepted, Alkan was willing to experiment in interpretation practically or verbally. The full set of teaching notes is included in the Aucoc article and Some of Alkan's most salient teaching points are included here on the interpretation of Bach, Beethoven, Mendelssohn, Weber, Chopin and Schumann.

On Bach performance: 'as for the bourrée [from the *English Suite in A major BWV 806* or in *A minor BWV 807*] when one plays serious works such as those of Bach one should not use the editions of Le Couppey, Lacombe and others. Their markings have no value or authority ...'. 'I [Marie Aucoc] played the fugue [unspecified] from memory ... [Alkan] raised his head in extreme astonishment ... Mademoiselle ... you have played your fugue by heart.'

Despite problems on the second page of this fugue Marie managed the third page from memory and Alkan was forced to admit that she could play the fugue from memory!

Marie Aucoc also studied the Beethoven op 110 *Sonata* with Alkan. Alkan demanded that the arioso be more rhythmic and the fugue be more flowing. Another favoured work for Marie was the 'andante' and rondo of a Beethoven *Concerto* [likely to be op 58].

Alkan's romantic teaching repertoire with Marie Aucoc consisted of Mendelssohn, Weber, Chopin and Schumann. (The absence of Liszt here and in the Petits Concerts is striking.) The only Mendelssohn work studied is the baroque-inspired but romantically massive *Prelude in B flat major* op 35. The Weber studied was the *Sonata in C major* op 24. Alkan seemed content with Marie's performance. He himself demonstrated admirably the slow movement of op 24. Rather more piano works of Chopin were studied including the third, fourth, fifth and sixth *Études* of Chopin [op 10]. Alkan pointed out several errors in the edition used and advised Marie not to play the bass too heavily. Interestingly, he advised that the hands should be desynchronized as we hear from the older generation of Chopin interpreters. With Marie, Alkan also worked through the tragic magnificent *Nocturne in C minor* op 48/1. On performing the taxing *Étude in A flat major* op 10/10 Marie seems to have become fatigued. Apparently Alkan understood this but he seems not to have prescribed how to stay relaxed. We might deduce that he favoured a finger-attack rather than weight-shifting approach to piano technique for performing the *Étude in C minor* op 10/12. Marie realized that she needed to work tremendously hard but Alkan on this occasion did not make many observations. The arpeggio-like *étude* op 25/1 elicited the response from Alkan that the melody was not sufficiently brought out and the accompaniment was too loud. Marie blamed Mlle Pasquet's piano! No specific teaching notes on Schumann's *Carnaval* were made by Marie unfortunately apart from Alkan recommending Mozart as an antidote to the effort of playing this work.

Despite Alkan's extremely brief teaching remarks it is clear that he required as an interpreter both textual fidelity and precise adherence to the composer's markings. Other interpretative ideas were rather less forthcoming. We might project that he demanded the same text-centred approach to the interpretation of his own music. Of all text-based performance instructions tempo indications are probably the first markings noticed in an Alkan score.

Tempo

Two opposing opinions exist regarding Alkan's tempo markings. George Beck in his preface to his selected edition of Alkan categorically states that 'Alkan's metronome marks are always too rapid and should not be taken too literally'.[45] His principal evidence is the marking minim = 112 for *Le Chemin de fer* which is self evidently a printing error for crotchet = 112. The other glaring printing error is quaver = 144 rather than crotchet = 144 for *Fa* op 38/2. But this is rather slim evidence for Beck's assertion. The argument is made more complex by the lack of metronome marking in many of Alkan's collections such as *Les Mois* op 74, the *Preludes* op 31 and the *Esquisses* op 63. Most of the organ music is bereft of exact tempo indications. But regarding Alkan's extremely rapid movements there are several more movements which veer towards the impossible in performance terms. These are:

Comme le vent op 39/1	Prestissamente quaver = 160
Scherzo-diabolico op 39/3	Prestissimo dotted minim = 132
Une fusée op 55	minim = 96
Scherzo-Minuetto	dotted minim = 84

On the other hand Raymond Lewenthal advises players when preparing a performance of Alkan's music to: 'read his markings scrupulously, starting with the metronome indications which at first will usually seem too fast. They are <u>not</u> [Lewenthal's underlining]. It is you who is too slow'.[46] Works which fall into the Lewenthal 'too fast' category include the *Étude* op 76/3 (Presto – crotchet = 160) and the finale of the *Symphonie* op 39 (Presto – semibreve = 96). Tempo markings specified in the Alkan literature should be attempted since they are essential to an authentic projection of the music.[47]

At the other end of the tempo spectrum Alkan's slow movements are sometimes given only moderately slow markings. Given the funereal character of the slow movement of the *Symphonie* op 39, the tempo of crotchet = 88 is not particularly slow. The same argument applies to the slow movement of the *Violoncello Sonata* op 43 with dotted crotchet = 60. Unfortunately both comparative slow movements of the *Duo Concertant* op 21 and *Trio* op 30, two of Alkan's most eloquent, profound and funereal movements lack metronome markings.

Tempo indications in Alkan's music are sometimes modified by the term 'assez', as in the *Chant* op 38/1 where the metronome mark of crotchet = 100 reflects the broad moderate tempo and character of this work.

The question of tempo rubato in the music of Alkan is an interesting one. The indication 'rubato' never appears in Alkan's scores. If rubato is required it tends to be written into the score as in *La Vision* op 63/1.

Ex. 13.3 *La Vision* op 63/1, bars 1–10

Ex. 13.4 *Concerto* op 39/11, bars 82–85

Romantic impassioned passages in Alkan of course may imply a degree of freedom in performance. Alkan's own indication *ampiamente* in the slow movement of the *Concerto* op 39 implies this.

But in general the approach to rubato application in Alkan should be similar to that when interpreting Chopin: 'rubato [must have] an unshakeable logic. It always justified itself by a strengthening or weakening of the melodic line, by harmonic details, by the figurative structure. It was fluid, natural; it never degenerated into exaggeration or affectation'.[48] Marmontel adds: 'Alkan was never subject to the frequent large alterations in tempo found in the modern school.'[49] The best example of Alkan's direct approach to unvarying tempo is found above the theme of *Le Festin d'Esope* op 39 where the tempo marking of quaver = 126 is supported by the instruction 'allegretto senza licenza quantunque'.

Performance instructions

As well as precise instructions Alkan often adds rather imprecise colourful and eccentric markings to his music. Again in *Le Festin* (see Diagram 13.1) we note a variety of imitative and aesthetic instructions. Using the discipline of musical semiotics such instructions imply intonations embedded in Alkan's contemporary society. These according to the ideas of Ujfalussy

> indicate the music formulae and the types of particular sonorities which transmit precise significations of social and human types ... Composers of strong personality concentrate and condense the characteristic events of the musical consciousness of surrounding society into types, uniting them into different genres and structures for the purpose of an artistic creation.[50]

Diagram 13.1

Variation instruction

5	marziale	march-like
10	scampanatino	tinkling
11	quasi-corni	horn-like
14	trombata	trumpets
16	preghevole	pleadingly
18	leggierissimamente	extremely lightly
19	lamentevole	lamentingly
20	impavidé[o]	fearless
21	caccia	the hunt
22	abbajante	barking

For example in *Le Festin* we find a heroic revolutionary march (variation 5), an invocation of the world of the French orchestral baroque (variation 14), the delicacy of French pianism (variation 18) and indeed more than a glimpse of Alkan's own temperament (variation 19).

It would be over-zealous to catalogue all of Alkan's colourful performance instructions. It is possible to subdivide his works into categories and, using Ujfalussy's principles, discover intonational types rather in the manner of Marta Grabocz's studies of the piano music of Liszt.[51] Although Alkan has minimal stylistic congruity with Liszt after his mid 1840s compositions, there are general types derivable from Beethoven and Italian and French opera. In the case of Alkan as has been mentioned several times in this study the influence of the French baroque, particularly that of dance types, is profoundly apparent. Obviously many examples of each intonational type exist but for the sake of concision only one example of each is given here. Understanding by the performer of these intonational categories will help recreate the authentic Alkanian style.

Appassionato themes of a rapid nature

For example the opening of the *Symphonie* op 39, as has been said in Chapter 4 has a dramatic pulsating nature akin to the opening of Beethoven's *Eroica* symphony. In performance the Alkan work needs a similar forward drive and urgency of interpretation.

Scherzo-like themes

In Alkan perhaps even more so than in Liszt these themes are very varied. The scherzo movement of the *Sonatine* op 61 combines a scherzo-like rapidity with minuet poise. The lightest most even touch is required here from the pianist.

March tunes

These are much more common in Alkan than in Liszt. Two outstanding Alkanian examples are the *Marches* op 26 and op 27. The latter is a rare example of a revolutionary march in major tonality. The funeral march-type is found in the slow movement of the *Symphonie* op 39 and directly in the *March funèbre* op 26. It is also embedded into the final movement of *Les Quatres Ages Sonata* op 33. Even more so than for Liszt the funeral march represents for Alkan a lamentation for the loss of the *ancien régime* as well as a personal statement of loss in older age. The performer needs therefore to approach this movement with the darkest of tonal colourings.

Pastoral themes

The geneses of these type reach back to the Italian and French baroque composers and then on to the pastoral symphony. In Alkan's *Les Moissoneurs* (*Les Mois* op 74/8) the pianist needs to delineate the atypical pastoral elements with drone bass accompaniment, graceful contour and descending fifths at the end of the phrases with great freshness.

Religious type themes

In Alkan these are of the broadly devotional type such as the exquisite *Cantique des Cantiques* (*Prelude* op 31/13) taken from verse two of the *Songs of Songs*. Strongly melodic with a repeated accompaniment this demands from the player the most sensitive of nuances balancing the melodic contour against the irregular quintuple meter.

Jewish based themes

These require much intensity and emotion from the performer. Examples from ancient Jewish melodies include the *Ancienne melodie de la synagogue* (*Preludes*, op 31/6) referred to in Chapter 6, and Jewish-inspired themes present in the 'alla giudesca' of the *Onze preludes* op 66/7.

Heroic themes based on early-nineteenth-century French opera

These are characterized by a disrupted melodic line and the idea of a dramatic agent expressed in musical terms. Most common in the Alkanian output is the grandiose type exemplified by the *Scherzo focoso* op 34 where the ultimate in power and accuracy is needed from the performer.

Bel canto themes often of doleful character

There is a striking similarity between Alkan's *Ma chère servitude* op 60/2 and Liszt's *Mal du pays*: both demand a well-developed sense of romantic pathos and an intense melancholy in performance.

Extended declamatory types

Based on intonations from French-Italian opera these are characterized by a simple clear rhythmic opening with some intense turning points then antecedent-consequent phrases reaching an impassioned cadence. These determinants need to be fully realized by the performer when interpreting the opening of Alkan's op 76/2 *Étude*.

Lament types

Marked 'lagrimoso lamento', or 'lamentevole' in the case of Alkan's *By the waters of Babylon* op 52, this tragic sentiment is 'inherited from a traditional intonation' as Grabocz notes.[52] For Alkan the spirit of the familiar Old Testament message is powerfully transmitted.

Instrumental recitative

Revival of the use of baroque recitative in romantic piano music is found in Schumann, Chopin, Liszt and Alkan. An excellent example of the latter's output is the *Prelude* op 31/18 where the performer needs to understand the expressive vocal introduction and the fragile arioso-like romance which follows. Unusually for Alkan the performer is instructed to play 'avec beaucoup d'expression'.

Associative or symbolic themes

The most obvious type is the pianistic imitation of bells in the *Étude* op 16/1 (campane and scampanio) and in *Les Cloches* op 63/4. Alkan's *Prières* op 64 are also a rich source of musical symbolism. The tragedy of descending minor intervals followed by the optimism of major intervals/tonality is reflected in the opening of the *Prière* op 64/1.

Technical requirements within scalic arpeggiated and chorded passages

Often Alkan's technical intricacies can be facilitated by adhering to the suggested fingerings. As Luguenot observes: 'each [fingering] solution implies ... a sonority, a phrasing, a dynamic, a balance of different voicings'.[53] So the use of the high speed 1–2–3–4–5 right-hand chromatic fingering in *Le Vent* op 15/2 gives exactly the correct sound for the effect of whistling wind. This Alkan example antedates a similar example in Liszt's *Wilde Jagd* étude by some fifteen years.

Equally interesting fingering is found in the bravura *Saltarella* op 23 where the rapid use of 3-1 achieves the high velocity required on the then new double-escapement pianos. Specified fingerings in pieces such as *Comme le Vent* op 39/1 show the expectations of the performer's finger technique by the composer. In this case there is a phenomenal challenge of the use of the prescribed fingering throughout this relentlessly high velocity étude. Other interesting fingerings are found in the mixed double note passage in the op 33 *Sonata* (third movement) and the use of 4/2 4/2 for thirds in *Les Omnibus* op 2 variation. This work includes an early example of glissando 4/2 fingering. The op 35 *Études* have several fingering solutions such as the passing of the fifth finger over octaves with the third finger in op 35/1, playing octaves with the third finger in op 35/2, avoidance of the fifth finger by using 1–2–3–4 in op 35/4 and the extremely extended fingering for the top voice in the op 35/6 *Étude*. This fingering is really mandatory if the 'très légèrement' instruction is to be carried out.

As expected *Le Festin d'Esope* op 39/12 contains a fair proportion of unusual fingerings to produce the required effect. Alkan's requirements include the use of the thumb in variation seven to help the downbeats, the use of the thumb slide in the 5–4–3–2–1 tied 1 group in variation twenty-two and the remarkable use of cross-fingering in variation twenty-three which permits the sonority of this variation to emerge perfectly.

Extended arpeggiated passages abound in Alkan's output. All demand the ultimate in control of the thumb and the acquisition of a relaxed contracted hand. The *Étude* op 15/1 contains an exuberant pre-Lisztian type of broken chord virtuosity unequalled by any contemporary piano composer.

The extraordinary op 76/2 *Étude* is also almost Lisztian in its use of powerful arpeggios. In Alkan's later piano music more directionally varied arpeggios are found such as in *Les Soupirs* op 63/11. This type of arpeggio texture prefigures textures found in later impressionist French composers for piano.

Mention has already been made of the sustained arm octaves in *Le Preux* op 17. Such jejune use of octave technique in Alkan is unusual. He is more inclined to employ octaves as part of a varied texture such as in the classic pre-allegro barbaro piece the *Allegro barbaresca* op 35/5. Any prospective pianist for this étude must possess a large relaxed hand to negotiate all the octaves and the 3–4–5 octave fingerings.

Elsewhere in Alkan's octave passages such as in the *March triomphale* op 27 and in the *Quasi Faust* second movement of op 33 where octaves are part of varied textures, the performer needs to follow the advice given by Alkan in *Le Preux* op 17 'du bras' that is play octaves from the arm. Pianists with large hands may even discover that if such passages are fingered with the thumbs and fifth fingers the arms are more relaxed and the pianistic execution is much more secure.

But perhaps Alkan makes the greatest demands on the performer in the field of chord technique. More than any other romantic composer he explores the sonic potential chords. The *Andante romantique* op 13/1 published in 1837 is truly astounding in its pre-Mazeppa anticipation of freely moving chromatic triads. Fingering for these Alkan chords is not specified.

A stylistic feature of Alkan's music discussed in this study is the massed effect, that is a series of repeated chords often continued for many bars yielding a pulsating powerful texture. The op 76/2 *Étude* especially explores these types of chords and often the use in this étude predates the pianistic chordal textures found in *Messiaen*. These types of massed effects require complete wrist and arm relaxation from the performer to recreate Alkan's orchestral sonority on the piano. A proper sense of wrist/arm relaxation aids the precise weight control of chords of a much lower dynamic level such as in the *Andante romantique* op 13/2 where the registral shifts need to be varied. Many of Alkan's fullest chordal textures necessitate the largest of hands as in the fugue of the *Quasi-Faust* movement of op 33. In many instances therefore the player has to guard against tension. As Lewenthal wryly notes, when practising the chordal stretches in the divinely beautiful *Étude* op 35/8 the 'hands may feel as though they have been on the rack'.[54]

These imaginative massed chordal textures emerge in the music of Alkan around the period of the *Étude* op 16/1 where the blind triadic chords mirror the coda of the Chopin *F major Ballade*, develop in the op 76 *Études* and in the op 27 *Marches* and reach extraordinary potency in *Quasi-Faust*. Not even Liszt's études exceed such technical intensity.

Pedalling

The starting point for investigating pedalling practice in Alkan's music is *Adam's Méthode* (1804). From this treatise we realize that the fashion for 'effects' pedalling was temporary and would inevitably expire. Only two pedals (the sustaining and the una corda pedal) were now deemed necessary.[55] In 1827 therefore, one year before the composition of Alkan's op 1, Hummel declared 'all other pedals are useless ...

but the use of the sustaining pedal combined occasionally with the other pedal [una corda] has an agreeable effect ...'.[56] In Alkan's *Serenade* op 74/5 we find both pedals employed in the recitative-like passage following giving an 'agreeable' colouring.

Ex. 13.5   *Sérénade* op 74/5, bars 37-39

Pedalling signs in Alkan's early works were rather different from those commonly used today. In op 1 for example we discover the indication 'grande pédale' which follows the tradition of nomenclature established by Boieldieu in his *Concerto* op 14. 'Grand pédale' is actually the sustaining pedal of the grand piano. The indication 'sourdine' means the use of the una corda pedal. To Alkan this pedal is implied in sourdement passages. Such muted passages occur in structurally important parts in his work, for example in the left hand octaves in *Le Preux* op 17 and in the diminished sevenths before the second group of the first movement of the *Symphonie* op 39.

Pedalling guidelines suggested by Lavignac[57] in his piano tutor of 1889 indicated that methods of notation were being developed for the depression of the sustaining and una corda pedals before or after the note or chord was played (legato pedalling) or simultaneously with playing the note or chord (direct or staccato pedalling). But the printing problems associated with this notation were enormous and there are no indications that Alkan embarked on this system.

The sustaining pedal's mechanism rapidly became more efficient after its invention by Stein in 1783. The 1820s/1830s compositions of Alkan reflect the improvements made to this pedal. For example the opening of the *Andante Romantique* op 13/3 marked 'legato e con due pedale' requires both sustaining and una corda pedals. The more limited sustaining power of the contemporary French pianos however ensured clarity in tremolando passages such as in variation twenty-four of *Le Festin d'Esope* op 39. But a bel canto melodic line might be obliterated by excessive pedalling of the tremolando and texturally dense accompaniments. A solution to this problem was suggested by the Parisian piano manufacturer Boisselot who patented a selective tone-sustaining device which curbed the effect of excessive pedalling and its resultant loss of textural clarity.[58] Certainly such cloudiness of pedalling existed, since Adam in his Méthode ruefully states that the [sustaining] pedal is only used 'to dazzle the ignorant in music or to disguise the mediocre of talent'.[59] Adam counsels against the overuse of the [sustaining] pedal in forte passages and implores that this pedal be lifted for each harmonic change. But the latter suggestion was not invariably followed by Alkan. For example the pedalling instruction in the celebrated nineteenth variation of *Le Festin d'Esope* op 39 results, on a modern piano at least, in harmonic chaos: to quote Lewenthal 'this effect is not for timorous souls! ... Pandemonium was obviously intended and achieved'.[60]

Finally a couple of puzzling pedalling issues to tax the imagination of the performer. Alkan in the *Prelude* op 31/13 suggests 'les deux ped et ped' which is probably only achievable on the pédalier. Even more cryptically in the slow movement of the *Symphonie* op 39 'senza ped. ou vero due ped' is found. The pianist has to choose between playing this passage without pedal or without either pedals.

Ex. 13.6   *Symphonie* op 39/11, bars 70–74

Any prospective Alkan pianist needs to be academically and practically involved in the performance practice issues outlined here. An ideal Alkan recital would employ contemporary Erard and/or Pleyel pianos, the Erard for the large-scale pieces and the Pleyel for the more intimate music. Ronald Smith's splendid recording of a selection of the *Preludes* op 31 and the *Esquisses* op 63 is an admirable model. Prospective performers of Alkan's piano music need supreme cantabile and technical facility as well as complete control of pedalling.

Pierre Reach[61] has written meaningfully on the psychological problems of interpreting Alkan and points out how the special massed effects of the composer's style anticipate those of Messaien. We might look back to Alkan's Petits Concerts and recreate some of the composer's own programmes with the addition of some Messiaen to show the relevance of Alkan for today's audiences. For the present we have on disc an excellent range of Alkan performances which are sensitive to many of the performances practice issues discussed here. To some extent my choice of these artists and their recordings listed in the appendix is a personal one but included are several classic performances from Lewenthal, Smith, Ogdon, Martin and Hamelin. These artists have proudly promoted Alkan's cause.

Chapter 14

Epilogue

It is difficult to write a summative conclusion to a study of Alkan's music because of the frequent coexistence of startling musical originality alongside stereotyped banality. Alkan, like Liszt, was a victim of his age. Both composers wrote rather too many empty 'pièces d'occasion'. But by judiciously sifting the first-rate from the formulaic amongst the pre-1844 works, op 8, op 10, op 12, op 13/2, op 15, op 21 and op 76 emerge as the finest. Of the post-1844 works it should be apparent from the frequency of citations that op 26/27, op 31, op 33, op 39, op 41, op 47, op 63 and op 70 are of great quality. This survey has attempted to show Alkan's links with the French clavecin school, his debt to the Austro-Germanic and French classical movement and, tentatively, his anticipation of the later French romantics such as Franck and Fauré.

Nevertheless, despite several complimentary reviews in *LFM* and *RGM* during his lifetime, Alkan's finest music has been neglected by performers, academics, critics and audiences alike. Fétis tried to explain this neglect merely noting that the 'music was difficult'.[1] After Alkan's death in 1888 there was little enthusiasm for his music. For example, one might have expected that Vincent d'Indy, the founder of the Schola Cantorum would provide some serious analysis of Alkan's music but as mentioned earlier, d'Indy[2] dismissed Alkan as a composer and only remarked on his prowess as a performer of Bach and Beethoven. D'Indy's indifference to Alkan the composer reflects the mood amongst contemporary French musicians. Alkan was viewed as 'an interesting figure but not a legenday one'.[3]

We have to turn to Germany for a more sympathetic reception of his music. As outlined in Chapter 4 Bülow wrote perceptively on the op 35 *Études* and Busoni championed the cause of the op 39/2 *Étude*. Busoni did not however perform any Alkan works in his piano recital tours in Paris. France remained unmoved by Alkan after the first world war too, possibly because of the anti-romantic movement of Stravinsky and his followers. Even that arch-romantic musician Alfred Cortot[4] in his historical survey of French piano music passed Alkan off as just an organist. Later French writers also gave extremely generalized views on Alkan. Parent observed that his music 'stretched technical requirements to the limits of the piano's art'[5] and Favre conceded that Alkan had an 'original but difficult style'.[6] Not until the publication of Beck's critical edition of Alkan's selected works in 1969 was there any serious notice taken of his music in France. Since 1969 of course François-Sappey's splendid collection of essays on Alkan has brought the composer into French musicological focus.

As well as further biographical and analytical studies, writing about Alkan might easily be extended to postmodernism, semiotic and psychological areas.[7] Alkan's personality is a fascinating one epitomized by the Hegelian idea of 'the self-extending subjectivity of the ego'.[8] His own developed ego state comprises a complex compounding of French *ancien régime* (op 24, op 46, parts of op 31 and op 63, op 51 and the transcriptions), the Beethovenian artist-hero (op 33, op 39 and op 47), the Faustian legend (*Quasi-Faust* in op 33 and *L'Enfer* in op 21). Alkan's musical personality extends to the French revolutionary march (op 26, op 27 and op 37), the devotional (op 54, op 64, op 69, op 72, the plainchant preludes and parts of op 31), the Mendelssohnian-lyrical (all the *Chants*) and the Jewish (op 31/4, op 31/5, op 31/19, op 52, op 64/8).

The analytical approach in this study has been empirical rather than Schenkerian or semiotic, although intonational analysis as a branch of musical semiotics has been invoked to illuminate for the performer various character types in Alkan's music. Analytically useful too may be narrative grammar methods using the Greimas-Tarasti theories.[9] These can explain and codify several stylistic angles. For example, the idea of 'savoir' (knowing) can unravel the opening pages of *Quasi Faust* op 33 after the projectile-like openng. 'Savoir' concludes that much of informational virtuosity is desirable from these opening pages. Alongside 'savoir', 'pouvoir' (being) comprises the capacity of the music to be expressed on the particular instrument using the resources such as those suggested in Chapter 13. Another term 'devoir' (having) concentrates on the models from which Alkan drew his inspiration. 'Devoir' categorizes the Italianate conformity of his early music and the relationship of say op 63 to French baroque models. The concept of 'vouloir' (intending), that is the internal trend of music may be seen in Alkan's more directioned works as in op 35, op 39, op 47 and op 61. Conversely, his non-progressive works are low in 'vouloir'. Alkan's best miniatures therefore realize 'vouloir' most fully.

Although the French classical opera influenced Alkan's melodic writing, he is definitely a romantic melodist. The classical-romantic divide is not however a clear one. Aguwa's[10] expression of this issue is admirable: 'the classical style did not die in 1830 nor was there an inaugural ceremony for romanticism in the same year'. In fact, Alkan shows in his music both a directness of classical discourse together with an indirectness of romantic language. Alkan's apprentice works act melodically as an outpouring of the dominant musical culture of the French bourgeois audience of early-nineteenth-century Paris. After *c*1840, Alkan's music becomes more original, internalized, often nostalgic and with recourse to the baroque and lyrical. A balance with classicism however is found by his embracing of the sonata dialectic after *c*1840.

These ideas illustrate the theories of Marothy[11] who discusses the concept of the 'inside' (lyricism and nostalgia) and the 'outside' (extraversion, march-like stylistics and heroism). During the nineteenth century with all its social instabilities and tensions the 'inside' became an oasis of calm, stability and security manifested in Alkan's baroque dances and lyric statements. Conversely the 'outside' is now demonstrated by much more tortured styles, chromaticism, rhapsodic storms and demonic elements. Examples of the 'outside' in Alkan include *Le Vent* op 15/2, a piece as explained in Chapter 12 only understood by a fellow 'outside' composer like Liszt, and op 33, op 39, and op 47 where many demonic elements are present. The finales of Alkan's large-scale works such as that of the *Symphonie* op 39 are also examples of the 'outside' portrayal of a tortured Faustian ride to hell. 'Outside' rhapsodic distortions of the stylized polonaise and the saltarella occur too in the finale of the *Concerto* op 39 and the finale of op 47. Dislocation of the simple binary funeral/triumphant nature in the *Marches* op 26 and op 27 yields the 'outside' satanic/ transcendental outpourings of *Quasi Faust* op 33.

Such opposites are less apparent in the apprentice works, many of the morceaux caracteristiques and the monotheistic études of op 35 and op 39. But without the discipline of binary markers bravura passages may dominate resulting in large areas of over-writing. When there are however inter and intra motivic relationships as well as these binary markers, such as in the *Symphonie* op 39 and op 47 excellent formal coherence results. When baroque ritornello form is strengthened with motivic unity, a gigantic but coherent movement such as the opening of the *Concerto* op 39 is created.

Some attention has been paid to Alkan's musical parameters. As a romantic harmonist Alkan favours classical harmonic restraint, but late works such as the *Chants* op 70 with frequent recourse to fluid non-resolving sevenths, look forward to the harmonic world of Fauré. Other anticipations of *fin de siècle* harmonic practices include a use of extended dominant pedals causing cadential delay as found in Alkan's stupendous cadenza to the first movement of the C minor Beethoven *Concerto*. Freely expressive ornamental chromaticism in a Chopinesque sense is absent in Alkan's music. His type of chromaticism in say the first movement of the *Symphonie* op 39 relates rather more to the chordal chromaticism manner of Franck. Chromatic harmony in Alkan's music usually highlights the expressive moments of a piece, sometimes reflecting the mimetic implications of its title. But he is predominantly a diatonic pre-Wagnerian harmonist as middle ground analysis of even the most harmonically experimental of op 63 shows. Yet Alkan in this study and elsewhere has been credited with anticipating various composers especially Debussy, Stravinsky, Satie, Prokofiev, Ives, Cowell, Gershwin and others. Writers such as Caux[12] have pointed out for example the blue notes in the *Barcarolle* op 65/6 and the chordal clusters in *Les Diablotins* op 63/45 look forward to the harmonic language of Gershwin and Cowell respectively but emphatically there is no evidence to prove that the composers mentioned knew any of these Alkan pieces.

Alkan is a less interesting melodist than harmonist. His apprentice works are highly derivative of Italianate operatic role models in which melodies embellish a simple harmonic structure. From 1835 onwards he develops a more personal melodic voice which is often note centred, although the important op 74 *Les Mois* have a varied melodic grace worthy of Mendelssohn. Chopin's melodic genius is flatteringly imitated in Alkan's nocturnes. In heartfelt 'innig' statements Alkan almost approaches the world of Schumann where melodies are pure entities requiring no development. An exquisite example of such purity is found in the trio of the *Symphonie* op 39 where the melody is an 'object for itself'. The more peaceful op 31, op 64 and op 72 and the plainchant preludes exhibit the same melodic simplicity. Sometimes, as in *Morituri te salutant* op 63/21, Alkan permits a complete dissolution of the melodic line to allow other musical parameters to emerge. Oppositely, if Alkan does employ a melodic chromatic colouring it is often at the cadence as a parody of Wagner's melodic writing. It may be recalled that Alkan loathed Wagner's music!

If his melodic tendencies became more lyrical with compositional maturity, the spirit of the baroque dance never ceased to infiltrate Alkan's rhythmic world: his last published work was the *Toccatina* op 75. Purely nationalistic dance rhythms did not much interest Alkan, with the sole exception of the *Bourée d'Auvergne* op 29. So the fashionable 'alla polacca' was transformed into symphonic grandeur in the finale of the *Concerto* op 39. Rhythmic maturity in Alkan's compositional career saw a distillation of the bombast of revolutionary marches into more personal examples such as in op 37, op 39, op 50/1 and op 50/2. Alkan, like Schumann, sometimes as in op 23, *Le Chemin de fer* op 27 and the *Allegro barbaro* op 35/5 is rhythmically obsessive but these pieces have, in their defence, an exciting primitivism. This barbarism is unequalled in piano music until the arrival of Bartok who is likely to have known op 35/5 before writing his own *Allegro barbaro*.[13] Such rhythmic regularity counterbalanced in other works by irregular time signatures and metres such as in the *Zorzico* and the op 32 set. Importantly, Alkan devised exact notations to counteract the rubato excesses of contemporary romantic pianists. Again, this is part of his essential classicism, a feeling for classical temporality[14] where the transportation backwards to *ancien régime* times is manifested by a real nostalgia for certainty and exactness.

Although Alkan's largest scale works are a personal outpouring of a romantic sonata writer, the smaller works are often more coherent in form building. With the exception of the wonderful *Festin d'Esope* op 39/12 and the last movement of op 33, Alkan was not an especially inspired writer of variations and rondos. Like Chopin perhaps, such forms were the products of the apprentice composer to be discarded with compositional maturity.

In conclusion however it is his very personal, original, polyvalent attitude to texture and sound where opposites excitingly co-exist, which places Alkan amongst the most significant of romantic piano composers. The variety of textures in his music is quite staggering from the power of the massed effect, where the piano seems to personify the power of a full orchestra to the tranquillity of simple linear writing. Alkan's richly creative attitude to counterpoint runs through all his best music from the purest in the chamber and other fugues to the most extravagently joyous in *Le Seigneur* in op 33. The *Études* sets op 76, op 35 and op 39 show an unparalled inventiveness in texture and sound far removed from French étude models, Czerny and Clementi. Alkan's love of the baroque and classical period is manifested by the exquisite transcriptions texturally faithful to their originals. The adaptability of Alkan's textural skills to the titles of the pieces is also astonishing, and even within the densest textures he maintains tremendous precision and clarity of parts. This stylistic feature is the one which most looks forward to French keyboard composers of the twentieth century.

Alkan's absorption of Italian and French opera, the thematically saturated world of the classical sonata, the power and purity of Jewish chant, the keyboard and organ music of Bach and the noble French classical tradition allowed him to select yet distance himself from these models. It is this sound world of Alkan that is unique where he reaches over other musical parameters to create a multi-dimensioned world of sound colour for itself. This applies in his non-keyboard pieces too of which there are all too few available for analysis. Rather than speculate on the influence of Alkan on later composers, we can centre his real contribution to music in the creation as a 'conservative radical' of an infinitely varied sound world which in his best music unites all the various components into a marvellous sense of coherence. His music demands further investigation by all musicians who love and wish to understand French romantic instrumental music more completely.

Notes to Chapters

Chapter 1   Alkan – The Historical and Social Background

1   See Chapter 3 of Mongredien (1986)
2   See Ganvert in François-Sappey (1991) 263–281.
3   Idelssohn (1944) 219.
4   Arch. Paris, V2E, 7 e Mairie.
5   Marmontel (1878) 119. Translation by author.
6   Jean Ravina (1818–1906) pianist, pupil of Zimmerman and Reicha. First prize in piano 1834, first prize in harmony 1836.
7   Leon Honoré (1818–1874) pianist and composer.
8   Antoine Marmontel (1816–1898) pianist, teacher and author. Pupil of Zimmerman, first prize in piano 1832. His students included Albeniz, Bizet, d'Indy, Dubois, Guiraud and Wieniawski.
9   Marmontel (1878) 118.
10   Arch.nat. AJ 3766 (16), 76, 86–89, 149–154, 226, 352.
11   Pierre Zimmermann (1785–1853) teacher and composer. Studied composition with Boieldieu. First prize in piano 1800, first prize in harmony 1802. Pupils included Franck, Alkan, Lacombe and Marmontel.
12   Victor Dourlen (1780–1864) teacher and composer. Professor of harmony at the Conservatoire from 1816.
13   François Benoist (1794–1878) organist, teacher and composer. Studied harmony with Catel and piano with L. Adam. First prize harmony 1811, first prize piano 1814. Won Prix de Rome in 1815. Professor of organ at the Conservatoire from 1819–1872. Pupils included A. Adam, Alkan, Franck, Bizet, Dubois and Saint-Saëns.
14   Antoine Batiste (1820–1876) organist, teacher and composer.
15   Fétis (1860) 'Alkan'.
16   Jacques Rode (1774–1830) violinist and composer. Another possible contender as a work for Alkan's debut could be Rode's *Variations in G major*, popular with singers.
17   Angelica Catalani (1780–1849) Italian virtuoso soprano, resident in Paris from 1814.
18   Leo (1931) 258.
19   AN O^3 1825. Letter dated 22 March 1826.
20   Giuditta Pasta (1797–1865) Italian soprano. Appeared in first Paris performance of Rossini's *Zelmira* in March 1826. Specialized in Rossini, Donizetti and Bellini roles.
21   Giovanni Rubini (1794–1854) Italian tenor. Specialized in Rossini roles, debut in Paris 1825.
22   Filippo Galli (1783–1853) Italian bass. Rossini specialist, Paris début 1821.
23   Lambert Massart (1811–1892) Belgian violinist and teacher. Protégé of Kreutzer, studied at the Conservatoire from 1829.
24   *Le Mentor*, April 1826 79.
25   *Gazette de Liége*, 15 February 1827.
26   *Gazette de Liége*, 28 February 1827.
27   The *Harmonicon*, April 1827 73.
28   de Bertha (1909) 135.

29 RM (1829) 353.
30 Auguste Franchomme (1808–1884) cellist and composer. First prize in cello 1825. Founder member of the Société des Concerts du Conservatoire in 1828. Chopin dedicated his op 65 *Sonata* to Franchomme.
31 Murdoch (1934) 232.
32 ASJ 49 (1994) 2–3.
33 ASJ 38 (1989) 7–11.
34 Fétis (1860) 'Alkan'.
35 The mixture of conservatoires, virtuosi, artists, composers and pianists is typical of such societies.
36 See entry in Decourcelle (1881).
37 Joseph Mayseder (1789–1863) violinist, teacher and composer. Second violinist of the Schuppanzigh Quartet.
38 Jean Lamatre (1772–?) composer and cellist.
39 Pauline Viardot-Garcia (1821–1910) mezzo-soprano. Engaged to Viardot, director of the Italian theatre in Paris. Principal singer until 1841.
40 Joseph d'Ortigue (1802–1866) music critic and author.
41 GM 4 (1837) 460.
42 GM 5 (1838) 96.
43 Heinirich Ernst (1814–1865) virtuoso violinist, pupil of Paganini. Début Paris 1831.
44 Pierre Batta (1795–1876) cellist and teacher.
45 Adolph Gutmann (1819–1882). German pianist: arrived in Paris in 1834. Dedicatee of Chopin's *Scherzo in C sharp minor* op 39.
46 See Watson (1988) 42 for details of the Thalberg and Liszt concerts.
47 See Walker (1983) 240–241 who observes that this work was not finished for the concert on 31 March.
48 de Bertha (1909) 135–147.
49 Olga Samaroff (1882–1948). Student of Delaborde at the Conservatoire. Taught at the Julliard School; pupils included Raymond Lewenthal.
50 Lewenthal (1964) v–xx. See also LSA (1987) 3–5.
51 François-Sappey (1991) 307.
52 Letter to Fontana dated 1841 in Hedley (1962) 195.
53 *LFM* May 1844 46.
54 *RGM* 13 (1846) 13–14.
55 Macdonald (1976) 402.
56 Emile Prudent (1817–1863) composer and pianist. Won first prize at the Conservatoire in 1833.
57 Edouard Wolff (1816–1880) Polish pianist and composer. Resident in Paris from 1835.
58 *RGM* 14 (1847) 25.
59 Letter dated July 8–17 in Hedley (1962) 324.
60 See Cairns (1969) preface.
61 Letter dated 26 July 1848 in Searle (1973) 108.
62 ASJ II (1980) also Fryklund (1930) 85–154.
63 B.H.V.P. G3288.
64 Ibid.
65 AN F^{21} 1291.
66 Ibid.
67 See Curtiss (1959) 22.
68 Cairns (1969) 584.

69   AN F^{21} 1291.
70   Other likely candidates are Prudent (reference 56) and L. Lacombe (1818–1884) pupil of Zimmerman.
71   AN AJ^{37} 71(1) dated 30 November 1858.
72   See Marmontel (1878) 119.
73   In Delacroix (1932) 290.
74   *RGM* 16 (1849) 147
75   Napoléon Reber (1807–1880) professor of composition at the Conservatoire from 1851.
76   B.H.V.P. G3295.
77   BN Fonds Conservatoire letter: Alkan 6.
78   *RGM* 19 (1852) 354–356.
79   *RGM* 19 (1852) 361–362.
80   Opera by Boieldieu (1775–1834) composed in 1825. The example refers to the Act 2 Cavatina.
81   The piece reflects this restricted range.
82   *RGM* 19 (1852) 356.
83   [Paris] 30 October 1852 in Sietz (1958) 9.
84   *Le Ménestrel*, November 1852.
85   Dated November 6–7 1852 in Sietz (1958) 95.
86   *RGM* 19 (1852) 361–363.
87   Thomas Tellefsen (1823–1881) pianist and composer.
88   *RGM* 20 (1853) 69. No precise citation given.
89   Nicolas Lemmens (1823–1881) organist, composer and teacher.
90   *RGM* 21 (1854) 199.
91   *RGM* 23 (1856) 50–52.
92   *RGM* 20 (1853) 28.
93   *RGM* 21 (1854) 29.
94   *RGM* 22 (1855) 7.
95   Vallas (1951) 109.
96   Louise Massart (1827–1887) pianist and teacher at the Conservatoire.
97   Pauline Viardot's skills embraced piano playing (she was taught by Liszt. She was probably familiar with comtemporary piano music.
98   Letter from Alkan to Hiller [1857] in Sietz (1961) 29–30.
99   Hans von Bülow (1830–1894) pianist, conductor and composer. See NZM (1857) 273.
100 Letter from Alkan to Hiller [1856] in Sietz (1958) 121.
101 Letter from Alkan to Hiller, 21 April 1958 in Sietz (1958) 131.
102 Letter from Alkan to Hiller, 2 July 1859 in Sietz (1958) 142.
103 Letter from Alkan to Hiller, 24 July 1859 in Sietz (1958) 145.
104 See reference 102 and also Barth (1975) 190.
105 See Letter from Alkan to Hiller, 31 January 1860 in Sietz (1958) 156.
106 Joseph d'Ortigue (1802–1866) French critic and chief editor of *Le Menestrel* from 1863.
107 Anton Rubinstein (1829–1894) pianist and composer.
108 Letter from Alkan to Hillier, 24 April 1860 in Sietz (1958) 167.
109 See the correspondence in Sietz (1958) 176–177.
110 Letter from Alkan to Hiller, May 1862 in Sietz (1961) 15–16.
111 Possibly *K491* because of the Hummel arrangement and cadenza.
112 Letter from Alkan to Hiller, 2 February 1863 in Sietz (1961) 29.
113 Letter from Alkan to Hiller, 10 April 1863 in Sietz (1961) 29–30.

114 Letter from Alkan to Hiller [1864?] in Sietz (1961) 51–52.
115 Letter from Alkan to Hiller dated 'early May 1865' in Sietz (1961) 61.
116 Letter from Alkan to Hiller, 17 December 1865 in Sietz (1961) 127.
117 Letter from Alkan to Hiller, 17 December 1865 in Sietz (1961) 73.
118 Letter from Alkan to Hiller, 5 April 1869 in Sietz (1961) 127.
119 *RGM* 37 (1870) 100.
120 Lewenthal (1964) vi.
121 Letter from Alkan to Hiller 11 August 1871 in Sietz (1964) 64–65.
122 *RGM* 40 (1873) 22.
123 Marie Durand (1830–1909) organist, critic, publisher and composer.
124 Georges Mathias (1826–1910) pianist and composer.
125 Louis Gouvy (1819–1898) pianist and composer.
126 *RGM* 40 (1873) 78
127 Pablo Sarasate (1844–1908) virtuoso violinist and composer.
128 *RGM* 40 (1873) 109.
129 Hubert Léonard (1819–1890) violinist and composer.
130 *RGM* 40 (1873) 126.
131 Johann Altenburg (1736–1801) trumpet virtuoso and composer.
132 Lugwig Berger (1797–1839) pianist and composer. His lyrical style influenced Mendelssohn.
133 Aloys Schmitt (1788–1866) pianist, composer, teacher and writer.
134 *RGM* 41 (1874) 62.
135 *RGM* 41 (1874) 79.
136 *RGM* 41 (1874) 109.
137 *RGM* 41 (1874) 142.
138 *RGM* 41 (1874) 46.
139 *RGM* 42 (1875) 69.
140 Macdonald (1976) 401–402 and *RGM* 43 (1876) 22.
141 Alfred Turban (1847–1896) 1st prize in violin Paris Conservatoire 1872.
142 Victor Verrimst (1825–1893) 1st prize in double bass Paris Conservatoire 1845.
143 *RGM* 44 (1877) 54.
144 *RGM* 44 (1877) 77.
145 *RGM* 44 (1877) 93.
146 *RGM* 44 (1877) 109.
147 *RGM* 44 (1877) 125.
148 *RGM* 44 (1877) 142.
149 *RGM* 45 (1878) 86.
150 *RGM* 45 (1878) 110.
151 *RGM* 45 (1878) 141.
152 Ibid.
153 *RGM* 45 (1878) 206.
154 *RGM* 45 (1878) 102.
155 *RGM* 47 (1880) 125.
156 *RGM* 47 (1880) 142.
157 Macdonald (1976) 401–402.
158 de Bertha (1909) 135–147.
159 Frederick Niecks (1845–1924) critic and author. See Niecks (1918) 4–7.
160 Possibly the wife of Clement Dubois (1837–1924) composer and teacher. Student of Marmontel: director of the Conservatoire from 1896.
161 d'Indy (1930) 473.

162 Fourcaud (1893) 111.
163 Isador Philipp (1863–1958) pianist, teacher and co-editor of an incomplete edition to Alkan's piano music. This verbal account was given to Robert Collet in 1937. See Smith (1976) 74.
164 Jean Maurin (1822–1894) violinist and teacher.
165 de Bertha (1909) 135–147.
166 Mme Rachel Guerret (1878–?). See Smith (1976) 75.
167 da Motta (1900) 255.
168 Macdonald (1973) 25 and Macdonald (1988) 118–120.

Chapter 2   Apprentice Works

1   Rousseau (1796) *Sonate*.
2   Adam (1804).
3   Fétis (1860) 'Dussek'.
4   See for example the 1837 transcription of part of Beethoven *Symphony No. 7* for two pianos eight hands. Also see the series of transcriptions of 1847, 1861 and c.1866.
5   Alkan's op1 was discovered in 1991 by Luguenot. See SAB 18 (1991) 1–2.
6   Weinstock (1949) 37 citing the letter of 12 August 1829.
7   Castil-Blaze (1825) 262–263.
8   Fabré (1962) 69.
9   Samson (1985) 32.
10 *Le Pianiste* (1833) 26.
11 Alkan's op 5 is still missing. Date of op 5 is taken from Fétis (1835–1844)
12 Rossini's overture to *Semiramide* (1826) contains an earlier example ofapplied passing note in its third theme.
13 Smith (1987) 1–2.
14 GM (1828) 35a. Fétis may have been discussing op 3 as well.
15 Possibly derived from the Chopin set of variations on *La ci darem la Mano* op 2 published in Paris in 1830.
16 Hinson (1978) 'Alkan'.
17 Vapereau (1858).
18 Shaw (1974) 12.
19 *Bath and Cheltenham Gazette*, 12 April 1834.
20 Compare the Andante and Rondo *Capriccioso* op 14 (1824).
21 Published by Richault in Paris 1859.
22 From the score published by Cocks in London 1834.
23 *RGM* 5 (1838) 96.
24 *Le Pianiste* (1833) 23.
25 Published by Richault.
26 See also Bizet's *Variations Chromatiques de Concert* published 1838.
27 'Bellini' in Grove 6.
28 F. Paër (1771–1839) violinist, opera composer and conductor at the Theatre Italien.
29 M.E. Carafa de Colobrano (1787–1872) opera, ballet and church composer. Professor of composition at the Conservatoire from 1840.
30 Possibly related to Henry Field whom Alkan met in Bath during his 1834 visit.
31 See the *Variations in E flat major* op 82 published 1849.
32 Appropriately minetic 'imitating the sound of oars'.
33 From the collection of *Neapolitan Songs* by G.L. Cottrau.

Chapter 3 Development of a Personal Voice

1 Ellis (1995) especially on the *RGM* reviews.
2 Cairns (1969).
3 See Chapter 1 p. 8.
4 Perhaps inspired by the Beethovenian precedent.
5 See for example the end of *Le Festin d'Esope* op 39/12.
6 See the rondo finale of the *Sonata in A major D959* (1828).
7 Presumably 'superbiamente' that is 'in a proud and arrogant manner'.
8 Bellamann (1924) 251.
9 See particularly the accompaniment patterns in the *Impromptu in C minor D899/1* (1817).
10 See the arpeggio passages in the *Sonata in A flat major* (1819), first movement.
11 Liszt's *Mazeppa* was composed in 1840 and was developed from No. 4 of the 24 *Grandes Etudes* composed in 1837, the publication date of Alkan's op 13.
12 See Chapter 2 p. 44.
13 *Le Pianiste* (1833) 23.
14 *RGM* (1838) 167.
15 Schumann (1881) 317.
16 *RGM* (1837) 460.
17 Possibly this is the musical declaration of intent towards an identified beloved who may have been the mother of Alkan's illegitimate son, Elie-Miriam Delaborde born 8 February 1839.
18 As in *Vision* (No 6 of the *Etudes d'execution transcendante*) final version composed 1851.
19 *RGM* (1837) 461.
20 Sorabji (1932) 213–219.
21 Lewenthal (1967) 37.
22 *RGM* (1837) 460. The other op 15 études contain no expression/dynamic marks also. But Philippe added fingering and expression/dynamic marks in his collected edition of Alkan's piano works.
23 Alkan uses the complete version of the plainchant.
24 See especially his *Harmonies poétiques et religieuses* published in 1835.
25 Also in *Quasi-Faust* op 33.
26 A technique later developed by Ravel in *Le Gibet* (*Gaspard de la Nuit*).
27 See especially the *Three-Page Sonata* (1905). There is no evidence that Ives knew the Alkan work.
28 As in Liszt's setting of *Soireé de Vienne* No. 6.
29 See the dramatic sforzando diminished sevenths in the *Sonata in C minor* op 13.
30 Alkan's Italianization of 'impassibilité' that is 'impassively'.
31 Literally 'bells'.
32 Literally 'the incessant chiming of bells'.
33 Smith (1987) 25.
34 Schumann (1881) 486–487.
35 This musical expression of winter is developed by Liszt in *Chasse Neige* (No. 6 of the *Etudes d'execution transcendante*).
36 Prophetic of *Chanson de la Folle au bord de la mer*, *Preludes* op 31 and *Le Tambour bat aux Champs* op 50.
37 See also *Heraclite de Democrite* op 63/39 and *Horace et Lydie* op 65/5

Chapter 4 *Études*

1   Marx (1884) 300.
2   Leopold von Meyer (1816–1883) pianist and composer. Pupil of Czerny.
3   See also the *Capriccio alla Soldatesca* op 50.
4   Published without opus numbers but plate numbers suggest a publication date of 1838–1840.
5   Notwithstanding the Czerny 10 *Grand Studies* for the improvement of the left hand op 399. Alkan's op 76/1 is the first extended left hand étude.
6   'Thalberg' in Grove 6.
7   Niccolo Paganini (1782–1840) Virtuoso violinist who directly inspired Schumann's 6 *Studien mach Capricen von Paganini* published 1832, and Liszt's *Études d'execution transcendante d'aprés Paganini*, published 1840.
8   The influence of op 76/1 on Bizet's *Farandole* (*L'arlésienne*) compared with 1872 is notable.
9   Liszt probably knew op 76/1 when writing *Wilde Jagd*.
10   Alexander Dreyschock (1818–1869) pupil of Tomaschek. Virtuoso pianist and professor of piano at the St. Petersburg Conservatoire.
11   See especially pp. 66–67 of *Regard de L'esprit de joie* from the 20 *Regards sur l'Enfant Jesus* composed 1944.
12   Such as the op 35/8 with similar rhythmic verve in both hands.
13   Literally 'carrying on'. This implies a highly legato touch is required.
14   See for example the arpeggiated cascades just before the fugue in *Quasi Faust* (1847).
15   Sorabji (1932) 215.
16   Smith (1987) 99.
17   NBM II (1857) 273–276.
18   Dille 12 (1970) 3–9.
19   Sorabji (1932) 216.
20   Smith (1987) 102.
21   Beck (1969) iii–xi.
22   Sorabji (1932) 217.
23   van Dieren (1935) 14.
24   Lewenthal (1964) xvii.
25   Alkan may have known Chopin's Étude op 10/10 also.
26   Smith (1987) 105.
27   *RGM* 19 (1852) 361–363.
28   Smith (1987) 113.
29   Quoted in Smith (1987) 113.
30   Smith (1987) 115.
31   Lewenthal (1964) xiii.
32   A better known example is the Schumann *Sonata in F minor* given the title*Concerto without Orchestra* by the publisher Haslinger, but the first movement runs only to sixteen pages.
33   Smith (1987) 240.
34   Smith (1987) 147.
35   Schumann (1881) 342.
36   Rellstab (1834) 19–20.
37   For a fuller study see Jachimecki (1930) 107–108, Leichtentritt (1922) 78–209, Samson (1985) 59–60.

38   Dale (1954) 191.
39   Busoni (1904) preface.

Chapter 5   Sonata Types for Piano

1   Newman (1969) 8.
2   Rousseau (1821) 218–219.
3   Boulez (1964) 61–75.
4   Favre (1953) 29.
5   Momigny (1806) 198.
6   Momigny (1806) 394.
7   Momigny (1806) 397.
8   Ellis (1995) is the best account of the importance of Beethoven in Paris during Alkan's lifetime.
9   Johann Edelmann (1749–1794) composer of operas, ballets and keyboard music.
10   See Howard (1963) for an excellent account.
11   Nicholas-Joseph Hüllmandel (1751–1823) composer and pianist.
12   Etienne Méhul (1763–1817) composer of comic operas and keyboard music.
13   Ringer (1951) 552–553.
14   Hyacinthe Jadin (1769–1802) pianist, composer and teacher at the Conservatoire.
15   Eitner (1899–1904) 436.
16   Schumann (1881) 317.
17   Prod'homme (1937) 248–250.
18   Fétis a (1830) 137–168.
19   See Chapter 13 – Reception. (
20   François Boieldieu (1775–1834) composer and teacher at the Conservatoire.
21   Thayer (1866–1879) 801.
22   AMZ iv (1801–1802) 226–227.
23   Ignace Ladurner (1766–1839) pianist and composer.
24   Steibelt's popularity in Paris and London as pianist, teacher and composer is also referred to in Chapter 2 p. 39.
25   Pupil of Beethoven, Haydn, Albrechtsberger and Clementi; Kalpbrenner was also influenced by Cramer's piano style.
26   Schoenberg (1963) 112–113.
27   Schumann (1914) 155–156.
28   Gertler (1931) 1–13.
29   Devaux in *The Harmonicon* viii/i (1830) 33–34.
30   Fétis b (1830) 230.
31   Schumann (1914) 394–395.
32   Schumann (1914) 452.
33   *RGM* 12 (1845) 68.
34   Soullier (1855) *Sonate*.
35   Bellaigue in *Guide Musical XLVII* (1901).
36   Newman (1969) 67.
37   Smith (1976) 63.
38   Lewenthal (1964) xvii.
39   Alkan (1847) preface.
40   François-Sappey (1991) 105.
41   Lewenthal (1964) XVIII.

42 François-Sappey (1991) 107, Smith (1987) 71–73.
43 François-Sappey (1991) 114–115.
44 Sorabji (1932) 216.
45 Letter dated 25 July 1847 in Fryklund (1930) 115.
46 Almost certainly the *12 Études* op 39.
47 Smith (1987) 159.
48 Sorabji (1932) 215.

Chapter 6   Morceaux Caracteristiques

1   Dalhaus (1978) 221, 226.
2   Ellis (1969).
3   Jean-Jacques Beauvarley-Charpentier (1730–1794) organist and composer.
4   Bernard Viguerie (c1761–1819) teacher and composer.
5   See Favre (1953) 146.
6   Ferdinand Hérold (1791–1833) piano teacher and composer of comic operas.
7   Alexandre Boëly (1785–1858) composer, organist and pianist.
8   Morellet (1771).
9   Goblot (1901) 62.
10 Gabriel Dupont (1878–1914) composer and organist.
11 Prunières (1933) 20.
12 Ellis (1969) 681.
13 Bellamann (1924) 254.
14 *RGM* 14 (1847) 244. See also *RGM* 14 (1847) 25 for a brief appreciation of op 26 and op 27.
15 *RGM* 14 (1847) 244.
16 Ibid.
17 *RGM* 14 (1847) 245.
18 Beck (1969) viii.
19 *RGM* 14 (1847) 245.
20 *RGM* 14 (1847) 244–246.
21 *Psalm 150* from Verses 3–5 in the Authorised Version.
22 Naumbourg (1874) *Rikud*.
23 *RGM* 14 (1847) 246.
24 See the baroque items in the 1847 *Souvenirs* series. Also from the mid-1840s baroque music or baroque-inspired works featured in his concert programmes.
25 Possibly an Erard double keyboard piano was available. See Smith (1987) 165.
26 Beck (1969) viii.
27 de Bertha (1909) 138.
28 Smith (1987) 55.
29 Smith (1987) 161.
30 Smith (1987) 166.
31 Lewenthal (1964) xvi.
32 See also the *Benedictus* op 54 (1859).
33 Smith (1987) 154.
34 Smith (1987) 170.
35 Smith (1987) 61.
36 Smith (1987) 63.
37 Ibid.

Chapter 7   The *Esquisses*

1   Smith (1987) 44.
2   Literally 'frenzied' [sketch]. The manuscript (MS 2943) is in the British Library and is dated 9/10/47.
3   Gorer (1946) 688.
4   Lewenthal (1964) xiv.
5   Smith (1987) 44–45.
6   Lewenthal (1964) xvi.
7   Lewenthal (1964), xv.
8   Einstein (1958) 119–127 comprehensively describes this duality originating in Kircher's *Musurgia* (Rome, 1650) in which the equating of the major key with a happy mood and the minor key with a gloomy state is proposed. Alkan probably became aware of the Heraclite/Dèmocrite proposed in binary divide from Batistin's third book of *Cantates françois* (1711). Here the darkness of Heraclitus is portrayed in French recitative style and the happiness of Democritus is presented as an Italianate da capo aria.
9   Stravinsky (1972) 45.
10   Smith (1987) 47.
11   Lewenthal (1964) xv.
12   Smith (1987) 47.
13   Letter from Alkan to Hiller, 31 January 1860 in Sietz (1958) 156.
14   Smith (1987) 50.

Chapter 8   Arrangements and Cadenzas

1   Riemann (1882).
2   Keller (1969) 22.
3   Smith (1987) 174–176.
4   RM 3 (1828), 372.
5   *RGM* 16 (1849) 147–148.
6   Warrack (1976) 341.
7   Kerman (1967) 196–199.
8   Türk (1789) preface.
9   Smalley (1972) 30–34.

Chapter 9   Organ and Pédalier Music

1   *RGM* 20 (1853) 161, 181. See also Smith (1987) 221–222.
2   Cavaillé-Coll (1929) 71.
3   Saint-Saëns (1913) 39.
4   Smith (1987) 222.
5   Smith (1987) 223.
6   Sabatier in François-Sappey (1991) 235.
7   Wells (1989) 14–16.
8   Smith (1987) 230.
9   Fromageot (1909) 193.
10   Smith (1987) 235.
11   Sabatier in François-Sappey (1991) 249.

Notes

12 Charles-Simon Richault (1780–1866) Parisian music publisher.
13 Sabatier in François-Sappey (1991) 241.

Chapter 10   Piano and Strings

1 Fétis in *RGM* 13 (1846) 1–3.
2 *RGM* 14 (1847) 244–246.
3 *RGM* 11 (1844) 74–75. See also Smith (1987) 212.
4 Kreutzer's review in *RGM* 13 (1846) 13–14 relates the imagery of this movement to Scheffer's painting in the Louvre and by derivation Dante's poem particularly the lines 'La bacco mi bacio tutto tremante'.
5 Smith (1987) 185.
6 *RGM* (1837) 81.
7 Halbreich in François Sappey (1991) 208–209.
8 See Samson (1985) especially Chapter 8 for a survey of Chopin's sonatas.
9 Samson (1985) 138.
10 Samson (1985) 138–141.
11 Halbreich in François-Sappey (1991) 213.

Chapter 11   Miscellaneous Compositions

1 *RGM* 11 (1844) 74.
2 For an excellent overview of Jewish influences in Alkan's life and music see Ganvert in François-Sappey (1991) 263–281.
3 Translation for the NIV.
4 *LFM* 7 November 1844.
5 See François-Sappey (1991) 316.
6 Smith (1987) 212.
7 Macdonald (1976) 401–402.
8 *RGM* 13 (1846) 13f
9 See Cox in Layton (1995) especially 193–196.
10 RGM 11 (1844) 74–75.
11 ASJ 43 (1991) 2.

Chapter 12   Reception

1 Schumann (1881) 317.
2 *RGM* 5 (1838) 107.
3 *RGM* 4 (1837) 460.
4 *LFM* March 1844.
5 *LFM* May 1844.
6 RM (1928) 5.
7 *Le Pianiste* (1833) 23.
8 *RGM* 5 (1938) 107.
9 *LFM* Feb 1844.
10 *LFM* Oct (1944).
11 *RGM* 12 (1845) 89.

12 *LFM* March 1844.
13 *RGM* 14 (1847) 25 reviewing op 26 and op 27.
14 *RGM* 13(1846) 13–14.
15 *RGM* 14 (1847) 245–246.
16 *RGM* 16 (1849) 147–148.
17 *RGM* 19 (1852) 361 363 details letter from Alkan to Fétis.
18 For a detailed account see Ellis (1995) especially chapter 10.
19 *RGM* 29 (1862) 97.
20 *RGM* 40 (1873).
21 *RGM* 40 (1873) 62.
22 *RGM* 40 (1873) 109.
23 *RGM* 42 (1875).
24 *RGM* 42 (1875) 69.
25 *RGM* 42 (1875) 110.
26 *RGM* 16 (1849) 148.
27 *RGM* 44 (1877) 54.
28 *RGM* 41 (1874) 62.
29 *RGM* 42 (1875) 85.
30 *RGM* 44 (1877) 54.
31 *RGM* 42 (1875) 69.
32 *RGM* 41 (1974) 79.
33 *RGM* 47 (1880) 142.
34 *RGM* 16 (1849) 148.
35 *RGM* 20 (1853) 18.
36 *RGM* 40 (1873) 78.
37 *RGM* 40 (1873) 78.
38 *RGM* 44 (1877) 125.
39 *RGM* 44 (1877) 142.
40 *RGM* 42 (1875) 142.
41 *RGM* 47 (1880) 142.
42 *RGM* 44 (1877) 125.
43 *RGM* 45 (1878) 86.
44 *RGM* 47 (1880) 142.
45 *RGM* 40 (1873) 126.
46 *RGM* 40 (1873) 141.
47 *RGM* 40 (1873) 109.
48 *RGM* 40 (1873) 126.
49 *RGM* 42 (1875) 70.
50 Himmelfarb in François-Sappey (1991).
51 Ellis (1995) provides an excellent overview. Schrade (1942) takes a more contextual stance.
52 GM June 12 (1836).
53 *LFM* April 1844.
54 *RGM* 42 (1875) 70.
55 *RGM* 40 (1873) 62.
56 *RGM* 40 (1873) 141.
57 *RGM* 42 (1875) 110.
58 *RGM* 44 (1877) 109.
59 *RGM* 47 (1880) 102.
60 *RGM* 41 (1874) 79.

61 *RGM* 42 (1875) 85.
62 *RGM* 44 (1877) 109.
63 *RGM* 11 (1844) 87.
64 Schumann (1914) 124.
65 Newman (1969) 117.
66 *RGM* 42 (1875) 85.
67 *RGM* 40 (1873) 126.
68 *RGM* 42 (1875) 69.
69 *RGM* 44 (1877) 93.
70 *RGM* 40 (1873) 109.
71 *RGM* 41 (1874) 79.
72 *RGM* 42 (1875) 69 and handbill.
73 *RGM* 42 (1875) 85.
74 *RGM* 42 (1875) 142.
75 *RGM* 44 (1877) 77.
76 *RGM* 45 (1878) 110.
77 This work was highly influential on Chopin. See Samson (1985) 52, 82.
78 *RGM* 45 (1878) 86.
79 *RGM* 41 (1874) 142.
80 *RGM* 45 (1878) 86.
81 *RGM* 42 (1875) 69 and handbill.
82 *RGM* 41 (1874) 79.
83 *RGM* 42 (1875) 85.
84 *RGM* 44 (1877) 109.
85 *RGM* 40 (1873) 126.
86 *RGM* 40 (1873) 134.
87 *RGM* 42 (1875) 85.
88 *RGM* 42 (1875) 142.
89 *RGM* 42 (1875) 142.
90 *RGM* 45 (1878) 141.
91 *RGM* 47 (1880) 102.
92 *RGM* 40 (1873) 62.
93 *RGM* 40 (1873) 109
94 *RGM* 40 (1873) 141
95 *RGM* 41 (1874) 62.
96 *RGM* 42 (1875) 69.
97 *RGM* 42 (1875) 110.
98 According to *RGM* 42 (1875) 142 this was performed at the fifth concert.
99 Announced in 'F Minor' in the *RGM* 42 (1875) 142
100 *RGM* 44 (1877) 54.
101 *RGM* 44 (1877) 93.
102 *RGM* 44 (1877) 125
103 *RGM* 45 (1878) 142.
104 *RGM* 47 (1880) 125 and *RGM* 40 (1873) 109
105 *RGM* 40 (1873) 141
106 *RGM* 42 (1875) 69.
107 *RGM* 44 (1877) 93.
108 *RGM* 42 (1875) 142.
109 *RGM* 44 (1877) 93.
110 *RGM* 44 (1877) 125.

111 Fétis (1860) Alkan.
112 RM (1829) 353.
113 Macdonald (1976) 402.
114 Le Pianiste (1833) 23.
115 *RGM* 2 (1835) 393.
116 *RGM* 5 (1838) 378.
117 *RGM* 11 (1844) 87.
118 *RGM* 12 (1845) 89.
119 *RGM* 16 (1849) 147.
120 *RGM* 20 (1853) 18.
121 *RGM* 20 (1853) 69.
122 *RGM* 40 (1873) 22.
123 *RGM* 40 (1873) 62.
124 *RGM* 40 (1873) 78.
125 *RGM* 40 (1873) 109.
126 *RGM* 40 (1873) 119.
127 *RGM* 40 (1874) 141.
128 *RGM* 41 (1874) 62.
129 *RGM* 41 (1874) 142.
130 *RGM* 41 (1874) 62.
131 *RGM* 42 (1875) 85.
132 *RGM* 42 (1875) 142. Note the discrepancy of handbill of concert.
133 *RGM* 44 (1877) 142.
134 *RGM* 45 (1878) 110.
135 *RGM* 45 (1878) 142.
136 *RGM* 40 (1873) 62.
137 *RGM* 40 (1873) 78.
138 *RGM* 40 (1873) 126.
139 *RGM* 40 (1873) 141.
140 *RGM* 40 (1873) 62.
141 *RGM* 41 (1874) 79.
142 *RGM* 41 (1874) 109.
143 *RGM* 42 (1875) 70.
144 *RGM* 42 (1875) 110.
145 *RGM* 42 (1875) 142.
146 *RGM* 44 (1877) 62.
147 *RGM* 44 (1877) 77.
148 *RGM* 44 (1877) 109.
149 *RGM* 44 (1877) 125.
150 *RGM* 44 (1877) 23.
151 *RGM* 44 (1877) 125.
152 *RGM* 44 (1877) 62.
153 *RGM* 45 (1878) 86.
154 *RGM* 47 (1880) 102.
155 *RGM* 47 (1880) 142.
156 *RGM* 47 (1880) 125.
157 Schmidt 15 December 1899.
158 da Motta (1900) 121–123, 137–141.
159 da Motta (1901) 109f.
160 Bolte (1913) 665–668.

161 Sorabji (1932) 218.
162 Henderson (1938) 111
163 Carner (1938) 14.
164 Bloch (1941) 38.
165 Lewenthal (1964) 44.
166 Allen (1970).
167 Sadie (1970).
168 Salzman (1972).
169 Orga (1973).
170 Smith (1977).
171 Macdonald (1978).
172 Cooper (1978).
173 Mellers (1978).
174 Macdonald (1980) 'Alkan'.
175 Rothstein (1982).
176 Rapoport (1982).
177 Starr (1985).
178 Smith (1987) 128.
179 François-Sappey (1991) 88.

Chapter 13   Performance practice

1   Johann Stein (1728–1792) organist, piano manufacturer and inventor of the Viennese action.
2   Johann Eckhardt (1735–1809) German pianist and composer.
3   In the *Annonces, Affiches et Avis divers* quoted in Loesser (1954) 314–315.
4   Georg (Abbé) Vogler (1749–1814) organist, theorist and composer in Loesser (1954) 314–315.
5   See chapter 1.
6   Pierre (1900).
7   Sumner (1966) 55.
8   See Harding (1978) 159.
9   Ibid.
10   Harding (1978) 184.
11   Harding (1978) 239.
12   Alpheus Babcock (1785–1842) American piano manufacturer.
13   Harding (1978) 195.
14   Harding (1978) 339.
15   See Chapter 1.
16   See Chapter 1.
17   See Chapter 1.
18   See Chapter 13.
19   Karasowski II (1877) 96.
20   Winter in Todd (1990) 24.
21   Erlich (1976) 108–127.
22   Lewenthal (1964) vii.
23   Menthuen-Campbell (1981) gives a very full account of traditions in Chopin performance.
24   See Chapter 1.

25 Gerig (1974) 315.
26 *Le Pianiste* (1833) 33.
27 *RGM* 11 (1844).
28 *RGM* 5 (1835) 341.
29 *RGM* 16 (1849) 147–148.
30 Lewenthal (1964) ix–x.
31 Lewenthal (1964) x.
32 *LFM* October 1844.
33 Lewenthal (1964) x.
34 *RGM* 40 (1873) 22.
35 d'Indy (1930) 473.
36 *LFM* April 1844.
37 LSA 32 (1996) 5–18.
38 See Gerig (1974) Chapter 15 for a full account of the French School.
39 Stevenson (1989).
40 Stevenson (1989) 131.
41 See chapter 1.
42 Long (1963) 109.
43 Long (1959) 2.
44 See LSA 32 (1996) 5.
45 Beck (1969) iii.
46 Lewenthal (1964) ix.
47 Lewenthal (1964) x.
48 Mikuli in Michelowski (1932) 72–77.
49 Marmontel (1878) 133.
50 Ujfalussy (1978) quoted in Grabocz (1986) 28–29.
51 Grabòcz (1986) 27–56.
52 Grabòcz (1986) 53.
53 Luguenot in François-Sappey (1991) 185.
54 Lewenthal (1964) xvii.
55 See Rowland (1993) for a comprehensive account of pedalling.
56 Hummel in Harding (1978) 112.
57 Lavignac (1889).
58 In *Descriptions des Machines et Procedes* no. 11754 (Paris 1811–1863).
59 Adam (1798) 218.
60 Lewenthal (1964) xi.
61 In François-Sappey (1991) 62.

Chapter 14   Epilogue

1 Fétis (1878–1880) 'Alkan'.
2 d'Indy (1930) 425–428.
3 d'Indy (1930) 471–474.
4 Cortot (1930–48).
5 Parent (n.d) 2.
6 Favre (1953) 290–291.
7 See for example the narrative analysis of op 33 in François-Sappey (1991) 102–119.
8 Hegel's *Aesthetik* in Le Huray and Day (1981) 344.
9 Monelle (1992) 258–260.

10 Agawu (1991) 135.
11 Marothy (1974) 112.
12 Caux (1983) 4–5.
13 Sietz (1952) 370–372 and Dille (1970) 3–9.
14 Monelle (2000) 115.

Bibliography

Adam, L., *Méthode ou Principe General du doigte pour le fortepiano* (Paris 1804)
Agawu, V.K., *Playing with signs: a semiotic interpretation of Classic music* (New Jersey 1991)
Ahn, J., 'A stylistic evaluation of Charles Valentin Alkan's piano music.' *Dissertation abstracts international section A: the humanities* (UM I, Ann Arbor) 50 (1989) 289
Alkan, C.V., *Grande Sonata* op 33 preface (Brandus, 1847)
Allen, E., [Review of op 39, Smith] *R R* January 1971
Anderson, E., *Letters of Mozart to his family* (London, 1966)
Anderson, W.R., 'Wireless Notes' *MT* 79 (1938) 109–111
Artz, F.B., *France under the Bourbon Restoration* (Cambridge, 1931)
Badura-Skoda, P. and E., *Interpreting Mozart on the keyboard*. Translated by L. Black (New York, 1962)
Barth, H. (ed.), *Wagner – a documentary study* (London, 1975)
Baum, R., *Joseph Wölfl* (Kassel, 1928)
Beck, G. (ed.), 'Ch. V. Alkan: oeuvres choisies pour piano', *Le Pupitre* 16 (Paris, 1969)
Bellamann, H., 'The piano works of C.V. Alkan' *MQ* 10 (1924) 251–262
Bertha, A. de., 'Ch. V Alkan aîné: etude psycho-musicale.' *Bulletin Française de la Société Internationale de Musique* 5 (1909) 135–147
Bloch, J., *Charles Valentin Alkan*: an undergraduate study undertaken at Harvard University (Indianapolis, privately printed, 1941)
Bolte, T., 'Charles Valentin Alkan zur 100. Wiederkehr Seines Geburtstages', *NZM* 80 (1913)
Boulez, P., 'Sonate que me veux tu' *Meditations* 7 Spring 1964
Bouyer, R., 'A propos du Festin d'Esope', *Le Ménéstrel* 69/35 (1903) 276f
Bullivant, R., *Fugue* (London, 1971)
Bülow, H. von, 'C.V. Alkan, douze etudes pour le piano en 7 suites op 5' *NBZ* 11 (1857) 273–276
Busoni, F., *The piano works of Liszt* [Liszt-Siftung] Leipzig, 1904
Cairns, D., *The Memoirs of Hector Berlioz* (London, 1969)
Carner, M., [Preview to Petri broadcasts] *Radio Times* 58 (1938) 14
Castil, Blaze, F.H.J., *Dictionnaire de musique moderne* (Paris, 1825)
Caux, D., 'Journée Alkan' Report in ASJ 20 (1983) 4–5
Cavaillé-Coll C. and E., *A. Cavaillé-Coll: ses origines sa vie, ses oeuvres* (Paris, 1929)
Cone, E.T., 'Stravinsky: the progress of a method' in B. Boretz and E.T. Cone *Perspectives on Schoenberg and Stravinsky* (New York, 1972)

Conway, D., 'Alkan and his Jewish Roots', ASJ 62 (2003) 2–11
Cooper, M., [Review of op 39, Smith] *Gramophone* 55 (1978)
Cortot, A., *La musique française de piano Paris* (1930-48)
Curtiss, M., *Bizet and his world* (London, 1959)
Czerny, C., *School of Practical Composition* translated by J Bishop (London, 1848)
Dahlhaus, C., 'Die Kategorie der Charakteristichen in *Die idea der absoluten Musik* (Kassel, 1978)
Dale, K., *Nineteenth Century Piano Music* (London, 1954)
Dannreuther, E., 'Alkan' in *Grove's Dictionary of Music and Musicians*, 4th edition ed. H.C. Colles (London, 1940)
Davie, C.T., *Musical Structure and Design* (London, 1970)
Decourcelle, M., *La Société academique des enfants d'Apollon 1741–1880* (Paris, 1881)
Delacroix, E., *Journal* (ed. A. Joubin) (Paris, 1932)
Demuth, N., *French piano music* (London, 1958)
Dent, E., *Ferrucio Busoni* (London, 1974)
Dieren, B. van, *Down amoung the dead men* (London, 1935) 12–17
Dille, D., '*L'allegro barbaro de Bartok*' Magyar *Tudomanyos Akademià*: SM 12 (1970) 3–9
Dommer, A. von, *H. Ch. Koch's Musikalischen Lexicon* (Heidelberg, 1865)
Einstein, A., *Letters on Music* (New York, 1958)
Eitner, R., *Biographisch – bibliographischen Quellenlexikon der Musiker und Mussikgelehrten* (Leipzig, 1899–1904)
Ellis, K., *Music Criticism in Nineteenth Century France. La Revue et Gazette Musicale de Paris, 1834–1880* (Cambridge, 1995)
Ellis, M.K., *The French Piano Character Piece of the Nineteenth and Early Twentieth Centuries* (PhD dissertation, Indiana University, 1969)
Erlich, C., *The Piano: a history* (London, 1976)
Fabré, M., *A History of Land Transportation* (Lausanne, 1962)
Faurot, A., *Concert Piano Repertoire* (New York, 1974)
Favre, G., *Boieldieu: sa vie son oeuvre* (Paris, 1944–1945)
Favre, G., *La Musique française de piano avant 1830* (Paris, 1953)
Fetis, F.J., *Biographie universelle des musicians* (Paris, 1860)
Fetis, F.J. a, *Curiosités historiques de la musique* (Paris, 1830)
Fetis, F.J. b, *La musique mise à la portée de tout le monde* (Paris, *1830)*
Ford, K.E., 'The Pedal-piano, part III (conclusion): after Schumann, The Diapason 75/12' (1984) 14f
Fourcaud, L. de., *La Salle Pleyel* (Paris, 1893)
François-Sappey, B. (ed.), *Charles Valentin Alkan* (Paris, 1991)
Fromageot, R., 'Un disciple de Bach: Pierre François Boëly' *Revue de l'histoire de Versailles* (August 1909), 193
Fryklund, D., 'Contribution à la connaissance de la correspondence de Fétis'. *Svensk Tidskrift för Musikforsking* 12 (1930) 85–154
Gay, S., *Salons Célèbres* (Paris, 1837)

Gerig, R.R., *Famous Pianists and their Technique* (Washington, 1975)
Gertler, W., *Robert Schumann in seinen frühen Klavierwerken* (Berlin, 1931)
Gillespie, A., *French Piano Music in The Nineteenth Century* (New York, 1951)
Girardin, E. de., *Lettres parisiennes* (Paris, 1856)
Goblot, H., *Revue philosophique de la France et l'étranger* 2 July 1901
Gorer, R., 'A nineteenth century French romantic.' *The Listener* 36 (1946) 688
Grabocz, M., *Morphologie des oeuvres pour piano de Liszt* (Budapest, 1986)
Hailstone, C., *Provisional discography of works by Ch. V. Alkan* (typescript, London, 1990)
Hallé, C., *Life and Letters: an autobiography* (1819–1860) (London, 1896)
Harding, J., *Saint-Saëns and his circle* (North Carolina, 1978)
Harding, R.E.M., *The Pianoforte – its history traced to the Great Exhibition of 1851* (Cambridge, 1978)
Hedley, A. (ed.), *Selected Correspondence of Fryderyk Chopin* (London, 1962)
Henderson, W.R., [Review of op 39, Petri] *MT* 79 (1938) 111
Hennig, D., *Charles-Valentin Alkan. An introduction with special reference to the etudes* op. 35 and op. 39 (B.Phil dissertation Oxford, 1975)
Himelfarb, C., 'Reflections sur la problematique de la forme dans le piano romantique français.' *Le Festin d'Esope* no 12 des *Etudes mans les tourmineurs* op 39 de C.V. Alkan (1857) *Analyse Musicale* 20 (1990) 24–32
Hinson, M., *The Piano in Chamber Ensemble – an annotated guide.* (Sussex, 1978)
Howard, P., *Gluck and the birth of modern opera* (London, 1963)
Idelssohn, A.Z., *Jewish Music in its historical development* (New York, 1944)
d'Indy, V, d'., 'Impressions musicales d'enfence et de jeunesse: III. adolescence:' *Les Annales Politiques et Litteraires* 95 (1930) 425–428, 471–474
Jacimecki, Z., *Frederic Chopin et son oeuvre* (Paris, 1930)
Jenkins, W.G., *The Legato touch and the ordinary in keyboard playing from 1750–1850. Some aspects of the early development of piano technique.* (PhD dissertation, Cambridge University, 1976)
Jensen, E., *Walls of circumstance: studies in nineteenth century music* (New York, 1992)
Jordan, R., 'Alkan's friendship with Chopin and Georges Sand' *ASJ* 38 (1989) 7–11
Karasowski, M., *Chopin: Sein Leben seine Werke und Briefe* (Dresden, 1877)
Keller, H., 'Arrangement: for or against,' *MT* 60 (1969) 22
Kenyon, M., *Harpsichord Music* (London, 1940)
Kerman, J., *The Beethoven Quartets* (London, 1967)
King, N., 'The enigmatic Charles Alkan and the pedal piano' *Royal College of Music Magazine* 82/2 (1986) 69–72
Kivy, P., *Authenticities: philosophical reflections of musical performance* (Ithaca and London, 1995)
Krehbiehl, H.E., *The Pianoforte and its music* (New York, 1909)
Kreutzer, L., 'Revue critique. Composition de M.V. Alkan', *RGM* 13 (1846) 13f
Langham-Smith, R., 'Review of François-Sappey' 1991 *ML* 73(1992) 613–615
Layton, R. (ed.), *A Guide to the Symphony* (Oxford, 1995)

Lavignac, A., *L'école de la pedale* (Paris, 1889)
Le Huray, P. and Day, J. (ed.), *Music and Aesthetics in the Eighteenth and Early Nineteenth Centuries* (Cambridge, 1981)
Leichtentritt, H., *Analyse der Chopinscher Klavierwerke* (Berlin, 1922)
Leo, S., 'Musical Life in Paris 1817–1848, *MQ* 17 (1931) 258
Lewenthal, R. (ed.), *The piano music of Alkan* (New York, 1964)
Lewenthal, R., 'The Berlioz of the piano' *Musical America* 84 (1964) 44
Lewenthal, R., 'In search of Alkan' *MM* 15/8 (1967) 37
Lippmann, F., 'Bellini' in *Grove's Dictionary of Music and Musicians*, ed. S. Sadie (London, 1980)
Liszt, F., 'Revue. Trois morceaux dans le genre pathétique, par C.V. Alkan. Oeuvre 15, 3e livre des 12 caprices.' *RGM* 4 (1837) 460f.
Lockspeiser, E., 'Alkan the neglected' *The Listener* 19 (1938) 103
Lockspeiser, E., *Debussy: his life and mind* vol. 1 (London, 1962)
Lockwood, A., *Notes on the literature of the Piano* (New York, 1968)
Loesser, A., *Men, Women and Pianos* (New York, 1954)
Long, M., *Le Piano* (Paris, 1959)
Long, M., *Au piano avec Gabriel Fauré* (Paris, 1963)
Lowinsky, E., 'Music in the Culture of the Renaissance' *Journal of the History of Ideas* 95 (1954)
Macdonald, H., 'The death of Alkan' *MT* 114 (1973) 25
—'The enigma of Alkan' *MT* 117 (1976) 401f
—[Review of op 39, Smith] *MT* 119 (1978)
—'Alkan' in *Grove's Dictionary of Music and Musicians* 6th edition ed. S. Sadie (London, 1980)
—'More on Alkan death' *MT* 129 (1988) 118–120
Marmontel, A., *Les pianistes celébres* (Paris, 1878)
Marler, R., *The role of the piano etude in the works of C.V.Alkan* (Cincinnati, 1990)
Marothy, J., *Music and the Bourgeois, Music and the Proletariat* (Budapest, 1974)
Marx, A.B., *Allegemeine Harmonielehre* (Leipzig, 1884)
Mellers, W., [Review of op 39, Smith] *The Guardian* 20 March, 1978
Mellers, W., 'Alkan's alchemy', *MM.* 22/10 (1988) 30–32
Menthuen-Campbell, J., *Chopin playing from the composer to the present day* (London, 1981)
Michelowski, A., 'How did Chopin play' *Muzyka.* IX (1932)
Momigny, J.J., *Cours complet d'harmonie et de composition* (Paris, 1806)
Mongredien, J., *French Music from the Enlightenment Romanticism* (Oregon, 1986)
Monelle, R., *Linguistics and Semiotics in Music* (Chur, 1992)
Monelle, R., *The Sense of Music: semiotic essays* (New Jersey, 2000)
Morrellet, A., *De L'expression en musique* (Paris, 1771)
Morrison, B., 'Alkan the mysterious' *MM* 22/10 (1974) 30–32
da Motta, J.V. da., 'Charles H.V. Alkan. Op 39, Douze etudes dans tous les tons mineurs' *Der Klavierlehrer* 23(1900)
—C.V. Alkan (ainé) *AMZ* 28 (1901)
Murdoch, W., *Chopin – his life* (London, 1934)

Naumbourg, S., *Recueil de chants religieux et populaires de Israelites* (Paris, 1874)
Newman, W., *The Sonata since Beethoven* (New York, 1969)
Niecks, F., *Frederic Chopin as man and musician* (London, 1888)
Niecks, F., 'More glimpses of Parisian pianists of another day. Personal recollections. Ch. V. Alkan' *MMR* 48 (1918) 4–7
Opienski, H. (ed.), *Chopin's letters* translated by E.L. Voynick. (New York, 1931)
Orga, A., [Review of op 39, Ogdon] *RR*(April 1973)
Parent, H., Répertoire encyclopédie du pianiste (Paris, n.d.)
Pasternak, V., *Songs of The Chassidim* (New York, 1971)
Pierre, C., *Le Conservatoire National* (Paris, 1900)
Piggot, P., *Life and Music of John Field* (London, 1973)
Piston, W. and Devoto, M., *Harmony* (London, 1978)
Prod'homme, J-G., *Les Sonates pour piano de Beethoven* (Paris, 1937)
Prunières, H., 'Musical Symbolism' *MQ* 30 (1933) 20f
Rappaport, P., [Review of op 39, Smith] *Fanfare*, February 1987
Rellstab, H., *Iris im Gebiete der Jonkunst* 5 (1834) 19–20
Riemann, H., *Musiklexicon* (Leipzig, 1882)
Ringer, A.L., 'A French Symphonist at the time of Beethoven: Etienne Nicolas Méhul' *MQ* 37 (1951) 543–565
Rink, J. (ed.), *The Practice of Performance Studies in Musical Interpretation* (Cambridge, 1995)
Ritterman, J.E., *Concert Life in Paris, 1808–1838: influences on the performance and repertoire of professional pianists* (PhD dissertation London University, 1985)
Rothstein, E., [Review of op 39, Smith] *The New York Times* 25 April 1982
Rousseau, J.J., *Dictionnaire de Musique* (Paris, 1821)
Rowland, D., *History of Piano Pedalling* (Cambridge, 1993)
Sachs, C., *Rhythm and Tempo* (London, 1953)
Sadie, S., [Review of op 39, Smith] *The Times* London, 16 March 1970
Saint-Saëns, C., *Ecole Buissonnière* (Paris, 1913)
Saltzmann, E., [Review of op 39, Ogdon] *SR* September 1972
Samson, J., *The Music of Chopin* (London, 1985)
Schilling, B., 'Virtuose Klaviermusik des 19. Jahrhunderts am Beispeil von Charles Valentin Alkan (1813–1888)' *Kölner Beitrage zur Musikforschung* 145 (Regensburg, 1986)
Schmidt, L., [Review of op 39 da Motta] *Berliner Tageblatt und Handelszeitung* (Berlin, 1899)
Schoenberg, H.C., *The Great Pianists* (New York, 1963)
Schrade, L., *Beethoven in France* (New Haven, 1942)
Schumann, R., 'Etuden für Pianoforte: C.V. Alkan. 3 grosse Etuden, op 15', *NZM* (1838) 167
Schumann, R., 'Ch. Valentin Alkan, 6 charactische Stücke, op 16' *NZM* 10 (1838) 167
Schumann, R., *Music and Musicians: essays and reviews* translated by F.R. Ritter (London, 1881)
Schumann, R. (ed. M. Kreisig), *Gesummette Schriften über Musik und musiken von Robert Schumann* (Leipzig, 1914)

Searle, H., 'A Plea for Alkan' *ML* 18 (1937) 276–279
Searle, H., 'Alkan' in *Grove's Dictionary of Music and Musicians*, 5th edition ed. E. Blom (London, 1954)
Searle, H., *Berlioz – a selection from his letters* (New York, 1973)
Shaw, R., *Charles Valentin Alkan 1813–1888: his life and his early piano works*. (B. Mus Hons. dissertation, Edinburgh University, 1974)
Shedlock, J.S., *The Pianoforte Sonata* (London, 1895)
Sietz, R., *Aus Ferdinand Hillers Briefwechsel (1826–1861), (1862–1869), (1870–1875), Beiträge zur Rheinischen Musikgeschichte 28, 48, 56* (Cologne 1958, Kassel 1961, Kassel 1964)
Sietz, R., 'Ein Vorlâufer von Bartók's "<<Allegro barbaro">> *Die Musikforschung* 5 (1970) 370–372
Sitsky, L., 'Summary notes for a study on Alkan' *SMA* 8 (1974) 53–91
Sitwell, S., *Liszt* (London, 1934)
Smalley, R., 'A case of neglect: two virtuosos cadenzas for Beethoven' *MM* 20/9 (1972) 30–34
Smith, R., 'Charles-Valentin Alkan', *The Listener* 86 (1971) 25f.
—*Alkan. Volume one: the enigma* (London, 1976)
—'Alkan and Frankenstein's Monster' Programme note to 1977 London recital
—'Alkan's concerti da camera', *MT* 124 (1983) 227–230
—*Alkan. Volume two: The music* (London, 1987)
Sorabji, K., *Around Music* (London, 1932)
—*Mi Contra Fa* (1947)
Soullier, C.S.P., *Nouveau dictionnaire de musique illustré* (Paris, 1855)
Starr, M., 'Concerto for piano and orchestra' (New York, 1985)
Stevenson, R., 'Saint-Saëns Views on The Performance of Early Music' *Performance Practice Review* 2(2) Fall 1989
Stravinsky, I., *Themes and Conclusions* (London, 1972)
Sumner, W.L., *The Pianoforte* (London, 1966)
Sydow, B.E. (ed.), Correspondence de F. Chopin (Paris, 1953–1960)
Szabolcsi, B., *A History of Melody* translated by C. Jolly and S. Karig (Budapest, 1965)
Thayer, A.W., *Thayer's Life of Beethoven* revised E. Forbes (Princeton, 1964)
Thayer, A.W., *Ludwig van Beethovens Leben* i–iii edited by H. Dieters (Berlin 1866–1879)
Timbrell, C., *French Pianism: An Historical Perspective* (London, 1992)
Todd, R.L. (ed.), *Nineteenth Century Piano Music* (New Jersey, 1990)
Turk, D.G., *Klavierschüle* (Leipzig, 1789)
Ujfalussy, A., *Bevezetes a marxista-leninista agazati esztetikaba* (Budapest, 1978)
Unger, M., *Muzio Clementi's Leben* (Langensalza, 1914)
Vallas, L., *César Franck* (London, 1951)
Vapereau, G., *Dictionnaire des contemporains* 6th edition (Paris, 1893)
Vorepierre, B.D., *Dictionnaire français illustré et encyclopédie universelle* (Paris, 1864)

Walker, A., *Liszt: The Virtuoso Years* (London, 1983)
Warrack, J., *Carl Maria von Weber* (Cambridge, 1976)
Watson, D., *Liszt* (London, 1988)
Weinstock, H., *Chopin: The Man and His Music* (New York, 1949)
Wells, J., 'Charles Valentin Alkan, 1813–1888' *The Diapason* 80/11 (1989)
Werner, E., *A voice still heard: the sacred songs of the Ashkenazic Jews* (Philadelphia, 1976)
Whistling, C.F., *Handbuch der Musikalische Litteratur* (Leipzig, 1817–)
White, E.W., *Stravinsky* (London, 1979)

Archival Sources

Shaw (1974) in his bibliography and François-Sappey (1991) 303–320 are invaluable sources for information on the Alkan archives. Relevant to this study are the following:

Arch. Paris, V2E7e Mairie	Birth certificates of Charles Napoleon and Gustave Alkan
Arch. nat. AJ 3766	Contains details of the birth dates of the Alkan family, the admission date to the conservatoire, the prizes won and the names of teachers.
AN O3 1825	Contains requests by Alkan and Alkan père for the use of halls, singers and instrumentalists as well as concert announcements.
ANF21 1291	Includes eight letters referring to Alkan's candidature for the post of piano professor at the conservatoire in 1848.
ANAJ37 71	Contains Auber's hearty commendation of Marmontel for the Légion d'honneur award. Letter dated 30 November 1858

Bibliothèque Historique de la Ville de Paris

Fonds Sands G3288–3298	Eleven letters written by Alkan to George Sand from the late 1840s to the late 1850s

List of Works

There are considerable problems in estimating the composition and publication dates of Alkan's music. Useful aids have been plate numbers of the original pieces, publishers' catalogues and, especially, the deposition dates of the pieces in the main Paris music libraries, namely the *Bibliothèque Nationale* (BN) and the *Bibliothèque du Conservatoire de Musique* (BCM.). The entries in the British Museum (BM) and the Reid School of Music, University of Edinburgh (RS) have also been helpful.

Particularly important too were the following sources:

W. Altmann, *Kammermusik-Katolog* (Leipzig, 1945).
BBC Music Library, *Piano and Organ Catalogue* (vol.1, 1965).
O. Deutsch, *Music Publishers' Numbers* (London, 1946; Ger. Trans., rev., 1961).
H. Macdonald, 'Alkan' in *New Grove Dictionary of Music and Musicians* (London, 1980).
F. Pazdirek, *Universal-Handbuch der Musikliteratur*. Unchanged reprint of the original edition Vienna 1904–1910 (Hilversum, 1967).
C.F. Whistling, *Handbuch der Musikalischen Litteratur* (Leipzig, 1817, onwards).

There are several important collections of Alkan's piano works but all of the following are highly selective and incomplete. These are:

E. Delaborde and I. Philipp, *Ch. V Alkan: oeuvres choisies* (Paris, c1900).

These use the original plates of Richault *et al* and were reissued by Costellat, now Billaudot.

R. Lewenthal (ed.), *The Piano Music of Alkan* (New York, 1964).

This uses the original plates and has highly informative and useful editorial annotations.

Beck, G., *C.V. Alkan: oeuvres choisies pour piano. Le pupitre*, xvi (Paris, 1969).

This has reset typeface and a useful commentary on the pieces.

M.A. Hamelin (ed.), *Le Festin D'Esope and other works for solo piano* (New York, 1998).

This is the most accessible modern source of classic Alkan works.

Main publishers consulted included:

Bote und Bock, Brandus et Cie, Bureau Centrale, Cocks, Costellat, Deugel, Diabelli, Richault, Schlesinger, and Scott.

Composition dates are without brackets and published dates are with brackets. Titles of works have been abbreviated and translated in several cases.

I Piano works with opus number

Op

1	Variations on a theme from Steibelt's *Orage Concerto*	*c*1828	(*c*1828)
2	Les Omnibus Variations	*c*1828	(1829)
3	*Il était un p'tit homme. Rondoletto*	*c*1828	(*c*1830)
4	*Rondo brilliant*, for piano and quartet ad lib	*c*1833	(*c*1833)
5	Rondo, on *Largo al factotum* from Rossini's *Il barbiere di Siviglia*		(*c*1833)
8	*Six Morceaux Caractéristiques* See op 74		(1838)
[12]	Rondeau Chromatique		(1834)
12	Trois Etudes de Bravoure (Improvisations)		(1837)
13	Trois Andantes Romantiques		(1837)
15	Trois Morceaux dans le genre pathétique		(1837)
16	*Trois Etudes de Bravoure* (Scherzi)		(1837)
[16] no. 4	Variations on *Ah! Segnata e La mia morte* from Donizetti's *Anna Bolena*		(1834)
no. 5	Variations on *La tremenda ultrice spada* from Bellini's *I Capuleti e i Montecchi*		(1834)
no. 6	Variations quasi fantaisie sur une barcarolle napolitaine		(1834)
17	Le Preux. Etude de concert		(1844)
22	Nocturne		(1844)
23	Saltarelle		(1844)

24	Gigue et Air de Ballet dans le style ancien		(1844)
25	Alleluia		(1844)
26	Marche funèbre	1844	(1846)
27	Marche triomphale	1844	(1846)
27 sic	Le Chemin de fer	1844	(1844)
29	Bourrée d'Auvergne		(1846)
31	25 *Préludes dans tous les tons majeurs et mineurs, pour piano ou orgue*		(1847)
32 no. 1	*1ᵉʳ Recueil d'Impromptus:* *Vaghezza* *L'Amitié* *Fantasietta alla Moresca* *La Foi*		(1848)
no. 2	*2ᵐᵉ Recueil d'Impromptus:* *3 Airs à Cinq Temps et 1 à Sept Temps*	1848/ 1849	(1849)
33	Grande Sonate	1847	(1848)
34	Scherzo focoso	1847	(1848)
35	Douze Etudes dans tous les tons majeurs		(1848)
37	Trois Marches Quasi da Cavalleria		(1857)
38	*1ᵉʳ Recueil de Chants*		(1857)
38	*2ᵉ Recueil de Chants*		(1857)
39	Douze Etudes dans tous les tons mineurs		(1857)
41	*Trois Petites Fantaisies*		(1857)
42	*Réconciliation, petit caprice*		(1857)
45	*Salut, centre du pauvre!*		(1856)
46	*Minuetto alla tedesca*		(1857)
50 no. 1	*Capriccio alla Soldatesca*		(1859)
50 no. 2	*Le Tambour bat aux champs*		(1859)
51	*Trois Menuets*		(1859)
52	*Super Flumina Babylonis.* *Paraphrase du Psaume 137*		(1859)
53	Quasi-caccia, Caprice		(1859)

55	Une Fusée, introduction et impromptu	(1859)
57	Deux Nocturnes (*2e et 3e Nocturnes* – see Op 22)	(1859)
60	Ma chère liberté Ma chère servitude	(1859)
60 bis	*Le Grillon. 4e nocturne*	(1859)
61	*Sonatine*	(1861)
63	Esquisses. 48 motifs	(1861)
65	*3e Recueil*	(*c*1866)
67	*4e Recueil de Chants*	(*c*1868)
70	*5me Recueil de Chants*	(*c*1872)
74	*Les Mois:* Nuit d'hiver, Carnaval, La retraite, La Pâque, Sérénade, Promenade sur l'eau, Nuit d'été, Les Moissoneurs, L'Hallali, Gros temps, Le Mourant, L'Opéra. See op 8	(*c*1840)
75	*Toccatina*	(*c*1872)
76	*Trois Grandes Etudes*	(*c*1839)

II Solo piano works without opus numbers listed in alphabetic order

Apassionata [sic] [op 63/29]	1847
Caprice ou Etude	(1843)
Chapeau bas! 2 fantasticheria	(1872)
Désir. Fantaisie pour Piano	(1844)
Fantasticheria pour Piano	(1868)
Impromptu	(*c*1845)
Jean qui pleure et Jean qui rit: *2 fughe da camera*	(*c*1840)
Palpitamento	1855
Petit conte pour le Piano	(1859)

Les Regrets de la Nonnette	1854
Variations à la vielle	(*c*1840)
Variations sur un air favori de l'opera ugo conte de Parigi	(*c*1840)
Zorcico. Danse Ibérienne à 5 temps	(*c*1852)

III Transcriptions for solo piano

(1)   Partitions pour piano: Souvenirs des Concerts du Conservatoire   (1847)

1. *I ciele immensi narrano*, from Marcello, *18th Psalm*
2. *Jamais dans ces beaux lieux*, from Gluck's *Armide*
3. *Choeur des Scythes*, from Gluck's *Iphigénie en Tauride*
4. *Andante*, from Haydn's *Symphony No. 36.*
5. *La Garde passé, il est minuit*, from Grétry's *Deux Avares*
6. *Menuet*, from *Symphonie en mi bémol* [*Symphony No. 40 in E flat*] byMozart

(2)   *Souvenirs des Concerts du Conservatoire,* 2nd Series   (1861)

1. Handel, *Choeur des prétres de Dagon* from *Samson*
2. Gluck, *Gavotte (Orphée)*
3. Haydn, *Finale du 38ᵉ Quatuor* [Op 64/5]
4. Mozart, *Ne pulvis et Cinis, motet*
5. Beethoven, *Bundeslied*, from Op 122
6. Weber, *Choeur des Filles de la Mer* from *Oberon*

(3)   Souvenirs de musique de chamber   (*c*1866)

1. *Rigaudon des petits violins de Louis XIV*
2. *Morceau de la 2ᵉ Sonate (flute et clavecin) de J.S. Bach*
3. *Menuet d'un Quatuor de Haydn* [Op 76 No.2]
4. *Andante du 8ᵉ Quatuor de Mozart* [K.464]
5. *Cavatine du 13ᵉ Quatuor de Beethoven* [Op 130]
6. *Scherzo du Trio, Op 63, de Weber*

Other transcriptions

Beethoven, *Piano Concerto No. 3 in C minor.* 1st Movement. With an extensive cadenza by Alkan	(1860)
Meyerbeer, overture to *Le Prophète*	(*c*1849)
Mozart, *Piano Concerto in D minor, K.466.* The whole work transcribed. With cadenzas by Alkan	(1861)

IV Pedal piano, organ or harmonium

Op

54 Benedictus pour piano à clavier de pédales (1859)

64 13 *Prières pour orgue avec pedal oblige: ou piano à Clavier de pédales* (1866)

66 11 *Grands preludes et 1 Transcription, du Messie de Haendel, pour piano à Clavier de pédales* (1866)

69 Impromptu sur le choral de Luther: Un fort rampart est notre Dieu, pour piano à pédales (1866)

72 11 *Pièces, dans le style religieux, et 1 transcription, du Messie de Haendel, pour orgue, Harmonium ou piano sans Pédalier* (1867)

Pro organo. Praeludium   1850

Petits preludes sur les 8 gammes du plain-chant. Pour orgue (1859)

Pour M. Gurkhaus   1863

12 *Études d'orgue ou de piano à pédales pour les pieds seulement* (1866)

V Piano duet

Op

26 *Fantaisie à 4 mains sur Don Juan*   1844

40 *Trois marches pour Piano à quatre mains* (1857)

47bis *Saltarelle, Finale de la Sonate de Concert pour Piano et Vionloncelle, arrangée à 4 mains* (c1866)

Finale à quatre mains (c1838)

Le Prophète. Opéra en 5 actes. G. Meyerbeer. Ouverture. Arrangée à 4 mains. (1850)

12 Études d'orgue, ou de Piano à Pedales pour les pieds seulement (c1866)

Bombardo-carillon, pour Clavier de Pédales, à Quatre Pieds seulement, 'ou Quatre Mains, sur Clavier ordinaire' (c1872)

Étude, pour Piano a clavier de Pédales   1872

VI Chamber Music

Op

21	Duo concertant, pour piano et violin	1840	(c1841)
30	*1er Trio pour piano, violin et basse*		(1841)
47	*Sonate de concert pour piano et violoncello*	1856	(1857)
	A son confrère P. Cavallo C minor. Fragment of six bars of a string quartet	1846	

VII Large scale instrumental music

Op

10	*Concerto da Camera composé pour le piano* [A minor]		(1832)
[10]	*2e concerto da Camera* [C sharp minor]		(1834)
	Arrangement for piano solo		(1859)
	Pas-redoublé for military band	1840	

VIII Vocal Music

Listed chronologically by date of composition

Hermann et Ketty Cantata on a text by Pastoret for soprano, tenor and orchestra	1832	
L'entrée en loge[s]. Cantata on a text by Gail for tenor and orchestra	1834	
Etz chajjim Hi for two sopranos, tenor bass, unaccompanied		(1847)
3 ancient Jewish melodies for voice and piano (nos 1 and 2) and for organ or harpsichord	1854	
2er verset du 41e Psaume (*2ev: du 42e de la Vulgate*) for voice and piano	1855	
Air of J.S. Bach from *The Cantate*: *Wie schön leuchtet der Morgenstern* for soprano with piano accompaniment	1855	
Hallelujah for choir (S.A.T.B.) piano or organ	1857	
Marcia funèbre sulla morte d'un Pappagallo	1858	(1859)
Stances de Millevoye for three female voices		(1859)

IX Works quoted but lost

Cadenza for the first movement of a concerto by Handel 1869

Choeur des Derviches, extract from *Die Ruinen von Athen* op 113 1860
by Beethoven, piano transcription

Symphonie in A major op 92 by Beethoven transcribed for (*c*1838)
eight hands

Symphonie grand orchestre 1844

Romance du phare d'Eddystone for voice and piano 1845

X Unidentified Works

Ops 6, 7, 9, 11, 14, 18, 19, 28, 36, 43, 44, 48, 49, 56, 58, 59, 62, 68, 71, and 73

Vocal and Choral

Etz chajjim Hi and *Hallelujah* Fitzgerald

Marcia funèbre sulla morte d'un Pappagallo Lewenthal

A Basic Alkan Discography

This list is to some extent a personal selection. Reference should be made to Smith (2000) for Shaw's very complete list Only artists' names are stated since CD numbering frequently changes. From the many Alkan recordings currently or recently available, I have made this selection.

Piano and Organ

Concerto from op 39	Ogdon
Esquisses op 63	Martin
Études op 76	Smith or Hamelin
Études op 35	Ringeissen
Études op 39	Smith
Grande Sonate op 33	Smith or Hamelin or Reach
Impromptus op 32/1	Martin
Marche funèbre op 26	Smith
3 *Petites fantaisies* op 41	Smith
Preludes op 25	Mustonen
Prieres op 64 (excerpts)	Wells
Les Regrets de la Nonette	Smith
Sonatine op 61	Lewenthal or Reach or Hamelin

Chamber Music

Grand Duo op 21, Trio op 30 and *Sonate de Concert* op 47	Alkan Trio

Orchestral

Concerti da camera op 10	Hamelin/ BBC Scottish SO/ Brabbins

Index of Musical Works

Alkan's works are arranged according to the classification on pp. 248–54. The works of other composers are arranged alphabetically under their names.

References to pages containing musical extracts are in **bold**.

Alkan, Charles Valentin

I Piano works with opus number
op 1, *Variations sur un thème de Steibelt* 5, 27, **28**, 29, 248
op 2, *Les Omnibus* **29**, 30, 35, 99, 115, 200, 211, 248
op 3, *Il était un p'tit homme* 30, 248
op 4, *Rondo brillant* 30, **31**, 32, 248
op 5, Rondo on *Largo al factotum* 30, 248
op 8, *Six Morceaux Caractéristiques* 49, **50–2**, 248
   see also op 74
[op 12] *Rondeau chromatique* 6, 35, 248
op 12, *Trois Etudes de Bravoure* (Improvisations) 39, **40**, **41**, 248
op 12/3, *Trois Etudes de Bravoure, Allegro marziale* 104
op 13, *Trois Andantes Romantiques* 35, 41, **42**, 43, 248
op 13/1: 75
op 13/2, *Andante con moto* 75
op 13/3, *Andante Romantique* 213
op 15, *Trois Morceaux dans le genre pathétique* 7, 8, 43, **44**, **45**, 46, 248
   reception 173–5, 177
op 15/2, *Le vent* 7, 43, 44, 45–6, 63, 95, 99, 211, 216
op 15/3, *Morte* 98
op 16, *Trois Etudes de Bravoure* (Scherzi) **47**, 48–9, 87, 248
op 16/1: 98, 199
op 16/4, variations on *Ah! Segnata e La mia morte* **36**, 37
op 16/5, variations on *La Tremenda Ultrice Spada* 35–6

op 16/6, *Variations quasi fantaisie sur une barcarolle napolitaine* 37
op 17, *Le Preux* 96, 104, 204, 212, 213, 248
op 22, *Premier Nocturne* 8, 14, 19, 96, 113, 248
op 23, *Saltarelle* 8, 96, 199, 211, 248
   reception 175, 176
op 24, *Gigue et Air de Ballet dans le style ancien* 8, 14, 23, 96, 97, 176, 249
op 25, *Alleluia* 8, 96, 97, 101, 249
op 26, *Marche funèbre* 9, 46, 54, 96, 97, 98–9, 189, 190, 249
   reception 176
op 26/7, *Marches* 19
op 27, *Marche triomphale* 8, 9, 96, 97, 98, 99, 104, 118, 189, 190, 212, 249
op 27 sic, *Le chemin de fer* 99, 118, 249
op 29, *Bourrée d'Auvergne* **99**, 100, 217, 249
op 31 *25 Préludes dans tous les tons majeurs et mineur* 8, 9, 93, 97, 100, **101**, 102–3, 143, 249
   reception 178
op 31/1: 100
op 31/2: 100
op 31/3, *Dans le genre ancien* 100–1
op 31/4–5: 101
op 31/6, *Ancienne Mélodie de la Synagogue* **101**, 190, 191
op 31/7: 101
op 31/8, *La chanson de la folle* 93, 101
op 31/9, *Placiditas* 101–2
op 31/10, *Dans le style fugué* 100, 102
op 31/11, *Un petit rien* 102, 103
op 31/12, *Le temps qui n'est plus* 102, 103
op 31/13, *J'étais endormie* 102, 103, 114, 214
op 31/14: 102

op 31/15, *Dans le style gothique* 102
op 31/16: 102
op 31/17, *Rêve d'amour* 102, 103
op 31/18: 102–3
op 31/19, *Prière du Matin* 102–3
op 31/20: 103
op 31/21: 103
op 31/22, *Anniversaire* 103
op 31/23: 103
op 31/24: 103
op 32, *Impromptus* 103–4
op 32 no. 1, *1er Recueil d'Impromptus*
    Fantasietta alla Moresca 103, 249
    La Foi 103, 249
    L'Amitié 103, 249
    Vaghezza 9, 103, 249
op 32/2: 62, 104
op 33, *Grande Sonate* 77, 81, 84, **85–7**, 91, 93, **202**, 211, 249
    Les Quatres Ages Sonata 77, 78, 79, 80, **82–7**, 88, 137
    Prométhée Enchaine 86, **87**
    Quasi Faust ix, 78, 80, **84–5**, 103, 145, 212
op 34, *Scherzo focoso* 87–8, 91, 249
op 35, *Douze Etudes dans tous les tons majeurs* 23, 53, 56–7, **58**, 59, **60**, 61–2, 103, 211, 249
op 35/1: 19, 56, 190
op 35/2: 56–7
op 35/3: 57
op 35/4: 57
op 35/5: 57, **58**, 212
op 35/6: 59, 211
op 35/7, *L'incendie au village voisin* 53, 59
op 35/8: 59, **60**
op 35/9, *Contrapunctus* 61
op 35/10, *Chant d'amour-chant de mort* 61
op 35/11: 61–2
op 35/12: 62
op 37, *Trois Marches Quasi da Cavalleria* **104**, 105, 249
op 37/1: **104**
op 37/2: 105
op 37/3: 105
op 38 *1er Recueil de Chants* 14, 18, 20, 191, 249
op 38 *2me Recueil de Chants* 19, 249
    Chant de guerre 23, 108, 191

op 38/1: 105, **106**, 189, 190
op 38/2, *Sérénade* 106–7
op 38/2/1, *Hymne* 107
op 38/3, *Choeur* 107
op 38/4, *L'Offrande* 107
op 38/5, *Agitatissimo* 107
op 38/6, *Barcarolle* 107, 109
op 39, *Douze Etudes dans tous les tons mineurs* 14, 22, 35, 53, 62–4, **65–7**, 68, **69–70**, 71–2, **73**, 74–5, 87, 93, 190–1, 249
op 39/1, *Comme le vent* 63, 99, 173, 206, 211
op 39/2, *En rhythme molossique* 63
op 39/3, *Scherzo diabolico* 64
op 39/4–7, *Symphonie* ix, 23, 64, **65–7**, 68, 81, 88, 160, 162, 166, 190, 213
    recordings 194–5
op 39/8–10, *Concerto* 22, 68, **69–70**, 71, 139
    reception 191–8
op 39/11, *Overture* 71, 75, **207**, 214
op 39/12, *Le Festin d'Esope* ix, **72–3**, 74, 108, **203**, 208, 211, 213, 218
op 41, *Trois Petites Fantaisies* 14, 109–10, 249
op 41/1, *Assez Gravement in A Minor* 109
op 41/2, *Fantaisie* 109–10
op 41/3, *Fantaisie* 110
op 42, *Réconciliation* 110, 249
op 45, *Salut, cendre/centre du pauvre!* 110, **111**, 249
op 46, *Minuetto alla tedesca* 23, 111, 112, 191, 249
op 50 no.1, *Capriccio alla Soldatesca* 80, 93, 111–12, 249
op 50 no.2, *Le Tambour bat aux champs* 111, 112, 249
op 51, *Trois Menuets* 112–13, 249
op 52, *Super Flumina Babylonis* 113, 191, 249
op 53, *Quasi-caccia* 94, 113, 249
op 55, *Une fusée* 94, 113, 250
op 57, *Deux Nocturnes* 113, **114**, 250
    see also op 22
op 60, *Ma chère liberté* 114–15, 127, 250
    Ma chère servitude 94, 115, 127, 250
op 60 bis, *Le Grillon* 94, 115, 250
op 61, *Sonatine* 16, 77, 81, **88**, 89, **90**, 91, 115, 126, 250

Index of Musical Works

op 61/1: 88–9
op 61/4: **90**
op 63, *Esquisses* 16, 48, 94, 121–30, 250
    Barcarollette 128, 190
    Début de Quatuor 124
    Délire 121, 128
    Duettino 123, 129
    En Songe 126
    Fais Dodo 125
    Fantaisie 128
    Fuguette 122
    Grâce 123
    Héraclite et Démocrite 94, 100, 117, 127, 128, 129
    Increpatio 127–8
    Inflexibilité 123–4
    Innocenzia 128
    La Poursuite 123
    La Vision 121, 126, **207**
    Laus Deo 122
    Le Ciel vous soit toujours prospère 94
    Le Frisson 127
    Le Legatissimo 126
    Le premier billet doux **125–6**
    Le Staccatissimo 126
    Les Cloches 94, 126–7
    Les Diablotin 94, 129
    Les Soupirs 93, 94, 128, 212
    L'homme aux sabots 94, 127
    Liedchen 128
    Minuettino 124
    Musique militaire 129
    Odi profanum vulgus **122**
    Petit Air 121
    Petit Marche Villageoise 127
    Petit Prelude à Trois 124
    Pseudo-naiveté 127
    Ressouvenir 122–3
    Rigaudon 93, 122, **123**
    Scherzettino 128
    Scherzetto 129
    Toccatina 124
    Tutti de concerto 123
op 65 *3e Recueil de Chants* 115, 250
    Esprits follets 115–16
op 65/4, *Canon* 115
op 65/5, *Horace et Lydie* 116, 127
op 65/6: 116
op 67 *4e Recueil de Chants* 19, 250

Allegro con bravura 19
Barcarolle 19
Chanson de la Bonne Vieille 19, 116–17, 190
Doucement 117
Neige et Lave 116, 127
op 70 *5e Recueil de Chants* 23, 117, **118**, 250
    Allegro vivace 118–19
    Andante flebile 119
    Andantinetto 118
    La voix de l'instrument 119, 191
    Scherzo-coro 119
op 74, *Les Mois* 22, 94, 250
    Une Nuit d'Eté 50, 95, 189
    La Pâque **50**
    Une Nuit d'Hiver 49, 95
    Les Moissonneurs 51
op 74/5, *Sérénade* **213**
op 74/12, *L'Opéra* **51**, 93
op 75, *Toccatina* 102, 103, 120, 124, 134, 250
op 76, *Trois Grandes Etudes* 53, 250
op 76/1: **54**
op 76/2: 54, **55**, 56, 211
op 76/3: 56, 103

II Solo piano works without opus numbers
Appassionato 117, 250
Jean qui pleure, et Jean qui rit **95**, 102, 127, 250
Les Regrets de la Nonnette 171, 251

III Transcriptions for solo piano 131, 132, 133–7, 138, 139–40, 141–2
Bach, J.S., *Sonata in E flat major* **136**, 251
Beethoven, Ludwig van
    B flat Major Quartet, cavatine 136, **137**, 251
    Bundeslied **135**, 251
    Piano Concerto No. 3 in C Minor, 1st movement 139, **140**, 141, 251
Gluck, Christoph
    Choeur des Scythes (*Iphigénie en Tauride*) 132, 179, 180, 251
    Gavotte (*Orphée*) **133**, 251
    Jamais dans ces beaux lieux (*Armide*) 132, 180, 251

Grétry, André, *La Garde passé* (*Deux Avares*) 132, 251
Handel, George Frideric
　Choeur des prêtres de Dagon (*Samson*) 133, 181, 251
Haydn, Joseph
　String Quartet in D minor, minuet 136, 251
　Symphony no. 36, andante 132, 251
　Thirty-eighth Quartet, finale 134, 251
Marcello, Benedetto
　I cieli immensi narrano (18th Psalm) 23, 132, 251
Meyerbeer, Giacomo
　Le Prophète, overture 137, 251
Mozart, Wolfgang Amadeus
　A major String Quartet, andante 136, 251
　A minor sonata 181, 251
　Jupiter Symphony 139, 251
　Ne pulvis et Cinis, motet **134**, 251
　Piano Concerto in D Minor 138, **139**, 251
　Symphony in G Minor, minuet 132, 251
　Rigaudons des petits violons de Louis XIV 136, 251
Weber, Carl Maria von
　Choeurs des Filles de la Mer 22, 135, 251
　Trio in G minor, scherzo 137, 251

IV Pedal piano/organ/harmonium 18, 189, 190
12 Etudes d'orgue ou de piano 143
op 54, *Benedictus* 144, **145–6**, 147, 252
op 64, *Prières* 22, 144, **147–9**, 252
op 64/8 *Deus Sabboath* 189, 190, 252
op 66, *Onze Grands Préludes* 19, 22, 23, **149**, 150, **151–2**, 252
op 69, *Impromptu sur le choral de Luther* 145, 152–3, 252
op 72 *Onze pièces dans le style religieux* 143, 144, 153, **154**, 155, 252
　Petits préludes sur les 8 gammes du plain-chant 143, 144, 252

V Piano duet
op 40, *Trois marches pour piano à quatre mains* 14, 18, 22, 189, 252

op 47, *Violoncello Sonata* 189–90, 252

VI Chamber music
op 21, *Duo Concertant pour piano et violin* 8, 9, 19, 20, 22, 81, 157, **158–9**, 190, 253
　reception 178
op 30, *Piano Trio* 9, 157, 160, **161**, 162, 253
op 47, *Sonate de concert pour piano et violoncello* 14, 19, 157, 162, **163**, 164, **165**, 166, 190, 253

VII Large scale instrumental music
op 10 *2nd Concerto da Camera* 6, 8, 20, 33, **34**, 35, 253
[op 10] *Concerto da Camera* 6, 7, 32, **33**, 167, 253
　pas-redoublé 170, 253

VIII Vocal music
Etz chajjim hi **169**, 170, 253
Hallelujah 170, 253
Hermann et Ketty 6, 167–70, 253
L'entrée en loge[s] 7, 167, 253
Marcia funèbre sulla morte d'un pappagallo 7, **168**, 169, 253
Stances de Millevoye 14, 167, 253
Wie schön leuchtet der Morgenstern 167, 253

IX Works quoted but lost
Romance du phare d'Eddystone 8, 167, 253
Symphonie grand orchestre 170–1, 177, 253

Bach, J.S.
　C major fugue and Pastorale 19
　Concerto for three pianos 13
　D Minor Concerto 179
　French Suite in G Major, gavotte 8
　Fugue in E Minor 96–7
　G minor alla breve Fugue 22
　Ich ruf dich 20
　Prelude and Fugue in F Minor 19
　St Matthew Passion 16
　Toccata in F major 18, 20, 22, 143
　Triple concerto 17
　Triple keyboard concerto 22
Bartok, Béla

Index of Musical Works

Rumanian Dance no.1 103
Beauvarlet-Charpentier, Jean-Jacques
   Recueil de sept préludes 93
Beethoven, Ludwig van
   32 Variations in C Minor 61
   Appassionata sonata 154
   C Minor Concerto 22
   Eroica Symphony 64, 87, 97–8
   Fantasie (op 77) 22
   Fifth Symphony 170
   G major Bagatelle 154
   G major Piano Concerto 161
   Hammierklavier Sonata 17, 78, 107, 113, 182
   Ninth Symphony 119
   Pastoral Symphony 59
   Piano Concerto no 4 86
   Seventh Symphony 7, 8
   Sonata
      op 2/2: 66
      op 31/1: 8, 109
      op 31/2: 63
      op 109: 19
      op 110: 18, 19, 22, 24
   Sonata in D, op 10/3: 20
Bellini, Vincenzo
   I Puritani 7
Berlioz, Hector
   Grande Symphonie Funèbre et Triomphale 97, 168
   Orphée 133
   Symphone Fantastique 44, 87
Bizet, Georges
   L'Arlésienne 19
Boëly, Alexandre
   Caprice, op 7 94
   Quatorze Préludes 152
Boieldieu, François
   Concerto (op 14) 213
   La Dame Blanche 12
Boulez, Pierre
   Third Sonata 77
Brahms, Johann
   Intermezzo in E flat major (op 117) 62
Bruckner, Anton
   Symphony No. 4 48
Chabrier, Emmanuel
   Paysage 95
Chopin, Frederic

24 Preludes 100
A major Polonaise (op 40/1) 116
Allegro de concert (op 46) 23
B minor Piano Sonata, (op 58) 116
E Minor Concerto 19, 33
Etude in A flat major (op 10/10) 205
Etude in C minor (op 10/12) 206
Etude in F minor (op 25/2) 107
Etudes (op 10) 205
F major ballade (op 47) 22
   reception 186
F minor ballade 24
F minor concerto (op 21) 6
Fantasy (op 49) 66
Funeral March 81, 98
Nocturne in A flat major (op 32/2) 60
Nocturne in C minor (op 48/1) 20, 205
Nocturne in D flat major (op 27/2) 117
Notturino-inamorato **124–5**
Piano Sonata No. 2 48
Prelude in A Flat Major 50
Prelude in E Flat Major 61, 75
Prelude in F major 50
Prelude in F sharp minor (op 28/8) 107, 117
Prelude no. 2 in A minor 102
Preludes (op 28) 93, 103
Rondo in C Minor (op 1) 30
Scherzo in B minor 83
Scherzo in E major 83–4
Sonata (op 35) 19
Sonata Funèbre 79
Third Scherzo 152
Couperin, François le Grand
   La Fine Madelon 180
   Un petit rien 93
Couperin, Louis
   Préludes non mesurés 93
Dreyschock, Alexander
   Variation pour la main gauche seule (op 22) 54
Dupont, Gabriel
   La Chanson du vent 95
Field, John
   A minor concerto 20
   Romance in B flat minor 184
Franck, César
   Prelude, Chorale and Fugue 54
   Ruth 8

Gluck, Christoph
   Ballet des Scythes 20
   Orphée 93
Gossec, François Joseph
   Marche lugubre 168
Handel, George Frideric
   Messiah 122, 143, 149, 152, 153, 155
   Samson 22
Haydn, Joseph,
   String Quartet in D minor (op 76/2) 63
Hérold, Ferdinand
   Neuf Caprices en trois Suites, (ops 4/6/7) 94
Hiller, Ferdinand, *Trio* (op 7) 19
Honegger, Arthur, *Pacific 231* 99
Hummel, Johann
   B minor Concerto 8, 19, 20, 23
Kullak, Theodor
   Two Concert Studies (op 2) 74
Liszt, Franz
   A major Concerto 61
   Ab Irato 96
   Andante amoroso 9
   Benediction de dieu dans la Solitude 86
   Etudes de Concert 53
   Feux Follets 57
   Harmonie du soir 75
   Mal du pays 115
   Mazeppa 75
   Rémininscences de Don Juan 95
   Sonata in B Minor 84
   Totentanz 46
   Transcendental Etudes 74, 75, 84, 149
   Venezia e Napoli 37
   Wilde Jagd 54, 75, 211
Mahler, Gustav
   Sixth Symphony 111
Mendelssohn, Felix
   D minor Trio 161
   E minor Prelude (op 35/1) 117
   Etude in F minor 184
   Fantasie in A minor 184
   G minor Piano Concerto 123
   Prelude in B flat major (op 35) 205
   Six Organ Sonatas 152
   Songs without words 105, **106**, 107, 116, 117, 124, **125**, 184
Messiaen, Olivier
   Regard de l'Eglise d'amour 62

Meyer, Leopold von
   Etude de bataille (op 35) 53
Mozart, Wolfgang Amadeus
   Don Giovanni 124
   Gigue (K574) 96
   Sonata in A Minor 19
   Sonata in C 8
   Symphony No. 39 170
   Symphony No. 40 in G minor 8, 72
   Wind Quintet 19
Mussorgsky, Modeste
   The Old Castle 101
Orga, Ates, *Concerto* (op 39) 195
Paganini, Niccolò, *La Chasse* 55
Poulenc, Francis
   Trois Pastorales 95
Rameau, Jean Philippe
   Les Sauvages 180
   Piè de clavecin 93
Ravel, Maurice
   Sonatine 88
Ries, Ferdinand
   Septet 6
Rode, Jacques
   Air and variations 187
   Ricordanza 2
Rubinstein, Anton
   Fifth Piano Concerto (op 94) 16
Satie, Eric
   Gymnopédies 126
Schubert, Franz
   A flat Impromptu (D899) 128
   A flat Moment Musical 125
   A minor Sonata (D784) 63
   D major Novelleten (op 21) 128
   Die Schöne Müllerin 22
   G major Sonata (D894) 22, 183
   Introduction and Rondo (op 70) 18
   Les enharmoniques 129
   Marche militaire 129, 183
   Moment Musical in C major (D780) 100
   Serenade 102
   Symphonische Etuden **52**
   Thécla 22, 183
   Variations for four hands (op 35) 19, 23, 183
Schumann, Robert
   Carnaval 206
   Esquisses 19, 185

Kreisleriana 19, 185
Novellette (op 21/1) 104
Papillons 48
Third Piano Sonata (op 39) 192
Sèverac, Déodac de
   En Languedoc 94
Steibelt, Daniel
   Third Concerto in E Major 27
Strauss, Richard
   Ein Heldenleben 82
Wagner, Richard
   Lohengrin 15

Tannhäuser 15
The Flying Dutchman 15
Tristan and Isolde 15
Weber, Carl Maria von
   A flat Sonata 184
   Der Freischütz 5, 187
   Filles de la mer (*Oberon*) 184
   Konzertstück 32
   Movement perpétuel 8
   Polonaise in E flat major 22, 184
   Sonata in C major (op 24) 22, **37**, 56, 205
Widor, Charles Marie, *Carnaval* 94

Name and Subject Index

Charles Valentin Alkan is referred to as CVA in the index, except for his own main entry.

Adam, Adolphe Charles 4, 8, 79, 157
Adam, Louis 200
  Méthode 212, 213
Alard, M. 19
Alembert, Jean le Rond d' 27
Alkan, Adolphe 9
Alkan, Celeste 4
Alkan, Charles Valentin
  apprentice works 2–37
  on arrangements 131–2
  assessment of 215–18
  Bach performances 13, 181
  Beethoven performances 182
  Belgian tour 5
  on Berlioz 14
  biblical study 17
  Blanchard on 176, 178–9
  Bolte on 192–3
  cadenzas, transcriptions 137–41
  chamber music, reception 186–9
  Chopin
    comparison 176
    performances 185–6
  composing years (1854–73) 14
  de Bertha on 105
  death 24–5
  début recital 2, 201
  Delaborde, musical collaboration 18
  d'Indy on 24, 204, 215
  discography 255
  early life 2–9
  Esquisses 121–30
    classification 130
  Fétis, correspondence with 12–13
  Fétis on 175–6, 178
  Field performances 184
  on French music critics 16
  full name 2
  on Gounod 16
  Haydn performances 181
  Hiller, correspondence 14–15, 16–17, 179

  Impromptus 12
  Jewish element x
  journal reception 175–9
  Kreuzer on 177–8
  LFM reviews 176, 177
  Liszt on 5, 174–5
  Marmontel, view of 12–13
  melancholia 15, 16, 17, 62
  Mendelssohn performances 184
  morceaux caracteristiques 94–5
  Mozart performances 181
  music
    Greimas-Tarasti theories 216
    inside/outside analysis 216–17
    melodic voice 217
  musical contemporaries 2
  obituary 25
  organist, Paris Temple 11–12
  Paris concerts 5, 7, 8, 13
  Paris Conservatoire, admission 2
  performance of
    arpeggios 211–12
    chord technique 212
    fingering suggestions 211
    instructions 208–11
    pedalling 212–14
    rubato application 208
  performance tradition 203–5
  performing, retirement from 7, 9–14, 111, 176
  personality 215–16
  Petits Concerts 1873–80 17–25, 179
    1875 series, programme 21
    Chopin performances 185–6
    reception 180, 189–91
    repertoire choice 180, 189–91
  pianistic style 204
  piano choice 201–3
  piano playing, tributes 24
  piano studies 2
  repertoire 186–9

Baroque 180–1
classical 181–2
Petits Concerts 180, 189–91
romantic 183–6
Revue Musicale on 175–6
RGM reviews 176–8, 179, 180, 182, 183, 184, 189, 190
romanticism 216
on Rubinstein 15
Schubert performances 183
Schumann on 43, 49, 50, 173
Schumann performances 184–5
siblings, musical talent 2, 4
sonata style 78–9, 80, 81
stile brillante 39
studies on ix
teaching repertoire 205–6
tempo markings 206–8
violinist 2, 187
on Wagner 15
Weber performances 184
works, list 248–54
Alkan, Emma Christian 9
Alkan, Ernest 4
Alkan family tree 3
Alkan, Gustav 4, 18
Alkan, Maxime 2, 4, 14
Alkan, Napoléon 4, 9, 14, 24
Alkan Society Journal ix
Allgemeine Musik Zeitung 192
Altenburg, Johann 19, 189
arrangements
CVA on 131–2
definitions 131
Auber, Daniel 6, 10, 11, 13, 15, 79
Aucoc, Marie 204
piano studies with CVA 205–6

Babcock, Alpheus, piano development 200–1
Bach, C.P.E. 19
Bach, J.S. 1, 13
CVA's performances 181
Baillot, Pierre 6
Méthode de violin adoptée par le conservatoire 157
Batta, Pierre 7
battle pieces, compositions on 93

Beck, George 59, 99, 105, 206
C.V. Alkan: Oeuvres choisies pour piano ix
Beethoven, Ludwig van 13
CVA's performances 182
influence in France 39, 182
sonata style, influence 78
Benoist, François (CVA's organ teacher) 2, 152
Bibliothèque de l'organiste 144
Berger, Ludwig 19
Berlioz, Hector 79
Beethoven, promotion of 39
CVA on 14
on decline of music 9–10
Memoirs 11
on Meyerbeer's *Dinorah* 14–15
Prix de Rome 11
on Wagner 15
Bizet, Georges 11, 79
Blanc, Charles 10, 11
Blanc, Louis 10
Blanchard, Henri 46, 103, 173, 174, 180
on CVA 11, 42, 45, 132, 176, 178–9, 187
Bloch, Joseph ix, 193
Boieldieu, François 201
sonatas 79
Bolte, T., on CVA 192–3
Brandus & Richault, publishers 13
Bras, Jean Yves 25
Brendel, Alfred 93
Broadwood, John, piano development 200
Bülow, Hans von 14, 22, 59, 184, 215
on CVA 56–7, 59, 61, 62
Busoni, Ferrucio 63, 75, 215
cadenzas, performance 141, 142

cadenzas
CVA's 137–41
performance, Busoni 141, 142
rules 138
Carner, Mosco 193
Castil-Blaze, François 28, 29
Catalani, Angelica 2
Cavaille-Coll, Aristide 143
chamber music, popularity 157
Cherubini, Luigi 1, 6
Chopin, Frederic 7, 8, 9, 10, 19

CVA's performances 185–6
death 11
friendship with CVA 6, 8, 11
piano choice 201
Choron, Alexandre, *Principes de composition* 1
Clementi, Muzio 6, 19, 53, 183
Gradus ad Parnassum 80
Colas, Marie-Antoinette 25
Collet, Robert 24
Concerts Spirituels 199
Cooper, Martin, on CVA's *Concerto* (op 39) 196
Corrette, Michel, *Divertissements* 93
Cortot, Alfred 215
Couperin, François le Grand 115
Czerny, Carl 7, 19, 20, 80, 180, 218

da Motta, José Vianna 25, 191–2
Dale, K. 75
Davison, J.M. 9
de Bertha, Alexandre 5, 7, 24–5
on CVA 105
Debussy, Claude, *Pour le piano* 57
Delaborde, Elie Miriam (CVA's natural son) 7, 8, 16, 17, 19
CVA, musical collaboration 18
Delaborde and Philipp, publishers ix
Delacroix, E. 9, 11, 178
d'Indy, Vincent, on CVA 24, 204, 215
Dourlen, Victor 2, 4, 25
Dumas, Alexandre 7
Dussek, Jan 27
Düsseldorf Music Festival 15

Edelmann, Johann 78, 158
Ellis, M.K. 95
Elwart, Antoine 167
Erard, Sébastien, piano development 199–200
Ernst, Heinrich 7
étude, definition 53

Fauré, Gabriel 114
Fétis, François Joseph 9, 10, 27, 79, 87, 100, 102–3, 157, 158, 215
correspondence, CVA 12–13
on CVA 175–6, 178
on the sonata 80–1

Field, Henry 33
Field, Isabella 36
Field, John 20, 23, 32, 53, 96, 180, 183
CVA's performances of 184
Fissot, Henri (CVA's duo pianist) 22, 23, 188–9
form, Schumann on 80
France
Beethoven's influence 39, 182
Revolution (1848) 93
Franchomme, Auguste 19
Franck, César 7, 14, 144
François-Sappey, Brigitte ix, 84, 86, 215
on CVA's *Concerto* (op 39) 198

Gazette Musicale 46, 182
Geneva Conservatoire 204
Goblot, H. 94
Gorer, R. 121
Gossec, François Joseph 171
Gounod, Charles François 14, 79
CVA on 16
Greimas-Tarasti theories, CVA's music 216
Grisez, M. 19
Guerret, Rachel 25
Gutmann, Adolphe 7, 9

Habaneck, François 6
Halbreich, Harry 161
Halévy, Jacques 6, 8
Hallé, Charles 6
Handel, George Frideric 13
Harmonicon 5
harmonium, popularity 144
Haydn, Joseph, CVA's performances of 181
Heller, Stephen 9, 183
Henderson, W.R. 193
Hennig, Dennis ix
Herz, Henri 5, 7, 10, 13, 49
Hiller, Ferdinand 6, 12, 13
CVA, correspondence 14–15, 16–17, 179
Himmelfarb, Constance ix, 182
Hugo, Victor 10
Hüllmandel, Nicholas Joseph 78, 157
Hummel, Johann 6, 184

Jacquard, M. 19, 190
Jadin, Hyacinthe 78

Kalkbrenner, Friedrich 6, 7, 49, 53, 79
    sonata style 80
Keller, H. 131
Kreutzer, Conradin 9, 170
    on CVA 177–8

La France Musicale (*LFM*) 8, 157, 170, 175
    reviews of CVA 176, 177
Ladurner, Ignaz, sonata style 80
Lavignac, A. 213
Lefébure-Wely, Louis 144
Lemmens, Nicolas 14
Léonard, Hubert 19
Lewenthal, Raymond 7, 44, 67
    on the *Concerto* (op 39) 194
    CVA performances ix
    on *Esquisses* (op 63) 121, 126, 128
    on *Etudes* (op 35/8) 59–60
    on *Le Festin d'Esope* 72–3, 213
    on *Les Quatre Ages* 82
    on playing CVA 203, 206, 212
    on *Quasi-Faust* 84
    on the *Symphonie* 68
Liszt, Franz 6, 7, 8, 182
    on CVA 5, 174–5
    on *Le vent* 45
Long, Marguerite 204
Luguenot, François ix, 211

Macdonald, Hugh ix, 25, 195
    Cello Sonata (op 47), edition ix
    on *Concerto* (op 39) 196, 197
Mansouroff, Zina de 167
Marmontel, Antoine 10, 204, 208
    CVA's view of 12–13
    Les Pianistes Célèbres 11
Marothy, J. 216
Martin, Josephine 8, 199
Marx, A.B. 53
Mas, M. 19, 188
Massart, Lambert 5
Massart, Louise 14, 19, 183, 188
Masson, Elizabeth 167
Maurin, Jean 24
Méhul, Etienne 78, 171
Mellers, Wilfred, on *Concerto* (op 39) 196–7
Mendelssohn, Felix 6, 19, 183
    CVA's performances of 184

Le Mentor 5
Méthode de Piano du Conservatoire 27
Meyerbeer, Giacomo 6, 8, 11, 79
    Dinorah, CVA on 14–15
miniatures *see morceaux caracterisques*
Momigny, J.J. 77, 78, 94
morceaux caracteristiques
    battle pieces 93
    CVA's 94–5
    examples 94
    meaning 93
Morhange, Alkan (CVA's father) 3, 14
Moscheles, Ignaz 5, 8, 19, 53, 183, 200
Mozart, Wolfgang Amadeus 13
    CVA's performances of 181
music, romantic 1, 8, 20, 23, 77, 157
musical semiotics, CVA's music 216
musical tastes, changes 1

Naumbourg, Samuel 8, 169
Newman, W. 77, 81, 183
Niecks, Frederick 24

Ogdon, John 194
Onslow, George 6
organ, French, developments 144
Orloff, Prince 24
Orloff, Princess 16
Ortigue, Joseph 7, 171

Paër, Ferdinand 6
Paganini, Niccolò 53
Pape, Henri, piano development 2, 200, 201
Parent, H. 215
Paris
    musical scene 6, 7
    revolutions 9, 17
Paris commune (1871) 17
Paris Conservatoire 1, 10, 12, 24, 157, 204
Paris Consistoire 8
pédalier
    CVA's skill at 143–4
    launch 143
Pfeiffer, M.G. 19
Philipp, Isidore 24, 25
pianist-composers 6, 201
Le Pianiste 35
piano players

demand for 5
French school 204
piano style 27
pianos
   Erard, Pleyel, comparison 201–2
   France, development 199–201
   popularity, with women 199
Pixis, Johann Peter 7
Poitevin, Marie 190
Prix de Rome 6, 11, 167
Prudent, Emile 9
Prunières, H. 95

Rapoport, P., on *Concerto* (op 39) 197–8
Reach, Pierre 214
Revue et Gazette Musicale (*RGM*) 9, 157, 175
   reviews of CVA 176–8, 179, 180, 182, 183, 184, 189, 190
Revue Musicale, reviews of CVA 175–6
Richault, Simon 153, 183
Riemann, H., arrangement, definition 131
Rode, Jacques 6, 157
Rothstein, E., on *Concerto* (op 39) 197
Rousseau, Jean-Jacques, on the sonata 77
Rubinstein, Anton, CVA on 15

Sabatier, François 148, 153, 155
Sadie, Stanley, on *Concerto* (op 39) 194
Saint-Saëns, Camille 81, 144
Salle Erard 10, 11, 18, 20, 23, 24, 190, 201
Salle Favart 187
Salle Pape 201
Salle Pleyel 20, 22, 23, 190, 201
Salle Taitbout 20
Salzman, Eric, on *Concerto* (op 39) 195
Samaroff, Olga 7
Samson, J. 162
Sand, George 7, 10
   friendship with CVA 6, 11
Saraste, Pablo 19
Satie, Erik 104
   Socrate 116
Scarlatti, Domenico 13, 18
Schelling, Brigitte ix
Schmitt, Aloys 19, 183
Schola Cantorum 24, 215
Schrade, L. 182
Schubert, Franz 19

CVA's performances of 183
Schumann, Clara 6, 16
Schumann, Robert 16, 19
   on CVA 43, 49, 50, 173
   CVA's performances of 184–5
   on form 80
   on the sonata 81
Shaw, Richard ix
Smalley, Roger 144–5
Smith, Ronald ix, 59, 63, 84, 107, 109, 113, 114, 116, 119, 121, 127, 144, 170, 214
   Alkan in Miniature (co-author) ix
   on the *Concerto* (op 39) 194, 195, 198
Société Alkan Bulletin ix
Société Grétry 5
Société Maurin-Chevillard 136
Société Nationale de Musique 81
sonata
   battle effects 80
   Beethoven's influence 78
   Boieldieu, 79
   eighteenth century 77, 81
   Fétis on 80–1
   France 79, 81–2
   German supremacy 79
   meaning of 77
   Rousseau on 77
   Schumann on 81
sonata style
   CVA 78–9, 80, 81
   Kalkbrenner 80
   Ladurner, 80
   Steibelt 80
Sorabji, Kaikhosru 56, 59, 61, 87, 88, 193
   Around Music 193
Spontini, Gaspare 8
Starr, Mark 198
Steibelt, Daniel 27, 79
   sonata style 80
Strauss, Richard 91
Subotnik, Rose 176
Szarvady, Mme 23

Tellefsen, Thomas 13
Thalberg, Sigismond 7, 34, 53
Thomas, Ambroise 11, 13, 167
Turban, Alfred 20

Türk, Daniel Gottlieb, rules for cadenza writers 138

Ujfalussy, A. 208, 209

van Dieren, Bernard 59
Verrimst, Victor 20
Viardot-Garcia, Pauline 14, 15
Viguerie, Bernard 93
Viotti, Giovanni Battista 6

Wagner, Richard, CVA on 15

Weber, Carl Maria von, CVA's performances of 184
Wells, J. 150
White, John ix
   Alkan in Miniature (co-author) ix
Wolff, Edouard 9

Zimmerman, Pierre (CVA's teacher) 2, 5, 6, 7, 8, 10, 28
Zorzico dance 12, 104, 110, 218
Zumpe, Johann Christoph 200